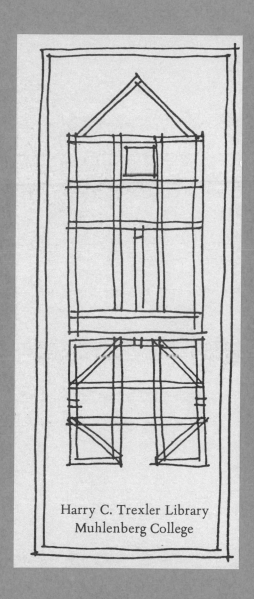

ZAIBATSU

ZAIBATSU

The Rise and Fall of
Family Enterprise Groups
in Japan

Hidemasa Morikawa

Foreword by
Alfred D. Chandler, Jr.

UNIVERSITY OF TOKYO PRESS

Publication of this volume was assisted by grants from the Suntory Foundation and the Keio Gijuku Fukuzawa Memorial Fund for the Advancement of Education and Research.

ISBN 4–13–047055-8
ISBN 0–86008–488–4
Printed in Japan

Second printing, 1993

CONTENTS

FOREWORD, Alfred D. Chandler, Jr.   ix
ACKNOWLEDGMENTS   xiii

INTRODUCTION   xv
Zaibatsu Defined   xvii
Coverage   xviii
Historical Framework   xx
Themes   xxi
Major Questions   xxii

PART I   FORMATION OF THE ZAIBATSU,
1868–93   1
CHAPTER 1   ZAIBATSU ORIGINS   3
Political Merchants   4
From Mining Enterprises to Zaibatsu   15
From Political Merchants to Zaibatsu   20
Summary   24

CHAPTER 2   EMERGENCE OF THE ZAIBATSU   26
Early Diversification   28
Enforcement of the Commercial Code and Zaibatsu
    Reorganization   43
The Rise of Salaried Managers   46
Summary   54

PART II   DEVELOPMENT OF THE ZAIBATSU,
1894–1913   57
CHAPTER 3   DIVERSIFICATION STRATEGIES   59
Mitsui   59

Mitsubishi   68
Furukawa and Sumitomo   73
Asano and Yasuda   82
Ōkura and Fujita   88
Summary   92

CHAPTER 4   FACTORS AFFECTING ZAIBATSU
DEVELOPMENT   93
Managerial Resources   93
Organizational Structures   105
The Zaibatsu Family   114
Summary   118

PART III   SHIFTING FORTUNES, 1914–29   121
CHAPTER 5   THE ZAIBATSU AND WORLD WAR I   123
Zaibatsu, Old and New   123
Diversification into Heavy Industries   128
Development of Overseas Trade   131
Movement into Banking and Insurance   136
Summary   139

CHAPTER 6   THE POST-WORLD WAR I ERA   140
Strengths and Weaknesses of the Zaibatsu   141
The Zaibatsu and Heavy Industries after World War I   144
The Postwar Advance into New Heavy Industries   150
Expansion of Financial Enterprises   159
Vicissitudes of the Zaibatsu Trading Companies   169
Summary   177

CHAPTER 7   THE FAMILY MULTISUBSIDIARY
SYSTEM   182
Formation of the Multisubsidiary System   182
Rationale for Adopting the Family Multisubsidiary System   211
Issues of Control in the Multisubsidiary System   213

PART IV   DEPRESSION, WAR, AND DISSOLUTION,
1930–48   221
CHAPTER 8   TRANSFORMATION, COLLAPSE, AND
POSTWAR DISSOLUTION   223
The Zaibatsu "Conversion"   224
Wartime Growth of the Zaibatsu in Heavy Industry   228
Wartime Reorganization and Collapse   233
End of the Road: Forced Dissolution   237

EPILOGUE   241
Review of the History of the Zaibatsu   241
Closed and Open Systems of Ownership   243
Exclusive Ownership, Progressive Management   245
The Zaibatsu and Postwar Japanese Business   247

NOTES   249
INDEX   275

FOREWORD

Professor Morikawa's book on the Japanese zaibatsu is a crowning achievement of his thoughtful scholarship and patient research which have resulted in the first detailed, carefully organized history of this significant institution. It will certainly be essential reading for any serious scholar who is interested in the phenomenal growth of the Japanese economy. It should also influence the future thinking on the historical development of managerial capitalism in international perspective. To a business historian like myself who has studied the three varieties of managerial capitalism—those of the United States, Great Britain, and Germany—Professor Morikawa provides an essential underpinning for understanding the evolution of a fourth variety of managerial capitalism, one that evolved in a very different way than did those of the West. His book thus enriches our understanding of the workings of modern industrial capitalism.

As Professor Morikawa so convincingly illustrates, the zaibatsu were the central institution of the development of Japan's modern economy. These family-controlled and multibusiness enterprises, managed through an extensive hierarchy of salaried managers, became one of the crucial instruments in the transformation of the Japanese economy from a traditional commercial agrarian one to a modern industrial one. For, until the Meiji Restoration in 1868, Japan had little contact with the West. Western capitalism evolved over five hundred years of personal, mercantile economy, and small-scale industrial capitalism. Japan, with the driving force of the zaibatsu, made the transformation within a single generation. Therefore, an appreciation of the history of the zaibatsu between their modern beginnings in the 1880s until World War II is not only essential in understanding how that transformation was carried out, but also for an analysis of the origins of today's Japanese brand of managerial capitalism.

In the 1880s, when the government in charge of this transformation turned over the industrialization of the country to private individuals, the nation still lacked the basic commercial and financial infrastructure and the technical and managerial skills essential to introduce and operate Western industrial technologies. The families that undertook this task had played a significant part in, and profited from, the government's initial efforts in industrialization. As Professor Morikawa describes, many of these families moved from finance and mining to shipping, shipbuilding, and metal-making. Some then formed trading companies both to export their products and to import the new materials and technology essential for industrialization. At the same time they established banks and insurance companies to support their industrial and trading activities. To administer each of the new and growing enterprises, they recruited full-time salaried managers.

By the turn of the century, these mutually supporting multibusiness groups had become a continuing source of capital for the continuing transfer of modern industrial technology and for the recruitment of managers to operate the new industries. The latter task required not only engineering and technical skills, but also a broad knowledge of foreign languages. So, as Professor Morikawa documents, the zaibatsu from their beginnings recruited university graduates into their managerial ranks. Well before World War I such managers in these family-controlled organizations were making both operating and strategic decisions for their individual enterprises. In some, including the largest, the Mitsui Group, established by a two-hundred-year-old merchant clan, the family quickly withdrew from all but honorific positions. In others a small number of successors of the founding family remained in the top command. Thus at Mitsubishi, one son of two founding brothers acted as the president from 1916 to 1945 and headed the managerial hierarchies that operated enterprises in major industries and in worldwide trading activities.

During World War I and then in the 1920s, the zaibatsu provided pools of capital and managerial skills needed to bring to Japan the more technologically advanced, science-based industries—chemicals (rayon and fertilizers), electrical equipment, and nonelectrical machinery, as well as improved metal-making. Professor Morikawa points out that corporate headquarters of the zaibatsu remained small. Their functions were those of passive oversight rather than active strategy-making. The heads of the subsidiaries, he stresses, continued to determine their own strategies of investment, moved into new markets, and adopted new techniques. In carrying out their objectives they worked closely with their cohorts in the banks, trading companies, and allied industrial enterprises in their groups. Senior executives in the corporate office kept a watchful eye on the performance of the operating managers, played a role in the appointment of senior executives, and gave final approval for funding of new or expanded activities.

In the 1930s, as Professor Morikawa illustrates, family ownership began to erode. The Depression reduced retained earnings, which had financed earlier growth. The families were under attack from right-wing nationalist parties. The military felt they put money before national honor. To meet such criticism the families disposed of large blocks of shares in their groups. By 1941 the military expansion since 1932 had changed Japan's economy into a command one, and the military had a major impact on the operations and investments of their group enterprises. During the Occupation that followed defeat, the Holding Company Liquidation Commission, under the guidance of the Supreme Commander for the Allied Powers, aggressively dissolved what still remained of these groups. They removed family control, eliminated the corporate headquarters, and forbade cooperation between individual enterprises of the prewar groups.

Nevertheless the heritage remained. Since the 1950s the Japanese economy has grown vastly in size. Its institutions have become far more complex. But groups of allied enterprises made up of banks, trading companies, and related industrial corporations, some direct descendants of the prewar zaibatsu, remain at the core of Japanese industrial strength. What has changed is ownership. Today the enterprises in these groups are owned by not families but banks, other financial institutions, and industrial corporations, and largely by those in their own group. That is, the large majority of shares of these managerial enterprises are held by other managerial enterprises. And it is this institutional structure that most sharply differentiates the Japanese species of capitalism from the American type.

Any comparative analysis of the differences of Japanese corporate industrial economic performance with those of other industrial nations must consider the implications of these differences in corporate control and corporate relationships. Therefore, any study involving Japan's managerial multibusiness group enterprises must begin with Professor Morikawa's superlative study of the origins and growth of such institutions. So, of course, must any history of the evolution of Japanese business, industry, and the economy during the twentieth century.

ALFRED D. CHANDLER, JR.

ACKNOWLEDGMENTS

I began my study of Japanese zaibatsu in 1964. I followed the business history method, for which I received invaluable advice and guidance from Professor Nakagawa Keiichirō. I amassed numerous monographs, and my research was published in 1980 as *Zaibatsu no keieishiteki kenkyū* (Tōyō Keizai Shinpōsha).

It was Professor Alfred D. Chandler, Jr., who first suggested that I publish an English edition of the book. My initial encounter with Professor Chandler was at the First Fuji Conference in 1974, and I have had the good fortune of meeting him at many academic meetings since: at Moline (Illinois), Tokyo, Vancouver, Budapest, Boston, and Berne. It was perhaps at those meetings, listening to my presentations, that he developed an interest in Japanese zaibatsu and the comparative study of large-scale enterprises in the United States, Great Britain, Germany, France, and Japan. My friend Hikino Takashi, a research fellow in Chandler's seminar at Harvard Business School, also encouraged me to publish an English edition.

I set about this monumental task in 1985, just as I was moving to Yokohama National University from Hosei University. I rewrote my book, and Ms. Ruth S. McCreery, a professional translator and my neighbor, produced the first draft of the translation. The manuscript was then thoroughly revised by Professor Steven J. Ericson of Dartmouth College, who as a business historian of Japan was very knowledgeable about the subject and familiar with the terminology. The manuscript also benefited from the editorial assistance of Ms. Patricia Denault.

The writing, translating, and perfecting of the English manuscript took eight years, by which time I had become professor at Keio Business School. On the recommendation of my friend Professor Yamazaki

Hiroaki of University of Tokyo, my manuscript was accepted by University of Tokyo Press. My one regret is that the academic research on zaibatsu that was carried out during those eight years has not been sufficiently represented in this edition.

I would like to express my deep gratitude to the many people who participated in the birth of this book: Professor Chandler, who first inspired me to produce my research in English, and Mr. Hikino, for his encouragement; to my translators, Ms. McCreery and Professor Ericson, my appreciation of their professional commitment to my work; and to the staff of the University of Tokyo Press, Mr. Izumi Wataru and Ms. Nina Raj, my thanks for their contribution in seeing the final product through.

Finally, I wish to express my appreciation to the Keio Gijuku Fukuzawa Memorial Fund for the Advancement of Education and Research and the Suntory Foundation for financial assistance of the publication of this book.

INTRODUCTION

The zaibatsu are central to the economic history of modern Japan. These diversified business groups, some of which grew to immense size, reached their mature form in the early decades of the twentieth century and dominated numerous sectors of the Japanese economy until their dissolution under the Allied Occupation following World War II. Many large-scale Japanese companies that today wield enormous influence over the contemporary world economy had their origins in the zaibatsu.

Japan's remarkable economic growth since the 1950s has enabled it to become, in per capita terms, the present leading industrial power in the world. The Japanese economy did not, however, simply spring into existence after the Second World War: the country's postwar "miracle" rests on the solid foundation of economic development that began with the opening of Japan's ports in 1858 and continued to the country's surrender in 1945. During that period, the Japanese economy underwent a tremendous structural change as it moved from a traditional agrarian system to a modern industrial regime.[1] Japan differs markedly from the developing countries of recent decades in that private rather than state initiative accounted for most of the country's prewar economic development. The harnessing of many profit-oriented private enterprises to the national goal of industrialization was a distinctive feature of Japan's modern economic experience.

The private businesses that spearheaded Japan's prewar economic development employed both the "open," or joint-stock, system of ownership and the "closed" system, in which ownership was limited to the individual founder of an enterprise and members of his family. In some industries, one system dominated; in others, the two coexisted. Among industries, the systems did not exist in isolation from one an-

TABLE I.1   Distribution of Closed and Open Ownership Systems by Industry, 1940

Steam railroad	S + O	Beer	O + C′
Electric railroad	O	Cotton spinning	O
Shipping	O	Rayon	C
Electric power	O	Silk reeling	C
Gas	O	Paper	C′
Banking	O + C	Chemical fertilizer	C
Trust	C	Dye	O + C
Life insurance	O + C + C′	Paint	O
Hazard insurance	C + C′	Pharmaceutical	C
Trading company	C	Petroleum	O + C
Department store	C	Glass	C
Coal mining	C	Cement	C + C′
Metal mining	C	Iron and steel	S + C′
Construction	C	Aluminum	C
Marine products	O + C′	Electric wire	C
Milling	O	General machine	O
Confectionary/dairy	O + C′	Electric machine	C
Sugar	O + C′	Shipbuilding	C

O = open ownership system; C = closed ownership system; C′ = quasi-closed ownership system; S = state enterprise.
NOTE: When a zaibatsu employed the open system for a particular subsidiary, it treated the latter as though it were in fact a closed enterprise by keeping ownership of the shares largely within the zaibatsu family (hence, the designation "quasi-closed system").

other; they frequently interacted. For example, a "closed" bank might supply capital to an "open" industrial enterprise. At times, "closed" enterprises also took the form of joint-stock companies, but in such cases shares were not sold to the public; only family members or close associates could become stockholders. The distribution of ownership systems in 1940 is indicated schematically in Table I.1.

The introduction and dissemination of the joint-stock company in Japan was extremely rapid. Indeed, a rudimentary form of joint-stock enterprise appeared immediately after the Meiji Restoration of 1868, the starting point of Japan's modern era.[2] The basic function of the joint-stock company—the mobilization of capital from the public at large—was fully realized by the 1880s, and this type of organization, in which anyone could become a stockholder through the free sale and purchase of shares, served as a driving force behind Japanese industrial development in a number of fields.

Despite the acceptance of the joint-stock company in Japan, the contrast with Western development is clear. In the West, joint-stock companies were the motivating power behind economic development, but in Japan their role was less significant. Conversely, the closed system, featuring family ownership, has in the West been associated with a lack of innovation and entrepreneurship and has in fact been regarded as a hindrance to economic development. Few scholars would argue that the family firm has been the driver of Western industrialization in its various stages. In Japan, however, a particular type of family business, the zaibatsu, provided much of the impetus for the country's modern economic development. The main objective of this book, then, is to clarify why and how the zaibatsu became leaders in the economy as it developed during the prewar period.

ZAIBATSU DEFINED

Before turning to these issues, however, we must settle several theoretical questions. First, what was a "zaibatsu"? I define a zaibatsu as a group of diversified businesses owned exclusively by a single family or an extended family. A zaibatsu's diversified businesses were not necessarily legally independent companies but were sometimes organized as internal divisions of a single large concern. The zaibatsu form was not unique to Japan, but the huge scale that such groups as Mitsui and Mitsubishi attained and the number of zaibatsu formed in the course of industrialization were distinctively Japanese phenomena.

My definition of zaibatsu differs in several respects from those used by other scholars. One definition equates the zaibatsu to big business or oligopolistic enterprises. Admittedly, many zaibatsu could be described as large-scale concerns competing oligopolistically, that is, as big business enterprises. But not all big businesses in prewar Japan were zaibatsu. In fact, several large-scale businesses, such as electric power and cotton-spinning companies, were organized as joint-stock companies. Moreover, not all zaibatsu were big businesses. Zaibatsu existed in a variety of sizes, from the enormous Mitsui, Mitsubishi, and Sumitomo to medium-sized and small business groups. All the large zaibatsu and most of the smaller ones had their headquarters in one of the big central cities—Tokyo, Osaka, Yokohama, or Kobe—but some of the smaller zaibatsu were headquartered elsewhere. Known as local zaibatsu, these included the forerunners of today's Toyota, Bridgestone, and Kikkō-man. The development of zaibatsu in every region and on every scale is one of the distinctive features of Japan's prewar business history. Hence, to regard the zaibatsu as big businesses competing oligopolistically would result in an overly narrow definition that would exclude from consideration not only the regional spread of the zaibatsu structure but also the range of sizes within the zaibatsu category.[3]

Another definition of zaibatsu identifies the form with the German

Konzern, or multisubsidiary organization, in which a parent, or holding, company controls several joint-stock companies in different business sectors.[4] It is true that by the 1920s all the major zaibatsu had adopted the multisubsidiary form. But they initially had been organized, and many had long operated, as family-owned groups of diversified businesses, and only at a later point in their development did they reorganize themselves along multisubsidiary lines. Of the major zaibatsu, for example, Mitsui transformed itself into a multisubsidiary business in 1909, Mitsubishi in 1917–19, and Sumitomo in 1921, yet all had been zaibatsu well before those dates. Therefore, to equate zaibatsu with the multisubsidiary enterprise would be to overlook the earlier stage of zaibatsu formation.

A third definition of zaibatsu stipulates that any combined group of businesses in different fields constitutes a zaibatsu, even if control by one parent holding company is lacking.[5] This approach avoids the error of excluding the zaibatsu as they existed before adopting the multisubsidiary structure, but it identifies the zaibatsu with the large corporate groups of postwar Japan. The multisubsidiary form was outlawed in the postwar settlement, which dissolved the zaibatsu and prohibited holding companies. In the 1950s the large corporations that had belonged to the zaibatsu prior to their breakup revived the old zaibatsu corporate names that had been forbidden under the Occupation. Firms originally in the same zaibatsu formed corporate groups. These trends convinced many Japanese scholars that the zaibatsu had been resurrected, but this is a mistaken interpretation. The postwar groups lack one of the distinctive features of the zaibatsu, for each group is not owned exclusively by a single family. They are characterized by mutual shareholding among their constituent firms and consultation among the group members' top managers, but these are looser groupings that cannot be regarded in the same light as the prewar zaibatsu. Moreover, if such descendants are to be categorized as zaibatsu, then we must also include similar postwar groups that did not originate from the prewar combines.

COVERAGE

In this book I focus on eight business groups that amassed great wealth in the political and economic reorganization occurring after the Meiji Restoration of 1868 and that subsequently began to develop into zaibatsu in the 1880s—Mitsui, Mitsubishi, Sumitomo, Yasuda, Furukawa, Ōkura, Asano, and Fujita—and on two groups that emerged as zaibatsu around 1910—Kuhara and Suzuki. Each of these ten zaibatsu owned and operated large-scale enterprises in a variety of industries.

TABLE I.2   Total Paid-in Capital Held by Selected Zaibatsu, 1928 (%)

Mitsui	4.9
Mitsubishi	4.0
Yasuda	2.7
Asano	1.9
Sumitomo	1.4
Ōkura	1.1
Furukawa	0.5
Total	16.5

SOURCE: Takahashi Kamekichi, *Nihon zaibatsu no kaibō* (An Analysis of Japanese Zaibatsu) (Tokyo: Chūō Kōronsha, 1930).

They exerted a strong influence, both quantitatively and qualitatively, over their industries and over the Japanese economy as a whole. In 1928 the total paid-in capital of joint-stock companies in Japan was ¥13,161 million, of which ¥2,190 million or 16.5 percent was accounted for by the subsidiaries of seven major zaibatsu—Mitsui, Mitsubishi, Yasuda, Asano, Sumitomo, Ōkura, and Furukawa. Table I.2 shows the individual percentages of the total paid-in capital held by these groups.

The qualitative influence of the major zaibatsu can be estimated from the variety of industries dominated by this form of enterprise. Mitsui and Mitsubishi, whose subsidiaries attained high levels of concentration in a wide range of industries, offer the most dramatic examples.[6] Around 1930 Mitsui subsidiaries ranked first in a number of fields. Mitsui Trading had the highest foreign trade volume of all trading companies, accounting for 15.2 percent of Japan's total exports and 14.4 percent of total imports in 1930. Mitsui Mining led in coal output, producing 14.0 percent of the total tonnage of coal mined in Japan in 1929. Mitsui Trust was the country's largest trust company, with 28.3 percent of all cash trusts (net) in 1930. Miike Dyestuff Works, a division of Mitsui Mining, manufactured all of Japan's artificial indigo in 1933. Also in 1930 Tōyō Cotton Trading, a Mitsui Trading subsidiary, accounted for 19.5 percent of Japan's raw cotton imports; Ōji Paper and Fuji Paper, in which the major shareholder was Ōji, together produced 65.4 percent of the total weight of paper (excluding cardboard and traditional Japanese paper) made in Japan, while Dai Nippon Celluloid manufactured 66.4 percent of the total tonnage of raw celluloid, and Denki Kagaku Kōgyō produced 55.5 percent of the total tonnage of lime-nitrogen; Shibaura Engineering Works was first or second, with 15.3 percent of all proceeds, in the Japanese electrical machinery industry; and Mitsukoshi was Japan's largest department store, with 29 percent of the total department-store floor space.

Most other Mitsui subsidiaries ranked second in industries including banking, warehousing, shipbuilding, rayon production, pig-iron production, and cement making. A Mitsui subsidiary was third in ammonium sulphate production. In fact, only the Mitsui subsidiaries in life and marine insurance had not reached the top ranks of their fields by 1930.

Mitsubishi subsidiaries followed Mitsui in the degree of concentration in important industries, ranking first in a number of fields, including shipbuilding, aircraft manufacturing, sheet glass and soda ash production, shipping, warehousing, and non-life insurance. They ranked second in coal mining and beer brewing, third in pig iron, electric machinery, and life insurance, and fourth in the trust business.

Mitsui and Mitsubishi's high level of multi-industrial concentration was exceptional, but the other zaibatsu subsidiaries were also more or less characterized by high concentrations in various key industries.

HISTORICAL FRAMEWORK

This study is organized around the four distinctive phases of zaibatsu development.

FORMATION OF THE ZAIBATSU, 1868–93. The Meiji Restoration of 1868 led to the establishment of a modern economic and political infrastructure, which laid the basis for Japan's industrialization. These years encompassed the introduction of the joint-stock company, formation of a modern banking system, development of railway and steamship line, modernization of cotton spinning through the importation of machinery and the factory system, and application of steam power to mines. The end of the period is marked by the implementation in 1893 of portions of the Commercial Code, which established the legal framework for modern enterprises in Japan. During this phase the founders of the zaibatsu accumulated their wealth, and Mitsui and Mitsubishi in particular began to diversify their businesses.

DEVELOPMENT OF THE ZAIBATSU, 1894–1913. During this formative stage of modern Japanese industry, companies in a number of fields, including cotton spinning, paper making, sugar refining, shipbuilding, coal and metal mining, electric power, and shipping, developed in ways that allowed them to take advantage of growing domestic and world markets. Each zaibatsu adopted its own diversification strategy. Mitsui, the most rapidly expanding zaibatsu, began to build a multisubsidiary system in response to the growth and diversification of its enterprises.

SHIFTING FORTUNES, 1914–29. This period comprised the economic boom accompanying World War I, the postwar depression, and the ensuing period of slow and unstable growth until 1929. Such heavy industries as chemicals, electrical machinery, iron and steel, and shipbuilding flourished during the wartime boom, but many firms encountered managerial difficulties in dealing with the postwar slump. Under these changing conditions, the second rank of zaibatsu tried to overtake Mitsui and Mitsubishi, triggering a fierce struggle for survival in which managerial ability was the deciding factor in sorting out the winners from the losers. By the close of the period, all ten zaibatsu examined had adopted the multisubsidiary system.

DEPRESSION, WAR, AND DISSOLUTION, 1930–48. After the Great Depression struck in 1930, Japan embarked on the road to militarism and war. During this critical period the zaibatsu marched toward their doom, driven by hostile pressure from antizaibatsu interests within Japan and by an inability, given their closed system of finance, to comply with military demands for the development of heavy industry.

THEMES

Three themes are traced throughout this business history of the ten major zaibatsu.

DIVERSIFICATION. The zaibatsu developed into immense combinations by employing a strategy of diversification. Accordingly, I examine the diversification strategies of the major zaibatsu, as well as the economic environment that necessitated such activity and other motives for diversification. The financial and human resources necessary for successful diversification will form a particular focus.

VARIETY OF DEVELOPMENT PATTERNS. The major zaibatsu did not develop at the same tempo or along the same path. Some achieved record growth, others expanded slowly, stagnated, or went bankrupt. While the variety of patterns among the zaibatsu is made clear, special attention is paid to the nature and implementation of diversification strategies as the key to the outcome of individual development trajectories.

THE MULTISUBSIDIARY SYSTEM. In the process of developing through diversification, the major zaibatsu adopted the multisubsidiary system, which met their need for overall control of a variety of business operations. The formation and structure of the family-owned multi-subsidiary system, the form common to the zaibatsu as a group, is discussed.

MAJOR QUESTIONS

In the course of zaibatsu development, complicated relations arose among the major actors involved: among members of the owner family; between family members and the salaried managers they employed; and among family members, their salaried managers, and such outside figures as financiers and politicians. In analyzing these relationships, this work seeks to answer an important question in zaibatsu history: for each major zaibatsu, how did members of the owner family and their salaried managers interact?

Over time the number and geographical spread of zaibatsu markedly increased. Why? The simplest answer is that many less wealthy families followed the lead of Mitsui, Mitsubishi, and Sumitomo, the richest families to form zaibatsu. Yet the existence of the pioneers must be accounted for. Japan's position as a latecomer pursuing industrialization under adverse conditions was one factor. Not only was Japan behind the industrialized Western nations, but it also had been virtually isolated from world markets for some two hundred years until its sudden opening under Western pressure in 1858. Given the degree of Japan's backwardness, the country could hope to modernize only by following Western models for a whole range of economic sectors. Moreover, the limited supply of entrepreneurs with the capital and management skills needed for rapid industrialization necessitated that those entrepreneurs operate in a variety of business fields.

Another factor encouraging zaibatsu formation was the role of the family firm as one of the driving forces behind Japan's industrialization. Although the joint-stock company was introduced early in the Meiji period and quickly gained widespread acceptance, the family firm, owned by the founder and his family, remained the most common business form and adapted itself to a broad range of economic fields. Such exclusively family-owned businesses helped to spearhead the industrialization process from the Meiji era on, in many cases transforming themselves into zaibatsu.

Mitsui, Mitsubishi, Sumitomo, and similar family firms became comprehensive organizers of diversified enterprises while they preserved closed ownership. How could such families form groups of diversified businesses requiring vast sums of capital while retaining exclusive ownership? And even if these wealthy families had enough money to exclude external capital, why did they risk their fortunes by investing in diversification instead of safeguarding their wealth? Where did the courage for aggressive investment originate? In short, how were these families able to retain exclusive ownership, protect their fortunes, and yet lead Japan into the industrial age?

The main sources of the enormous wealth of the larger zaibatsu families lay in profits accumulated from government patronage and mining. The families invested their fortunes in new areas because of strong internal pressure to regard diversification as more important than conservation of assets. Such pressure sometimes came from within the zaibatsu family, as in the case of the Iwasaki brothers at Mitsubishi, but more often it originated among the salaried managers. The zaibatsu were thus a product of the owner families' money and their salaried managers' desire to diversify.

If diversification had failed at Mitsui, Mitsubishi, and Sumitomo, they would not have become models for less wealthy families. The zaibatsu form then would not have gained the currency that it did. Thus, the central question, and the issue that this book addresses, is: How did the pioneering major zaibatsu successfully apply their diversification strategies over an extended period?

The question can be answered in two ways. First, the zaibatsu built an organizational structure appropriate to a strategy of diversification, one that enabled them effectively to control a wide range of enterprises. Hence, Alfred Chandler's paradigm, "structure follows strategy," applies to the business history of Japan's zaibatsu. No business strategy unaccompanied by a suitable organizational structure can succeed. What kind of organizational structure, then, did Mitsui, Mitsubishi, and Sumitomo create while pursuing their diversification strategies?

The multisubsidiary system, adopted by all the major zaibatsu, was the organizational structure most conducive to the strategy of diversification. In this structure, each of the businesses into which the zaibatsu diversified took the form not of a division but of a subsidiary company, and, like a division within a multidivisional enterprise, each subsidiary was able to function autonomously within the framework of the zaibatsu's overall policy. The central office of the zaibatsu exercised control over the subsidiary companies, which were joint-stock concerns, by holding their shares.

The second way to discover the reasons for the zaibatsu's success is to determine who devised and implemented the diversification strategy and multisubsidiary system at Mitsui, Mitsubishi, and Sumitomo. The answer is that the salaried managers, who possessed administrative ability derived from their education and business experience, guided the zaibatsu along the road to the multisubsidiary form.

This raises another question: Why were so many highly educated salaried managers brought into the zaibatsu and promoted to top management? A forward-looking, progressive attitude was required to realize that in order to expand the zaibatsu would need to employ large numbers of such managers entrusted with strategic functions. When members of the owner family or influential advisers recognized the need for educated managers, the zaibatsu used their ample funds to employ such people, who upon reaching top management positions strove to hire and promote other salaried managers. As a result, a large group of salaried administrators developed within the zaibatsu, accompanied by the rapid formation of managerial hierarchies. Despite their characteristic family exclusiveness, therefore, the zaibatsu were the most advanced Japanese businesses in the employment of salaried managers and their promotion to top decision-making posts as well as in the creation of managerial hierarchies.[7] Although seemingly typical family businesses, they were in fact pioneers of "managerial enterprise" and managerial capitalism in Japan.[8] Thus, from the standpoint of modern Japanese business as well as economic history, the zaibatsu continue to command our attention.

PART I

FORMATION OF THE ZAIBATSU, 1868–93

CHAPTER 1
ZAIBATSU ORIGINS

Of the ten major zaibatsu examined in this book, two—Mitsui and Sumitomo—originated during the Tokugawa Shogunate (1603–1868) and the other eight during the first half of the Meiji era (1868–1912). These businesses attained the zaibatsu form—that is, exclusive family ownership of several different types of enterprises—toward the middle of the Meiji era.

Their reluctance to rely on outside investors meant that the founder of a zaibatsu and his heirs had to possess considerable personal wealth. Where did that wealth originate? What were the sources of funding that made possible the emergence of the zaibatsu? The phrase "from political merchant to zaibatsu" suggests one answer—the conventional explanation that the zaibatsu founders got their start as so-called Meiji political merchants. "Political merchants" (*seishō*) were traders and financiers who used their ties to powerful political figures to obtain government favors, enabling them to earn substantial profits in return for providing goods or services to the state. Government patronage took the form of subsidies, grants of monopolies or special privileges, favorable credit arrangements, and sales of state enterprises at nominal prices.

This is but a partial explanation, however. The Mitsui, Mitsubishi, Yasuda, Ōkura, and Fujita zaibatsu all were established on the basis of wealth accumulated through political merchant activities, but others, including Sumitomo and Furukawa, grew out of mining enterprises and never became political merchants. Moreover, Mitsui, Mitsubishi, and Fujita used capital amassed through political merchant operations to acquire mines, from which the profits, combined with those from state purveyor activities, created the wealth needed to form zaibatsu. Thus, political merchant activities or mining or some combination of the two yielded the enormous fortunes that made possible the founding of many zaibatsu.

Political merchant activity and mining shared a characteristic: both were carried out on a monopolistic basis with strong barriers to entry. Political merchants had personal ties to powerful government figures, and mining companies had exclusive rights to mineral resources; these advantages presented almost insurmountable obstacles to latecomers. The profits from political merchant and mining operations, maintained as they were through monopoly, were naturally large.

POLITICAL MERCHANTS

Political merchants had appeared in the Tokugawa period because the rulers of the time, the Tokugawa shōgun and the various domain lords (*daimyō*), had, in accordance with the restriction on direct samurai involvement in business activities, entrusted the purchase and sale of commodities and the handling of money to merchants. The explanation for the growth of political merchants after the Meiji Restoration is more complex. First, because the leaders of the new Meiji regime emerged from the old samurai ruling class, they continued to entrust commercial and financial matters to merchants. For example, until 1873 most of the government's revenue came from the land tax, which was paid in kind, that is, in rice. The state turned to merchants with special government connections to convert the rice into money by selling it in the major markets of Osaka and Tokyo and depositing or remitting the proceeds. Even after the reform of 1873, under which the land tax had to be paid in cash, designated merchants rather than the producers themselves continued to sell the rice and deposit tax revenues, because rice markets outside of Osaka and Tokyo remained undeveloped.

Second, as an underdeveloped country, Japan had to respond to the Western challenge by pursuing industrialization and achieving national independence and economic stability. One potential source of capital and enterprise for these tasks was the old merchant class. But many of the traditional merchants who had amassed wealth prior to 1868 went bankrupt in the economic confusion surrounding the restoration, and those who survived were reluctant to invest in modern industries in which they lacked experience. In the end, the Meiji government had no choice but to take the lead in industrialization, managing directly a variety of enterprises ranging from arsenals and shipyards to telegraphs and mines. But even in industries that the government tried to promote as private undertakings through a policy of protection and subsidy—

the classic example is shipping—the traditional merchants failed to participate. The Meiji regime had to look elsewhere for entrepreneurs willing to cooperate in its industrialization program. On discovering such businessmen, the regime formed close connections with them and supplied generous assistance, creating a new type of political merchant.

The political merchants that developed into major zaibatsu can be divided into three groups according to the kinds of services they provided the Meiji government: first, Mitsui and Yasuda, financiers licensed to handle national tax revenues; second, Ōkura and Fujita, merchant enterprises that supplied goods and services required by the regime; and third, Mitsubishi, which received special subsidies from the government for shipping operations.

Mitsui

The Mitsui family had been political merchants since the late seventeenth century. The founder of the house was Mitsui Hachirōbei Takatoshi, who with his sons set up dry goods shops in Edo (now Tokyo) and Kyoto in 1673 to sell fine-quality kimonos. Ten years later they opened money exchange shops, which in 1691 began operating an exchange service for the Tokugawa Shogunate.[1] This service enabled the shogunate to avoid forwarding tax revenues in cash to its administrative headquarters in Edo. Taxes were collected in kind, principally as rice, from the peasants, and the rice was sold on the market in Osaka, at that time the country's major mercantile center. The shogunate of course needed its revenues in Edo, but conveying cash was both risky and expensive. The function of the exchange service was to forward the revenues to Edo without a physical transfer of funds. The Mitsui and other official exchange shops accomplished this task by accepting government funds on deposit in Osaka, using these funds to buy promissory notes given by Edo merchants to their Osaka and Kyoto counterparts, sending these notes to Edo where the shops collected payments on them, and finally delivering the funds to the shogunate. The exchange shops did not collect a fee from the shogunate for performing this service; instead, they were allowed a time lag, generally two to five months, in delivering the government funds they held. By making use of what were in fact interest-free deposits of enormous size, the exchange shops could garner huge profits. The performance of this service was limited to highly trusted financiers, officially about ten in number, who were able to put up large amounts of security.

The Mitsui exchange shops in Edo, Kyoto, and Osaka took full advantage of these privileges to build up their profits. Indeed, from about the middle of the eighteenth century the exchange shops began to overtake the stagnating dry goods shops in profitability, and after 1830 they surpassed dry goods to become Mitsui's main business.[2] When the Tokugawa Shogunate fell in the Meiji Restoration, the Mitsui family was accustomed to the advantages of performing services for the government, and the house continued to function as fiscal purveyor to the new regime.

Mitsui's experiences as a political merchant were not always positive, however. Businesses that obtained their profits by relying on official patronage could be enormously successful, but they were vulnerable to sudden changes in government policy or personnel. This was certainly true for Mitsui, whose role as a political merchant exposed it to three bankruptcy crises in the period surrounding the Meiji Restoration.

The first crisis occurred before the restoration when the shogunate ordered Mitsui to make large contributions that were not legally owed to the regime. At the time, the shogunate was faced with civil war and the collapse of its hegemony, and it was attempting to meet its military expenses by squeezing the merchants. (Mitsui was thus not the only victim of these extraordinary assessments.) The shogunate made four levies on Mitsui in 1864–65, totaling about 700,000 *ryō*, and imposed forced contributions of the same amount on other merchants as well. But a 1.5 million *ryō* assessment in February 1866 was imposed on Mitsui alone.[3] Since at that time the total operating assets of the Mitsui Ōmotokata, the head office, were about 970,000 *ryō*, the government assessment was a burden that Mitsui simply could not afford to bear.

Behind this 1.5 million *ryō* assessment were events dating from 1859, when the port of Yokohama was opened to foreign trade. At that time the shogunate ordered large merchants, including Mitsui, to open branches in Yokohama. Immediately thereafter it directed the new Yokohama branch of Mitsui's Edo dry goods shop to furnish financial services to the shogunate office engaged in international diplomacy there. Mitsui's Yokohama branch provided storage for government funds as well as accounting, exchange, and transfer services. It then used the shogunate funds it held on deposit to make loans, primarily to silk yarn traders, and to speculate in foreign currency. In the course of these activities Mitsui lost a large sum. In February 1867 the Yokohama branch of the Mitsui dry goods shop had on its books 220,000 *ryō* in Japanese currency and $40,000 in foreign currency on deposit, but it actually held only 93,000 *ryō* and $25,000 in cash. The remainder was tied up in loans or currency speculation. Moreover, of the latter investments, about 100,000 *ryō* were uncollectible—an enormous amount since at the time the annual profits from the Mitsui dry goods and exchange shops totaled only 25,600 *ryō*.[4] The shogunate zeroed in on this weak point of the Mitsui enterprise to make its forced levy of 1.5 million *ryō*.

The Mitsui family had no alternative but to petition for a reduction in the assessed amount. Mitsui needed someone to act as go-between with Oguri Kōzukenosuke, who was then acting as minister of finance in the shogunate. The Mitsui house learned that a small exchange dealer with whom it had done business, Minokawa Rihachi, had been Oguri's servant. Rihachi had then become, at the age of twenty-five, the son-in-law and adopted heir of a small merchant, acquiring from him the sur-name Minokawa. He had gradually built up capital until 1855, when at the age of thirty-five he had been able to open his own small exchange shop.[5] An uneducated, illiterate man, Minokawa was nonetheless extremely clever and had outstanding negotiating skills. Mitsui therefore entrusted the negotiations to him. As a result of his mediation, the shogunate agreed to reduce its levy on Mitsui to one-third of the original demand, to be paid in installments over three years. In fact, Mitsui was required to pay only the first year's installment of 180,000 *ryō*, the remainder being cancelled in March 1867.[6]

Minokawa's negotiating talent was not the only reason that the shogunate ended its raids on Mitsui: the regime had another service to demand of the merchant. In October 1866 it ordered Mitsui to operate a lending institution set up in Edo and Yokohama by the shogunate with an investment of 100,000 *ryō* from the Yokohama customs duties. Mitsui consented and established the Goyōsho, an office to manage this government enterprise, under the direct control of its head office. The foreign exchange services provided by the Yokohama branch of the Edo dry goods shop were also transferred to the Goyōsho, and Minokawa was appointed manager as a reward for his successful negotiations to reduce the levy. On joining Mitsui, he changed his name to Minomura Rizaemon.[7] The Goyōsho was operated on a plan devised by the shogunate,[8] but, according to one interpretation, circumstances surrounding its establishment—including the fact that its initial capital of 100,000 *ryō* equaled the amount of uncollectible public funds owed by Mitsui's Yokohama branch—suggest that its founding, as well as Mitsui's undertaking to manage it, were agreed to by Minokawa and the shogunate as the price of reducing the government's assessment on Mitsui.

As long as the House of Mitsui continued to develop as a political merchant, Minomura's talents and connections were essential. After the Meiji Restoration he skillfully established ties with bureaucrats in the new regime and made efforts to ensure Mitsui's position as special fiscal purveyor to the government. Mitsui thus continued to function as a political merchant with only a simple change of partner, the new Meiji government taking the place of the Tokugawa Shogunate. After the victory of the restoration forces was assured and the imperial capital moved from Kyoto to Tokyo, Mitsui was appointed as one of three financial agents (*kawasekata*) to the new government. In that capacity, it made donations to the regime, floated national bonds, and issued non-convertible paper currency (*Dajōkan-satsu*) on the government's behalf. Through the Goyōsho, the House of Mitsui also handled the receipt, deposit, and transfer of national tax revenues, profiting handsomely by lending out the huge sums of public money it held on deposit. As the Goyōsho manager, Minomura became central to Mitsui's provision of financial services to the new government.[9]

Mitsui carried out another task for the government in response to the chaotic monetary situation prevailing in the early Meiji period. A multitude of currencies were at that time in circulation, ranging from paper money formerly printed by the individual domains to Mexican silver dollars imported through the treaty ports. New currency regulations were issued in May 1871, making the yen, equivalent to one *ryō*, the basic unit of currency. Immediately thereafter the government announced that Mitsui alone would perform the functions of collecting the necessary gold and silver for the new currency, exchanging the various old coins for the new standardized ones, and issuing convertible notes.

At the same time Mitsui was informally directed to begin preparations for establishing a central bank. The offer of these privileges was based on a proposal from several finance ministry officials who wished to have a major merchant house set up a central bank and cooperate in issuing the new currency and strengthening the nation's finances. Minomura played an active part in shaping that plan through his contacts with the officials involved.[10] To carry out these services, Mitsui in July 1871 established a new institution, the House of Mitsui Exchange (Kawaseza Mitsui-gumi), whose functions were actually performed by the Mitsui Goyōsho and exchange shops. After the granting of Mitsui's request to establish a central bank with the power to issue convertible notes on the basis of the House of Mitsui Exchange, construction began on a five-story Western-style building to house the bank.[11] In order to concentrate on banking, Mitsui moved to divest itself of the dry goods business that had been the family trade for generations; to that end it created a new branch family (*bekke*) named Mitsukoshi, outside the Mitsui clan proper, to which it entrusted the dry goods shops.[12]

Then the attitude of the Ministry of Finance changed. First, in September 1871 it cancelled the right to issue convertible notes that it had given to the House of Mitsui Exchange. Next, sometime around

April 1872 the ministry altered its plan to have Mitsui alone found a central bank and instead requested that Mitsui and Ono, one of the other houses designated as a financial agent for the government, establish such a bank together as a so-called national bank.[13] The ostensible reason for this change was that the Ono house, following Mitsui's lead, had also applied for permission to found a bank. But behind this development was the existence of two opposing factions within the finance ministry: one group, led by Inoue Kaoru, favored a proprietary bank (basically the plan as originally announced), and the other, headed by Itō Hirobumi, favored national banks. The latter group won out and the national bank plan became government policy.[14] Based on the American model, the national banks were to be organized as joint stock companies issuing notes on the security of government bonds. Despite its elaborate preparations to establish a central bank on its own, Mitsui was therefore compelled by the Ministry of Finance to found a national bank, Daiichi Kokuritsu (First National), as a joint venture with Ono. Furthermore, it was forced to abolish the House of Mitsui Exchange and to transfer its privileged status in relation to the new currency—and its five-story building—to the national bank.[15]

Although the finance ministry had broken its promises to Mitsui, Minomura and other top Mitsui managers did not abandon their commitment to Mitsui's traditional role as official financier or to its policy of establishing a bank controlled exclusively by Mitsui to facilitate that function. Both Mitsui and Ono took an indifferent attitude toward the Daiichi Kokuritsu Bank and participated only nominally in the bank's management. The top manager of the bank was its full-time director, former finance ministry bureaucrat Shibusawa Eiichi.[16]

Because Mitsui could still handle funds for government bureaus other than the Ministry of Finance, the Goyōsho continued to perform that function as before. In November 1872 the Goyōsho also took over the exchange shop operations, as its earnings from lending government funds on deposit had grown enormously since the Meiji Restoration and surpassed the profits of the exchange shops.[17] In a change that reflected the growing support within the Ministry of Finance for the establishment of banks other than national banks, in May 1874 the Mitsui Goyōsho was renamed the House of Mitsui Exchange Bank (Mitsui-gumi Kawase Bank).

Mitsui faced a second crisis stemming from its political merchant activities in the fall of 1874. The Ministry of Finance had required each of the three houses—Mitsui, Ono, and Shimada—that were handling government revenues to post as security an amount equal to one-third of the government funds on deposit. But in October 1874 the ministry suddenly revised the system, ordering that the security equal the entire amount on deposit and that the required sum be posted by December 15 of that year. The ministry's goal was tighter control over the use of government funds. Ono and Shimada, which had large sums of public money tied up in long-term loans and investments, were unable to raise the funds for the increased security and went bankrupt. They presented their property for the repayment of public funds.[18] Mitsui managed with great effort to avoid bankruptcy. Minomura had gotten word of the impending change from within the government, and the House of Mitsui Exchange Bank made a desperate attempt to collect the government funds it had lent out. Mitsui was in a better position than were the other houses because public funds accounted for a relatively small proportion of its bank's total deposits and because it had lent out government funds more cautiously than had Ono.[19] The key, however, had been Minomura's decisive role, including the advance warning that he had given Mitsui.

Mitsui Bank was founded in July 1876 with a capital amount of ¥2 million; it replaced the House of Mitsui Exchange Bank. At the time of the bank's establishment, government funds accounted for about one-half of the ¥9 million on deposit.[20] This huge sum, the product of Mitsui's privileged connection with the state, amounted to over one-third of all bank deposits nationwide.[21] Thus, through its new bank Mitsui continued to follow the political merchant path.

Meanwhile, with the Ono house bankruptcy, the Daiichi Kokuritsu Bank's capital of ¥2.5 million (as of its establishment in June 1873) was reduced by the Ono house's share of ¥1 million. Two-thirds of the new capital of ¥1.5 million was provided by Mitsui, and five of the bank's seven directors were at that point Mitsui representatives.[22] Eventually, however, Mitsui withdrew from direct management of the Daiichi Kokuritsu, confining itself to participation as an investor.

In the course of its long history as a political merchant, Mitsui thus experienced both enormous profits and dangerous risks. This was particularly true in the turbulent period spanning the late Tokugawa and early Meiji years. Mitsui passed through the events of those years with great success, largely as a result of the contributions of its top manager, Minomura Rizaemon. Minomura helped Mitsui to gain access to government patronage, to establish the Mitsui Bank, and to overcome the crises that befell political merchants during the Meiji reforms.

Yasuda

The Yasuda zaibatsu began, like Mitsui, as a privileged purveyor of fiscal services to the government. The founder, Yasuda Zenjirō, amassed great wealth through the handling of public funds, as did the Mitsui. Yasuda, however, started his financial career at the end of the Tokugawa period, when the Mitsui had already been in business for generations. Moreover, he came from a background very different from that of the Mitsui family.

Born into a low-ranking and impoverished samurai family in what is now Toyama Prefecture, Yasuda moved to Edo with the hope of rising in the world. He initially worked for a moneychanger, and in 1863, at the age of twenty-five, he became independent. By 1866 his enterprise had developed into Yasuda Shōten, a firm specializing in moneychanging, and his fortune reached the impressive sum of 5,000 *ryō*. The remarkable growth of Yasuda's business resulted from his outstanding skill in currency transactions, particularly his expertise in appraising gold and silver.[23]

Yasuda became a political merchant in 1867, when the shogunate ordered Yasuda Shōten to undertake the collection of gold and silver coinage going out of circulation, an activity that earned Yasuda a handsome profit. After the Meiji Restoration, he cooperated in putting into circulation the nonconvertible paper money issued by the new government. The new currency enjoyed little public confidence until the government announced in May 1869 that the notes would be honored at the same value as specie. Yasuda had earlier bought up large amounts of the depressed paper money, and following the government's announcement he reaped huge profits—some 8,800 *ryō* in the second half of 1869 alone.[24] In 1874 Yasuda began handling public funds for a number of government bodies other than the Ministry of Finance, and making use of interest-free government deposits, he expanded his financial activities. He founded the Third National Bank as a joint venture with other businessmen in 1876; the bank made a public offering of its stock, but Yasuda and his family held 40.7 percent of the shares.[25] In 1880 Yasuda Shōten's financial division was spun off as the Yasuda Bank (Gōhon Yasuda Ginkō), an unlimited partnership with a capital of ¥200,000, and the Third National came to act as an auxiliary to it.

Ōkura

The Ōkura zaibatsu was founded by Ōkura Kihachirō, who was born into a peasant family in what is now Niigata Prefecture. At the age of seventeen Ōkura went to Edo, where he worked for a merchant for three years. He opened his own grocery store in 1857 but eight years later switched to dealing in guns, profiting from the internal disturbances preceding the Meiji Restoration.[26] After the restoration, in April 1872 Ōkura set off to travel through the United States and Europe, seeking out new business opportunities. During the trip he met members of the Iwakura Mission, a diplomatic and fact-finding mission of Meiji government leaders who toured the West from 1871 to 1873. Immediately upon returning to Japan in October 1873, Ōkura established a trading company, Ōkura-gumi Shōkai, capitalized at ¥85,000 with investment from former daimyō, including those of Ōkura's native domain. The new company embarked on direct overseas trade by establishing a branch office in London. The firm made its profits, however, not from foreign trade but from the services it provided on commission to the Meiji government. Ōkura obtained the government business through the connections he had made with government leaders during his trip abroad. His company furnished the regime with military supplies, engaged in leather tanning and military boot production, and also carried out public works.[27]

Fujita

Fujita Denzaburō, founder of the Fujita zaibatsu, was born into a family that ran a saké and soy sauce brewery in Chōshū, now Yamaguchi Prefecture. In 1869 Fujita started a company in Osaka, and using his connections to high government officials from Chōshū, such as Inoue Kaoru, he earned immense profits by supplying goods to the new regime and by engaging in civil engineering works. Fujita's business was touched by scandal; at one point he was jailed for about four months on suspicion of using counterfeit paper money. But he survived that experience to found the Fujita-gumi in partnership with his two older brothers, Fujita Shikatarō and Kuhara Shōzaburō, in 1881. Of its ¥60,000 in capital, Denzaburō provided ¥30,000 and his brothers ¥15,000 each. Denzaburō was named president of the new concern.[28]

Mitsubishi

Mitsubishi zaibatsu founder Iwasaki Yatarō's origins were in the bottom stratum of the samurai class of the Tosa domain, now Kōchi Prefecture. His abilities were recognized by a leading figure in the domain, Yoshida Tōyō, and as a result Iwasaki was chosen to serve in the domain bureaucracy. At the age of thirty-three, in 1867 he was appointed head of the Nagasaki branch of the Kashoku-kyoku, or money-making agency, of Tosa's industry promotion office. Known as the Kaiseikan, this office was set up to increase production of the domain's special products, to sell those products to foreign and native merchants in Osaka, and to use the proceeds to purchase ships and weapons from foreign merchants.[29]

After the Meiji Restoration, the Nagasaki branch office was closed and Iwasaki was transferred to the Osaka office, where he became manager in July 1869. There he oversaw the transactions of his domain with both foreign and Osaka merchants and directed the assistance rendered by the office to other domains dealing with foreign merchants.[30] During his service at the Nagasaki and Osaka offices of the Kaiseikan, therefore, Iwasaki had many business dealings with foreign merchants and won their trust, which later served him well.

Prompted by the national government's prohibition of domain-operated enterprises and by the domain's policy of fiscal retrenchment, in 1870 Tosa officials turned the Kaiseikan's Osaka branch into a private concern named Tsukumo Shōkai. Having been in charge of the Osaka office, Iwasaki took on the directorship of Tsukumo Shōkai, which centered its operations on shipping, using domain boats, but also continued dealing with foreign merchants as its predecessor had.[31]

When the Meiji government abolished the domains in 1871, replacing them with the modern prefecture system, Iwasaki's position as a domain official ended. At the urging of former Tosa leaders, he decided to convert Tsukumo Shōkai into an independent firm, taking over two steamships and part of Tsukumo Shōkai's remaining assets. He paid for the steamships, valued at 40,000 *ryō*, by capitalizing on the foreign merchants' confidence in him and assuming 40,000 *ryō* of the debts owed by the Tosa domain. The other assets taken over by Iwasaki were valued at about 23,000 *ryō* and represented security for loans made to Tosa by Osaka merchants. He acquired these assets by repaying the loans for the domain.[32] Iwasaki himself did not possess such a large sum of money; he probably borrowed it from foreign merchants.

Tsukumo Shōkai in 1872 was renamed after three executives of the new trading company, all former Tosa samurai: Kawada Koichirō, Ishikawa Shichizai, and Nakagawa Kamenosuke (also known as Morita Shinzō). The character for river, or *kawa*, was part of each of their surnames; thus, the company was named Three Rivers, or Mitsukawa. The name reveals that Iwasaki had yet to establish his leading role within the new firm.

He had evidently managed to do so by March 1873, when the company was renamed Mitsubishi Shōkai; as Iwasaki explained in a letter to his younger brother, "I changed the name because I dislike the name 'Mitsukawa Shōkai.'" Mitsubishi, or Three Diamonds, had been used as the logo of Tsukumo Shōkai since its founding in 1870.[33] After Mitsubishi Shōkai moved its headquarters to Tokyo in 1874, its name was changed again, to Mitsubishi Steamship Company (Mitsubishi Jōkisen Kaisha), when the company received a government commission to provide transportation for the Taiwan Expedition of 1874, a punitive expedition against Taiwanese aborigines. Mitsubishi Steamship Company's articles of incorporation set forth the principle that the firm

was Iwasaki's personal enterprise to be managed under his absolute
authority:

> Although this company (*kaisha*) is called a company and takes
> the form of a company, it is an enterprise of the Iwasaki family and
> is completely different from firms that are based on joint invest-
> ment with others. Therefore, the decision of the president is re-
> quired on all problems and on all personnel affairs concerning the
> company.[34]

Mitsubishi Steamship Company was renamed Mitsubishi Mail
Steamship Company (Yūbin Kisen Mitsubishi Kaisha) in 1875.

Iwasaki's shipping business was able to grow rapidly only because of
government protection. The state regarded a strong domestic shipping
industry as essential for transporting the mails and the rice that formed
the basis of its tax revenues, for moving troops in time of internal rebellion or foreign war, for excluding foreign steamship companies from
Japan's coastal navigation, and for initiating scheduled shipping between Japan and other countries. The Japan National Mail Steamship
Company (Nihon-koku Yūbin Jōkisen Kaisha), or YJK, already existed. It had been founded on capital that the government had forced
wealthy families to provide, and its growth had been fostered by
government-supplied steamships and funds. But with passive and dis-
organized management, YJK remained overdependent on government
patronage and lacked able managers and consistent strategies. Such
shortcomings were due to squabbling among its principals, who had
been virtually thrown together to operate the firm; as a result the company failed to satisfy the government's needs.[35]

The firm's deficiencies became painfully clear in 1874. When the government found itself unable to charter foreign vessels for the Taiwan
Expedition, the Western nations having declared their neutrality, it
turned to YJK for assistance. YJK, however, resisted the state's request,
whereupon the government approached Mitsubishi, which willingly
acceded to the government's demands and provided the necessary
ships.[36] Furthermore, while Mitsubishi was winning the regime's trust,
YJK was dealt a serious blow by the bankruptcy of the House of Ono,
one of its major stockholders and financiers. When the government refused to come to its rescue, YJK was dissolved in 1875. Mitsubishi thus
came to monopolize the official patronage of the domestic shipping
industry.

Mitsubishi profited vastly from its new relationship with the government. The company agreed to provide the regime with military transport during wartime, to inaugurate a state-supervised shipping service,
and to establish a merchant-marine training school. In return, the gov-

ernment transferred to Mitsubishi the ships it had bought and provided the firm with subsidies, loans, and enormous fees for chartering the ships. The value of the vessels was conservatively estimated at ¥1.2 million, and the subsidies totaled about ¥2.2 million.[37] Beginning with the Yokohama-Shanghai run in 1875, Mitsubishi developed a series of scheduled overseas routes. In 1875–76, with government backing, it succeeded in driving first American Pacific Mail Steamship and then British Peninsular and Oriental Steam Navigation (P&O) from the Shanghai route. It also opened domestic routes to the northeastern part of the main island and to Hokkaido, so that its lines circumnavigated Japan. During the Satsuma Rebellion of 1877, the last major uprising of former samurai protesting the reforms of the Meiji regime, the company supplied the government with military transport and reaped a profit of some ¥1.2 million. By the end of 1877 Mitsubishi owned sixty-one steamships with a total tonnage of 35,400 and held a monopoly in the Japanese shipping industry.[38]

FROM MINING ENTERPRISES TO ZAIBATSU

The five zaibatsu described in the preceding section originated as political merchants, but not all zaibatsu shared such beginnings. Sumitomo and Furukawa instead developed out of mining concerns.

Sumitomo

The Sumitomo family enterprise has a history even longer than that of Mitsui. Sumitomo claims two founding ancestors, Sumitomo Masatomo and Soga Riemon.[39] Sumitomo, born in 1585, was the progenitor of the Sumitomo familial line, whereas Soga, the father of Sumitomo's son-in-law, was the founder of the Sumitomo family business. After learning copper smelting and processing techniques in Osaka, Soga had opened a copper refinery named Izumiya in Kyoto in 1590. Sumitomo, who was a druggist and publisher in Kyoto, invited Soga's eldest son, Tomomochi, to marry his daughter and become his adopted heir, taking on the Sumitomo surname. With this marriage the lines of the two Sumitomo ancestors merged.

Soga divided the copper works with Tomomochi and allowed Tomomochi to start his own firm using the Izumiya name. Tomomochi's Izumiya advanced into Osaka in 1623, and there developed into an extensive business in copper smelting, processing, and trading, and finance. Sumitomo was one of the shogunate's chartered merchants in copper trading, holding several of the *kabu*, or shares, that signified a license from the regime. Sumitomo had exclusive possession of four of the sixteen *kabu* nationwide for copper trading in 1678.[40] The firm was commissioned in 1691 to operate the shogunate's Besshi copper mine in what is now Ehime Prefecture on Shikoku. The copper output of the Besshi mine peaked at 1,521 metric tons in 1698, but Sumitomo remained the largest copper producer throughout the Tokugawa period.[41]

By the end of that time, however, Sumitomo was experiencing a number of problems. Output at the Besshi mine was down, the operation having reached the limits of its premodern technology; the firm was squeezed by the rising cost of copper production and the fixed purchase price of the shogunate; funds were tied up in loans made to domain lords; and the shogunate cut back on the amount of discounted rice that it sold Sumitomo as a subsidy for copper production.[42]

Moreover, immediately after the Meiji Restoration, Sumitomo faced a series of major crises. First, since the Besshi Copper Mine had been owned by the shogunate, the new Meiji government tried to expropriate it. The Sumitomo copper stockpiles in Osaka were also frozen. Sumitomo survived this crisis because the Besshi manager, Hirose Giemon, convinced the regime that the shogunate had entrusted operation of the mine to Sumitomo in perpetuity and that therefore it was actually Sumitomo property. Then, the new government not only closed the old copper exchange (*dōza*), the shogunate's institution for buying copper but also abolished the official copper procurement system altogether. At the same time, the government demanded that Sumitomo pay for the rice that the shogunate had advanced it in 1867, not in copper as agreed on with the shogunate, but in cash, at a cost of ¥57,000.[43] Next, the cancellation of domain debts to merchants incurred before 1844 made it impossible for Sumitomo to collect on its loans to the former daimyō. At the same time, output at the Besshi mine continued its long-term decline.

It was Hirose Giemon, promoted to the position of top manager (*sōrinin*) of the Sumitomo head office, who found a way out of the bleak situation. Hirose (who had taken the new given name Saihei) successfully petitioned the government to grant Sumitomo two years' grace on settling the rice advance, followed by a five-year period of payment in installments. To replace the market for copper lost by the abolition of the government purchase system, Hirose sold copper to foreign merchants, opening a Kobe branch office for that purpose in 1871. He also hired a French engineer from 1874 to 1875 to help modernize the Besshi mine, offering the Frenchman the enormous salary of $600 a month—six times what Hirose himself was making at the time. The engineer's advice led to a ¥673,700 investment in the mine, which yielded a dramatic expansion in productive capacity.[44] Besshi's copper output grew from about 422 metric tons in 1868 to 862 in 1877 and to over 2,000 in 1890.[45]

Furukawa

The founder of the Furukawa zaibatsu, Furukawa Ichibei, was manager of one of the Ono family stores, the Itoten, when the Ono house collapsed in 1874. He had directed the profitable business whereby the House of Ono had used the government funds held on deposit to engage in raw silk export and mining. Ichibei had thus learned the details of trading as well as of mining operations while at the Itoten. After the Ono fell, he became independent and initially set his sights on both silk export and mining, but when his raw silk business failed, he devoted himself exclusively to mining, particularly copper.[46]

Ichibei was personally without financial resources; the approximately ¥15,000 he had earned while working for the Ono had been on deposit with the Ono-gumi, and when the house went bankrupt his funds were impounded by the government.[47] Ichibei tried to convince the government to transfer to him the Kusakura and Akashiba copper mines, which it had taken over from the Ono-gumi. He appealed for assistance to the Sōma, a former daimyō family with which he had done business while managing the Itoten. The funds deposited with Ono by the Sōma family had also been impounded; in exchange for abandoning their claim to ¥22,000 of those funds, the Sōma accepted title to the Kusakura and Akashiba mines and then entrusted their management to Ichibei. He began operating the Kusakura mine in November 1875; the Akashiba mine was abandoned. The following year, opposition developed within the Sōma family to its connection with mining, and Ichibei seized the occasion to make himself owner as well as operator of the Kusakura mine by agreeing to return to the Sōma their ¥22,000 investment. To raise the money, he turned to the Daiichi Kokuritsu Bank's president, Shibusawa Eiichi, with whom Ichibei had close ties from his days in the Ono-gumi. With the output of the Kusakura mine as security, he borrowed the ¥22,000 from the bank, receiving ¥10,000 at the outset and ¥1,000 monthly for a year.[48]

After the Kusakura acquisition, Ichibei used the same technique to gain possession of two other copper mines. In purchasing the Sachiu mine, also formerly managed by the Ono group, Ichibei had the cooperation of another daimyō family, the Matsudaira of Takamatsu. He began operating the Sachiu mine in May 1876.[49] And the Ashio Copper Mine, which had long suffered from shaky management, was purchased by Ichibei in a partnership with the Sōma family in February 1877.

Some members of the Sōma family were opposed to this new mining venture, but Ichibei persuaded them to accept his plan. The mine's owner demanded a down payment of ¥15,000 and the assumption of his debt of ¥33,000 to Mitsui Bank. The Sōma and Ichibei bore the cost equally. The Sōma, however, provided the necessary security for taking over the debt since the annual income from the Kusakura mine was only about ¥3,000; Ichibei borrowed his half of the down payment from the Daiichi Kokuritsu Bank. It was agreed that Ichibei would be responsible for managing the Ashio mine and that he would share the profit or loss equally with the Sōma family.[50]

To overcome a shortage of funds resulting from the Ashio's low output, Ichibei brought Shibusawa into his partnership with the Sōma family in 1880. Shibusawa, the Sōma family, and Ichibei each contributed one-third of the start-up and operating capital. Ichibei did everything possible to develop the Ashio mine, even sinking his earnings from the Kusakura mine into it. His efforts were rewarded in 1884, when a large vein of ore was discovered at Ashio. Output grew dramatically, and he reaped ample profits. He bought out the Sōma family's share in the Ashio in 1886 for ¥120,000, payable in installments over five years, and Shibusawa's share in 1888 for ¥400,000, payable in installments over eight years.[51] The Ashio mine was then entirely his.

Ichibei also acquired from the government the Innai mine in 1884 and the Ani mine the following year. Both mines were originally Ono operations that had been run by the government after Ono's collapse. Both were equipped with machinery imported from abroad and employed a number of mining engineers with university degrees. These acquisitions contributed to the modernization of the Furukawa mining enterprises, which now centered on the Ashio mine.[52]

Ichibei used the profits from the Ashio mine as the basis for further modernization of his mining empire. The mines were electrified, and the Bessemer process introduced. Ichibei built a refinery in Tokyo with a reverberatory furnace in 1884 and then introduced electric smelting in 1889. At Ashio in December 1890 he opened Japan's second hydroelectric plant and the first to power an industrial enterprise.[53] The electric smelting equipment and hydroelectric plant were both purchased from the German firm Siemens. Ichibei thus became a pioneer in modern mining and metallurgy as well as in hydroelectric power in Japan.

Furukawa Ichibei's eagerness to introduce new technology stemmed from his need to achieve rapid increases in productivity to fulfill an advantageous contract he had signed with Jardine, Matheson & Company in 1888. He had agreed to supply 19,000 metric tons of copper over a twenty-eight-month period, or 680 metric tons a month, at the high price of about ¥345 a ton. At the time of the signing of the contract, the output of the Furukawa mines was only 400 metric tons a month.[54] As a result of his efforts to upgrade the mines, Ichibei was able to raise their monthly output to a level sufficient to fulfill the contract. Production at the Ashio mine grew very rapidly—in 1891 its output was 7,550 tons, or 3.6 times that of the Besshi mine. By that time Furukawa had become Japan's largest producer of copper.

Asano

The origin of the Asano zaibatsu was in neither political merchant activities nor mining. The founder, Asano Sōichirō, moved to Tokyo from his home prefecture of Toyama with only ¥33 in his pocket. At first he was a street vendor of sugar water; he then moved to Yokohama where he undertook a series of businesses, from selling bamboo sheaths (used to wrap food) to retailing firewood, charcoal, and coal, and gradually he built up his capital. He noticed in 1876 the potential uses for coke, a by-product of coal gas production, of which the gaslight company in Yokohama was having trouble disposing. He was able to supply the coke as fuel to the government-run cement factory and to Shōshi Kaisha, a paper manufacturer, both located in Tokyo. This operation proved to be a breakthrough for Asano: because of its success, he came under the patronage of Shibusawa Eiichi, president of both the Daiichi Kokuritsu Bank and Shōshi Kaisha.[55]

Thereafter, through introductions by Shibusawa, Asano cornered the market in coal, in particular reaping high profits through the sale of coal from the state-run Hokkaido Colliery (Hokkaido Tankō). Again with Shibusawa's assistance, Asano was able to buy a government cement factory in 1884 and to found Asano Shipping (Asano Kaisōten) in 1886, with the goal of shipping cement and coal in his own vessels. In 1893 Shibusawa stood guarantor for him so that he could acquire the exclusive right to sell in eastern Japan kerosene produced in Russia and imported by Samuel, Samuel, & Company. That acquisition marked the beginning of Asano's petroleum division.[56]

Shibusawa was a leader in the business world and had close ties to the government, but he was not a powerful political figure—thus his assistance does not qualify Asano as a zaibatsu with political merchant origins. Furthermore, though Asano did found the Iwaki Colliery (Iwaki Tankō Kaisha) with Shibusawa and others, his business origins were not primarily in mining operations. Of the eight zaibatsu discussed thus far, then, Asano stands alone with roots outside the two main categories of zaibatsu origins.

FROM POLITICAL MERCHANTS TO ZAIBATSU

Political merchants, with their close ties to the wielders of state power, could grow fat on government favors, but the business was extremely risky. A change in the views or policies of those in authority was enough to throw a political merchant into an operating crisis. Such firms were required to pay kickbacks in return for the special privileges received, but if their official patron fell from power, they could fall with him. Such powerful businesses as Ono and Shimada did indeed collapse in this manner in early Meiji. Even Mitsui and Mitsubishi weathered several near-fatal crises. The political merchants, having built fortunes on the basis of their special government charters, needed to switch off the political merchant track as soon as possible to ensure their preservation and continued growth. Those that followed the path to zaibatsu formation all succeeded in making the switch, jettisoning their reliance on government patronage. This clearly argues against the simple thesis that the zaibatsu developed directly out of political merchants.

Mitsui

Mitsui and Mitsubishi offer prime examples of firms that underwent the metamorphosis from political merchant to zaibatsu. In the case of Mitsui, Mitsui Bank initially relied on government deposits to enlarge its operations. The disadvantage of this situation was that those who furnished Mitsui with government connections could and did take advantage of the fact that it depended on their favor to secure official patronage. When they demanded loans as kickbacks for having public revenues deposited in Mitsui Bank, the bank provided the loans on a rather casual basis without requiring the posting of security or strict repayment. As a result, bad debts accumulated. In the first half of 1880, when government deposits accounted for 43 percent of the bank's total deposits, bad debts represented 28 percent of its total debts. These two figures had risen respectively to 55 and 39 percent by the end of 1882. After the Bank of Japan was founded that year, the figure for government deposits declined until at the end of 1890 it stood at only 12 percent; however, the contemporaneous figure for bad debts remained largely unchanged at 36 percent.[57] Adding to the bank's woes was the shortage of able managers following the death of the de facto president, Minomura Rizaemon, in 1877. Furthermore, with the establishment of the Bank of Japan, Mitsui Bank was required to yield its handling of government deposits to the new central bank by 1886. As a matter of course, Mitsui Bank had to abandon its dependence on deposits of public funds. Yet the old-fashioned Mitsui managers (*bantō*) were unable to shift the bank from the political merchant course it had been following; in fact, they did nothing but petition for a delay in the cutoff of government business. Consequently, the management of the bank, burdened with bad debts, continued to deteriorate.

Government leaders, learning from sources within the bank of Mitsui Bank's worsening situation, feared that its failure would deal a serious blow to the economy. Accordingly, they appointed one of their number, Inoue Kaoru, who had close ties to the Mitsui family, to undertake the reconstruction of the bank.[58] Inoue regarded the old-line *bantō* as incapable of rebuilding Mitsui Bank. In addition, the bank's advisers—Shibusawa, Masuda Takashi, and Minomura Risuke—were all preoccupied with other concerns.[59] So Inoue reached outside Mitsui to find talented personnel for the task at hand, commissioning Takahashi Yoshio, a graduate of Keiō Gijuku (now Keiō University) and a journalist specializing in economics, in January 1891 to examine the bank's operations and draw up a reorganization plan. Takahashi submitted a plan that called for the collection of bad debts, among other reforms.[60]

Inoue wanted a more forceful character than Takahashi to put through the reforms and so asked Nakamigawa Hikojirō, another Keiō graduate and president of the San'yō Railway Company, to become director of Mitsui Bank. Nakamigawa agreed, but his appointment initially met with opposition not only from the *bantō* but also from Masuda and the other advisors, who regarded Nakamigawa as a disagreeable nuisance. In July 1891, however, almost immediately after Nakamigawa agreed to the move, there was a run on the Kyoto branch of Mitsui Bank. Given the shaky state of the bank, the *bantō* and advisors had no alternative but to accept his appointment.[61] Even after Nakamigawa was named director of the bank, the old *bantō* Nishimura Torashirō and Nakai Sanpei had, as vice presidents, a higher position. Nakamigawa objected to Inoue; as a result, Nishimura and Nakai resigned, and Nakamigawa was promoted to vice president in February 1892. Having thus gained control over the bank's management, he immediately set about instituting major reforms.[62] Correctly recognizing that Mitsui Bank's operational difficulties stemmed from its dependence on government patronage, he directed the bank to stop accepting deposits of public funds and close the many branches that had been opened to accommodate government business. Having denied Mitsui Bank the political merchant course of action, he succeeded in forcing the elimination of the bank's enormous backlog of bad debts.[63]

Mitsubishi

Like Mitsui, Mitsubishi accumulated a huge amount of capital through its political merchant activities, but it too suffered because of its dependence on government patronage. With official backing and its deep capital base built up during the Satsuma Rebellion, Mitsubishi contributed greatly to the development of the Japanese shipping industry. Its monopoly power, however, made Mitsubishi vulnerable to charges that it was capturing excessive profits through the high fares it charged, neglecting to replace its fleet with new steamships, pouring capital earned in the shipping industry into a wide range of nonshipping enterprises, and acquiring large numbers of shares in several major companies. The government was finally unable to ignore these criticisms of Mitsubishi.[64]

The state policies protective of Mitsubishi were largely the work of two government leaders, Ōkubo Toshimichi and Ōkuma Shigenobu. Ōkubo was assassinated in 1878, however, and Ōkuma ousted from political power in 1881; thus, Mitsubishi lost its two principal patrons within the regime and found its position as a political merchant seriously weakened. Moreover, the state leaders who had driven Ōkuma from power regarded Mitsubishi, Ōkuma's confederate, as a target for attack. As they saw it, Ōkuma in politics, Mitsubishi's Iwasaki in business, and Keiō founder Fukuzawa Yukichi in education had joined forces to create a powerful triumvirate.[65]

Accordingly, in 1882 the government promulgated a directive forbidding Mitsubishi to engage in business activities outside of the shipping industry.[66] Moreover, in October of that year, it established a new shipping company to compete with Mitsubishi. The new enterprise, Kyōdō Un'yu Kaisha, or KUK, was a merger of three small shipping firms with financial support from the government and powerful figures in the business world. It was capitalized at ¥6 million, of which ¥2.6 million was provided by the state. As William Wray has argued, the government did not intend to use KUK to beat down Mitsubishi so that KUK could become the shipping-industry champion. This is clear from the fact that Mitsubishi continued to receive ¥200,000 to ¥300,000 a year in government subsidies to cover its operating costs, whereas KUK got almost no subsidy.[67] Nevertheless, it does not automatically follow that the government's intention in establishing KUK was simply to generate competition in the shipping industry and to secure a shipping company that would be more cooperative than Mitsubishi in providing military transport.[68] Given that the founding of KUK came within a year of Ōkuma's ouster, it is certain that a politically motivated desire to strike at Mitsubishi, Ōkuma's business ally, was also at work. Furthermore, criticism of Mitsubishi as monopolistic and uncooperative had been common well before the establishment of KUK.

Mitsubishi sustained heavy damage as a result of its confrontation with KUK. As competition heated up, fares were lowered, reducing revenues. This painful situation was exacerbated by the economic slump beginning in 1881 and by the establishment in 1884 of yet another shipping company, Osaka Shōsen Kaisha (OSK). During this period Mitsubishi posted losses not recompensed by the government subsidies received.

At the same time, however, Mitsubishi was making every effort to expedite repayment of the debts incurred with the regime, including the price of the thirty steamships provided by the government and the borrowed money. The period for repaying the ¥1.2 million it owed for the thirty steamships was fifty years from 1877. Far from taking the full fifty years, Mitsubishi liberated itself from this debt in July 1883. It made an immediate payment of ¥370,000, which represented the principal of the debt outstanding—approximately ¥1.05 million—and was calculated by deducting interest compounded at 6 percent and figured backwards over the remainder of the repayment period.[69] Again, in February 1885 Mitsubishi cleared its debt for money borrowed from the government, some ¥1.32 million, by making an immediate payment of ¥630,000, calculated backward at 10 percent interest.[70]

The early repayment of these loans, particularly that of July 1883, was directly related to the terms of the government directive, which specified that Mitsubishi could not sell the steamships until the ¥1.2 million loan covering the ships' purchase price had been paid.[71] Immediate repayment was therefore necessary to ensure that Mitsubishi could sell the old ships and acquire new ones. The early repayment was a practical move, but it also had symbolic significance: we can see Mitsubishi's desire to be free of its political merchant status as soon as possible.

The government's use of KUK to attack Mitsubishi did cause a downturn in the latter's shipping business, but while Mitsubishi managed to cover its shipping losses with profits generated by its diversified nonshipping operations, KUK went deeply into the red.[72] Compared with Mitsubishi, which was receiving government subsidies and as a personal enterprise did not have to worry about pleasing stockholders, KUK was in a disadvantageous position: it did not enjoy government subsidies, and its management was beset by stockholders clamoring for dividends.

Concern over the danger of collapse of both Mitsubishi and KUK and over the confusion prevailing in the Japanese shipping industry prompted efforts within and without the government to arrange a merger between the two firms beginning in early 1885. After Iwasaki Yatarō died that February following an illness, the top management at Mitsubishi recognized that a union was unavoidable and began pressing for favorable terms. At KUK Morioka Masazumi, a supporter of the government's demand for a merger, was appointed president in April.[73] These changes speeded the merger negotiations, and as a result, in September Mitsubishi and KUK combined to form a new company, Nippon Yūsen Kaisha (Nippon Mail Steamship Company), or NYK. NYK had authorized capital of ¥11 million in 220,000 shares, of which the former KUK owners got 120,000 and the Iwasaki family 100,000. This unequal distribution of shares was apparently the product of two considerations: concern that KUK stockholders would otherwise vehemently oppose the merger and fear that the Iwasaki family would dominate the new firm should it hold a majority of the shares.[74] As it was, with five-elevenths of the shares, the Iwasaki family was unquestionably the largest stockholder in NYK. Its position was far superior to that of both the government, which held 52,000 shares, and the former KUK shareholders from the private sector (4,608 as of the end of 1885), who held a total of 68,000 shares.[75]

Although the Iwasaki family had created an enormous fortune by acting as the government's shipping agent, it became embroiled in political confrontations because of that very dependence on the government. After its very painful experience as a political merchant in the early 1880s, the family was left with no alternative but to abandon overall ownership and control of its shipping business. But in exchange it was able to escape the political merchant role. By expanding into fields other than shipping, Mitsubishi was reborn as a zaibatsu. Meanwhile, the government, as a means of promoting the merger between Mitsubishi and KUK, guaranteed annual returns of 8 percent for a period of fifteen years on shares held in NYK. The Iwasaki family therefore could expect to receive an annual dividend of at least ¥400,000 on its initial share of NYK stock.[76] A more important source of capital for Mitsubishi's diversification, however, was its sale of large blocks of its NYK shares in the late 1880s and 1890s. The holding and particularly the sale of NYK stock thus proved to be a powerful asset for Mitsubishi.

SUMMARY

How did the zaibatsu compare in the amount of wealth amassed through their activities? Table 1.1 shows the annual incomes of six of

TABLE 1.1   Annual Income of the Major Zaibatsu Families, 1895

Zaibatsu family	Annual income (thousand yen)
Iwasaki	1,084
Mitsui	529
Sumitomo	156
Yasuda	94
Ōkura	65
Furukawa	62

SOURCE: Ishii Kanji, *Nihon keizai shi* (Japanese Economic History) (Tokyo: University of Tokyo Press, 1976), p. 202.

the zaibatsu families in 1895—the earliest comparative data available that have some degree of reliability. Except for Sumitomo and Furukawa, each figure is a total for the entire extended family. The table leaves no doubt that the wealth attained by the Mitsui and especially the Iwasaki families was enormous.

The backgrounds of the wealthy individuals who founded zaibatsu differed in several ways: there were the political merchants who established Mitsui, Mitsubishi, Yasuda, Ōkura, and Fujita; the mining entrepreneurs who formed Sumitomo and Furukawa; and the founder of Asano, who falls into a special category. Hence, to conclude that the zaibatsu all originated as political merchants is clearly erroneous. The development of the zaibatsu in fact shows that the risks and uncertainty involved in dependence on government support were not conducive to long-term growth. Mitsui and Mitsubishi, for example, were able to begin development as zaibatsu only after they had *stopped* being government purveyors. Similarly, Yasuda rapidly reduced its banking operation's dependence on government deposits, and at Ōkura and Fujita political merchant activities became just one part of a diversified management structure.

CHAPTER 2

EMERGENCE OF THE ZAIBATSU

Throughout the 1870s and 1880s, the Mitsui, Yasuda, Ōkura, Fujita, Mitsubishi, Sumitomo, and Furukawa family businesses used the fortunes that they had accumulated through political merchant activities or mining ventures to set about diversifying their enterprises, thus paving their way for emergence as zaibatsu. Asano, which built its wealth through means other than political merchant or mining operations, also embarked on diversification and thereby transformed itself into a zaibatsu as well.

The sale of government enterprises to the emergent zaibatsu during this period played an extremely important role in accelerating their diversification. The new Meiji government, challenged by Japan's late industrial development and the poor prospects for private initiative in the field, itself started a number of modern enterprises. It invested large sums of money in the purchase of machinery and equipment from abroad and hired scores of foreign engineers at princely salaries. Most of the state enterprises, however, turned out to be ill-managed and money-losing operations, and by 1880 the financial burden had become unbearable for the government. Consequently, with the exception of enterprises that were deemed unsuitable for private management, such as military arsenals and postal services, the government sold off its industrial operations to private entrepreneurs. The prices were generally low and the conditions of payment easy. Such circumstances did not mean that the government was showing undue favoritism toward private business; rather, the performance of state enterprises was so poor that if the government had not made the sale terms attractive no buyers may have appeared. Eventually, the regime sold off even such profitable enterprises as the Miike Coal Mine in line with its policy of transferring the responsibility for industrialization to private business.[1]

Despite the significance of the sale of state enterprises for the emergence of the zaibatsu, its importance should not be exaggerated to the point where the sale is regarded as having created the zaibatsu. For one thing, some zaibatsu, such as Sumitomo and Yasuda, did not pick up any of the enterprises put up for sale. On the other hand, some businesses did buy state enterprises and yet never acquired zaibatsu status—for instance, the firms owned by Nishimura Katsuzō, who purchased Fukagawa Hakurenga Seizōsho (Fukagawa White Brick Factory) and Shinagawa Garasu Seizōsho (Shinagawa Glass Factory), and Tanaka Chōbei, who bought the Kamaishi Iron Mine.

While diversifying operations, the nascent zaibatsu did not try to establish their own enterprises in the leading sectors of Meiji industrialization, namely, the railway and cotton-spinning industries. At that time even the wealthy zaibatsu families had relatively limited financial reserves, especially in light of the huge investment required to set up a major railway. Of the three biggest railroad companies of the Meiji era, the Nippon Railway was capitalized at ¥20 million, the San'yō Railway at ¥13 million, the Kyushu Railway at ¥11 million. The ability of the zaibatsu, with commitments to numerous enterprises, to singlehandedly supply the capital of the largest cotton-spinning company in 1890— ¥1.2 million—would have been severely tried. These fields were consequently left to joint-stock companies, which could pool the necessary capital from numerous sources, and the zaibatsu confined their involvement in railway and spinning firms to participation as major shareholders. The Iwasaki, Yasuda, and Fujita all owned large blocks of railway shares. The Mitsui held a number of shares in Kanegafuchi Cotton Spinning, as did the Sumitomo and Fujita in Osaka Cotton Spinning. The principal exception came in the 1890s when Mitsui did attempt to manage Kanegafuchi directly. For the most part, however, the fields into which the zaibatsu diversified during this period, such as finance and trade, provided the infrastructure for these leading sectors.

The implementation of the Commercial Code in 1893 led to major changes in the structure of the budding zaibatsu. The corporate system had been introduced into Japan immediately after the Meiji Restoration, with joint-stock companies and similar enterprises having been formed one after another. But only from around 1880 had the Japanese begun to understand the concept of limited liability and the essence of the joint-stock company form, and to establish joint-stock ventures possessing that essential feature. The enforcement of the Commercial Code marked the end of this period of trial and error and the establishment of the modern corporate system.[2] The adoption of modern company structures under the Commercial Code combined with diversification to transform the family businesses of early Meiji into the zaibatsu.

EARLY DIVERSIFICATION

Mitsubishi

Mitsubishi was the zaibatsu that most actively diversified during the early Meiji period. Mitsubishi engaged in a variety of secondary businesses peripheral to its principal line of shipping. By government order, however, the shipping company Yūbin Kisen Mitsubishi Kaisha could not be involved directly in any of those sidelines.[3] Mitsubishi's nonshipping businesses during its first decade and a half can be classified into several groups.

FORMER TOSA DOMAIN ENTERPRISES. Iwasaki Yatarō undertook the operation of the enterprises formerly run by the Tosa domain, including the production of camphor oil, raw silk, and tea, and the sale of Kōchi cottons. All were terminated fairly early on. The camphor oil operation had earned annual profits of about ¥18,000, but the irksome regulations imposed on it by Kōchi Prefecture (successor to the Tosa domain) led to its abandonment in 1875.[4] The other lines were dropped because they did not prove commercially viable.

Two other former Tosa enterprises that came into Mitsubishi hands were the Manzai and Otokawa coal mines in Wakayama Prefecture. Mitsubishi's predecessor, Tsukumo Shōkai, a de facto Tosa domain enterprise, had received the right to operate the mines in payment for a steamship sold to the Shingū domain. The mines produced about 1,200 metric tons of coal annually, most of which was used to fuel the Mitsubishi steamships. Otokawa was an inconvenient location for loading and shipping coal, however, so the coal-mining operation was terminated in 1874. Foreign engineers were dispatched to the Manzai mine in an effort to increase its production, but in 1884 it too was closed.[5]

YOSHIOKA COPPER MINE. Mitsubishi bought this old copper mine in Okayama Prefecture from its owner, a former daimyō, for ¥10,000. The deed lists Kawada, Ishikawa, and Morita (also known as Nakagawa) as the buyers. Since these were the three men from whom the name Mitsukawa Shōkai was derived, it seems likely that the mine was purchased on their initiative.[6]

SHIPPING-RELATED BUSINESSES. These enterprises included Mitsùbishi Seitetsusho (Ship Repair Facility) and Mitsubishi Kawaseten (Exchange Office). Mitsubishi Seitetsusho dated from a December 1875 joint purchase with Royd & Company, an English trading firm operating in Shanghai and Nagasaki, of a small shipyard then under construction in Yokohama. It was established with capital contributions of $100,000 each from Mitsubishi and Royd & Company. Operating many steamships, Mitsubishi had need of its own dry dock for their repair. The shipyard was transferred in 1879 to Mitsubishi's full ownership. When Nippon Yūsen Kaisha (NYK) was established, it took over the repair facility, but some of the employees and facilities were transferred to the Nagasaki Shipyard, leased by Mitsubishi from the government in 1884.[7]

Mitsubishi established the exchange office during its shipping war with the P&O to draw off shippers from the latter. Opened at Mitsubishi's Osaka branch in June 1876, it provided shippers with credit against their cargo. Iwasaki Yatarō favored entering this business in order to build a base that would prove useful in founding a bank.[8] Since the government did not permit Mitsubishi Kaisha to engage in finance as a sideline, the exchange office was spun off as Mitsubishi Exchange Office in 1880, and it also engaged in banking and warehousing.[9] Its capital, which was raised or lowered as circumstances warranted, was initially set at ¥1 million, a large sum. Hida Shōsaku, a Keiō Gijuku graduate and assistant manager of the Fifteenth National Bank, was appointed as manager.[10] In view of the office's shortage of loan funds, the riskiness of lending against cargoes, and the business difficulties of the parent company owing to the depression of the early 1880s and competition with KUK, Mitsubishi decided to give up the operation in 1884. In August of the following year, the exchange office was formally closed as part of Mitsubishi's withdrawal from the shipping business.[11]

TAKASHIMA COAL MINE AND NAGASAKI SHIPYARD. Both these enterprises were brought into Mitsubishi almost accidentally, without Iwasaki Yatarō's express approval. Both also formed starting points for Mitsubishi's growth into coal mining and heavy industries, key fields for the developing Mitsubishi zaibatsu.

Takashima Coal Mine had since the Meiji Restoration been operated jointly by the Saga domain, ruled by the Nabeshima family, and a Western merchant, first a Britisher, Thomas B. Glover, and then a Dutchman, A. J. Bauduin, after Glover went bankrupt.[12] In 1873 the Japanese government established laws forbidding non-Japanese to operate mines in Japan, and accordingly bought out the Takashima mine in January 1874, undertaking to operate it as a state enterprise. In November of that year the mine was sold to Gotō Shōjirō's company, the Hōraisha; Gotō borrowed the $200,000 to buy the mine and another large sum to operate it from the British firm Jardine, Matheson & Co. The Hōraisha, however, failed, and Gotō was saddled with debts of $900,000 and ¥350,000 to Jardine, Matheson.

The great Meiji intellectual and educator Fukuzawa Yukichi was concerned about Gotō's distressed circumstances, for Fukuzawa had high hopes that Gotō, who was also a politician, would contribute to the establishment of parliamentary government in Japan. Fukuzawa consequently turned to his friend Iwasaki Yatarō in 1878 and asked him to take over Gotō's debts in exchange for the Takashima Coal Mine. As the sum of money required was so large, Iwasaki steadfastly resisted making the deal, but the affair did not end there. Iwasaki owed Gotō a debt of gratitude for his help when they were both men of the Tosa domain; in addition, Gotō was the father-in-law of Iwasaki's younger brother Yanosuke. Moreover, a group within Mitsubishi, including Iwasaki Yanosuke, Kawada Koichirō, and Shōda Heigorō, strongly favored the acquisition of the Takashima mine. In the end, Iwasaki paid Gotō some ¥970,000 in 1881 to acquire and then run the mine.

The government-operated Nagasaki Shipyard was leased to Yūbin Kisen Mitsubishi Kaisha for a period of twenty years beginning in June 1884.[13] The government had two goals in deciding to lease the shipyards to a major shipping company: to reduce expenditures and improve efficiency. Why the authorities chose Mitsubishi rather than KUK, which was then receiving government patronage, is unclear. At any rate, the transfer to Mitsubishi came about at the instigation of the government, not Mitsubishi.[14]

119TH NATIONAL BANK. Rakusan Shōkai (Rakusan Trading Company) of Hakodate, Hokkaido, which had Mitsubishi Exchange Office as one of its creditors, failed in 1884. Two national banks that had invested in Rakusan, the 119th and the 149th, were affected by the failure to the extent that they showed signs of collapse themselves. The former daimyō and many former samurai of Usuki domain (in present-day Ōita Prefecture) owned stock in the two banks. Since Shōda Heigorō, the senior executive director (*kanji*) of Mitsubishi Kaisha, also hailed from Usuki, the banks' stockholders from the former Usuki domain appealed to Mitsubishi, through Shōda, to come to their rescue. Negotiations over a Mitsubishi bail out began while Iwasaki Yatarō was still alive, culminating in May 1885, three months after his death, with the merger of the two banks into the 119th National Bank, capitalized at ¥430,000, with the Iwasaki family acquiring all of the stock.[15] Hida Shōsaku, former manager of the defunct Mitsubishi Exchange Office, was appointed president.

SENKAWA SUIDŌ KAISHA. Iwasaki privately operated this public water company that had been founded in 1880 with ¥50,000 in capital. In 1908 its facilities were given to the city of Tokyo and the company dissolved.[16]

STOCKHOLDING. Iwasaki family members were also major stock-holders in a variety of firms, including railway (San'yō, Kyushu, and Nippon railways), insurance (Tokio Marine Insurance and Meiji Life Insurance), and trading companies (Bōeki Shōkai).

The case of Bōeki Shōkai deserves particular mention. Based on a plan by Fukuzawa Yukichi, Bōeki Shōkai was founded in July 1880 to carry out direct exports of raw silk. Of ¥200,000 in capital, ¥80,000 was put up by Iwasaki Yatarō. Hayashi Yūteki, head of the book importing firm Maruya, was appointed president, and Asabuki Eiji, a Mitsubishi employee, manager. With employees stationed in London, New York, Lyon, and Vladivostok, the company directly exported raw silk and imported and exported other goods without going through foreign merchants in Japan. A number of circumstances, including inadequate preparation, a business slump, and the failure of anticipated government protection to materialize, made its course difficult.[17] Added to these factors was its deficient personnel training: "A man fresh out of school with no trading experience becomes an employee because he has studied a little English and asks in what part of Hokkaido is Vladivostok located."[18] Despite these shortcomings, Bōeki Shōkai attempted to develop from the start as a general trading company handling direct sales of a wide range of items in a variety of regions. This overly ambitious approach failed, and in 1886 the firm merged with Dōshin Kaisha, another company trading directly in raw silk, which, after various changes, was in turn absorbed by Mitsubishi Shōji (Mitsubishi Trading Company) in 1924.

After transferring its shipping operations to NYK, Mitsubishi turned to the other diversified enterprises it had nurtured outside of the shipping business. It moved from sea to land.

Yūbin Kisen Mitsubishi Kaisha is considered to have dissolved upon the formation of NYK. Mitsubishi thereafter engaged in the diversified enterprises mentioned earlier, loosely using the name Mitsubishi Sha or Mitsubishi Kaisha. The name Mitsubishi Sha (Mitsubishi Company) was officially registered in March 1886.[19] Iwasaki's younger brother, Yanosuke, was named president, and he was assisted by Kawada, the senior executive director, and Shōda, manager of the central office.[20] In 1888 Shōda took over as senior executive director while serving concurrently as manager of the central office.[21]

TABLE 2.1   Sources of Income for Mitsubishi Company, 1886, 1889, and 1892 (% of total income)

Source	Year		
	1886	1889	1892
Interest on government securities	13.0	19.3	17.8
Stock dividends	25.8	24.6	27.1
Interest on loans	10.2	3.6	0.0
Real estate	0.4	2.4	3.0
Coal mining	41.5	45.1	37.5
Other mining	3.9	0.9	10.5
Shipbuilding	5.2	4.1	4.1
Total income	100.0	100.0	100.0

SOURCE: Hatate Isao, *Nihon no zaibatsu to Mitsubishi* (Japanese Zaibatsu and Mitsubishi) (Tokyo: Rakuyu Shobō, 1978), pp. 32–33.

Mitsubishi Company was founded to provide a new administrative structure for Mitsubishi's increasing forays into diversified enterprises. The three principal sources of funds for the company's diversification strategy were dividends on NYK stock and proceeds from the sale of that stock; dividends on railroad, insurance, and other stocks and proceeds from the sale of those stocks; and earnings from the diversified enterprises, in which coal mining revenues loomed especially large. (See Table 2.1.) Income from coal mining and dividends from stockholdings accounted for two-thirds of Mitsubishi Company's profits, which financed the company's diversification into several fields.

COAL MINING. Mitsubishi bought Shinnyū and Namazuda coal mines in 1889 and Hashima mine in 1890. Shinnyū was purchased from the Nippon Sekitan Kaisha and Count Kawamura for more than ¥235,000;[22] Namazuda coal mine from Asō Takichi for ¥105,000;[23] and Hashima mine for ¥100,000 from a Nabeshima branch family. (The Nabeshima had ruled the domain of Saga in Kyushu.)[24]

METAL MINING. Mitsubishi Company bought several metal mines, including Osarizawa in Akita Prefecture and Makimine in Miyazaki Prefecture in 1887 and Omodani in Fukui Prefecture in 1889. Osarizawa had been operated by the family of Okada Heizō, who had deep ties to Senshū Kaisha, one of Mitsui Bussan's predecessors, and the purchase price, including purchase of the surrounding mines, was about ¥280,000.[25] The cost of the Makimine mine is unknown.

Omodani was purchased for ¥150,000 from a company formed by the village of Omodani and outside investors.[26]

BANKING. The 119th National Bank's capital increased from ¥430,000 to ¥1 million in 1890, as the bank achieved rapid growth under the direction of Toyokawa Ryōhei, who had replaced Hida as president the year before. The scale of operations, however, was still much smaller than that of Mitsui Bank: deposit figures for 1893 for the 119th National were ¥5.52 million as opposed to ¥16.77 million for Mitsui.[27]

SHIPBUILDING. Mitsubishi in 1887 purchased the state-owned Nagasaki Shipyard, which it had been operating on lease from the government since 1884. The terms of the sale were ¥450,000 payable over fifty years, but Mitsubishi acquired the shipyards with a one-time payment of ¥91,017 after deducting projected interest at 10 percent over the fifty-year term.[28] Shōda, who had gone on a study tour of England in 1889, then made a proposal, which was accepted, that Mitsubishi make the development of shipbuilding operations a strategic goal. Accordingly, beginning in 1893, Mitsubishi began acquiring land for shipyard construction in Kobe.[29] In a letter to Iwasaki Yanosuke, Shōda recommended that Mitsubishi also advance into iron and steel making. Iwasaki Yanosuke, however, decided against Mitsubishi's entry into that field on the grounds that the company would not be granted the government assistance necessary to establish a private iron and steel enterprise.[30] Instead, Mitsubishi Company's planning focused on the expansion of shipbuilding.

REAL ESTATE. The government sold to Mitsubishi in March 1890 a tract of land known as the Marunouchi. Totaling approximately 35.7 hectares (88.2 acres), the tract, located between the Imperial Palace (formerly Edo Castle) and the present site of Tokyo Station, is now prime commercial land—in 1890, however, it was a barren expanse formerly used by the military as barracks and parade grounds. The government had earlier requested Mitsubishi Company to accept the Marunouchi tract, but given the high asking price, ¥1.28 million, and the condition that it be paid within a year, as well as the economic slump then under way, Mitsubishi, like the other wealthy houses approached, hesitated. When Shōda, who was in England at the time and who held a long-cherished wish that Mitsubishi create in Japan a central business district such as the one he saw in London, learned about the offer, he decided that it was the opportunity he needed. He telegraphed Iwasaki Yanosuke, urging him to buy the land. Yanosuke decided to accept the government conditions and purchased the land.[31]

Upon returning to Japan, Shōda explained his plan for constructing a business district and received Yanosuke's approval. Mitsubishi promptly employed Sone Tatsuzō, an architect who had graduated from the University of Tokyo, to plan the development of the area. Construction on Mitsubishi Hall No. 1 began in 1892 and was completed in June 1894.[32] The purchase of the Marunouchi land and the construction of the Western-style brick building marked the beginning of today's Mitsubishi Jisho Kabushiki Kaisha (Mitsubishi Estate Co., Ltd.) and the Marunouchi business district.

AGRICULTURAL LAND. Mitsubishi moved into the business of renting the farmland it owned, but that played only a minor and brief role in its history. Still, Mitsubishi sank ¥34,800 in operating expenses beginning in 1887 in its reclaimed lands in Okayama, which measured 133 hectares at the time of their greatest extent.[33] The 1,126 hectares of paddy lands it owned in Niigata Prefecture received a total investment of ¥350,000, also beginning in 1887.[34] The Okayama agricultural lands were sold to Fujita-gumi for ¥80,000 in 1901.[35] The Niigata lands were handed over to the Iwasaki family's Tōzan Nōji (Tōzan Farms Co., Ltd.) in 1919 and then sold off beginning in 1926.[36]

The six types of enterprises into which Mitsubishi diversified represent only those that can be followed through the historical record. These enterprises alone, however, accounted for an investment of approximately ¥3.2 million, including the capital increase for the 119th National Bank. Mitsubishi's ample wealth presents a striking contrast to the situation of Mitsui, which had to strain its resources to find the ¥1 million down payment needed to buy the Miike Coal Mine from the government in 1888.

The Iwasaki family itself, during the Mitsubishi Company period (1886–93), made substantial investments that did not fall under the company's control. At the time of the founding of several railroad companies, including the San'yō, Kyushu, Chikuhō Kōgyō, and Hokuetsu, the Iwasaki contributed capital and became major shareholders. For instance, of the 260,000 shares in the San'yō Railway Company, capitalized at ¥13 million, the Iwasaki owned 25,490 shares, a figure that gave them a dominant position among the shareholders.[37] When the shares owned by Mitsubishi managers were added to the Iwasaki holdings, the total topped 30,000 shares. A great event in early railroading was the completion of the main line of the first private railway, Nippon

Tetsudō Kaisha (Nippon Railway Company), which ran from Ueno, in Tokyo, to Aomori, in the north of Honshū.

The Iwasaki family commemorated the achievement of building the railway line by opening—with Ono Yoshizane, the railway president, and Inoue Masaru, a government official—a 3,622 hectare (8,950 acre) farm run according to American farming methods on the outskirts of Morioka, in northeastern Japan. The Iwasaki supplied the necessary capital of ¥100,000 over ten years, but the management of the farm was left to Inoue. According to their contract, the farm was to be in Inoue's name and profits were to be split evenly between Inoue and the Iwasaki.[38] Although not a party to the contract, Ono was clearly involved in the venture. The farm was later given the name Koiwai, an acronym taken from the first characters of the surnames of the three principals.

The funds for these enormous investments by Mitsubishi or the Iwasaki family came in part from the profits of its coal mining and other ventures, from the dividends on its railway and life insurance company stock, and from the interest on government bonds, but ultimately, the most telling benefits were provided by the NYK stock. Mitsubishi had shed its political merchant role, but it had inherited the capital accumulated as a state-dependent shipping company in the form of NYK shares. It sold most of those shares, using the proceeds to invest in other enterprises while receiving a guaranteed dividend of 8 percent on the NYK shares it retained. Thus, without becoming embroiled in politics or suffering the kind of government interference that had plagued its political merchant days, Mitsubishi was able to proceed toward becoming a truly diversified enterprise. Its road to development as a zaibatsu was clear.

Mitsui

During the period in which the House of Mitsui acted as a political merchant providing financial services to the government, the only business formally operated by the Mitsui family was Mitsui Bank. The house did continue, however, to control the Mitsukoshi dry goods store, which took the form of an enterprise of the Mitsukoshi, a branch family outside the Mitsui family proper. The Mitsui also established their trading company, Mitsui Bussan, and its subsidiary, Miike Tankōsha (Miike Coal Mining). Thus, Mitsui was informally expanding the family business into a variety of new fields by setting up independent companies.

Mitsui Bussan, like Mitsui Bank, was founded on July 1, 1876. It was created by a merger of two predecessors, the Mitsui-gumi Kokusan Kata and Senshū Kaisha. The Kokusan Kata originated with the local finance agent offices (*fu-ken kawasekata*) established in April 1873 by the Mitsui-gumi Goyōsho, the forerunner of Mitsui Bank, in response to a government request that Mitsui, Ono, and the other official financiers handle the nationwide distribution of rice. The government made this request in anticipation of the conversion of the form of land tax payment that year from rice to cash. Local finance agent offices were to issue landowners bills of exchange against the rice they produced; the landowners required this service since they lacked access to a central rice market but would need currency to pay their land taxes. The landowners were to use the bills of exchange to pay those taxes. The local finance agent offices were to collect the rice, ship it to the central market, and sell it there, and the financiers, then, were to hold the proceeds and make them available to the government as needed. Under this system, the official financiers, with their control over access to the central rice market, reaped huge profits. The Mitsui-gumi Goyōsho (after February 1874, the Mitsui-gumi Kawase Bank) expanded its rice dealings and also handled regional products other than rice to garner further profits. The Kawase Bank in August 1874 organized the trading activities of the local finance agent offices into an independent trading division, the aforementioned Mitsui-gumi Kokusan Kata.[39]

The other forebear of Mitsui Bussan, Senshū Kaisha, was a trading company founded in March 1874 by Inoue Kaoru, who the previous year had resigned as Vice Minister of Finance; Masuda Takashi, former deputy director of the mint who had resigned with Inoue;[40] and the Mori, the former daimyō family of Chōshū, Inoue's own former domain. The company was established with investment cooperation from the American firm known as 14-ban Kan (14th Hall), a partnership of merchants Edward Fisher and Robert W. Irwin. It engaged in rice transactions and the importation and sale to the army of weapons, blankets, and cloth for uniforms. In its first two years Senshū Kaisha recorded ¥196,000 in profits.[41]

Inoue returned to the government in late 1875 and, after consultation with Masuda, decided to distribute the profits and close Senshū Kaisha in March 1876. Inoue then asked the Mitsui family to take on Masuda and the other Senshū Kaisha employees as well as its commercial contracts.[42] The Mitsui approved his request, and Mitsui Bussan was born out of a combination of the personnel and operations of Senshū Kaisha and Mitsui-gumi Kokusan Kata. But because the Mitsui family regarded trading as a risky business, the House of Mitsui did not invest at all in Mitsui Bussan—rather, two family members, Mitsui Takenosuke and Mitsui Yōnosuke, formed branch families[43] outside of

TABLE 2.2   Main Products Handled by Mitsui Bussan, 1890 and 1894 (% of total value of products handled)

Product	Year	
	1890	1894
Rice	25.8	14.7
Fertilizer, fish oil, and marine products	14.3	10.1
Coal	12.6	11.7
Raw cotton	11.0	18.7
Machinery	} 7.8	8.7
Metals		4.2
Raw silk	3.0	3.9
Cotton yarn	0.0	2.3
Total percentage	74.5	74.3

SOURCE: *Kōhon Mitsui Bussan Kabushiki Kaisha 100-nen shi* (100 years of Mitsui Bussan) (Tokyo; Japan Business History Institute, 1978), vol. 1, p. 92.

the Mitsui family proper and, without putting up capital but on the condition of a ¥50,000 overdraft approved by Mitsui Bank, founded Mitsui Bussan. Takenosuke and Yōnosuke were mere figureheads in the new company. The real top manager was Masuda, named president in 1880; R. W. Irwin cooperated as an adviser.[44]

At the time of its founding, Mitsui Bussan was mostly involved in distributing rice for the land tax, importing military materiel, and acting as the sole marketing agency for coal produced by the government's Miike mine. The trading company was eager to export Miike coal, and to foster that export it established branches in Nagasaki (1876), Shanghai (1877), and Hong Kong (1878). Until about 1890, however, rice sales accounted for an overwhelmingly dominant share of its business. (See Table 2.2.) Mitsui Bussan also opened overseas branches in Paris (1878), New York (1879), and London (1880). All but the London branch were soon closed; the Paris branch was never revived, but the one in New York was reopened in 1896. The closures suggest the difficulty of undertaking direct foreign trade at the time.

Not until 1881 did Mitsui Bussan's balance sheet fall into the red, but even in the better years the profit level was not high. (See Table 2.3.) The firm's performance finally improved in the 1890s, by which time it had grown into a general trading company handling not only rice and coal but a broader range of items, including raw cotton, machinery, metals, raw silk, and cotton yarn. (See Table 2.2.) The reason for its success lay in Masuda's solid strategic thinking, in which the training of able personnel was regarded as the chief determinant of

TABLE 2.3   Mitsui Bussan's Profits, 1876–93 (in yen)

Year	Profits
1876	7,921
1877	200,040
1879	150,861
1881	−103.209
1883	70,442
1885	60,165
1887	30,019
1889	40,000
1891	80,832
1893	282,412

SOURCE: Same as Table 2.2, pp. 80, 83.

success in overseas trade. He promoted operations on the slow but sure path of government-related sales of rice, Miike coal, and military supplies, for such official business, although not very profitable, was relatively stable, and meanwhile devoted time to training his personnel. Waiting until the employees were ready before gradually expanding the firm's list of products and geographical areas covered, he strategically opened the way to Mitsui Bussan's growth into a general trading company. This soundly cautious approach was in direct contrast to the reckless strategy employed by the Mitsubishi-affiliated Bōeki Shōkai.

Mitsui Bussan also branched out into the ownership of mines. When the government decided to sell its Miike mine in 1888 (in order to appease criticism that government ownership of Miike was having a detrimental market influence over private mines), Mitsui Bussan determined to buy it. If other hands obtained the mine, then Bussan would have to forego the profits that the firm, as sole agent for Miike, derived from commissions, rebates, and government-guaranteed low-interest lending and sales and transport expenses;[45] in addition, its establishment of overseas branches would also become meaningless. The minimum price for the mine, however, was ¥4 million—a ¥1 million down payment with the remainder to be paid over fourteen years.[46] The sum was large, Mitsui Bussan's performance at that point was far from dazzling, and Mitsui Bank was reeling under the burden of bad debts.

Despite the stiff purchase requirements, at Masuda's direction Mitsui Bussan participated in the bidding. The down payment was borrowed, after much pleading, from Mitsui Bank. When the bids were opened, Mitsui Bussan's offer of ¥4,555,000 was found to be the highest; second was that of Mitsubishi, at ¥4,552,300. Thus, by outbidding its nearest competitor by only ¥2,700, Mitsui Bussan narrowly succeeded in acquiring the Miike mine. Bussan formed Miike Tankōsha to begin operating the mine in late 1888. The company was capitalized at ¥5 million, with the investment shared equally by Bussan and Mitsui-gumi, the nominal agent of Mitsui Bank. Dan Takuma, a Massachusetts Institute of Technology graduate who had been an engineer at the Miike mine prior to its sale by the government, was named manager (*jimuchō*).

Miike Coal Mining had to pay the government ¥254,000 a year toward the purchase price and Mitsui Bank ¥80,000 a year as interest on the loan. To earn that sum, the enterprise had to increase output, since its annual profits (before paying annual installments) for the four years following the purchase averaged only ¥110,000.[47] If the mining company could only produce the coal, Mitsui Bussan could sell it. Dan believed that the way to increase output was to develop the Kattachi mine, a branch mine of Miike. The Kattachi was, however, plagued by flooding, and its water-pumping equipment was damaged in the major earthquake of July 1889. Undiscouraged, Dan convinced Masuda to introduce two Davey pumps (at the time the world's largest and most up-to-date) at a cost of ¥400,000; with them, Dan succeeded in removing the water and developing the Kattachi.[48]

Mitsui-gumi, the body representing Mitsui Bank, also owned and operated the Kamioka and Mosumi metal mines; and Mitsui Bussan owned and operated the Iwaoto sulphur mine and Kano antimony mine in addition to the Miike. Regarding the history of the Kamioka mine, before the founding of Mitsui Bank, Mitsui-gumi Kawase Bank had taken over loans made by the Nakanishi-gumi to Gifu Prefecture mine owners. The mines, which had been posted as security for the loans, were eventually acquired by Mitsui-gumi Kawase Bank. Both Mitsui-gumi Kawase Bank and its successor, Mitsui Bank, made unsuccessful efforts to sell them. In the end, the mines were consolidated in 1886 and operated under the Kamioka name by Mitsui-gumi, acting as Mitsui Bank's agent.[49]

Sumitomo

Sumitomo also diversified into a number of different fields during the first half of the Meiji era. Hirose Saihei, Sumitomo's top manager, had total authority over the Sumitomo family enterprises. Although he did pursue a general reconstruction strategy based on diversification, his policies were often irrational and arbitrary, as illustrated in the cases of banking and iron manufacture. Under Hirose's leadership Sumitomo diversified into the following fields.

FOREIGN TRADE. Through Kobe Copper Sales, which Sumitomo established in 1871 to sell copper to foreign merchants, silk, tea, and camphor were also sold. In addition, the conclusion of the Japan-Korea Treaty of Amity in 1873 presented an opportunity for opening up trade with Korea. Sumitomo set up branches in Pusan in 1878 and in Wonsan in 1880, but it was no match for the Chinese merchants already there and abandoned the field in 1882.[50]

SHIPPING. In the course of operating steamships carrying copper and other materials between Osaka, Kobe, Niihama, and additional points, Sumitomo began to accept general freight as well as passengers on the ships. It was operating two steamships in 1884, when fifty-five ship owners in western Japan came together to form Osaka Shōsen Kaisha (OSK) on the basis of an investment in kind of their ninety-three ships. Sumitomo was among the participants, and Hirose was appointed the first president of OSK.[51]

WAREHOUSING AND FINANCIAL ACTIVITIES. Sumitomo bought several *kurayashiki*, warehouses and offices that the old domains had maintained in Osaka to sell their annual rice revenues and other products there. While expanding its warehousing activities, the firm also moved into the financial activities known as *namiai*, whereby it made loans against the security of the merchandise entrusted to its warehouses. Some Sumitomo employees strongly favored developing the *namiai* business into a full-fledged banking operation, and the government as well wanted Sumitomo to establish a bank. Hirose, however, flatly refused to move from *namiai* into banking.[52] His stated reason was that Sumitomo should concentrate on its basic business, mining, but the evidence of the Korean trade venture shows that this was nothing but an excuse. Hirose's reluctance was basically a result of his ignorance of the banking system.

PRODUCTION FOR EXPORT. Sumitomo was itself engaged in processing the silk, tea, and camphor exported through its Kobe branch. It opened in 1880 a silk filature in Kyoto, which in 1887 was moved to a new plant in Samegai, Shiga Prefecture. Sumitomo began processing tea in 1888 and camphor in 1889; both of these operations were located in Kobe.[53]

IRON MANUFACTURE. Hydrometallurgical processing of pyrite began at the Besshi mine in 1878, and in 1886, following Hirose's wishes, Sumitomo started construction of a new Yamane plant for full-scale adoption of the hydrometallurgical method. Iwasa Iwao, a German-trained engineer, was employed for that purpose. Pointing out that the considerable quantities of iron and sulphur in the copper ore were recoverable by the hydrometallurgical method, Iwasa proposed that the mine produce pig iron and sulphuric acid as by-products. During a trip to Europe and the United States in 1889, Hirose noted the flourishing state of the iron and steel industries there and after his return ordered that, in line with Iwasa's proposal, pig iron and sulphuric acid production be initiated at the Yamane plant. Strong opposition to his plan arose from some Sumitomo employees because of the huge operating costs of iron production and also because of a quality problem related to the impossibility of fully removing the ore's copper content. Hirose nonetheless forged ahead and in 1893 set up a wrought iron division. The sulphuric acid operation, also expensive to run, was expanded without provisions for marketing.[54]

COAL MINING. Beginning in the 1890s Sumitomo switched to coal and coke as fuel for smelting copper at the Besshi mine, a change that led to increased coal consumption. In order to supply its own coal, Sumitomo bought a coal mine at Shōji, Fukuoka Prefecture, in 1893 and at Tadakuma, also in Fukuoka, in 1894.[55]

FOREST AND TENANT FARM LAND. Finally, Sumitomo maintained forest lands that were logged for fuel and for mine-pit props. To provide food for the miners at low cost, it owned extensive farmlands in Osaka and Niihama that were farmed by sharecroppers.

Other Zaibatsu Groups

YASUDA. Although Yasuda is commonly regarded as a financial zaibatsu, its diversification into fields outside finance must not be overlooked. Even after the founding of Yasuda Bank in 1880, Yasuda Shōten managed several nonfinancial operations. After Yasuda Shōten closed its doors in 1887, the Motojime Yakuba, founded in 1874 to manage Yasuda Zenjirō's private fortune, took over operation of the nonfinancial businesses.[56] Kushiro Sulphur Mine, which Yasuda had earlier acquired, in 1888 also came under Motojime Yakuba control. Other operations related to the Kushiro mine, including the Kushiro Railway, the warehouse business in Hakodate, and the sale of sulphur, were managed by the Motojime Yakuba as well.[57]

The scale of the nonfinancial activities was small, however, and Yasuda applied more capital to participation in such joint ventures as railway, insurance, and linen-spinning enterprises. Yasuda Zenjirō was particularly keen on the insurance business. In 1893 he acquired a large amount of Tokyo Kasai Hoken Kabushiki Kaisha (Tokyo Fire Insurance Company, Ltd.) stock and undertook its management himself. The same year, he founded Teikoku Kaijō Hoken Kabushiki Kaisha (Imperial Marine Insurance Company, Ltd.), with his family providing 30 percent of its ¥300,000 capital. Insurance is of course a form of finance, but the entry into this area is worth noting as a move toward diversification within the Yasuda zaibatsu's overall concentration on finance.

During this period, the holding of stocks in these enterprises was the task of Yasuda Bank. Yasuda set up in 1887 the Hozensha—initially nothing more than a body for managing the Yasuda Bank's capital—and quintupled the capital of the bank to ¥1 million. By 1894 the Hozensha had begun to function as a holding company; nonetheless, Yasuda Bank continued to carry out parallel holding-company functions.[58]

FUJITA. Fujita-gumi, under Kuhara Shōzaburō's name, bought the government's Kosaka mine in Akita Prefecture in 1884 for ¥273,600, payable over a period of twenty-five years. It also began operating other mines, including one in Ichinokawa, Ehime Prefecture. In addition, Fujita-gumi laid plans for a drainage operation in Kojima Bay, Okayama Prefecture. Initially a joint application to Okayama Prefecture for permission to undertake the project was made, but the applicants came to a parting of their ways; Fujita-gumi then applied independently in 1887, and the prefecture granted permission in 1889.[59] Fujita-gumi decided to concentrate its full resources on mining and drainage operations, and in 1887 it joined with Ōkura Kihachirō and Shibusawa Eiichi to establish two limited liability companies, Nippon Doboku (Nippon Construction), capitalized at ¥2 million, and Naigai Yōtashi (Naigai Contractors), at ¥500,000. Fujita-gumi then shifted the construction and contracting businesses it had been handling to the new companies, whose management was entrusted to Ōkura.[60]

Despite its decision to concentrate solely on mining and drainage, Fujita-gumi suffered from insufficient capital. Consequently, with Inoue Kaoru's introduction, the nascent zaibatsu borrowed a substantial sum from the Mōri family, the former daimyō house of the domain from which the Fujita family came. In 1891 the loans totaled ¥400,000.[61] Thanks to the Mōri family money Fujita-gumi was able to survive the blow of the 1890 financial crisis, but given its shortage of funds, Fujita was obliged to give up ownership of Nippon Construction and Naigai Contractors. Fujita-gumi reorganized in December 1893 as Gōmei Kaisha Fujita-gumi, an unlimited partnership capitalized at ¥600,000. It continued to be short of capital, and by 1903 loans from the Mōri had swollen to some ¥1.75 million.[62]

ŌKURA. The Ōkura family absorbed the business of Nippon Construction when the latter disbanded in the fall of 1892. This Ōkura enterprise named itself Ōkura Doboku-gumi (Ōkura Construction) in June 1893, and that November the unlimited partnership Gōmei Kaisha Ōkura-gumi was formed when Naigai Contractors, the other joint venture with Fujita and Shibusawa, merged with Ōkura-gumi Shōkai.[63] The initial capitalization is not known, but in 1905 it had a capital of ¥1 million.[64] Ōkura thus diversified operations by absorbing formerly joint enterprises. By this point in its development, however, it had not added any new operations.

FURUKAWA. Similarly, Furukawa at this stage did not venture beyond operations related to copper production, such as lumbering and coal mining.

ENFORCEMENT OF THE COMMERCIAL CODE AND ZAIBATSU REORGANIZATION

The formative phase of the zaibatsu came to a close with the implementation of the new Commercial Code (Book 2, Corporations) in July 1893. This act led to significant change in the organizational structures of the emergent zaibatsu. A system of three types of commercial entities was established under the code: unlimited partnerships (*gōmei kaisha*), limited partnerships (*gōshi kaisha*), and joint-stock companies (*kabushiki kaisha*). The establishment of joint-stock companies had already boomed beginning in the latter half of the 1880s. The new Commercial Code therefore gave a legal basis to the joint-stock company form. The zaibatsu also introduced formal company structures in accordance with the provisions of the code. The zaibatsu usually avoided the joint-stock company structure, which entailed public disclosure of financial details, a requirement that contradicted the zaibatsu rule of exclusive family ownership, and confined themselves to the limited or unlimited partnership form. Ultimately, after about 1910 they reorganized their operating enterprises into joint-stock companies, but that change did not affect their overall structures.

The Mitsui family, after its 1890 management crisis, accepted Inoue Kaoru's direction in reorganizing Mitsui Bank and the other family enterprises. Inoue was, of course, most concerned about the immediate problem, the improvement of Mitsui Bank's performance, but he also insisted on the establishment of a family constitution, the Mitsui *kaken*, as well as on a new administrative structure for the Mitsui family enterprises. The Mitsui responded by quickly making the necessary reforms, incorporating the opinions of their top salaried managers as well.[65] Among the steps they took was to establish in December 1891 an ultimate decision-making body, the Mitsui family Provisional Council (Kari Hyōgikai), to take up questions regarding both the family constitution and the administrative structure. Nakamigawa Hikojirō took part in defining and drafting rules for the council,[66] whose membership consisted of eight Mitsui family members; eight nonfamily members, including six Mitsui top salaried managers; and two outsiders, Shibusawa Eiichi and Minomura Risuke.[67] Under the Provisional Council system, Mitsui Bussan and Mitsukoshi Gofukuten (the dry goods store) were regarded as directly managed enterprises of the Mitsui family. Miike, Kamioka, and the other mines were grouped together in a new company, Mitsui Kōzan Kaisha (Mitsui Mining Company). It was decided that the function of the Provisional Council was to have overall control of the four operating companies, Mitsui Bank, Mitsui Mining, Mitsui Bussan, and Mitsukoshi Gofukuten.[68]

With the decision to regard Mitsui Bussan and Mitsukoshi as directly managed enterprises, membership in the House of Mitsui had to be given to Mitsui Takenosuke and Yōnosuke, who were partners in Mitsui Bussan, and to Mitsukoshi Tokuemon, the nominal owner of Mitsukoshi Gofukuten. Accordingly, in December 1892, the family decided to revive the three associate families that had been abolished at the end of the Tokugawa period, with Takenosuke, Yōnosuke, and Tokuemon designated as the heads, and to enroll the three men in the House of Mitsui.[69] The Mitsui house was thus restored to full strength with eleven families, and it remained that way until the dissolution of the zaibatsu after World War II.

Concurrent with the enforcement of the Commercial Code, the House of Mitsui in July 1893 organized Mitsui Bank, Mitsui Bussan, and Mitsui Mining (Mitsui Mining had been established in 1892 as a limited partnership) into unlimited partnerships. Mitsukoshi Gofukuten was made an unlimited partnership and renamed Mitsui Gofukuten that September. Also that year Mitsui Bussan had been reorganized in the unlimited partnership format but with the expectation that it would be changed into a limited partnership upon the implementation of the Commercial Code; Mitsui Gofukuten had been expected to adopt that mode as well. Likewise, in May 1893, the Provisional Council had decided to make Mitsui Bank into a limited partnership. Mitsui family members and the zaibatsu's top salaried managers had thought it desirable to limit the liability of the family members who owned the bank.[70] Until the 1899 reform of the Commercial Code, limited partnerships were all stipulated to be entities based fully on the limited liability system, but at the June 1893 Provisional Council meeting, adoption of the limited partnership format was vetoed and it was decided to set up all four operating companies as unlimited partnerships. The reasons for this sudden change are not clear, but Shibusawa's forceful defense of the unlimited partnership form at the meeting was said to have had a great effect.[71]

It is understandable that the House of Mitsui did not select the joint-stock company form, which would have necessitated making public the family's financial situation, but there is no obvious reason for its rejection of the limited partnership form in favor of the unlimited. Possibly the house regarded the joint and indivisible nature of the Mitsui fortune as incompatible with a limited liability system.[72] There also appear to have been suggestions that unlimited partnerships were preferable because they commanded greater trust from the public or because their capital could be increased or reduced without the registration that was required of limited partnerships.[73]

With unlimited liability, however, the danger was posed that the failure of one enterprise could lead to the collapse of all—and the fall of the House of Mitsui. To prevent such an occurrence, the heads of the eleven Mitsui houses were distributed among the four operating companies as partners, and the unlimited liability for a given company was to be borne by the partners in that company alone.[74] The lineup of partners follows.

> Mitsui Bank: Hachirōemon, Motonosuke, Takayasu, Hachirōjirō, and Morinosuke
> Mitsui Bussan: Takenosuke and Yōnosuke
> Mitsui Mining: Saburōsuke and Gen'emon
> Mitsui Gofukuten: Fukutarō and Tokuemon

The distribution of partnerships was, of course, a sham, and one that violated the Mitsui tradition (dating from the founding of the house) of joint ownership of the family fortune by the eleven houses. Therefore, in order to restore the structure to a form faithful to Mitsui tradition, in 1898 the heads of the eleven houses became partners in all four companies.[75]

Soon after the establishment of the four unlimited partnerships, the Mitsui decision-making bodies were also reorganized. The Ōmotokata Yoriai, the decision-making organ for matters concerning the Mitsui family, and the Provisional Council, the comparable organ for issues concerning the operating companies, merged in November 1893 to form the Mitsui-ke Dōzokukai (Mitsui Family Council).[76] This step resulted from the recognition that having parallel decision-making bodies could lead to difficulties in terms of coordination. The new Mitsui Family Council was composed of regular members (the heads of the eleven houses), associate members (the retired heads of the houses), six top salaried managers, and two outsiders (Shibusawa and Minomura Risuke).[77] The new council inherited the Provisional Council's function of carrying out overall management of the four unlimited partnership subsidiaries. Though it did not take a company form, it served as the central office of the Mitsui zaibatsu. With its establishment, Mitsui-gumi, which managed the joint fortune of the Mitsui family, was renamed the Mitsui Motokata.[78] The following year, real estate and manufacturing divisions were added to the Motokata. Overseeing four subsidiaries and two divisions as well as performing other functions was a huge burden for the Mitsui Family Council and Motokata. Consequently in 1896 the Mitsui Shōten Rijikai (Mitsui Board of Directors) was set up under the Mitsui Family Council to assume supervision of the subsidiaries and divisions.

Similarly, in December 1893, the Iwasaki, owners of Mitsubishi, reorganized Mitsubishi Company into Mitsubishi Gōshi Kaisha (Mitsubishi, Ltd.), capitalized at ¥5 million. Iwasaki Yanosuke and Iwasaki Hisaya (Yatarō's eldest son) each provided half the capital and were limited liability partners.[79] Hisaya was named president of Mitsubishi, Ltd., and Yanosuke backed him up as inspector (*kanmu*). The diversified enterprises operated by Mitsubishi, Ltd., formed units within that company, and such enterprises did not become independent companies until the middle of World War I.

In addition to the changes at Mitsui and Mitsubishi, the establishment of Gōmei Kaisha Ōkura-gumi, the reorganization of Yasuda Bank as a limited partnership, and the reorganization of Fujita-gumi as an unlimited partnership all stemmed from the implementation of the Commercial Code in 1893. On the other hand, no changes in the structure of the Sumitomo, Furukawa, and Asano zaibatsu occurred at this time.

THE RISE OF SALARIED MANAGERS

By the mid-1890s most of the nascent zaibatsu had undergone a transformation not only of their administrative structures but also of their top management personnel. The managerial change centered on the rise of full-time salaried managers. In order to pursue the strategies of expansion and diversification, the zaibatsu required a large number of such managers. Two routes existed whereby salaried managers emerged in the zaibatsu. In the zaibatsu formed by wealthy families that had been active enterprises since the Tokugawa period, managerial authority was usually entrusted to the historically older type of salaried managers known as *bantō*. The *bantō*, men of narrow scope with skills derived solely from their direct experience, could not keep up with the swift pace of modernization after the Meiji Restoration. Consequently, the appearance of a new type of salaried manager with knowledge appropriate to the new age was vital to the growth of these zaibatsu.

In the zaibatsu that arose after the Meiji Restoration, zaibatsu that had initially developed owing to the individual abilities and leadership of their founders, the changing business environment and increasing scale and complexity of operations made necessary the cooperation of the new type of full-time salaried managers. With the aging or death of the founder, the contributions of such salaried managers became increasingly important.

Mitsui and Sumitomo

Mitsui and Sumitomo offer examples of the first path by which salaried managers entered the top management of zaibatsu. Although *bantō* were long-established props of the Mitsui family enterprises, *bantō* could not act as leaders in Mitsui's development as a zaibatsu after the Meiji Restoration. In fact, they represented more of an impediment than an asset to the rise of the Mitsui zaibatsu. Minomura, for instance, was a hero to Mitsui for saving it from crises just before and after the Restoration. Yet the political merchant business that Mitsui inherited from the Tokugawa period, a line of business that Minomura was determined to continue by dealing with the Meiji government, drew Mitsui into repeated difficulties. A completely uneducated man, Minomura Rizaemon was totally unable to conceive of any business apart from that of political merchant.

Granted Inoue's support, Minomura carried out a revolution at Mitsui beginning in April 1873. He used the full authority entrusted him by the family to reduce the family influence over the Mitsui enterprises. He established rules for the Ōmotokata, permitting the interpretation that the Mitsui family fortune that was jointly held through the Ōmotokata was not the private possession of the family members but rather to be shared by other relatives and employees. Upon the establishment of Mitsui Bank in 1876 he wrote a covenant, the Sōritsu Shuisho, stating that the relationship between family members and employees was not a master-servant relationship but that all were equal members of the new firm.[80] Then he actually distributed the 20,000 shares of Mitsui Bank stock (each share worth ¥100), allotting 10,000 shares to the Ōmotokata, in which family members and employees had equal standing; 5,000 shares to family members; and 5,000 to the bank employees. The latter shares were allocated widely so that 70 percent of the employees received shares.[81] Minomura took this revolutionary step because he regarded the family members' conservative attitudes as a hindrance to his ambitious plans for expanding the political merchant business of Mitsui Bank. He aimed to exclude the family from the bank's management, but his thinking did not entail any new strategy for expanding the enterprise, let alone any concept of modernizing it.

After Minomura's death in 1877, his son-in-law and adopted heir, Minomura Risuke, inherited the top management position at Mitsui Bank as senior vice president. His limited abilities in that role are indicated by the steady growth in the ratio of government deposits and bad debts during his tenure.

The Mitsui family struck back Minomura's reforms after his death; they completely undid the changes he had effected. For example, the rule stipulating that the assets of the Ōmotokata were not the sole property of the Mitsui family was revised in 1878 to read: "Although the assets are not the property of individual family members, they are the joint property of the Mitsui family." In addition, the 5,000 shares of Mitsui Bank stock distributed among the bank's employees were gradually bought back by the Ōmotokata, and in 1893, when the bank was reorganized as an unlimited partnership, the roughly 4,000 shares still held by the employees were bought up by the Ōmotokata at ¥200 a share.[82]

These reversals naturally placed Risuke in a very difficult position. So when the Bank of Japan was founded in 1882, Risuke left Mitsui to become the bank's first director. Nishimura Torashirō succeeded him as senior vice president of Mitsui Bank. Nishimura, unlike Risuke, was an educated man, but he was incapable of more than routine work.[83] His aptitude for management is indicated, for instance, by his critical response to the notion that the bank should demand repayment of overdue loans from those within the government: "Since they have influence over government deposits, pressing too much for payment would cause us trouble."[84] Even as late as 1887, he haphazardly continued to increase the number of Mitsui Bank branches in order to accept further government deposits.[85] His one plan of action was to petition the central government for an extension of the period during which Mitsui Bank was authorized to handle such deposits.

Mitsui was not staffed by *bantō* alone. It also had such progressive managers as Masuda, but because he was fully occupied with the Mitsui Bussan's management, which was not until 1891 one of the Mitsui family's directly managed enterprises, he was in a weak position to make suggestions about the management of the directly managed Mitsui Bank. In the end, the introduction from the outside of a manager of Nakamigawa Hikojirō's caliber was needed to extricate Mitsui from the difficulties created by its political merchant business.

In Sumitomo's case, the retirement of Hirose Saihei in 1894 marked the end of the age of *bantō*. Until then, since the time of the fourth-generation family head, the Sumitomo had maintained the tradition of entrusting the top management of their enterprises to *bantō*. Like his counterpart Minomura at Mitsui, the *bantō* Hirose had saved Sumitomo shortly after the Meiji Restoration and as a result had been given autocratic power.

The extent of his authority was never more clearly illustrated than in 1890 when the Sumitomo faced a succession crisis. On November 23 the retired family head Sumitomo Tomochika died. Seven days later nineteen-year-old Tomotada, his successor and the thirteenth-generation family head, also died, leaving the House of Sumitomo without a male heir. Hirose directed Tomochika's widow to assume the family headship while he sought a successor. He chose Tokudaiji Takamaro, sixth son of an ancient aristocratic family and younger brother of Saionji Kinmochi, a leading figure in the Meiji government. Upon his selection, Tokudaiji married Sumitomo Masu, sister of the late Tomotada; took the Sumitomo surname and a new given name, Tomoito; and became an adopted member and the fifteenth-generation head of the Sumitomo house.[86] Merchant families traditionally delegated substantial authority to their *bantō*, but even in those terms, for a *bantō* to select the family head was entirely out of the ordinary and attests to his enormous authority.

Hirose erred, however, in the way he used his authority. He has been accused of nepotism and abuse of power. For example, he appointed his nephews Iba Sadatake and Kubo Moriaki to executive positions in the House of Sumitomo, had the Sumitomo silk filature built in his home town, Samegai, and hired other relatives as managers at the filature.[87] He disregarded the opinions of other Sumitomo employees, rejecting their request to establish a bank and overriding their opposition to entering the iron production field. He also ignored the board of directors, the Jūnin Kyoku, established in 1882. Hirose diversified Sumitomo in an unplanned manner. He was unable to recognize that changing conditions within the house demanded more systematic and controlled management of its growth and diversification.[88]

By the early 1890s strong internal opposition to Hirose's dictatorial ways had given rise to a movement to censure him, producing turmoil within Sumitomo.[89] Beginning in 1892 the Niihama and Yamane refineries caused increasingly serious environmental damage due to the increase in the volume of ore smelted, the adoption of hydrometallurgical processing of pyrite, and the initiation of iron and sulphuric acid production. This growing problem antagonized the people living nearby, but internal strife prevented Sumitomo's top management from deciding on an effective way to handle the crisis.[90]

Resolution came with Hirose's forced retirement in 1894. When Tomoito described Sumitomo's predicament to his elder brother Saionji, Saionji advised Tomoito to have Hirose step down; Tomoito also conferred with Hirose's nephew Iba, Besshi mine manager, and secured his agreement to the change. Hirose was unhappy but could not hold out against the politically powerful Saionji. Hirose, isolated and sapped of power, resigned in November 1894; the action settled the house's internal disturbances. The Sumitomo family granted Hirose a considerable sum as superannuation in compensation for his long service.[91]

After Hirose's retirement, the Sumitomo zaibatsu was managed by a council of directors. Iba became the central figure, despite his relationship with Hirose, because his impartiality and managerial capability had won him the others' confidence.[92] Hirose's departure also paved the way for the establishment of Sumitomo Bank and the termination of iron and sulphuric acid manufacturing as well as tea, raw silk, and camphor production for export.

Sumitomo Bank was opened in 1895 with initial capital of ¥1 million.[93] Iba became vice senior executive director (*sōriji kokoroe*) of the Sumitomo head office in 1897. A former judge, he had not received a modern education, but he put the top management of the Sumitomo zaibatsu on a firm basis by bringing in talented personnel from outside.

Furukawa, Ōkura, Yasuda, and Fujita

The other zaibatsu represent the second path by which salaried managers emerged in the zaibatsu. It was common for the zaibatsu families that sprang up after the Meiji Restoration to employ men educated in the new ways and to have them participate in management to some extent—the zaibatsu founders were not necessarily the autocrats they are often made out to be.

In the case of Furukawa, when Furukawa Ichibei acquired the government-operated Innai and Ani mines, he also inherited many well-educated engineers, including Kondō Rikusaburō, a graduate of the mining department of Kōbu Daigakkō, Japan's first engineering college and a forerunner of the Faculty of Engineering of Tokyo Imperial University. Ichibei had Kondō work with him at Furukawa headquarters, where the engineer made major contributions to decision making on technological improvements at the Ashio and other mines. Ichibei also had a highly trusted *bantō*, Kimura Chōshichi, who had been apprenticed as a shopboy to the Ono family and had been Ichibei's subordinate during his days with the Ono-gumi. Ichibei saw that success in the mining industry required that he employ not only his *bantō* but also such well-educated personnel as Kondō.[94]

Similarly, in the Ōkura-gumi, Ōkura Kihachirō had two assistants, Takashima Kokinji, a graduate of Keiō Gijuku, and Tejima Eijirō, whose background is unknown but who was remarkably talented linguistically and accompanied Kihachirō as interpreter on his post-Meiji Restoration trip abroad. Tejima was appointed vice president and Takashima director of the Gōmei Kaisha Ōkura-gumi, founded in 1893. The same year Kihachirō married his third daughter to Takashima and his fourth daughter to Itō Kumema, an employee of Ōkura Construction, entering Kumema in the Ōkura family register as an in-marrying son-in-law and adopted son. Kumema succeeded to the top spot in Ōkura Construction the following year. A progressive-minded engineer, he had worked at Nippon Construction after graduating from the civil engineering department of Tokyo Imperial University in 1888.[95]

As in the case of Ōkura, the zaibatsu often employed highly educated men, then took them into the zaibatsu family as adopted sons or in-marrying sons-in-law and allowed them to participate in top management. These practices show that the zaibatsu family heads were making efforts to incorporate new knowledge as much as possible, but within the framework of exclusive control by the zaibatsu families. The cases of Shiraishi Motojirō of the Asano zaibatsu, Yasuda Zenzaburō of the Yasuda, and Motoyama Hikoichi of the Fujita all followed this pattern.

Shiraishi was graduated from the Law Faculty of Tokyo Imperial University in 1892. He was immediately hired by Asano Shōten and the following year selected as manager in charge of founding the Asano petroleum division. He married Asano Sōichirō's second daughter in 1895.[96]

Yasuda, formerly Iomi Teiichi, was hired by Yasuda Bank after his graduation from the Law Faculty of Tokyo Imperial University (in the same class as Shiraishi). He married Yasuda Zenjirō's second daughter in 1897, was adopted into the Yasuda family, and took the new given name Zenzaburō to go with his new surname.[97]

After working as a civil servant in the Ministry of Finance Motoyama left the government to become editor-in-chief of the *Jiji Shinpō*, a newspaper published by Fukuzawa Yukichi. He joined Fujita-gumi in 1886, becoming part of the management. Two years later he married the eldest daughter of Kuhara Shozaburō, older brother of the

founder Fujita Denzaburō. The Fujita-gumi operation for which
Motoyama was particularly responsible was the reclamation by drainage of Kojima Bay. He also served as a director of the company that
published the *Ōsaka Mainichi Shinbun*, a newspaper in which Fujita
had invested. Finally in 1906 Motoyama left Fujita-gumi to become
president of the newspaper company.[98]

Mitsubishi

Mitsubishi was the zaibatsu most enthusiastic about hiring and promoting highly educated personnel. Founder Iwasaki Yatarō was a friend
of Fukuzawa Yukichi and, perhaps because of Fukuzawa's influence,
soon recognized the importance of higher education. Iwasaki com-
mented to Fukuzawa that although his uneducated employees were
agreeable and performed ordinary tasks well, they caused the business
to suffer major losses due to their limited capacity for rational thought.
His highly educated employees, by contrast, were inclined to be inso-
lent and discourteous to customers, but they were bold and honest; he
used only them for business negotiations and the preparation of documents. Both types of employees had their strengths and weaknesses, he
noted, but "however much you train young fellows with no education,
it's hard to endow them with the concepts that the educated men have.
But, it's easy to train an educated man and give him a world-minded
exterior."[99]

Another reason for Mitsubishi's interest in hiring educated staff was
that its shipping business required Mitsubishi to employ many foreigners. Of the 1,793 employees of Mitsubishi in 1876, for example,
foreigners accounted for 22 percent, or 388, of whom 355 were crew
members.[100] This situation necessitated the engagement of highly educated native personnel with good linguistic skills.

The men of higher education employed by Iwasaki Yatarō included
Shōda Heigorō, Yoshikawa Taijirō, Toyokawa Ryōhei, Asabuki Eiji,
and Hida Shōsaku, all graduates of Keiō Gijuku; Yamamoto Tatsuo of
Mitsubishi Shōgyō Gakkō (Mitsubishi Commercial School), and Kondō Renpei, Suenobu Michinari, Hasegawa Yoshinosuke, Nanbu
Kyūgo, Katō Takaaki, and Isono Hakaru of Imperial University's
predecessors.

These men performed key roles in several enterprises affiliated with
Mitsubishi. Iwasaki's cousin, Toyokawa, managed Mitsubishi Commercial School and eventually became its headmaster. The school closed
in 1884, and after five years Toyokawa was appointed president of the
119th National Bank, an Iwasaki family enterprise. Thereafter he continued to be Mitsubishi's top manager in the field of banking.[101] Hase-

gawa and Nanbu were among the first group of students sent by the Ministry of Education to study abroad. Trained as mining engineers in the United States and Germany, they came to play critical roles in Mitsubishi's mining and metallurgical enterprises.[102]

Yoshikawa, Kondō, Suenobu, Katō, and Yamamoto transferred to NYK when it was founded. Yoshikawa and Kondō, along with part-time director Shōda, represented Iwasaki family interests at NYK. Yoshikawa became NYK's vice president in 1888 and its second president in 1894, but died the following year. He was succeeded by Kondō, who had been working his way up the NYK management since 1889. Kondō was president of NYK for a quarter of a century, from 1895 to 1921.[103]

Katō later left NYK to join the Ministry of Foreign Affairs; Yamamoto similarly moved to the Bank of Japan. Katō rose to become foreign minister and also served as prime minister from 1924 to 1926. Yamamoto rose to the presidency of the Bank of Japan, then became a politician and served as finance minister and as minister of agriculture. Suenobu also left NYK and moved to Tokyo Kaijō Hoken (Tokyo Marine Insurance). He became its chairman in 1897 and served in that position until 1925.[104] Isono left Mitsubishi after eight months and with the assistance of the Iwasaki family founded Meidi-ya, the ship chandler and importer of provisions.[105]

Katō, Suenobu, and Isono were all graduates of the Law Faculty of Tokyo Imperial University, the pinnacle of Japanese higher education. Yatarō was able to hire them in spite of the fact that the Law Faculty in about 1880 was graduating fewer than ten students a year, all of whom intended to become bureaucrats, politicians, or scholars rather than private businessmen. Yatarō managed to lure the three by promising to send them to Great Britain for study at Iwasaki family expense; so intent was he on securing their services that he was willing to spend large sums of money on them.

The Iwasaki family also used marriage to bring talented men into the family. Yatarō, for example, married his eldest daughter to Katō Takaaki. Shōda Heigorō was married to Yatarō's niece and Kondō Renpei to Toyokawa Ryōhei's younger sister, Yatarō's cousin.

Yatarō was not an autocrat; at times he was overruled by his partners and salaried managers. For instance, he was firmly opposed to the purchase of the Takashima coal mine, yet was overcome by the activist views of his younger brother Yanosuke, Kawada Koichirō, and Shōda. Particularly in his declining years, Yatarō was often ill and did not exercise arbitrary power.

After Yatarō's death, the management of Mitsubishi Company was centered on the teamwork of Yanosuke, the president, and Shōda, the senior executive director. By the late 1880s, of the three men whose surnames had formed the basis of the firm's first name, Mitsukawa, only Kawada survived. Ishikawa had died in 1882 and Nakagawa in 1887. Kawada's presence was disturbing to Yanosuke, fifteen years his junior, and therefore, after Kawada's appointment as president of the Bank of Japan in 1889, at Yanosuke's insistence he severed his connection to Mitsubishi in 1891. Iwasaki's eldest son, Hisaya, came home that year after studying in the United States. His return created an opportunity for Yanosuke to reform the Iwasaki family structure in preparation for Hisaya's appointment as the third president of Mitsubishi Company. The reform consisted of dividing the Iwasaki family into two branches headed respectively by Yatarō and Yanosuke, and distributing the family fortune between them. With this reform, Kawada was formally excluded from Mitsubishi.[106]

SUMMARY

The eight businesses examined so far all developed into zaibatsu by diversifying, but they differed considerably in their respective diversification patterns. Mitsubishi and Mitsui were the first to branch out into new fields, beginning in the 1870s. Sumitomo under Hirose also diversified energetically from early on, but the process contributed little to its emergence as a zaibatsu, although Sumitomo, along with Yasuda and Asano, ranked just below Mitsubishi and Mitsui in the extent of diversification. Asano was weak in the area of exclusive family ownership due to its reliance on joint ventures with other investors. In its vigorous program of diversification, however, Asano stood out. Ōkura and Fujita were diversifying as well, but the scope of their enterprises was limited. At Furukawa, diversification was restricted to enterprises connected with the copper industry, a process more accurately described as "vertical integration."

The fields into which these eight zaibatsu branched out in this period included banking, mining, trading, real estate, warehousing, shipping, and civil engineering. In manufacturing, Mitsubishi's shipyards and Asano's cement factory were about the only zaibatsu enterprises at the time. Although many of the zaibatsu became major stockholders in railway and cotton-spinning companies, they did not directly manage enterprises in those two leading sectors of Meiji industrialization.

With the implementation of the Commercial Code in 1893, some of the incipient zaibatsu began to adopt a company structure as well as to diversify their operations. These developments together transformed what had been family businesses into zaibatsu. The salaried managers, employed in growing numbers from this time by the owner families, promoted both diversification and structural change in the emergent zaibatsu. Among these managers were highly educated men able to recognize the trends of the new era, and in doing so offered a striking contrast to the *bantō* managers of the older tradition. Salaried managers played a vital role in the rise of the zaibatsu.

PART II

DEVELOPMENT OF THE ZAIBATSU, 1894–1913

Following their initial formation in the first half of the Meiji era, the developing zaibatsu continued to grow and diversify during the period from 1894 to 1913, a time that culminated in their emergence as full-fledged zaibatsu. This process coincided with the takeoff of Japan's industrial economy, which was led by the cotton-spinning industry. Between 1894 and 1913, per capita real income in Japan rose from ¥72 to ¥110, and the number of factories employing ten or more workers increased from 5,985 (of which 2,409 were using motors) to 15,811 (of which 9,403 were using motors).[1] In the same period the output of cotton yarn soared from 40,000 tons to 273,237 tons, and exports of that product leaped from 190 to 87,613 tons, while imports plunged from 11,731 to 228 tons.[2] Japan also began to lay the foundation for heavy industry during this time.

In addition, the Japanese company system took root during these two decades. After the implementation of the Commercial Code, companies grew remarkably in number and capitalization, as the figures below indicate.[3]

	Number of companies	Paid-up capital (¥1 million)
1896 (A)	4,549	398
1913 (B)	15,406	1,983
B/A	3.4%	5.0%

During the first twenty years of Meiji rule, the government had intervened to support industrialization in the private sector by encouraging the spread of the company system and the accumulation of capital by entrepreneurs. By the 1890s, however, the state had cut back on its direct role in the economy, giving way to private corporations.

Under such circumstances the zaibatsu matured in the latter half of Meiji. Although the major zaibatsu differed in terms of extent of diversification, exclusiveness of family ownership, and type of organization, these originally family-owned businesses all clearly achieved the distinctive zaibatsu form during this period.

CHAPTER 3

DIVERSIFICATION STRATEGIES

Mitsubishi and Mitsui had been most active among the major zaibatsu in diversifying their businesses in the years preceding 1894. Sumitomo, Yasuda, and Asano had followed their lead in this regard, Ōkura and Fujita had fallen behind, and Furukawa had not begun to diversify at all. In the 1894–1913 period, however, all the zaibatsu except Furukawa actively diversified their operations. Whereas Furukawa ruled out diversification in favor of vertical integration, the other major zaibatsu pursued a variety of strategies for branching out into new fields of enterprise.

MITSUI

Diversification at Mitsui in this period began under Nakamigawa Hikojirō, who as executive director of Mitsui Bank from 1892 to 1901 occupied the pivotal position in the zaibatsu's top management. Nakamigawa succeeded in ridding Mitsui Bank of its heavy burden of bad debts and in rebuilding operations by turning Mitsui away from its traditional political merchant line of business. At the same time he led the zaibatsu into a new area of operations: diversified industries fostered by Mitsui Bank. These industries included Kanegafuchi Bōseki (Kanegafuchi Cotton Spinning Company) and Ōji Seishi (Ōji Paper Company), over which the bank gained control by increasing its holdings of their stock; Shibaura Seisakusho (Shibaura Engineering Works, an electrical equipment manufacturer), Maebashi Kenshi Bōsekisho (Maebashi Silk Spinning Mill), and Ōshima Seishijō (Ōshima Silk Filature), acquired when their previous owners defaulted on Mitsui Bank loans for which they had posted these factories as security; Shinmachi Kenshi Bōsekisho

TABLE 3.1   Mitsui Bussan's Earnings in the Nakamigawa Era, 1892–1901
(in thousand yen)

Year	Earnings
1892	145
1893	302
1894	633
1895	1,087
1896	850
1897	1,123
1898	1,718
1899	1,868
1900	1,355
1901	1,686

SOURCE: *Kōhon Mitsui Bussan Kabushiki Kaisha 100-nen shi* (100 Years of Mitsui Bussan) (Tokyo: Japan Business History Institute, 1978), vol. 1, pp. 83, 289.

(Shinmachi Silk Spinning Mill) and Tomioka Seishijō (Tomioka Silk Filature), purchased from the government; and Mie Seishijō and Nagoya Seishijō (Mie and Nagoya silk filatures), newly built by Mitsui. The bank also supplied the generous funds needed by Mitsui Mining to upgrade the mining technology at Miike Coal Mine and to buy the Yamano and Tagawa coal mines in Kyushu. In addition, it bought about 18 percent of the total shares of stock issued by the Hokkaido Tankō Tetsudō Kabushiki Kaisha (Hokkaido Colliery and Railway Company).[1] Shibaura Engineering Works, the two silk-spinning mills, and the four silk filatures were all managed by the manufacturing division (*kōgyō bu*) of Mitsui Motokata.

The broad advance into industrial activities during Nakamigawa's tenure at Mitsui Bank was particularly striking, but new industrial investment was only part of Mitsui's strategic efforts in this period—for at the same time Mitsui Bussan and Mitsui Mining were also steadily expanding business operations. (See Tables 3.1 and 3.2.)

Mitsui Bussan extended its network of overseas branches dramatically in this period. In early 1892 the trading company had five overseas branches, in Shanghai, Hong Kong, Singapore, London, and Tianjin. The next year, when it was reorganized into an unlimited partnership, Mitsui Bussan added an agency in Bombay. By 1901 fourteen new overseas branches had been opened, ten in Asia (Yinkou, Taibei, Inchon, Shamen [Amoy], Zhifu, Hankou, Seoul, Guandongzhou, Manila, and Java) and the remaining four in New York, San Francisco, Hamburg, and Sydney.[2]

Most remarkable was the growth of Mitsui Bussan's commercial

TABLE 3.2   Mitsui Mining's Earnings in the Nakamigawa Era, 1892–1901
(in thousand yen)

Year	Earnings
1892	327
1893	631
1894	955
1895	1,208
1896	1,125
1897	807
1898	1,877
1899	1,808
1900	1,317
1901	1,862

SOURCE: Mitsui Bunko, *Mitsui jigyō shi* (History of the Mitsui Enterprises) (Tokyo: Mitsui Bunko, 1980), vol. 2, p. 708.

transactions on the Chinese mainland. This growth resulted in part from the increase in the number of branches operated there, but successful innovations in its trading methods also contributed. Such changes included initiation of third-country trade with China in 1895,[3] abolition of the use of compradors in 1897, and institution of a trainee system for the China trade in 1898.

"Comprador" refers to the Chinese commercial middlemen who formerly operated in China's trade ports. Compradors, paid on commissions, mediated between the Chinese merchants and producers and the foreign merchants, who were unversed in China's languages, customs, and procedures. It was usual for foreign merchants to rely on compradors in their dealings with China, and Mitsui Bussan had used them. But in order to reduce the payment of commissions, which amounted to considerable sums (1 percent of the proceeds), and to expand its dealings by keeping in touch as closely as possible with local conditions, Mitsui Bussan established the policy of prohibiting the use of compradors.

Implementation of that policy entailed serious efforts to train employees to be fluent in Chinese and knowledgeable about local customs and procedures, so that they could enter directly into transactions with local merchants and producers. In the trainee system for China trade, selected middle school graduates were sent, on salary, to China to live among the population and acquire the skills necessary for conducting business directly. The training program produced such accomplished personnel as Mori Tsutomu, who became head of the Tianjin branch and later went into politics, and Kodama Ichizō, who became head of the cotton division of Mitsui Bussan and later founded Tōyō Menka Kabushiki Kaisha (Oriental Cotton Trading Company, Ltd.).[4]

Mitsui Mining also expanded during this period. Almost all of Mitsui Mining's profits came from the Miike Coal Mine, for which the output had grown remarkably with the successful development of the Kattachi branch mine.[5] Thanks to Miike, Mitsui Mining was able in 1902 to pay off its debt to the government for the mine's original purchase.[6] Earnings from Miike also enabled Mitsui Mining to buy the Yamano coal mine in 1895 and the Tagawa coal mine in 1900.[7]

Although Nakamigawa's vision had great breadth, his policy of diversified industrial investment did not succeed. First, the business performance of all but one (Shinmachi Silk Spinning) of the units under the Mitsui manufacturing division worsened. Consequently the division was abolished in 1898 and its units transferred to other parts of the zaibatsu. Shibaura Engineering Works was placed under Mitsui Mining control, and the silk spinning mills and filatures were placed under the management of Mitsui Gofukuten.[8]

Nakamigawa had held great expectations for Shibaura Engineering Works, but given the low level of technical knowledge in Meiji Japan, Shibaura was bound to have difficulties. After its transfer to Mitsui Mining control, the efforts of its new head, Ōtaguro Jūgorō, and engineers put Shibaura in the black and even achieved a gradual increase in profits: ¥3,128 and ¥18,560 for the first and second halves respectively of 1900, and ¥25,053 and ¥27,560 for the first and second halves of 1901.[9] But the Mitsui family members and top managers other than Nakamigawa and Dan were displeased by the presence of Shibaura, a grubby machinery manufacturing unit, within Mitsui. They stubbornly demanded that it be sold. No one willing to take over Shibaura could be found, however, and in the face of vigorous opposition to its sale from the plant's engineers and workers, the Mitsui family members and managers had no alternative but to approve the zaibatsu's continued operation of Shibaura, leaving it under the control of Mitsui Mining until 1904.[10]

The Kanegafuchi Cotton Spinning Company also performed poorly in comparison with other cotton-spinning firms, at least in terms of its dividend rate.[11] Similarly, the Ōji Paper Company stagnated after coming under Mitsui control and in fact experienced considerable turmoil as a result of Mitsui intervention in its management. Mitsui Bank in 1893 assigned Fujiyama Raita to be an Ōji director. Ōji's capitalization was raised in 1896, at which point the bank acquired many of the newly issued stocks and increased its share of the company's total capital; thereupon Fujiyama was appointed as a senior executive director. Behind these moves was a plan by Mitsui Bank to shake up Ōji's management.[12] The upshot was that Shibusawa Eiichi, who as chairman of Ōji had been the company's leading figure since its founding in 1873, and his nephew Ōkawa Heizaburō, a senior executive director, stepped down in 1898. A fierce labor dispute then broke out at the paper mill, sparked by workers' opposition to these changes.[13]

Mitsui Bank, general promoter of Nakamigawa's industrialization program, also found itself in difficulty. With funds tied up in stock investments and long-term industrial loans, the bank was becoming less sound. The amount of stocks and government bonds the bank held as a percentage of its total assets had exceeded the 20 percent level, reaching 27.2 percent in 1893 and 25.7 percent in 1901, for example. In addition, its stockholdings had become concentrated in certain affiliated firms, such as Kanegafuchi Cotton Spinning, Ōji Paper, and Hokkaido Colliery and Railway.[14] Lending was also concentrated within Mitsui; for instance, at the end of June 1899, Mitsui enterprises accounted for 87 percent of overdrafts on the current account at the Mitsui Bank main office, of which 63 percent represented loans to Mitsui Mining (including Shibaura Engineering Works) and to the silk spinning mills and silk filatures under Mitsui Gofukuten.[15]

Another unfortunate circumstance for Nakamigawa was that, while he was committing the bank to fostering industrial enterprises at Mitsui, Mitsui Bank's footing in the banking world, at least in terms of its share of total deposits, was growing less secure. (See Table 3.3.) Both during and after Nakamigawa's tenure, Mitsui Bank had a consistent policy of holding down its deposits.[16] Nonetheless, after the Nakamigawa period ended in 1901, the bank's share of total bank deposits bottomed out and then began to rise, which suggests that the decline in the bank's share under Nakamigawa was not the result of its deposit policy at that time. Rather, what led to the withdrawal of deposits from Mitsui Bank was the publication by a scandal sheet, *Niroku Shinpō*, of exaggerated stories concerning the lack of confidence in Nakamigawa's industrialization policy and opposition to it within Mitsui's top management.[17]

That policy's lack of success did indeed provoke criticism of Nakamigawa within Mitsui. Opposition to his policies from Mitsui Bussan in particular was intensified by conflicts between the bank and trading company. Under Nakamigawa, Mitsui Bank had demanded that Bussan stop handling small-lot goods and had restricted lending to Bussan. The bank also stirred up a dispute with the cotton-spinning companies in western Japan over the fact that the Hyōgo plant of Kanegafuchi Cotton Spinning offered better working conditions than did the other firms; this dispute hurt the position of Mitsui Bussan, which had business relationships with all the spinning companies involved. Nakami-

TABLE 3.3   Mitsui Bank's Share of Bank Deposits, 1896–1911

Year	Mitsui Bank deposits as % of deposits of 5 major banks combined	Mitsui Bank deposits as % of total bank deposits
1896	48.3	17.0
1897	46.8	12.1
1898	45.5	10.1
1899	38.1	7.0
1900	34.3	6.1
1901	31.1	6.5
1902	31.6	6.5
1903	32.1	6.7
1904	33.4	7.7
1905	32.5	7.1
1906	33.6	6.1
1907	35.2	7.5
1908	32.9	7.0
1909	36.2	8.2
1910	35.4	7.6
1911	33.0	6.7

SOURCE: Yasuoka Shigeaki, ed., *Mitsui zaibatsu* (Tokyo: Nihon Keizai Shimbunsha, 1982), p. 152.

gawa's autocratic actions were also criticized by the family, its adviser Inoue, and other Mitsui managers, including Masuda. Inoue was particularly dissatisfied with Nakamigawa's forced settlement of bad debts, which had harmed some of Inoue's government associates.[18] Such dissatisfactions, linked to criticisms of Nakamigawa's industrialization policy, reached explosive force. Nakamigawa consequently lost his authority within the top management of the Mitsui zaibatsu, and he died, virtually excluded from Mitsui, in 1901.

After Nakamigawa's death, Masuda became senior executive director (*senmu riji*) of the Management Department of the Secretariat of the Mitsui Family Council (Dōzokukai Jimukyoku Kanribu), a body established in 1902 to exercise overall control over the Mitsui family enterprises. Masuda redirected the Mitsui zaibatsu away from the industrialization program of Nakamigawa's day. Inoue and Hayakawa Senkichirō, Nakamigawa's successor as executive director of the bank, cooperated with Masuda in this task. The results were the spinning off of Shibaura Engineering Works in 1904 as an independent company capitalized at ¥1 million, with capital and technology tie-ups with the U.S. firm, General Electric, beginning in 1909; the outright sale of all the silk-spinning mills and filatures; and efforts to sell the Mitsui Bank holdings in Kanegafuchi Cotton Spinning, Ōji Paper, and Hokkaido Colliery and Railway.

Mitsui Bank changed its policy from long-term industrial finance to commercial finance, with the emphasis on discounting bills and making short-term loans. The company shares and the real estate that the bank had not been able to sell were taken over by Mitsui Family Council; the bank made it a rule thereafter not to own stock.[19] Mitsui Gofukuten was spun off in 1904 as Mitsukoshi Gofukuten, capitalized at ¥500,000.

These moves can be summarized as a transformation in terms of Mitsui zaibatsu's business strategy from "industrial Mitsui" to "commercial Mitsui." Nonetheless, a strong orientation to the industrial Mitsui concept lived on, its proponents centered around executive director Dan of Mitsui Mining. The managements of both Mitsui Mining and Shibaura Engineering Works were opposed to the sale of Shibaura. The resulting compromise, in which the enterprise was spun off with about half its capital provided by the Mitsui family and about a quarter by General Electric, shows the continued working of the industrial Mitsui idea.[20] In addition, after the completion of harbor construction at Miike in 1909, Mitsui Mining decided to introduce the Koppers-type coke oven for recovering by-products at Miike. This innovation opened the way for Mitsui Mining's move into the coal chemical industry[21] and thus further demonstrates the persistence of the industrial Mitsui model.

Despite the collapse of Nakamigawa's industrialization policy and the industrial-commercial shift, the operations of the bank, trading company, and mining company continued to expand steadily. Table 3.4 illustrates Mitsui Bank's performance in terms of net profits, and the growth of Mitsui Bussan is shown in Tables 3.5 and 3.6. Upon Mitsui

TABLE 3.4   Mitsui Bank's Annual Net Profit after the Nakamigawa Era, 1901–8 (in thousand yen)

Year	Net profit
1901	630
1902	674
1903	628
1904	827
1905	1,316
1906	2,625
1907	3,312
1908	2,787

SOURCE: *Mitsui Ginkō 80-nen shi* (80 Years of Mitsui Bank) (Tokyo: Mitsui Bank, 1957), p. 744.

TABLE 3.5   Mitsui Bussan's Earnings in the Masuda Era, 1902–9 (in thousand yen)

Year	Earnings
1902	1,553
1903	1,668
1904	2,210
1905	2,347
1906	2,188
1907	2,052
1908	1,364
1909	1,972

SOURCE: Same as Table 3.1, p. 289.

TABLE 3.6   Exports and Imports of Mitsui Bussan, 1877–1909

Year	Exports (thousand yen)	As % of total exports	Imports (thousand yen)	As % of total imports
1897	10,432	6.4	33,540	15.3
1901	20,952	8.3	37,219	14.5
1905	51,604	16.0	84,769	17.4
1909*	85,241	25.9	76,282	22.8

SOURCE: Same as Table 3.1, p. 173.
* January to October only.

Bussan's reorganization as a joint-stock company in 1909, it alone was handling 26 percent of Japan's exports and 23 percent of its imports. The percentages are, of course, based on total imports and exports, including those handled by foreign merchants, and thus reveal that a remarkable share of Japan's foreign trade at the time was being conducted by Mitsui Bussan.

Mitsui Bussan was able to achieve such growth because among the highly diverse products handled it placed greatest emphasis on the goods most important for Japan's economic development: coal, raw cotton, cotton products, raw silk, machinery (including railway equipment), and sugar. Those six alone accounted for 60.9 percent of Mitsui Bussan's total sales in 1904 and 66.7 percent in 1909.[22] Another factor behind Mitsui Bussan's growth was that its network of overseas branches was much more fully developed than that of its competitors. Bussan widened its lead in this regard by opening twenty-four new branches between 1902 and 1909 (Beijing, Guangdong, Tainan, Dalian, Fuzhou, Shantou, Gaoxiong, Andong, Tieling, Fungtian, Calcutta, Bangkok, Qingdao, Rangoon, Jilin, Harbin, Changchun, Saigon, Pusan, Taizhong, Oklahoma City, Portland (Oregon), Vladivostok, and Lyon).[23] The striking abundance of Chinese branches parallels the expansion of Japan's interests there after its victories in the Sino-Japanese and Russo-Japanese wars. The growth of Bussan's China business was not a simple case of parasitism, however; the expansion was achieved by the aggressive program of action detailed earlier in this chapter.

Best known of the third-country trade arrangements instituted in this period was the export of soybeans from Manchuria to Europe beginning in 1908, which developed into a major source of revenue for Mitsui Bussan while turning Manchuria into a world-class soybean producer.[24] Mitsui Bussan's Shanghai branch also initiated third-country trade that did not involve China, such as the export of jute from India to Europe and the United States and tin from Malaya to the United States. As these major examples indicate, Mitsui Bussan emerged as a brilliant figure on the stage of world trade; in 1897, its third-country trade volume was only ¥180,000 or 0.3 percent of its total transaction volume, but by 1907 the figures had risen to ¥15,190,000 or 5.6 percent and by 1912 to a striking ¥55,656,000 or 15.5 percent.[25]

Mitsui Mining also grew steadily. Profits leaped from ¥1,860,000 in 1901 to ¥3,720,000 in 1911, at which time it was reorganized as a joint-stock company.[26] Moreover, by 1902 it had paid the government in full for the Miike Coal Mine and accumulated considerable capital reserves.

Mitsui Mining used the bulk of these funds to construct a port at Miike mine, which had been hampered, despite short-term improvements, in the large-scale loading of coal by the too-shallow Ariake Sea. By the turn of the century, planning of a port was already well under way, based on studies of ports overseas by a number of Mitsui engineers. The decision to build a port at Miike at a cost of ¥3 million was made at the end of 1901. All expenses were to be borne by Mitsui Mining. Construction began in November 1902, shortly before full payment was made for the mine in December, and the project was finally completed in March 1908 at a total cost of ¥3,760,000. As planned, Mitsui Mining was able to cover the cost with its own funds.[27]

The next year Mitsui Mining moved into the coal chemical industry. Thus the company experienced a steady progression: paying the government for the Miike mine, in the same year beginning construction of the port, and then, upon completion of the port, initiating coal chemical operations.

MITSUBISHI

Mitsubishi, Ltd., pursued even further the diversification strategy inherited from its predecessor, Mitsubishi Company. The firm, which was established in 1893, found its main sources of capital for diversification in profits from coal mining; proceeds from the sale of stock held by the Iwasaki family in NYK and several major railway companies; and dividends on the corporate stock retained by the family. Like its predecessor, Mitsubishi, Ltd., diversified its operations into coal mining, metal mining, banking, warehousing, real estate, and shipbuilding, but in the decades after 1893, striking changes occurred, particularly in shipbuilding, and a new field—trading—was added to the list. Moreover, considerable development of enterprises owned by the Iwasaki family but not directly controlled by Mitsubishi, Ltd., took place. The following sections provide an overview of Mitsubishi's growth and diversification during the period 1893–1913.

Coal Mining

While expanding production and upgrading technology at its existing coal mines, Mitsubishi bought a series of new mines not only in Kyushu but also in Hokkaido; Mitsubishi's coal-mining operations clearly underwent a geographic expansion. Mitsubishi in 1896 also bought the Tobata coke plant, renamed the Makiyama Gaitan Seizōsho (Makiyama Coke Factory), which supplied coke to the state-owned Yawata Iron Works (which had begun production in 1901).[28]

Metal Mining

Mitsubishi acquired the Sado gold mine, Ikuno silver mine, and Osaka refinery from the Imperial Household Agency in 1896. These enterprises had been added to the estate of the imperial family in 1888, but the Imperial Household Agency had been reluctant to invest the large sums required for their upgrade and decided to dispose of them. Mitsubishi was the buyer with a successful bid of ¥1,730,000.[29] In consequence, by 1910 Mitsubishi had risen to a leading position in the metal-mining industry; in that year it was the largest producer of gold and third largest of both silver and copper.[30] Mitsubishi, Ltd., then added to the zaibatsu's metal-mining interests by buying the Kyomipo iron mine in Korea in 1911.

Banking

The banking division of Mitsubishi, Ltd., founded in 1895, had capital set at ¥1 million, or one-fifth the total capital of Mitsubishi, Ltd.

According to the 1883 revision of the regulations governing national banks, a national bank had to dissolve or turn into an ordinary bank twenty years after its founding. Mitsubishi's 119th National Bank would reach the end of its term in 1898, and so the banking division was established to take over its business.[31] No other banks in Japan at that time were independent legal entities, and it was a difficult task to secure the necessary Ministry of Finance approval for the banking division's unprecedented form. Mitsubishi, Ltd.'s top management may have learned through its experience with the 119th National Bank that having a bank as an independent corporation was inconvenient in terms of controlling it. The 119th National Bank had tended to rely on loans from the Bank of Japan, but in 1901 the central bank turned down such a request by Mitsubishi's banking division. The resulting temporary shortage of funds spurred a shift in policy at the division toward enlarging its deposit operations.[32]

Warehousing

In 1887 the Iwasaki family and others associated with Mitsubishi founded the Tokyo Sōko Kaisha (Tokyo Warehouse Company) to assume, outside of Mitsubishi Company control, the warehousing business that had been operated by Mitsubishi Exchange Office. Tokyo Warehouse became a joint-stock company in 1893. Mitsubishi, Ltd., bought all its stock in 1899 and turned it into a designated subsidiary. With its capital increased to ¥2 million in 1907, Tokyo Warehouse became the leading force in the harbor warehousing field in such major ports as Kobe.[33]

Real Estate

The development of an English-style business district in Tokyo's Marunouchi area accelerated after Mitsubishi Hall No. 1 was completed there in 1894. By 1912 Mitsubishi Hall No. 20 had been built. Non-Mitsubishi buildings were also constructed in the district, including the Tokyo Prefectural Offices, the Metropolitan Police Headquarters, and the Imperial Theater.[34]

Shipbuilding

NYK in November 1893 opened long-distance oceanic lines with destinations as far away as Bombay. In February of the following year, it decided to extend the Bombay line to Europe. For that purpose, while requesting government assistance, it proposed a funding plan for twelve ships to be assigned to the European route.[35] The plan was delayed by the outbreak of the Sino-Japanese War in 1894, but at the same time the conflict served to intensify the military's demand for large, high-speed steamships. After its victory in the war, the government's increased revenues (due to the huge indemnity paid by China) encouraged the government to give large-scale subsidies to shipping companies in order to operate long-distance routes as well as to shipbuilding companies in order to build the necessary steamships. Laws to promote shipping and shipbuilding were consequently enacted in March 1896.

NYK had anticipated the enactment of such laws, and in late 1895 it began preparations to inaugurate a shipping line to Europe, with twelve 6,000-ton-class vessels to be built for the route.[36] It would have been natural for the order to have been placed in Britain, then the world's preeminent shipbuilding nation. At an NYK board of directors meeting, however, Shōda Heigorō, who attended as representative of the Iwasaki family, which was still a major NYK stockholder, strongly requested that orders for two of the twelve ships go to Mitsubishi's shipyard. The request was granted on the condition that Mitsubishi produce ships of the same class and at the same price as those to be built in England.[37]

Until then, the biggest ship ever built at Mitsubishi's Nagasaki Shipyard was only 1,600 tons. Mitsubishi, Ltd., had sought to establish a larger shipyard in Kobe to replace the small-scale Nagasaki operation,[38] but its plan to buy the Kawasaki Shipyard in Kobe had come to naught.[39] Negotiations over the purchase of government land there to serve as the new shipyard's site had bogged down—in fact, the application for the land transfer was not sent to the navy minister until March 1896.[40] In order to act upon the NYK order for construction of the two 6,000-ton ships, therefore, Mitsubishi had no choice but to pour huge sums into expansion of the existing Nagasaki Shipyard. From 1884 to 1898 Mitsubishi had sunk a total of about ¥1,430,000 into the shipyard, but from 1899 to 1902 its capital investment amounted to some ¥2,390,000.[41] These figures actually underestimate the increase in investment associated with the construction of the ships, because the 1884–98 total includes the share for the first three years after the order for the ships was recieved in 1896.

Nagasaki Shipyard made an all-out effort and completed the first of the two ships, the *Hitachi-maru* (6,172 tons), in April 1898. The shipyard had looked to British sources for the design and materials as well as for technical guidance. Still, the *Hitachi-maru* was built entirely by the Japanese and thereby represented a turning point in the history of modern shipbuilding in Japan. Nagasaki Shipyard completed the second ship, the 6,309-ton *Awa-maru*, in 1899 and went on to complete three more ships, the *Kaga-maru* (6,301 tons) and *Iyo-maru*

(6,320 tons) in 1901, and the 6,444-ton *Aki-maru*, for NYK's U.S. line, in 1902.[42]

The huge amount of energy poured by Mitsubishi, Ltd., into the expansion of Nagasaki Shipyard and the construction of the *Hitachi-maru* and other large vessels is most vividly illustrated by the fact that Shōda, Mitsubishi's top salaried manager, was on location in Nagasaki for five years to direct the construction. Iwasaki Hisaya, then president of Mitsubishi, Ltd., was young and not very forceful. Consequently Shōda became the de facto president and prime mover in the top management. It was extraordinary for a man in his position to double as head of Nagasaki Shipyard and spend five years (1897 to 1901) away from Mitsubishi headquarters.[43] (The concurrent appointment as head of the shipyard lasted until 1906.) Thus Mitsubishi's determination to fill the NYK order and make use of it as an opportunity to modernize Mitsubishi's shipbuilding operations is clear.

Since the purchase of Nagasaki Shipyard, the Nagasaki branch of Mitsubishi, Ltd. had been responsible for its management. The branch had also been an important unit in Mitsubishi's coal sales, but the staff could not readily shed the idea that priority was to be given to coal over shipbuilding. This tendency was particularly discernible in the branch manager, Yamawaki Masakatsu, who was also director of the shipyard. Disagreements occurred as well between Yamawaki and his vice manager, Mizutani Rokurō, an engineer, and opposing factions sprang up around them within the shipyard.[44] The problem was an obstacle to the planned expansion of Nagasaki Shipyard, and the need to overcome it was what prompted Shōda to take on the additional task of heading the shipyard and staying in Nagasaki for an extended period of time. Almost simultaneously with Shōda's appointment as head of the ship yard, Yamawaki retired from Mitsubishi.

With the senior executive director and de facto president of Mitsubishi, Ltd., in Nagasaki for so many years, a leadership vacuum arose in Mitsubishi's top management. The inspector (*kanmu*) and former president of Mitsubishi, Iwasaki Yanosuke, filled the void. He had been appointed president of the Bank of Japan in 1896 but resigned in 1898, probably because he needed to devote his energies to the management of Mitsubishi. Iwasaki and Shōda had a close cooperative relationship.

Mitsubishi, Ltd., went on to establish shipyards in Kobe in 1905 and in Hikoshima in 1914. Thanks to its expansion since 1896, however, Nagasaki Shipyard remained the foremost shipbuilding enterprise in Japan. It received an order in 1908 from the Tōyō Kisen Kabushiki Kaisha (Oriental Steamship Company), part of the Asano zaibatsu, to build Japan's first large turbine vessels, the *Tenyō-maru* and *Chiyō-maru*. The capabilities of Nagasaki Shipyard thus continued to tower over the rest of the Japanese shipbuilding industry.

Trading

Mitsubishi, Ltd., separated sales from production in its coal-mining operations in 1896 and established a new division to manage coal sales at the head office. The coal sales division in 1899 was renamed the sales division (*eigyō-bu*) and given control of coal sales at all Mitsubishi, Ltd., branches.[45] The division also made efforts to market the coal abroad and to arrange for transport by ship. It came to handle coal produced by non-Mitsubishi mines as well.

After the Russo-Japanese War, the sales division expanded its operations in order to act as the overseas sales agent for such Mitsubishi affiliates as Mitsubishi Paper Mills, Asahi Glass, and Kirin Brewery. Next it began handling noncoal products of companies unrelated to Mitsubishi, initially doing so in 1909 in a transaction involving Chinese agricultural goods undertaken by the Hankou branch. At the same time, the division also embarked on third-country trade, beginning with the export of tung oil and sesame seeds to Europe and the United States by the Hankou branch.[46] The sales division of Mitsubishi, Ltd., later became Mitsubishi Shōji (Mitsubishi Trading Company, now known as Mitsubishi Corporation).

Iwasaki Family Enterprises

The Iwasaki family's investments in a number of major corporations outside of Mitsubishi Company went beyond that of stockholding: the Iwasaki were involved in management as well. The firms were outside the jurisdiction of Mitsubishi, Ltd., and operated as enterprises of the Iwasaki family. They included Koiwai Nōjō (Koiwai Farm), Mitsubishi Seishisho (Mitsubishi Paper Mill), and Kirin Brewery.

Koiwai Nōjō (Koiwai Farm), a farm on the outskirts of Morioka City, was started by Inoue Masaru and the Iwasaki family with the cooperation of Ono Yoshizane. Operations had come to a standstill by 1899, when Iwasaki Hisaya bought out the other owners and began running it himself. By switching the emphasis from farming to stock raising, Hisaya achieved a favorable turnaround in its operation. With this reform, the farm was named "Koiwai," formed by combining the first characters of the three founders' surnames. Iwasaki was fond of Koiwai Farm and poured energy into managing it directly.[47]

Mitsubishi Seishisho (Mitsubishi Paper Mill) originated with Kobe Paper Mill, a company run by two American brothers, Thomas and John Walsh, in Kobe. Iwasaki had had close dealings with the brothers, who were partners in the American trading firm Walsh, Hall & Co., since the late Tokugawa period. With other foreigners, the Walshes founded the firm as Japan Paper Making Company in 1875 and renamed it Kobe Paper Mill when they acquired full ownership two years later. The company was dependent on the Iwasaki family for loans, and the Iwasaki, in turn, converted their outstanding loans into investments in the company. John Walsh died in 1896, and his brother handed over the Kobe Paper Mill to the Iwasaki family the following year. The Iwasaki reorganized it into a limited partnership, Kobe Seishisho, capitalized at ¥500,000, and Mitsubishi, Ltd.'s Kobe branch was responsible for its management. Though renamed Gōshi Kaisha Mitsubishi Seishisho (Mitsubishi Paper Mill, Ltd.) in 1904, it was consistently treated as an Iwasaki family enterprise rather than as a part of Mitsubishi, Ltd.[48]

Meidi-ya and Kirin Brewery were two other Iwasaki family-related enterprises. Isono Hakaru left Mitsubishi's management in 1885 and with Iwasaki family assistance founded Meidi-ya, a ship chandler and food importer in Yokohama. That same year foreign residents of Yokohama pooled funds to establish Japan Brewery Company. This firm carried on the operation of a brewery built in Yokohama by an American, William Copeland, around 1869. Iwasaki Yanosuke and Shōda Heigorō were among the investors in Japan Brewery, a connection that led to its signing an exclusive sales contract with Meidi-ya. Meidi-ya sold the Japan Brewery product under the Kirin Beer label. Later, Meidi-ya, the Iwasaki family, and officials of several Mitsubishi companies provided funds to found Kirin Brewery, Inc., capitalized at ¥2.5 million, and to buy out the Japan Brewery Co.[49] Kirin Brewery, with a 50 percent market share, is now the largest beer company in Japan.

The Iwasaki family was also a major shareholder in many other firms and cooperated in the establishment of new companies, such as Nippon Chisso Hiryō (Nippon Nitrogenous Fertilizer). When the principal railway companies were nationalized in 1906–7, Iwasaki family members, who had been major shareholders in several, received a huge sum in compensation. The windfall became the driving force behind Mitsubishi's aggressive diversification in ensuing years.[50]

FURUKAWA AND SUMITOMO

Though Furukawa and Sumitomo both began in the copper industry and then developed into zaibatsu, their histories are quite different. Furukawa did not attempt to cross the boundaries of the copper industry; instead of diversifying, it pursued a strategy of vertical integration focused on copper-related industries. Sumitomo used the copper industry as the base for branching out into other fields. Thus a remarkably sharp contrast exists between the two zaibatsu.

Furukawa Zaibatsu

Furukawa's business from 1890 on was focused on the mining, refining, and rolling of copper, and its other interests all related to copper production: forestry, coal mining, coke production, and manufacture of electrical wire, which uses copper as its raw material. Furukawa managed forests in order to secure props for its mines and fuel for its copper-smelting operations and also in order to conserve its mine sites by preventing floods and landslides. Coal and coke were used as fuel in the refineries. Initially Furukawa had used charcoal as fuel, but the supply of charcoal could not keep up with the rising output of the mines and refineries; in 1887, therefore, Furukawa switched to coke. To become self-sufficient in coke, it built Furukawa Coke, a coking plant in Tokyo that began production in 1888.[51] For coal, the raw material for the coking plant, it bought and operated several coal mines in Kyushu beginning in 1894. In addition, Furukawa was a pioneer in Japan in the production of electric wire, a field in which it left Sumitomo far behind.

The Furukawa industries, however, were limited to those with a connection to copper production. As the largest domestic copper producer, unequaled in volume of production, technology, and marketing power, Furukawa succeeded in amassing a huge store of capital. But, unlike Sumitomo, it did not adopt a strategy of diversification, for one reason: founder Furukawa Ichibei's belief in unified operations within the copper industry. Until his death in 1903, Ichibei's business philosophy dictated the running of the zaibatsu, and it lavishly dipped into its vast financial reserves to buy more copper mines.[52] The many such mines purchased beginning in the latter half of the 1880s yielded little copper, however. Furukawa copper represented a substantial share of domestic production: 41.9 percent in 1890 and 36.7 percent in 1900 (Table 3.7). Yet the contribution of the mines other than Ashio to Furukawa's total output was insignificant: in 1890 the Ashio mine accounted for 76.3 percent of the total, and twenty years later it was almost unchanged at 74.2 percent. The efficiency of Furukawa's investment was extremely low.

Not surprisingly, therefore, opposition arose within Furukawa as well as from its creditor, the Daiichi Bank, to Ichibei's purchasing of copper mines. At the time of his 1899 purchase of the Kune copper mine in Shizuoka Prefecture for ¥300,000, when Ichibei was perhaps discouraged by the public outcry over pollution caused by the Ashio mine, he entreated at a managers' meeting, "Let me buy it. Think of it as my throwing away ¥300,000 on my hobby." He thus had to persuade opponents within Furukawa to permit the purchase.[53]

TABLE 3.7   Copper Output for Japan, Furukawa, and Furukawa's Ashio Mine, 1890–1910

Year	Total national output, (A) (tons)	Furukawa output (B) (tons)	Ashio output (C) (tons)	B/A (%)	C/B (%)
1890	18,115	7,589	5,789	41.9	76.3
1895	19,114	6,587	4,898	34.5	74.4
1900	24,317	8,924	6,077	36.7	68.1
1905	35,495	8,949	6,577	25.2	73.5
1910	49,324	9,480	7,034	19.2	74.2

SOURCE: Furukawa Kōgyō, *Sōgyō 100-nen shi* (100 Years of Furukawa Mining) (Tokyo: Furukawa Kōgyō Kabushiki Kaisha, 1976), pp. 76, 82.

TABLE 3.8   Plant Investment by Furukawa after the Russo-Japanese War

Investment Category	1906–10		1911–14	
	Amount (thousand yen)	% of total	Amount (thousand yen)	% of total
Ashio copper mine	623	20	2,070	41
Other copper mines	107	3	1,141	22
Nikkō hydroelectric plant, electrolytic refinery	1,401	46	574	11
Kyushu coal mines	339	11	965	19
Other	643	20	421	7
Total	3,113	100	5,171	100

SOURCE: Takeda Haruhito, "Nichiro sengo no Furukawa zaibatsu" (The Furukawa zaibatsu after the Russo-Japanese War), in *Keizaigaku Kenkyū*, no. 21 (1978): 24.

The mine-buying fervor at Furukawa subsided after Ichibei's death, and Furukawa's resources were committed to four projects: expansion of the Ashio mine, production of electrolytic copper and electric wire, coal mining in Kyushu and coke production, and development and expansion of refining facilities of mines other than Ashio. (See Table 3.8.) The enterprises were still all copper-related: although Furukawa abandoned the mine-buying program, it retained the commitment to Ichibei's concept of vertical integration within the copper industry.

There is no obvious rationale for Ichibei's single-minded commitment to copper production. His witnessing firsthand of the collapse of the Ono-gumi and his own subsequent failure in the raw silk trade may have contributed to his aversion to diversification. And he once made a revealing statement to the effect that he hated black and liked red.[54] Copper, in Japanese, has long been referred to as *akagane* (red metal). Perhaps, then, his fixation had less to do with economic considerations than a kind of monomania.

The argument that Furukawa's diversification was hindered by the well-known Ashio Copper Mine Incident, in which effluent from the Ashio caused severe pollution, must also be considered. The problem began attracting public attention in 1891, and the farmers who were the victims of the pollution received widespread support throughout the country. In the end, hard-pressed by public opinion, the government between 1897 and 1903 handed down five orders to Furukawa to install pollution controls; closure of the mine was thus averted.[55]

The pollution scandal was a great shock to the Furukawa family. The installation of the pollution controls moreover placed a heavy financial burden on the family. The third antipollution construction project proved to be especially costly. According to a government order dated May 27, 1897, the work had to be started within a week and completed within 30 to 180 days. In completing the project, Furukawa spent ¥598,348 in the latter half of 1897 and ¥646,619 in the first half of 1898, sums that correspond to 14–15 percent of Furukawa's total assets at the time.[56] Yet the immediate result of the antipollution measures was simply to reduce the Ashio output from 5,861 tons in 1896 to 5,298 in 1897;[57] production thereafter resumed its upward trend. The Furukawa family earnings also increased with no major check apart from the years 1896–97, as the following figures indicate:[58]

Year	Furukawa family earnings
1895	¥ 90,067
1896	−173,554
1897	77,775
1898	566,612
1899	1,477,210
1900	2,424,810
1901	2,503,711

Thus, the Ashio Copper Mine Incident seems not to have dealt a sufficiently large blow to have blocked the diversification of Furukawa.

As a result of the incident, Furukawa certainly found itself constricted with respect to financial reserves, as indicated by the fact that it had to borrow a large sum from the Daiichi Bank in order to install the antipollution controls. It is also conceivable that, feeling the weight of public censure, Furukawa avoided expanding operations and starting up new enterprises. For instance, it was forced to delay considerably construction of a large refinery in Nikkō to produce electrolytic copper and electric wire. But construction of the refinery was only delayed, not cancelled.

Furukawa had in fact begun production of copper wire in 1897 at its Honjo copper-refining plant. At first, electrolytic copper wire had accounted for less than 20 percent of its total copper wire production, but demand had risen dramatically, pushing the limits of the Honjo plant's capacity. From as early as 1896, Ichibei had wanted to build an electrolytic refinery and electric wire production facility in Nikkō in order to take advantage of the inexpensive electric power that could be produced there by a large-scale hydroelectric plant.[59] Such a plan had been drawn up at that time, but because of the Ashio Copper Mine Incident, the plan was not enacted until 1904.

Furukawa completed the Nikkō plant and associated hydroelectric facility in 1906. That same year it signed a contract to be the exclusive supplier of electrolytic copper wire to Yokohama Densen Seizō (Yokohama Electric Wire Manufacturing Company) and sole marketer of Yokohama Densen's electric wire. Furukawa put together an integrated system that included copper production at Ashio, electrolytic copper and wire production at Nikkō, electric wire production in Yokohama, and finally electric wire marketing nationwide and abroad. In 1908 it bought over half the stock of Yokohama Electric Wire Manufacturing.[60] Furukawa had overwhelming competitive strength in the electric wire industry, and the output of Yokohama Electric Wire under Furukawa control was more than five times that of Sumitomo.[61]

Although it met a delay due to the Ashio Copper Mine Incident, Furukawa successfully countered the impact of the incident and went on to expand operations and advance into new areas. In the final analysis, the Ashio incident did not hamper the development of Furukawa's operations. Why, then, did Furukawa continue to opt for vertical integration of copper-related industries instead of diversification?

The reasons may be sought within Furukawa's top management. Around the turn of the century, Furukawa did show temporary signs of moving toward a strategy of diversification. The power wielded by Ichibei, who had autocratically led the Furukawa family enterprises since their founding, was greatly weakened during the Ashio incident. Ichibei lacked the ability to resolve the crisis himself—he had to rely upon his adopted heir, Junkichi, and his salaried managers to deal with the government, borrow funds from Daiichi Bank, and direct the installation of pollution controls. When Furukawa was under pressure to carry out the third pollution control project in 1897, Junkichi bowed to a Daiichi Bank demand and established the Furukawa Kōgyō Jimusho (Furukawa Mining Office), which was the first step toward incorporating the Furukawa family business and reorganizing its management. Junkichi also hoped to found a bank and turn Furukawa away from its sole reliance on copper. When Ichibei died in 1903, the possibility of making such changes seemed to have increased substantially.[62]

Ichibei's loyal *bantō*, Kimura Chōshichi, and the engineer Kondō Rikusaburō continued, however, to adhere to the copper-only policy. Moreover, Junkichi, who succeeded Ichibei as head of the family, fell prey to a nervous disease owing to strain over the Ashio incident and the Furukawa reforms. At Junkichi's request, his elder brother, Mutsu Hirokichi, in March 1905 established Furukawa Kōgyō Kaisha (Furukawa Mining Company), an unlimited partnership capitalized at ¥5 million.

Junkichi was the second son of Mutsu Munemitsu, a former foreign minister whom Ichibei had known well since his Ono-gumi days, and thus, when Furukawa Mining Company was founded Furukawa not only appointed Junkichi as president, Kimura as executive director (*kanji chō*), and Kondō as director, it also named two of Mutsu's political protégés, Hara Kei and Okazaki Kunisuke, as vice president and director, respectively. The presence of these politicians within the Furukawa top management further complicated the situation.

Junkichi died in December 1905, extinguishing hopes for a change in Furukawa's strategy. His successor, Furukawa Toranosuke, was Ichibei's son and still a child. Furthermore, he was in a delicate position as Ichibei's son by his mistress, born after Ichibei had adopted Junkichi as his heir. On the pretext of Toranosuke's youth, Inoue and Shibusawa, who had been close to Ichibei, tried to act as his advisers, but their interference heightened the confusion.[63] After Junkichi's death, infighting among the top managers of the Furukawa zaibatsu left them no energy to give serious thought to long-term strategy.

Sumitomo Zaibatsu

Sumitomo, the other zaibatsu based on copper, presented a direct contrast to Furukawa in its firm pursuit of diversification. The strategy of this period, unlike the capricious policy during Hirose's autocratic rule, was to cultivate enterprises selected to meet the needs of the times. Strategy leaders were Iba Sadatate and Suzuki Masaya, senior executive directors, and Kawakami Kin'ichi, a director. Suzuki was a senior civil servant in the Ministry of Agriculture and Commerce when Iba invited him to join Sumitomo in 1896. Kawakami was a former director of the Bank of Japan who in 1899 also entered Sumitomo at Iba's request.

TABLE 3.9   Sumitomo Bank's Business Performance 1895–1910

Year	Deposits (thousand yen)	Loans (thousand yen)	Loans as % of deposits	Borrowing from Bank of Japan (thousand yen)	Profits (thousand yen)	Number of branches
1895	883	2,142	242.6	1,180	11	5
1899	7,487	8,164	109.0	1,511	317	11
1900	10,546	10,031	95.1	494	404	12
1905	26,780	18,976	70.9	0	646	17
1910	44,110	31,517	71.5	0	708	18

SOURCE: Sakudō Yōtarō, ed., *Sumitomo zaibatsu* (Tokyo: Nihon Keizai Shimbunsha, 1982), p. 141.

Suzuki succeeded Iba when the latter resigned as senior executive director in 1904.

The starting point for diversification at Sumitomo during this period was the establishment of Sumitomo Bank. Hirose's retirement was an excellent opportunity for those who had favored starting a bank but had been thwarted by Hirose. Sumitomo Bank was founded in 1895 with capitalization at ¥1 million. It had the advantage of being able to use Sumitomo's experience in the *namiai* business (loans made against warehoused goods); the disadvantage was that the new bank was unable to grow beyond the *namiai* level of operation.

On joining Sumitomo, Kawakami and the former Bank of Japan executives who accompanied him put the bank's operations on a modern basis. They split off the warehousing business, reorganized the bank and its regulations, expanded the number of branches, ended its dependence on borrowing from the Bank of Japan, and achieved a sounder deposit-to-loan ratio.[64] Table 3.9 shows the improvement in the bank's performance from 1895 on. The result was that by the end of 1905 Sumitomo Bank was the third largest bank in Japan, after Mitsui Bank and Daiichi Bank, in terms of deposits and loans and ranked fourth in number of branches, after the Daiichi, Yasuda, and Twelfth banks.[65]

Sumitomo's diversification continued with its entry into the iron and steel industry. Two engineers involved in preparations for establishing the government-run Yawata Seitetsusho (Yawata Iron Works) founded Nippon Chūkōsho (Nippon Steel Works) in 1899 with the assistance of another engineer, Hiraga Yoshitomi.[66] Kawakami, a friend of Hiraga, persuaded the head of the House of Sumitomo to invest in the steel works,[67] which established the first cast steel mill in Japan and was the first private firm in the country to build and operate an open-hearth furnace. The steel company fell into difficulties in 1901, at which time the Sumitomo family bought it and renamed it Sumitomo Chūkōsho (Sumitomo Steel Works).[68] Kawakami clearly played an active role in this acquisition.

Sumitomo Steel Works developed a sound business base through the production of ship's stores for the navy and such railway equipment as rolling stock and wheels and axles.[69] Together with Sumitomo Shindō-jo (Sumitomo Copper Rolling), which in 1912 became the first private firm in Japan to make steel pipe, Sumitomo Steel Works was the fore-runner of Sumitomo Kinzoku Kōgyō (Sumitomo Metal Industries).

Sumitomo moreover went further than Furukawa in one area of vertical integration: the production of sulphuric acid and fertilizer as by-products, which was intended to alleviate the pollution caused by copper refining. The pollution problem was beginning to pose serious obstacles to Sumitomo's expansion plans. Immediately after Hirose's retirement, in February 1895 Sumitomo closed the Yamane hydro-metallurgical processing plant, which had also produced pig iron and sulphuric acid, in order to solve the pollution problem there. Then, in November of the same year it bought an uninhabited island, Shisaka-jima, off Niihama in Ehime Prefecture, to which it planned to move the Niihama and Besshi copper-smelting plants. The Shisakajima refinery was completed in late 1904 but was found to spread sulphur-oxide-bearing smoke over an area much beyond the island, creating a nation-wide air pollution problem. In 1909 Sumitomo opened negotiations with residents harmed by the emissions and paid considerable sums in compensation. At the same time, it sought scientific solutions to the problems.[70]

Kajiura Kamajirō, an engineer at the smelting plant, proposed a plan that would kill two birds with one stone—he suggested that produc-tion of sulphuric acid and fertilizer using the gaseous sulphurous acid emitted by the plant would prevent smoke pollution and at the same time form a new business for Sumitomo. Suzuki sent Kajiura on a study mission to Europe and the United States to enable him to develop the plan further. The proposal eventually met with strong internal opposi-tion stemming from concern over the increased financial burden en-tailed and doubts as to its potential profitability. A decision was put off until it was learned that an improved method developed by the German firm Hartmann made it possible to produce sulphuric acid at low cost. With this information, the Sumitomo top management adopted Ka-jiura's plan in the autumn of 1911,[71] and in 1913 Sumitomo built a fertilizer plant and moved into production of both sulphuric acid and superphosphate of lime fertilizer. Kajiura was appointed the first manager of the plant.

In contrast to Sumitomo, Furukawa continued to suffer from the need for pollution control measures. Despite committing considerable resources to solving the problem, it considered producing sulphuric acid and fertilizer only in connection with the plans being drawn for construction of the Kune copper refinery. The plans were studied from 1906 on but never put into effect.[72]

Sumitomo lagged behind Furukawa, however, in the vertical integration of its coal mining and electrolytic copper and electrical wire-making operations. Furukawa's three coal mines in Fukuoka Prefecture by 1910 were producing 540,000 tons annually, or 3.5 percent of Japan's total production. At the same time, Sumitomo, having sold the Shōji mine in 1903, had only the Tadakuma coal mine, whose annual output of 324,000 tons was 2.1 percent of total domestic production.[73] The Tadakuma mine produced far more coal than Sumitomo consumed as fuel, and increasing access to coal markets, both domestic and foreign, was a problem. Sales did not grow as hoped, and the opinion emerged at the head office that Sumitomo should sell the Tadakuma mine and retire from coal mining.[74] Such action never came to pass.

Regarding copper rolling and copper wire production, Furukawa and Sumitomo had started at almost the same time. The Furukawa Honjo copper-refining plant opened a copper-rolling unit and began to manufacture copper wire in January 1897. The same year Sumitomo bought the Nippon Seidō Kabushiki Kaisha (Japan Copper Company, Ltd.), in which the Sumitomo family had previously invested. Renamed Sumitomo Shindōjo (Sumitomo Copper Rolling), the plant began production of copper wire in April 1897.[75] But Sumitomo's was a special silicate copper wire, and the firm lacked an electrolytic copper production capacity as big as Furukawa's. Thus a significant gap developed between Furukawa and Sumitomo in electrolytic copper and electrical wire production.

The copper from Sumitomo's Besshi mine was not suitable for electrolytic refining, but Sumitomo nevertheless decided on large-volume production of electrical wire in 1906 and entered the market in 1908. Sumitomo was forced to begin using electrolytic copper bought elsewhere when the wire made from the unsuitable Besshi copper was not well received due to its low rate of conductivity. The inadequacy of the highly paid British engineer and the factory's considerable distance from the major electrical wire markets, Tokyo and Yokohama, were additional problems besetting Sumitomo in its competition with Furukawa. Large losses in the electrical wire production division exerted pressure on Sumitomo Copper Rolling's business performance as a whole. Consequently in August 1911 that division was spun off as Sumitomo Densen Seizōsho (Sumitomo Electrical Wire).[76] The effect of making the division independent was remarkable: within one year the value of Sumitomo Electrical Wire's output more than doubled, to ¥700,000, and it earned a profit of about ¥100,000. Sumitomo nonetheless continued to lag behind Furukawa in electrical wire production.

ASANO AND YASUDA

Asano Zaibatsu

Asano had developed a cement plant, shipping agency, and petroleum division in the years 1868–93. It went on to expand and diversify even further while retaining characteristic features: reliance on joint investment with outsiders and inability to achieve exclusive family control.

For instance, in 1898 Asano reorganized its cement plant into Asano Cement Gōshi Kaisha (Asano Cement, Ltd.), capitalized at ¥800,000. But Asano Sōichirō, the partner with unlimited liability, contributed only ¥335,000 or 42 percent of the total capital. Having evaluated the assets of the plant at ¥500,000, he allotted equity equal to a third of that amount, or ¥165,000, to Shibusawa Eiichi, who had acted as go-between when Asano purchased the plant from the government and who had promised to accept a third of the liability if losses occurred. Accordingly, Asano's share was reduced to ¥335,000. Shibusawa divided his portion of the equity, giving a ¥110,000 share to his nephew-in-law Ōkawa Heizaburō and a ¥55,000 share to another relative, Odaka Kōgorō. The remainder of the total capital of ¥800,000 consisted of investments of ¥100,000 each by Shibusawa, by the family of Shibusawa's former master, the Tokugawa shōgun (with Shibusawa serving as the nominal investor), and by Yasuda Zenjirō.[77]

Asano Cement built a new plant at Moji, where it installed the first rotary kiln in Japan. The plant went into full operation in 1904, and Asano Cement's capital was increased to ¥5 million in 1909. The plant strengthened the firm's productive capacity so that by 1913, when Asano Cement was converted into a joint-stock company with ¥5 million in capital, it had become the leading cement maker, accounting for 37 percent of domestic cement production.[78] Cement became the foundation of the Asano zaibatsu's diversification strategy.

In another move toward diversification, in 1906 Asano established Ishikari Sekitan (Ishikari Coal), capitalized at ¥3.75 million, and thus embarked on developing coal mines in Hokkaido. (Asano already operated Iwaki Colliery in Fukushima Prefecture.) Asano needed joint investments from Nakano Buei and other wealthy men to establish Ishikari Coal.

Indeed, for all the projects arising from its diversification strategy in this period, the Asano zaibatsu was dependent upon joint investments. The initiation of each of the following four Asano enterprises illustrates this dependence.

ORIENTAL STEAMSHIP COMPANY. When Asano Sōichirō heard from his son-in-law Shiraishi Motojirō about the government's laws to promote shipping and shipbuilding, he conceived a plan to operate a scheduled trans-Pacific steamship line. He founded the Tōyō Kisen Kabushiki Kaisha (Oriental Steamship Company) in June 1896. Himself holding only one-thirteenth of the 130,000 shares in the company when it was capitalized at ¥6,500,000 in 1897, he was dependent for the remainder upon funds from Ōkawa, Shibusawa, Yasuda, and others. Difficulty arose when the major stockholders did not cooperate; for example, as a result of some of the stockholders' refusal to pay in, the original capital of ¥7.5 million had to be reduced to ¥6.5 million after only one year.[79]

Another significant example of Asano's instability due to lack of funds concerned the Oriental Steamship Company's San Francisco route, chosen in order to avoid Seattle and Vancouver, which were served respectively by NYK and the Canadian Pacific. Asano agreed to cooperate with the U.S. Pacific Mail and British Occidental and Oriental lines in making connections with the Southern Pacific Railway. Operations started in 1898 with a new British-made 6,000-ton-class steamship. Then, Pacific Mail began sailing a large, high-speed ship of 12,000 tons. To keep up, Oriental Steamship ordered two 13,000-ton-class turbine ships from Mitsubishi's Nagasaki Shipyard in June 1905. The cost of the ships was to be covered by a twofold capital increase and by borrowing £200,000 (¥2 million) from the British firm Samuel, Samuel, & Co.[80] Asano received permission at the 1905 general stockholders' meeting to carry out the capital increase, but its timing and the means by which it was to be carried out were left to be decided later. From 1907 on, however, the recession in the shipping industry worsened, as did Oriental Steamship's business performance. Consequently, with the two new ships on the verge of completion, a special stockholders' meeting was called in March 1908 and permission was withdrawn for the proposed capital increase. The following month another special stockholders' meeting was called by Shibusawa and other influential stockholders; at that time, the capital increase and the details of its execution were finally agreed upon.[81]

Sōichirō took an aggressive approach to developing Oriental Steamship. He opened new routes to Manila and South America in 1905 and ordered another 13,000-ton-class turbine ship, the *Shun'yō-maru*, in 1907. In that year he also acquired four tankers to transport crude oil for Nanboku Sekiyu, a petroleum company that he established to import and refine crude oil. The result of these bold actions, in combination with the prevailing recession in the shipping industry, was that Oriental Steamship's business grew even worse. From the second half of 1908 it was in the red for three straight semesters and paid no dividend for five. At the general stockholders' meetings of 1909 and 1910, Sōichirō, as president, was attacked by the stockholders and found himself in a difficult position. When Yasuda Bank accepted Oriental Steamship corporate debentures totaling ¥5 million,[82] and with the support of major shareholders including Shibusawa and Ōkura, Sōichirō managed to weather the attacks. At the 1909 meeting he selected as vice president Ōkawa Heizaburō, and at the 1910 meeting he appointed as directors Itō Suketada, formerly an official in a marine-related government office, and Isaka Takashi, head of the Yokohama branch office of Oriental Steamship.[83] The challenges had nonetheless considerably weakened Sōichirō's authority and exposed the weakness of a zaibatsu unable to maintain family-based financial exclusivity and forced to rely on joint funding.

NANBOKU PETROLEUM AND NKK. The same weak point can be seen in the case of Nanboku Sekiyu (South-North Petroleum). From 1893, Asano ran the Asano petroleum division, the exclusive sales agent for Russian kerosene. At the stage when the 1898 opening of a rail link between Niigata and Tokyo was expected to create a new market for Niigata kerosene, Asano expanded to include sales of kerosene produced by Hōden Sekiyu (Hōden Petroleum) and other refineries of Niigata Prefecture. Sōichirō furthermore decided to embark on a petroleum drilling and refining business in Niigata and accordingly hired in 1895 Kondō Kaijirō, an engineer formerly employed by the Ministry of Agriculture and Commerce. He then completed the Kashiwazaki oil refinery in 1900 and succeeded in drilling an oil well using the rotary method in 1902. Most of the oil fields in Niigata Prefecture, however, were under the control of two companies, Nippon Sekiyu (Nippon Petroleum) and Hōden Petroleum, and so Sōichirō was plagued by crude oil supply problems. He transferred his affiliated resources one after the other to Hōden Petroleum and finally in 1904 retired from the Niigata oil industry.[84]

The setback did not mean that Sōichirō had turned his back on the petroleum-refining business. Rather, he would force open a narrow path by changing his source of crude oil. His action was urged by the approaching expiration in 1906 of the contract with Samuel, Samuel, & Co. for selling Russian kerosene. In 1905 he founded Nanboku Petroleum as a joint venture with Ōkura Kihachirō and Yamada Matashichi, president of Hōden Petroleum. The new company explored for oil in Taiwan, then a Japanese colony, and in Aomori and Hokkaido, but without success.[85] A favorable opportunity for the revival of Asano's oil-refining business finally came in 1906 when an American dealer offered to sell California crude oil to Asano through the San Francisco branch office of the Oriental Steamship Company. After discussions with Kondō and Shiraishi, Sōichirō signed a supply contract and set about refining his imported crude oil. With the cooperation of the Nanboku Petroleum stockholders, he founded Tōzai Sekiyu (East-West Petroleum) and merged it with Nanboku, then capitalized at ¥3 million.

Asano's 3,234 shares in the new Nanboku Petroleum Sekiyu represented 5.4 percent of the total and gave it a standing as second largest shareholder. The major shareholder was Watanabe Tōkichi, senior executive director of Hōden Petroleum. Watanabe was appointed president, and Terada Kōichi, long-time manager of Asano's petroleum business, was named senior executive director. Kondō Kaijirō, who left Asano for Hōden Petroleum after Sōichirō had withdrawn from the Niigata oil fields, was appointed chief engineer.[86]

Nanboku Petroleum began importing crude oil in 1907. The Oriental Steamship Company, which the previous year had signed a contract for exclusive shipping of the crude oil, carried the oil in its own or chartered tankers. The Nanboku refinery was completed in Yokohama in 1908. Additional refineries in Maiko, Hyōgo Prefecture, and Dalian, Manchuria, were planned,[87] but at this point Nanboku was confronted by a movement opposing crude oil imports led by those elements, including Nippon Petroleum, calling for the protection of domestic crude oil. The anti-import movement lobbied the Diet until succeeding in 1908 in having the duty on imported crude raised 2.2 to 3 times. Increased costs were inevitable for refineries relying on imported oil. Moreover, the American dealer who had contracted to supply Asano merged with Standard Oil of California and could not fulfill the contract. Sōichirō's crude oil importing and refining business collapsed and virtually upon completion his Yokohama refinery was absorbed by Hōden Petroleum.[88]

When he learned that his supply of California crude had been cut off, Sōichirō promptly sent Kondō to South America to buy crude oil and set up a supply contract, despite the hike in the import duty. His intention to continue in the oil business was clear.[89] If Nanboku Petroleum had been Sōichirō's alone, it might have weathered the difficulties. The hasty decision to abandon the field was a result of the joint investment on which Nanboku was based. The case serves as another example of the characteristic weakness of the Asano zaibatsu.

Nippon Kōkan (Nippon Steel Pipe, NKK), established in 1912 and capitalized at ¥2 million, represents yet another instance of Asano's jointly funded enterprises. At its founding, Asano Sōichirō and his wife owned 1,800 shares and their daughter and son-in-law's family, the Shiraishi, owned 2,267 shares, so that only 10 percent of the total stock was under the control of the Asano family. For the remainder of the funds, Asano looked again to Shibusawa, Ōkawa, and Ōkura.[90]

The steel company had originated as an Ōkura-gumi venture. Imaizumi Kaichirō left his position as engineer at the government-operated Yawata Iron Works in order to cooperate with Ōkura-gumi in founding NKK. When Ōkura-gumi backed out for lack of joint investors, Imaizumi continued to work on the project, agreeing to a cooperative arrangement with Shiraishi, with whom he had been friendly since their student days. Shiraishi—as an officer of the Oriental Steamship Company, which was planning to open a shipping route to India—hoped for the development of the Japanese market for Indian pig iron, which would be a promising cargo for the new route. He consequently found the steel-pipe venture extremely attractive and convinced his father-in-law, Asano Sōichirō, to back the project. NKK was thus founded on the initiative of the Asano zaibatsu, with Shiraishi being appointed president.[91]

TOKYO BAY RECLAMATION PROJECT. Asano Sōichirō had long dreamed of a major Tokyo Bay construction project that would include the building of a port and canals and the creation of new landfill sites for factories. He first proposed such a project to the central and local governments in 1899 and again in 1908 and 1910. Permission was not forthcoming. He then secured Yasuda Zenjirō's promise of financial backing and formed Tsurumi Maichiku Kumiai (Tsurumi Reclamation and Construction Society), an anonymous association, in 1912. Tsurumi Maichiku Kumiai applied for permission to carry out a reclamation project that would fill in part of the bay, and the Kanagawa prefectural government at last granted permission in January 1913.[92] The society began work that August and in March 1914 reorganized itself into a joint-stock company, Tsurumi Reclamation Company capitalized at ¥3.5 million. Asano Sōichirō was named president. The Asano family held a relatively small interest in this firm, contributing only 33 percent of the total capital.[93] Tsurumi Reclamation operations grew rapidly, and the firm achieved consistently high returns. It increased its capital in March 1920 to ¥12.5 million and changed its name to Tokyo Wan Umetate (Tokyo Bay Reclamation).

Yasuda Zaibatsu

The House of Yasuda invested its energies in expanding and strengthening its banking business. Yasuda Bank itself went through a series of capital increases, expanding fivefold in 1887 to ¥1 million, then raising it to ¥2 million in 1900 when the bank was reorganized as an unlimited partnership, to ¥5 million in 1908, and to ¥10 million in 1912 when it was reorganized as a joint-stock company. As Table 4.4 shows, the bank also expanded deposits and loans to a remarkable extent.[94] In addition, Yasuda Bank was active in expanding its subsidiary banks. Besides founding the Nippon Shōgyō Ginkō (Nippon Commercial Bank) and Meiji Shōgyō Ginkō (Meiji Commercial), it strove to provide economic assistance to banks in difficulties and to reorganize and operate them as subsidiaries. Between 1893 and 1913 it acquired fifteen subsidiary banks.[95]

Yasuda also moved actively into nonbanking fields, establishing in 1894 Kyōsai Seimei Hoken (Kyōsai Life Insurance), successor to Kyōsai Gohyakumeisha, which had been founded in 1880 as the first life insurance company in Japan. Yasuda set up Yasuda Unpan Jimusho, a shipping and warehousing unit, in 1894 and founded Yasuda Seichōsho, a nail factory, in 1897. Nishinari Bōsekisho, a cotton-spinning company, was established in 1899 through the purchase of Naniwa Bōseki (capitalized at ¥600,000). In 1900 Yasuda bought Tenma Tekkōjo, a machinery manufacturer, and in 1911 acquired by foreclosure Toba Zōsensho, a shipyard capitalized at ¥200,000.[96] The Kushiro sulphur mine, in contrast, was closed in 1898 owing to a dispute over lease of the mine.[97] This group of family enterprises was controlled by the Yasuda Motojime Yakuba until its functions were taken over by the Yasuda Shōji Gōmei Kaisha (Yasuda Trading), established in 1899 with a capital of ¥1 million.[98]

The Yasuda zaibatsu also participated as an investor in many non-financial enterprises, including Tokyo Tatemono, a construction and real estate company, several railways, and Teikoku Seima (Imperial Linen), formed by the merger of four linen-spinning companies in which Yasuda had invested.[99]

The nonfinancial enterprises controlled by Yasuda Trading were small in scale compared with the expanding firms in the Yasuda financial group, and they performed rather badly. Nishinari Bōsekisho had poor returns and was sold to Mie Bōseki in 1905.[100] Toba Zōsensho was closed about a year and a half after its purchase and then handed over to Yokkaichi Tekkōsho (Yokkaichi Iron Works).[101] The nail factory Yasuda Seichōsho was set up to manufacture Western-style nails, and Yasuda employed Yamaguchi Takehiko, a government engineer who later founded Yamatake Shōkai (now Yamatake Honeywell) and Nippon Sanso (Nippon Oxygen) to run the plant. The factory, using expensive imported wire as its basic material and hard-pressed by competition from cheap imported nails, fell into serious difficulties. Production was suspended for about six years beginning in late 1902. Eventually, the initiation of domestic wire production by Yawata Iron Works and the imposition of a tariff on imported nails enabled Yasuda Seichōsho to resume operations on a stable basis. It was virtually the only one of Yasuda Trading's industrial subsidiaries to survive beyond World War I, but its sales in 1928 were only ¥600,000, much smaller than the ¥3.45 million recorded by Sumitomo Steel or the ¥5.3 million by Asano Kokura Steel.[102]

Overall control of Yasuda Trading, Yasuda Bank, and the various insurance companies was exercised by Hozensha and Yasuda Bank, between which the relationship is unclear. Hozensha beginning in 1894 possessed holding company functions, but the bank also held a substantial number of shares; thus, the two seem to have performed parallel functions.[103] The January 1912 reorganization of Hozensha into an unlimited partnership and of Yasuda Bank and Yasuda Trading into joint-stock companies, however, turned the Hozensha into a holding company with sole exercise of central office functions for the Yasuda zaibatsu. A supervisory division had been established within Hozensha in 1905; it was gradually strengthened to support Hozensha's central office functions.[104]

ŌKURA AND FUJITA

Ōkura Zaibatsu

At the outset the Ōkura zaibatsu expanded into a range of fields, including government purveying, leather tanning and shoemaking, construction, and foreign trade. Thereafter, however, it gave greater weight to developing its existing enterprises than to establishing new ones. Gōmei Kaisha Ōkura-gumi, established in 1893 and capitalized at a million yen, ran mainly the trading business, eventually adding the mining business. The shoemaking and tanning businesses were spun off, with partial funding from outside the Ōkura zaibatsu, as Nippon Seika (Nippon Shoemaking), established in 1902 and Nippon Hihaku (Nippon Tanning), established in 1907. In 1911, Ōkura trading and mining businesses were separated from Gōmei Kaisha Ōkura-gumi, an unlimited partnership, and merged with Ōkura Doboku-gumi (Construction) to form a joint-stock company capitalized at 10 million yen, Kabushiki Kaisha Ōkura-gumi. In the same year, the trading division of Kabushiki Kaisha Ōkura-gumi, with branches in London, New York, Hamburg, Sydney, Seoul, and major trading centers in China,[105] handled mainly such heavy industrial products as electric machines, general machines, and iron products made by Yawata Iron Works. But the scale of the Ōkura trading business was much smaller than Mitsui Bussan's.[106]

The new enterprises launched by the Ōkura zaibatsu were located in Korea and China. Ōkura-gumi had been quick to capitalize on the business opportunities presented by those countries. After the signing of the Japanese-Korean Treaty of Amity in 1876, Ōkura-gumi had been the first to plunge into trade with Korea, stepping up its activities there in the 1900s with the Pusan Bay reclamation project, purchases of farmland, and other investments. By 1907 it owned 2,300 hectares of Korean farmland, let to sharecroppers.[107]

With the Russo-Japanese War, Ōkura-gumi's overseas investments extended into Manchuria, centering particularly on coal mining and iron production at Lake Benxi (J.: Honkei-ko). Ōkura-gumi surveyed the Manchurian mines that were seized by Japan during the war and bought the Lake Benxi coal mine and an iron mine at Miaoergou (J.: Byōji-ko). Ōkura-gumi reportedly took advantage of the wartime confusion to buy the mines from bandits. It began operating the Lake Benxi coal mine in 1906,[108] but the Qing government demanded that the mine be operated as a joint Ōkura-Chinese enterprise; accordingly, in 1910 Ōkura formed a joint venture with the Qing government called the Honkei-ko Baikō Yugen Kōshi (C.: Benxihu Meigong Youxian Gongsi, or Lake Benxi Coal Mine, Ltd.). The Chinese and Ōkura each put up half of the total capital of 2 million yuan. Ōkura-gumi's share was paid in kind in the form of the mine itself, valued at 1 million yuan.[109]

Meanwhile, Ōkura-gumi asked the government's Yawata Iron Works to conduct a survey of the Miaoergou iron mine. Learning that the mine looked promising, Ōkura-gumi proceeded to add another business, iron and steel manufacturing, to its joint venture with the Qing government. The Lake Benxi coal mine venture was renamed Baitetsu Kōshi (C.: Meitie Gongsi, or Iron Company) in 1911, and its capital was doubled to 4 million yuan.[110] The new company built an iron mill with technological assistance from Yawata Iron Works; its first blast furnace was put into operation in 1915.[111] Many other Ōkura coal mines in Korea and China were operated by the mining division of

Kabushiki Kaisha Ōkura-gumi. That division also acquired coal mines within Japan, such as the Moshiri mine in Hokkaido, but their development awaited the establishment of Ōkura Kōgyō Kabushiki Kaisha (Ōkura Mining Company, Ltd.) in 1917.[112]

Fujita Zaibatsu

The business enterprises of Gōmei Kaisha Fujita-gumi were confined to two areas during this period: the operation of mines, such as that at Kosaka, and the Kojima Bay drainage project. Fujita-gumi did not move in new directions. In the second phase of the Kojima Bay drainage project, completed in 1912, Fujita-gumi reclaimed 5,540 hectares of land, including 3,720 hectares of paddy land.[113] The Kosaka silver mine was the hub of Fujita-gumi's mining activities, but its output began to decline after 1893. With Japan's conversion to the gold standard in 1897, silver prices collapsed, and the Kosaka mine became commercially unviable. To rescue Fujita-gumi from this crisis, the Mōri family, which had lent it large sums of money, and Inoue Kaoru, who had acted as intermediary between Fujita and the Mōri, demanded that the zaibatsu scale down its mining activities and halt operation of the Kosaka mine in particular.[114]

Kuhara Fusanosuke solved Fujita's most pressing problem, the unprofitability of the Kosaka mine. Appointed in 1897 deputy head of the mine and charged with handling the administrative business accompanying the suspension of operations at Kosaka, Fusanosuke was the fourth son of Fujita Denzaburō's brother Kuhara Shozaburō. Only twenty-nine in 1900 when he became head of the mine, he managed to convince Inoue to let him delay the mine closing. He thereupon mobilized the Kosaka engineering staff to carry out technological improvements. The Kosaka mine in 1902 turned to making use of the *kokkō*, a complex and low-grade copper ore that until then had remained unutilized. Pyritic smelting of *kokkō* was initiated, and an increase in copper output resulted. At the same time the mine's operations were electrified and pollution-control measures instituted.[115]

Through utilization of the abundant *kokkō* ore, Kosaka transformed itself from a silver mine into a copper mine. Immediately after pyritic smelting was put into operation, Kosaka became the fourth most productive copper mine in Japan; from 1907 it hovered between number one and number three. Its success turned around the entire zaibatsu; by 1903, Fujita-gumi was able to repay all its debts to the Mōri family.[116]

With Fujita-gumi's business on the upturn, Fujita Denzaburō decided in 1905 to switch the enterprise from a partnership of the houses established by three Fujita brothers to a father-son partnership in his line alone. He attempted to wrest away the partnership rights of Fujita Kotarō, eldest son of his late brother Shikatarō, and of Kuhara Fusano-suke, heir to the house of Kuhara Shozaburō, Denzaburō's other brother. Inoue and other political leaders stepped in to mediate the resulting dispute. In the end, Kotarō and Fusanosuke agreed to relin-quish their partnership rights in exchange for compensation amounting to a fourth of the assessed value of the Kosaka mine, or ¥5 million each, to be paid over a period of ten years.[117]

Fusanosuke left Fujita-gumi in December 1905. The day after quit-ting, he used his initial payment from Fujita to buy the Akazawa mine in Ibaraki Prefecture for ¥430,000. He renamed it the Hitachi mine and began to manage it himself.[118] Kotarō, on the other hand, invested his compensation largely in real estate and stocks and did not engage directly in industrial enterprise. Kotarō's family is known as the Tokyo Fujita to distinguish it from Denzaburō's family, the Osaka Fujita.

The engineers who had been Fusanosuke's subordinates at Kosaka and had helped him turn it around quit Fujita-gumi and followed him to the Hitachi mine. With their assistance, he made a success of Hitachi. By 1913 it had become second only to the Ashio mine in copper pro-duction, and Kuhara had risen to become a leading copper producer, ranking third after Furukawa and Fujita. In the World War I years, Fusanosuke worked to expand the Hitachi facilities and to diversify operations by following an ambitious strategy: branching out from copper to other nonferrous metals, including gold and silver. (See Table 3.10.)

Fusanosuke also moved into refining purchased ores by building a number of refineries and other facilities in Japan and Korea.[119] In 1912 he founded Kuhara Kōgyō Kabushiki Kaisha (Kuhara Mining Com-

TABLE 3.10   Production of Nonferrous Metals by Kuhara Mining, 1905–17

Year	Gold Production (Kg.)	Gold % of total domestic production	Silver Production (Kg.)	Silver % of total domestic production	Copper Production (Kg.)	Copper % of total domestic production
1905	1	0.02	9	0.01	21	0.06
1908	75	1.64	1,260	1.14	1,902	4.64
1911	497	5.20	9,066	7.11	4,774	8.79
1914	2,373	18.57	19,683	14.00	10,277	14.32
1917	4,577	35.34	81,980	40.22	37,072	33.99

SOURCE: *Nihon Kōgyō Kabushiki Kaisha 50-nen shi* (50 Years of Nihon Mining Com-pany) (Tokyo: Nihon Kōgyō Kabushiki Kaisha, 1957), p. 334.

pany, Ltd.), capitalized at ¥10 million. Then, with the sound base provided by his company's huge earnings during the wartime boom, he diversified into fields outside of mining and opened the way to the establishment of the Kuhara zaibatsu.

SUMMARY

The eight zaibatsu examined thus far pursued various strategies of diversification in the period 1893–1913. Mitsui during these years underwent steady development based on the three pillars of banking, trading, and mining. Although the diversified industrialization policy of Mitsui Bank under Nakamigawa Hikojirō ended in failure, Mitsui Bussan grew vigorously as a general trading company (*sōgō shōsha*), and Mitsui Mining recorded huge profits, enabling it to pay off the government for the Miike Coal Mine, build the Miike port entirely with its own capital, and advance into the coal chemical industry. Mitsui also spun off its dry goods store. Mitsubishi, meanwhile, developed across a wide range of fields, including coal mining, metal mining, banking, warehousing, real estate, shipbuilding, and trading; and in the case of Iwasaki family enterprises, farming, paper manufacturing, and brewing. Mitsubishi poured energy especially into shipbuilding.

Furukawa and Sumitomo zaibatsu had both started in the copper industry, but during these years they followed divergent paths. Whereas Furukawa grew through vertical integration of exclusively copper-related industries, Sumitomo adopted a strategy of diversifying into banking and steel and, even while pursuing vertical integration in the copper industry, advanced into the chemical industry in order to control pollution. Asano moved energetically into cement, shipping, petroleum, steel, and land reclamation, but suffered from a lack of personal wealth and from the resultant need to establish joint ventures with outsiders. Yasuda diversified its financial operations and further branched into such nonfinancial fields as sulphur mining, shipping, warehousing, nail manufacturing, cotton spinning, machine making, and shipbuilding; its nonfinancial enterprises, however, were small in scale and performed poorly. Central to Ōkura's diversification during these decades was the development of coal-mining and iron-manufacturing operations in Korea and Manchuria. In Fujita's case, the key developments were the reorganization of the Kosaka mine and the spin-off of Kuhara.

By the 1910s the major zaibatsu had all achieved the mature zaibatsu form. The scale and breadth of their activities had increased enormously, reflecting and accelerating Japan's takeoff into sustained industrial growth.

CHAPTER 4

FACTORS AFFECTING ZAIBATSU DEVELOPMENT

Among the variables that affected the ability of the zaibatsu to implement diversification strategies during the years 1893–1913 were managerial resources, organizational structures, and the zaibatsu family as owner and controller. I will attempt to counter the view common among zaibatsu historians in Japan that the zaibatsu developed by relying on their wealth of funds, especially the financial resources of their banks. The zaibatsu's managerial resources consisted not only of financial elements but also human ones. Such resources alone do not bring about the development of an enterprise: the organizational structures and personal relationships through which strategic decisions are made are also involved.

MANAGERIAL RESOURCES

Finances

A sole emphasis on financial resources will not lead to the development of the diversified business institution known as a zaibatsu. For instance, wealthy merchants who ranked with the Mitsui in the Tokugawa period did not necessarily transform themselves into zaibatsu in the Meiji period. Those that lacked managerially talented personnel to put their funds to work effectively could not develop into the complex and diversified zaibatsu form; they simply remained wealthy families.[1] With that caveat, it is proper to stress the significance of ample funds in developing diversified enterprises. In particular, large financial reserves were essential to the extent that the zaibatsu families were attempting to achieve diversification under exclusive familial ownership.

Zaibatsu with poor financial reserves were subject to external influences that hindered the efficacy of their diversification strategies. One way for a business to cover a lack of financial resources is to rely on outside investors through the joint-stock company form. In such a case, however, profits must flow out from the company in response to stockholders' demands for dividends. Such a process makes the accumulation of financial reserves even more difficult—which may explain why the zaibatsu, by generally avoiding the joint-stock company form at the outset, were able to form diversified enterprises early on, while the diversification of nonzaibatsu joint-stock companies was delayed until World War I. Those that had to rely on joint investors faced considerable intervention in their programs, as in the case of Fujita-gumi, which was ordered to dispose of the Kosaka mine by the Mōri family and Inoue Kaoru, and that of Asano Sōichirō, whose actions as top manager were restricted by his joint stockholders. To escape such interference; Fujita and Asano both sought sources of unrestricted funds, Fujita-gumi turning to Kitahama Bank and the Asano zaibatsu to Yasuda Bank.[2]

Financial resources included, first of all, owned reserves, both those of the zaibatsu family and those of the zaibatsu as a corporation. In the case of Mitsui, the three designated subsidiaries, Mitsui Bank, Mitsui Bussan, and Mitsui Mining, had been achieving high profits since 1890, and thus the owned reserves of the Mitsui family and the three subsidiaries had grown rapidly. Table 4.1 shows the growth in assets of Mitsui Motokata, charged with holding the family property owned in common by the members of the House of Mitsui; Table 4.2 gives the capital and reserves of the Mitsui Family Council and the three desig-

TABLE 4.1   Assets of Mitsui Motokata, 1892–99 (in yen)

Year	Total Assets*
1892	3,361,183
1893	3,897,150
1894	5,359,061
1895	5,630,567
1896	7,895,528
1897	9,345,633
1898	10,861,440
1899	11,224,444

SOURCE: Mitsui Bunko, *Mitsui jigyō-shi* (History of the Mitsui Enterprises) (Tokyo: Mitsui Bunko, 1980), vol. 2, p. 625.
* As of the end of each year.

TABLE 4.2   Owned Capital of the Mitsui Family Council and Mitsui's Three
Designated Subsidiaries, Mid-1906 (in yen)

	Capital	Reserves	Total
Mitsui Family Council	0	4,653,424	4,653,424
Mitsui Bank	5,000,000	7,700,000	12,700,000
Mitsui Bussan	1,000,000	15,470,000	16,470,000
Mitsui Mining	2,000,000	7,868,035	9,868,035
Total	8,000,000	35,691,459	43,691,459

SOURCE: Same as Table 4.1, p. 736.

nated subsidiaries at the end of the first half of 1906, just before the
Mitsui zaibatsu adopted the multisubsidiary system.

The Mitsubishi zaibatsu similarly acquired the financial resources to
carry out its diversification strategy through the owned reserves of a
family, the Iwasaki. In the Mitsubishi Company era (1886–93), stock
dividends, interest on the government bonds owned by the Iwasaki,
and profits from the zaibatsu's enterprises, particularly coal mining,
combined to create ample financial resources (Table 2.1).

During the period from Mitsubishi, Ltd.'s founding to the outbreak
of World War I (1893–1914), the firm was unable to finance its diversification entirely with its own capital and internal reserves, but had to
borrow considerable sums for that purpose from Iwasaki Hisaya. The
total of funds borrowed from Hisaya grew from ¥700,000 in 1894 to
¥8.9 million in 1906. Meanwhile, Hisaya's equity in Mitsubishi, Ltd.,
stood at ¥2.5 million, and at the same time Mitsubishi, Ltd.'s reserves
rose from zero in 1894 to ¥10.7 million in 1906.[3] Mitsubishi in 1907
used those reserves to increase its capital from ¥5 million to ¥15 million (see Table 4.3). The ¥10 million capital increase was regarded as
compensation for the loans from Hisaya, and so his share in Mitsubishi,
Ltd., was raised by that amount.

"Compensation" did not mean, however, that those loans were written off. The sum borrowed shrank to ¥107,000 in 1907 and dis-
appeared from the accounting record the following year, but from 1907
to 1917 an additional category entitled "debt account" was recorded
separately from the Iwasaki account. In that category was posted a total
of ¥13.4 million, which included loans of about ¥11.2 million from
Hisaya, ¥2.2 million from Iwasaki Yanosuke, and, after the latter's
death in March 1908, from Iwasaki Koyata.[4] The outstanding Hisaya
loans were thus carried separately from the Iwasaki account beginning
in 1907. In return for having his share in Mitsubishi, Ltd., increased by

TABLE 4.3   Mitsubishi, Ltd., Balance Sheets, 1906–8 (in million yen)

Item	1906	1907	1908
Capital account	5.0	15.0	15.0
Reserve account	10.7	0.0	1.8
Iwasaki account	8.9	0.1	0.0
Debt account	—	13.4	13.4
Cash	—	4.9	0.0
Other	2.4	0.9	7.1
Profit	3.0	2.7	1.7
Total	30.0	37.0	39.0

SOURCE: Mitsubishi Gōshi Kaisha, ed., *Mitsubishi Sha-shi* (Records of Mitsubishi company) (Tokyo: University of Tokyo Press, 1980), vol. 21, pp. 925, 1025, 1117.

¥10 million, Hisaya did not seek repayment of those loans—indeed, he lent the company additional funds, which were then consolidated with those from Yanosuke and Koyata to form the "debt account."

Banking created the second type of financial resources available to the nascent zaibatsu. These resources consisted of funds on deposit with banks founded by the zaibatsu (that is, total deposits less deposits of the zaibatsu family and its enterprises) and borrowings by those banks from the Bank of Japan. As Table 4.4 suggests, Mitsui, Mitsubishi, Sumitomo, and Yasuda, all of which owned banks in the 1893–1913 period, were positioned much more strongly in terms of financial resources, given the rapid growth in their banks' deposits, than were Furukawa, Ōkura, Asano, and Fujita, which did not have banks during this period.

The zaibatsu with banks were cautious, however, in using their own banks. For a zaibatsu to sink its bank's deposits into its enterprises and then to be unable to recover them would do devastating damage not only to the reputation of the bank but also to the family's honor. Reflecting the zaibatsu families' fear of this outcome, the zaibatsu with banks avoided as much as possible investing their banks' funds in their own enterprises, a restraint that became particularly marked after 1900.

The Mitsui zaibatsu provides the classic example of the practice. During Nakamigawa Hikojirō's promotion of industrial investments by Mitsui, the lending policy of Mitsui Bank was to give preferential treatment regarding terms of lending limits and interest rates to the Mitsui subsidiaries. Consequently, at the end of June 1899 enterprises within the Mitsui zaibatsu accounted for 87 percent of the overdrafts on current accounts at the bank's head office.[5] In order to counteract this development, after Nakamigawa's death Mitsui adopted a policy of maximum regulation of lending by its bank to Mitsui subsidiaries.

TABLE 4.4 Deposits and Loans of Zaibatsu-owned Banks, 1895–1912 (million yen)

Bank	1895		1903		1912	
	Deposits	Loans	Deposits	Loans	Deposits	Loans
Mitsui Bank	18.07	12.22	37.23	25.63	86.63	76.82
Mitsubishi, Ltd., banking division	4.47[a]	6.92[a]	15.98	14.71	40.55	37.27
Sumitomo Bank	0.88[a]	2.14[a]	18.60	15.62	49.98	43.91
Yasuda Bank	3.71	3.09	16.16	13.52	32.43	26.23

SOURCES: Compiled from various histories of the Mitsui, Mitsubishi, Sumitomo, and Fuji banks.
NOTE: All figures for mid-year, unless otherwise noted.
[a] At the end of the year.

The policy went so far as to require that Mitsui Bank hold down increases in the deposits themselves. As Masuda, executive director of the Mitsui head office, put it at a meeting of Mitsui Bank branch managers in 1904: "Deposits should be kept from growing, insofar as possible without offending customers. Funds should be safely tied up in loans without becoming uncollectable, even at low interest rates." This policy had been adopted, he explained, in response to outside criticism that "Mitsui is accepting deposits from others and operating a variety of its own enterprises. It is, however, extremely unsound and improper for it to invest in its own enterprises funds received on deposit from others."[6] As a result, conflicts concerning deposit increases often occurred between the negative policy of the Mitsui Bank head office and the aggressive policy of the branches.[7]

It is commonly argued that the zaibatsu operated banks only as a means of getting their hands on the copious funds needed for diversification. That argument holds for a certain period in the development of the zaibatsu banks, but, as the experience of Mitsui after Nakamigawa illustrates, it would be highly erroneous to fix upon this as a general explanation of the zaibatsu-bank relationship.

Borrowing from the Bank of Japan was another potential source of funds for the zaibatsu. Both the zaibatsu and other banks, however, attempted to end their dependency on Bank of Japan credit from 1899 on. The funds borrowed by Mitsui Bank, "thought for the most part to have been borrowed from the Bank of Japan," reached a peak of ¥13.8 million in the first half of 1900 and declined thereafter. From the second half of 1902, Mitsui Bank's borrowings were nearly zero.[8] Similarly, advances by the Bank of Japan to the banking division of Mitsubishi, Ltd., peaked at ¥3.4 million in the latter half of 1899 and then declined. The banking division subsequently did resort to borrowing during recessions, particularly in the 1907–8 slump, but it was not dependent on such financing for its regular operations.[9] The same trend held for Sumitomo Bank, whose borrowings peaked at ¥1.5 million at the end of 1899.[10]

Salaried Managers

A successful diversification strategy depends on an ample supply not only of funds but also skilled personnel. By "skilled personnel" is meant managers who combine ideas, insight, and strategic thinking with the ability to organize, coordinate, and motivate others. Zaibatsu with bigger pools of such managers and the ability to use them more effectively were quicker to form comprehensive groups of diversified enterprises.

Such human talent was derived from the zaibatsu families and their salaried managers. In general, however, the number of skilled personnel who were members of the founding families was limited, even when the definition of "family member" is extended to cover the husbands of daughters or nieces of the zaibatsu founders. The so-called Buddenbrook effect took hold among the zaibatsu: the wealthy lifestyle of the founders' descendants to some extent spoiled them; they tended to invest their energies in the arts, politics, and social life and to be rather indecisive as businessmen.[11] Accordingly, the skilled managers who promoted diversification were, except for the founders themselves, almost always salaried managers rather than family members. The salaried managers who played leading roles in the process of zaibatsu formation prior to World War 1 are examined in the following.

NAKAMIGAWA HIKOJIRŌ. This leading figure in the business history of the Mitsui zaibatsu was the nephew of Fukuzawa Yukichi, the great Meiji educator and popularizer of Western ideas. Nakamigawa left his native Nakatsu to study at Fukuzawa's Keiō Gijuku (now Keiō University) and then spent about four years studying in England on funds provided by his uncle. While in London he met Inoue Kaoru, who had been dispatched by the government on a fact-finding mission to the United States and Great Britain. Inoue formed a high opinion of Nakamigawa's abilities and invited him to join the civil service. Nakamigawa served under Inoue in the ministries of industry and foreign affairs and eventually rose to the upper levels of the bureaucracy. In 1881, however, almost all of Fukuzawa's former students, including Nakamigawa, were purged from the government, for Fukuzawa, like Iwasaki Yatarō, had come under suspicion as a confederate of Ōkuma Shigenobu, who was dismissed from political power circles that year.[12]

After leaving the government, Nakamigawa founded a newspaper, the *Jiji Shinpō*, with Fukuzawa and became its president. He was appointed president of the San'yō Railway Company in 1888, thanks to the machinations of Shōda Heigorō and Motoyama Hikoichi, his schoolmates, who represented the major shareholders, the Iwasaki and Fujita families.[13] While serving as president of the railway, Nakamigawa was asked by his former superior in the bureaucracy, Inoue, to join Mitsui. Before accepting the offer, Nakamigawa conferred with Fukuzawa, who encouraged him, saying that he was the person best qualified for the position.[14] Fukuzawa later argued in *Jitsugyō ron* (On Business) that intellectuals, with their high level of educational attainment, must "fill the Japanese business world with civilization" and take up the task of founding a commercial and industrial basis for the state.[15] Thus, he expected that his nephew, by restructuring Mitsui Bank and using the financial resources of the Mitsui family, would be in a position to "influence finance within the country" and to contribute to Japan's development. Nakamigawa had similar aspirations. His uncle's vision of establishing a commercial and industrial basis for the state underlay Nakamigawa's industrialization policy at Mitsui.

Nakamigawa intended to use college-educated men in rebuilding Mitsui Bank and carrying out his industrialization policy and accordingly hired, at high salaries, many Keiō Gijuku graduates. Most were hired after gaining experience elsewhere rather than immediately after leaving Keiō. For Nakamigawa, the use of a large number of university graduates was an important element in Mitsui's reform, but the introduction of so many Keiō graduates stimulated criticism of Nakamigawa within Mitsui for having created a "Keiō clique."

Many of the Keiō graduates employed by Mitsui during the Nakamigawa era went on to become leaders of Japanese industry. These illustrious products of Keiō and Mitsui included Fujiyama Raita (Dai Nippon Sugar), Fujiwara Ginjirō (Ōji Paper), Mutō Sanji (Kanegafuchi Cotton Spinning), Wada Toyoji (Fuji Cotton Spinning), Hibi Ōsuke (Mitsukoshi Department Store), Ikeda Seihin (Mitsui Bank), and Kobayashi Ichizō (Hankyū Railway).

Fujiyama showed his ability by clearing Mitsui Bank's bad loans and taking over Ōji Paper Company. He left Mitsui after Nakamigawa's death and became president of Dai Nippon Sugar, there acquiring the sobriquet of Japan's sugar king.[16] Similarly, Fujiwara, who became president of Ōji Paper, earned the nickname of Japan's paper king. Mutō stayed with Kanegafuchi Cotton Spinning (Kanebō) after Nakamigawa died and acquired a firm grip on its top management as well as its capital stock.[17] Wada too became a top manager in the spinning industry and founded Nippon Kōgyō Club (Japan Industrial Club). Hibi was distinguished by transforming the Mitsukoshi dry goods shop, after it was spun off from the Mitsui-designated subsidiaries, into Mitsukoshi Department Store, the first department store in Japan.[18]

MASUDA TAKASHI. As head of Mitsui Bank, Nakamigawa engaged in a bitter rivalry with Masuda Takashi, head of Mitsui Bussan. This rivalry was not the outcome of adherence by Masuda to the "political merchant" line that was opposed by Nakamigawa, or of opposition by Masuda to Nakamigawa's concept of establishing a commercial and industrial base for Japan. Masuda, like Nakamigawa, believed that the political merchant business favored by the old-fashioned *bantō* was harmful to the House of Mitsui. In addition, Masūda regarded the recovery of Japanese control over the country's international trade, then monopolized by foreign merchant houses, as an issue of national concern. Masuda believed that Mitsui Bussan should lead the drive to take back Japan's foreign trade. Thus, Masuda and Nakamigawa shared a common emphasis on devotion to the commonweal.[19] Masuda, however, was opposed to Nakamigawa's radical industrialization policy and to his autocratic actions, which denigrated the achievements of Mitsui Bussan. Delicate personnel relationships also entered into their rivalry, as suggested by Fukuzawa's concern, when Nakamigawa joined Mitsui, that Shibusawa and Masuda would dislike him.[20]

Whatever his relationship with Nakamigawa, Masuda remained the top manager of Mitsui Bussan since its founding in 1876. During Nakamigawa's tenure as Mitsui Bank head and following his death, Masuda, who became the leader of the Mitsui zaibatsu, continued to pour the greatest part of his energies into the growth of the trading company.

Masuda arrived at Bussan already possessing considerable experience in foreign trade. During his father's service as a retainer of the shōgun in Hakodate, one of the treaty ports opened to foreign trade, Masuda learned English, which he continued to study in Edo. Employed by the shogunate as an interpreter, he visited Europe on an official shogunate mission in that capacity.[21] After the Meiji Restoration, Masuda earned his living by working as an interpreter and assistant in business negotiations for domestic and foreign merchant houses in Yokohama, including the American trading firm Walsh, Hall & Co. In this period he came to Inoue's attention and was hired as deputy director of the Mint Bureau in the Ministry of Finance because of his proficiency in foreign languages. At the time, the mint had a number of foreign engineers and needed personnel with the requisite foreign language ability to manage them.

After joining Mitsui as top manager of the newly formed Mitsui Bussan, Masuda devoted himself to developing personnel rich in knowledge, experience, and international trade ability. From his own experience in the field, he was well aware of the decisive importance of skilled personnel. His wife's brother, Yano Jirō, was the first principal of the Shōhō Kōshūsho (Commercial Training School), and Masuda hired many graduates of that school and its successors, Tokyo Shōgyō Gakkō and Tokyo Kōtō Shōgyō Gakkō, training them on the job.[22] Mitsui Bussan executives who had been students at Shōhō Kōshūsho included Watanabe Senjirō, Iwashita Seishū, and Fukui Kikusaburō. When Masuda became full-time executive director of the management department of the Mitsui Family Council's secretariat in 1904, Watanabe succeeded him as executive director of Mitsui Bussan.

In addition, men who had prior work experience elsewhere, including Ueda Yasusaburō, Iwahara Kenzō, and former Bussan shopboys Yamamoto Jōtarō and Fujino Kamenosuke, were hired and trained to be the kind of managerial personnel that Bussan needed.

Ueda was the adopted son of a merchant family in Nagasaki. At the age of fifteen he was hired by the American merchant Robert W. Irwin, who was based in Nagasaki; with Irwin's assistance he studied in the United States at a private commercial college.[23] As Irwin was an adviser to Inoue's Senshū Kaisha and to Mitsui Bussan, Ueda joined the newly founded Mitsui Bussan after returning from the United States. He worked in the Shanghai branch and in 1880 became its manager, in which capacity he served for twelve years. Right after Mitsui Bussan was reorganized as an unlimited partnership, in 1893 Ueda was elevated to executive director, along with Masuda. Yamamoto Jōtarō was born into a low-ranking samurai family in the domain of Fukui. The nine-year-old boy was left in straitened circumstances when his mother died. His mother's brother Yoshida Kenzō, a Yokohama merchant, helped by appealing to his friend Makoshi Kyōhei, manager of the Yokohama branch of Mitsui Bussan, to take Yamamoto on as a shopboy. Yamamoto showed a remarkable flair for business and eventually, in 1901, became head of the Shanghai branch of Mitsui Bussan. He was appointed a director of Bussan in 1906 and with its reorganization into a joint-stock company in 1909 was named an executive director.[24]

SHŌDA HEIGORŌ. Shōda Heigorō of Mitsubishi is often compared with Mitsui's Nakamigawa Hikojirō. Both were top managers leading the industrialization of their respective zaibatsu. Both also were Keiō graduates who had been guided by Fukuzawa Yukichi. Among the diversified enterprises that developed at Mitsubishi after Iwasaki Yatarō's death, the project to build a new shipyard (in addition to the Nagasaki Shipyard) and the project to develop a business district in Tokyo's Marunouchi section both resulted from senior executive director Shōda's year of study in England.[25] Fukuzawa's teachings—in particular his concept of establishing a commercial and industrial base for the nation—were undoubtedly at work in Shōda's commitment to carrying out such projects at Mitsubishi.

Born into the family of a Confucian scholar in Usuki domain, he studied English on domain orders. He entered Keiō Gijuku in 1870 and two years later was promoted to instructor, devoting himself to school affairs. Fukuzawa, who apparently trusted Shōda deeply, recommended him to Iwasaki Yatarō; Shōda thereupon moved to Mitsubishi Shōkai in 1875. He worked as a translator and bookkeeper and, on Yatarō's orders, also formulated company rules and regulations. He set about modernizing the bookkeeping system, introducing

Western-style double-entry bookkeeping. Shōda joined the top management of Mitsubishi as executive director in 1880.

SUMITOMO SALARIED MANAGERS. Sumitomo enjoyed the services of several outstanding salaried managers following Hirose's retirement. In order to strengthen the top management at that time, Iba Sadatake invited in new managers from the outside, including Kawakami Kin'ichi, Suzuki Masaya, Nakada Kinkichi, Shidachi Tetsujirō, and Ogura Masatsune. Of these, Kawakami and Suzuki played crucial roles in directing Sumitomo's diversification before World War I.

Kawakami was a former director of the Bank of Japan, where he was a sufficiently important figure to rival Yamamoto Tatsuo (formerly of Mitsubishi) for influence. He and a number of other Bank of Japan executives resigned in 1899 after a dispute with bank president Yamamoto over personnel affairs. Iba then invited Kawakami to become director of the Sumitomo head office. In order to attract Kawakami, Iba accepted a demotion from the position of senior executive director to that of director, the same rank offered Kawakami. (Iba was reappointed senior executive director the following year.) Kawakami was influenced by the charm of Iba's personality and not only accepted his invitation but also became his willing supporter. A number of other executives from the Bank of Japan followed Kawakami to Sumitomo, where they contributed to the rapid growth of Sumitomo Bank.[26]

Suzuki Masaya joined Sumitomo in 1896 after serving as a high-ranking official in the Ministry of Agriculture and Commerce. Iba brought him in on the condition that he be sent on a three-year study tour abroad.[27] Suzuki had much in common with Kawakami. Both were sons of samurai, had been graduated from Tokyo Imperial University, and had served in the government bureaucracy. (Kawakami had been a bureau chief in the Ministry of Foreign Affairs before moving to the Bank of Japan.) Sumitomo was in fact more inclined than the other zaibatsu to employ former government officials as top managers (known in Japan as *amakudari kanryō* or "bureaucrats descending from heaven"), a tendency that began with the hiring of Kawakami and Suzuki.

Iba retired as senior executive director of Sumitomo in 1904, asserting that "old men shouldn't stay in top management forever." He was only fifty-eight at the time. His friend Kawakami simultaneously retired as director, leaving the top management of Sumitomo to the newly appointed senior executive director, Suzuki.

UNIVERSITY-EDUCATED MANAGERS. Many of the zaibatsu managers were graduates of Tokyo Imperial University, the first Western-style university in Japan. These men were doubly useful for their high educational level and for their wide-ranging contacts in government, business, and the universities.

Asano provides a good example of the general zaibatsu pattern of hiring university graduates. One of the reasons for the vigorous growth of the Asano diversified enterprises was the participation of such able engineers as Kondō Kaijirō in Asano's petroleum enterprises and Imaizumi Kaichirō in Nippon Kōkan (NKK). It was Asano Sōichirō's son-in-law, Shiraishi Motojirō, who linked these men to the Asano zaibatsu. All had been contemporaries at First Higher School, one of the elite preparatory schools, and at Tokyo Imperial University, though in different departments, frm which they had graduated in 1892. Kondō joined Asano's petroleum division on Shiraishi's introduction.[28] Shiraishi was likewise instrumental in keeping Imaizumi involved in the steel-pipe project that developed into NKK.

The Ōkura zaibatsu also employed university graduates as managers, including Kadono Chōkurō and Itō Takuma. Kadono's graduation from Tokyo Imperial University, with a degree in civil engineering, took place three years after that of Ōkura Kumema, the adopted son of the founder, Kihachirō. Kadono joined Ōkura-gumi after working for the Pennsylvania Railroad and the San'yō Railway. Itō graduated from First Higher School and from the law school of Tokyo Imperial University. He entered Ōkura-gumi through his ties with Kumema, his brother by birth, and worked in the tannery. When the tannery was spun off as Nippon Hikaku Kabushiki Kaisha (Nippon Leather Company, Ltd.), Itō continued to serve as its top manager.[29]

A university graduate served as a manager in the Yasuda zaibatsu as well. Yasuda Zenzaburō, together with Shiraishi, Kondō, and Imaizumi of the Asano zaibatsu, was graduated from First Higher School in 1889 and Tokyo Imperial University in 1892. The extremely close financial ties between the Yasuda and Asano zaibatsu that had begun with the friendship between their founders, Yasuda Zenjirō and Asano Sōichirō, both natives of Toyama Prefecture, continued on the basis of the relationship between Zenzaburō and Shiraishi. Those ties were not without complications, however. For instance, when Shiraishi was preparing to found NKK, Zenzaburō promised financial assistance from the Yasuda zaibatsu but failed to secure Yasuda Zenjirō's agreement.[30]

ENGINEERS. As in the Asano and Ōkura cases above, a number of engineers became salaried managers of the zaibatsu. In the Meiji era, Japan's mining and manufacturing companies in particular required engineers with systematic training to enable them to introduce industrial technology from the West. Such engineers were in short supply—thus, all firms in these fields, whether zaibatsu-affiliated or not, gave preferential treatment to engineers and let them participate in top management.

Mining and metallurgical engineers played a particularly prominent role in the zaibatsu, so many of which were involved in mining. Dan of Mitsui and Kondō of Furukawa were two such engineers who went on to exert contrasting influences on the overall strategies of their zaibatsu. Both had worked as engineers at government-run mines before moving into the private sector when those mines were sold. Both also led the modernization of the mining technology used in their zaibatsu. Dan came to be concerned with the overall diversification and industrialization of the Mitsui zaibatsu, not just with its mining division. Kondō, however, preserved the Furukawa tradition of exclusive involvement in the copper industry and hindered the zaibatsu's diversified development.

CONCLUSIONS. This survey of salaried managers during the formative period of the zaibatsu leaves the strong impression that such managers were highly oriented to national goals and relatively well educated. Graduates of Tokyo Imperial University and Keiō Gijuku were especially numerous. Their education had prepared them to seek as businessmen to enhance their country's place in the world.

About two-thirds of these managers came from the samurai class; nearly three-fifths had been abroad, and an equal proportion had entered zaibatsu employment after serving in the government bureaucracy or on a university faculty. Such factors must have helped to instill in them a strong sense of nationalism. They conceived of business strategies that met the new age's demand for industrialization and induced the zaibatsu families to implement their plans. Moreover, these men were young; nearly half began participating in top management before reaching the age of forty. They were men of great vitality as well as vision.

ORGANIZATIONAL STRUCTURES

Access to money and talented personnel enabled the zaibatsu to branch out into a number of different enterprises, but in the course of diversifying they had to develop management structures suited to the overall control of those enterprises. The cases of Mitsui and Mitsubishi clearly illustrate this development. Because of differences between the two zaibatsu's diversification processes, however, their structures provide a striking contrast. Mitsui employed a multisubsidiary structure, whereas Mitsubishi a multidivisional one. After adopting these structures, they both sought to improve their respective organizational systems. In Mitsui's case, the diversified enterprises took the form of independent subsidiaries, so it strove to integrate and coordinate the subsidiaries. Mitsubishi pursued the policy of controlling its operating units, as their number increased, by consolidating them according to field of activity. Interestingly, in the course of these endeavors, Mitsui and Mitsubishi showed signs of convergence as each moved in the direction of the structure originally adopted by the other.

The Structure of Mitsui

In 1893 the House of Mitsui organized its diversified enterprises— bank, trading company, mining company, and dry goods store—into four unlimited partnerships. The central office function of controlling these enterprises was vested in the Mitsui Family Council. The latter inherited that function from the Mitsui Provisional Council, established in 1891, at which time the diversified enterprises had come to be directly controlled by the Mitsui family.

The function of the zaibatsu central office, namely, overall control of diversified business operations, was more difficult at Mitsui than at Mitsubishi or any other zaibatsu (Figure 4.1). The four Mitsui enterprises had existed as independent firms before the four unlimited partnerships were established. The only enterprise directly controlled by the Mitsui family until 1891 had been the bank; the Mitsui dry goods shop, Mitsui Bussan, and Mitsui Mining had all been formally independent entities not under the ownership or control of the House of Mitsui. Of the four unlimited partnerships, the dry goods shop, due to its shaky performance, was formally placed outside the Mitsui zaibatsu in 1904. Each of the three remaining subsidiaries had a long history, was a large-scale enterprise, and played a leading role in its particular industry. Therefore, a strong tendency existed in these three subsidiaries to prefer independence and freedom of action over cooperation within the Mitsui group. Coordinating decisions among the three and attaining overall control over them was extremely difficult. The independent course of Mitsui Bank in the Nakamigawa era and the antagonism between the bank and the trading company can only be understood in terms of the centrifugal tendency of the Mitsui enterprises.

The Mitsui zaibatsu made efforts to achieve effective general control over the diversified enterprises by more closely integrating the bank, trading company, and mining company. Its chosen means was to establish a strong central office, but the centrifugal Mitsui structure made it necessary to reorganize the central office again and again.

The first such attempt occurred in August 1896, when the Mitsui

FIGURE 4.1 Administrative Chart of the Mitsui Zaibatsu, 1893–1909.

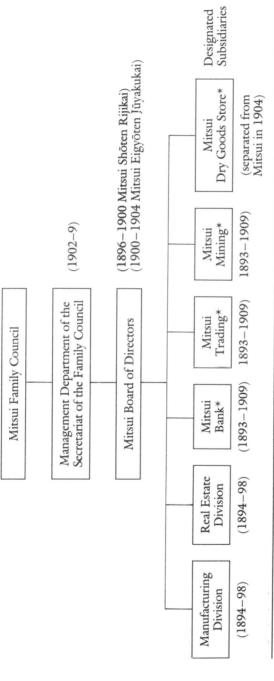

Mitsui Family Council				
Management Department of the Secretariat of the Family Council		(1902–9)		
Mitsui Board of Directors		(1896–1900 Mitsui Shōten Rijikai) (1900–1904 Mitsui Eigyōten Jūyakukai)		

Manufacturing Division	Real Estate Division	Mitsui Bank*	Mitsui Trading*	Mitsui Mining*	Mitsui Dry Goods Store*	Designated Subsidiaries
(1894–98)	(1894–98)	(1893–1909)	1893–1909)	1893–1909)	(separated from Mitsui in 1904)	

SOURCE: Mitsui Bunko, *Mitsui jigyō-shi* (History of the Mitsui Enterprises) (Tokyo: Mitsui Bunko, 1980), vol. 2, pp. 598–653.
*Unlimited partnerships established in 1893

Board of Directors (Mitsui Shōten Rijikai) was set up under the Mitsui Family Council to deliberate on the operations of the four unlimited partnerships, the manufacturing division, and the real estate division. The board's members were the chairman of the Family Council, the Mitsui family inspectors (*kansayaku*, an office instituted in 1894), the head of Mitsui Motokata, Mitsui family members serving as officers of the subsidiaries or divisions, and top salaried managers selected by the Family Council from each subsidiary or division. The real powers on the board were the top salaried managers. Their authority is clear from the fact that they alone were regarded as the directors (*riji*) on the board and that unless more than half the directors were present the board could not make decisions.[31] The first set of directors was comprised of seven men: Masuda Takashi and Ueda Yasusaburō of the trading company, Nakamigawa Hikojirō of the bank, Dan Takuma of the mining company, Takahashi Yoshio of the dry goods store, Asabuki Eiji of the manufacturing division, and Nishimura Torashirō of the real estate division.

The Mitsui Family Council was also responsible for overseeing the fortunes and livelihood of the Mitsui family members and so was not able to focus exclusively on overall control of the Mitsui diversified enterprises. Thus, the Board of Directors was established beneath it to specialize in controlling the enterprises. The board took over from the Family Council the right to approve the decisions of the Mitsui subsidiaries and divisions concerning their respective organizations, personnel, budgets, financial settlements, investments, disposal of assets, and contracts. Of this broad range of items, some could be decided at the level of the directors of each subsidiary or division, while others required the approval of the Mitsui Board of Directors.

For instance, when the branches of Mitsui Bussan brought to the board of directors in their head office proposals for initiating speculative commodity trading and making advances or increasing the limits on such transactions, they could not act on those proposals solely with the approval of their company's board. Such proposals had to be sent up for the approval of the Mitsui Board of Directors. If approved, then the Bussan board could decide on each transaction that fell within the limits set by the Mitsui Board of Directors (for instance, buying 2,000 tons of coal long) without referring back to the higher board.[32] Until just after the Mitsui Board of Directors was established, Mitsui Bussan had been able to make its own decisions about speculative trading and short-term lending. But beginning in October 1897, a dramatic increase appeared in the number of transactions approved by the Bussan board that then went to the Mitsui Board of Directors for approval.[33]

The establishment of the Mitsui Board of Directors signified a centralizing tendency in the management of the Mitsui zaibatsu.

It had been decided that any member of the Mitsui Board of Directors could propose measures.[34] Each director was also given the right to speak out on matters beyond those concerning the subsidiary or division for which he was responsible. This provision was quite reasonable given that the Mitsui Board of Directors was meant to be a comprehensive control body for all the Mitsui zaibatsu enterprises. In fact, however, the directors representing the subsidiaries and divisions found it extremely difficult to transcend the particular interests of their own enterprises to participate in making policy for Mitsui as a whole.

The Mitsui Family Constitution (Mitsui Kaken) was put into effect in July 1900. Under the new constitution the Mitsui Board of Directors (Mitsui Shōten Rijikai) was renamed the Mitsui Eigyōten Jūyakukai (also translated as Mitsui Board of Directors). The Mitsui Motokata was renamed the Mitsui-ke Dōzokukai Jimukyoku (Secretariat of the Mitsui Family Council). There were no major changes in the composition or functions of the renamed Board of Directors. The *eigyōten* or enterprises were restricted to the four unlimited partnership companies, the manufacturing and real estate divisions having been abolished in 1898. The membership of the new Mitsui Board consisted of only the family members who were presidents of the four unlimited partnership companies and the top salaried managers. The only difference in the new board's composition was the exclusion of the chairman of the Family Council and other family members who were not subsidiary presidents.[35]

Inoue Kaoru, adviser to the Mitsui family and the Mitsui Family Council, believed that the Board of Directors (in both its old and new versions) was failing to carry out fully its function of providing general control over the diversified Mitsui subsidiaries. He began voicing that opinion in 1901. The collapse of Nakamigawa's industrialization policy, opposition between Mitsui Bank and Mitsui Bussan, and criticism within the zaibatsu of the headstrong actions of Mitsui Bank under Nakamigawa's leadership were all considered to underscore the limitations of the Board of Directors as a central office for the zaibatsu.

A document proposing the establishment of the office of senior executive director (*sōmu riji*) on the Mitsui Board, presumably drafted by Mitsui family members and Inoue, criticized the board harshly. It stated that the board was flawed because it lacked necessary staff and also noted sternly that board members were not considering issues from the point of view of Mitsui as a whole:

The Board of Directors meets every week to consider proposals presented by the subsidiaries. Without an effective adjunct body to provide detailed studies of those proposals, however, the board finds it difficult to consider them prudently. Moreover, board members are too intent on grasping problems and conceiving of solutions from the one-sided viewpoints of their respective subsidiaries and tend to forget their duty not to be prejudiced in favor of any particular unit but to decide policy in terms of the overall, balanced management of the Mitsui zaibatsu.[36]

The proposal to place a senior executive director on the Board of Directors was not realized, but in April 1902, six months after Nakamigawa's death, the Management Department of the Secretariat of the Mitsui Family Council was instituted as a new central office for the zaibatsu. This body was placed above the Board of Directors and charged with deliberation and decision-making on policy and finance for the subsidiaries; it also performed adjunct services, such as carrying out studies for the various enterprises. The department was composed of five family members—the presidents of the bank, trading company, and mining company and the inspectors of the trading and mining companies; the top salaried managers of the bank, trading company, mining company, and dry goods store; and the full-time salaried managers of the Mitsui Family Council.[37] At first glance the new body appears to have been the same as the previous incarnation of the central office, but it was different in that it had an extensive managing director (*senmu riji*), a post to which Masuda Takashi was appointed, and it excluded the president of the dry goods store, a move presumably related to the store's separation from the Mitsui zaibatsu in December 1904.

Thus, a complex organizational structure with four levels—Mitsui Family Council, Management Department of the Council's Secretariat, Board of Directors, and unlimited partnership subsidiaries—was formed. This structure made necessary repeated decision-making on any given proposal. Yet such a heavy decision-making structure seemed perfectly natural to family members, to their adviser Inoue, and to Masuda, the executive director. As Masuda explained in an address to a 1903 meeting of the Mitsui Bussan branch managers:

For a proposal to be discussed and decided upon at the Mitsui Bussan head office by your president and directors is not enough. Deliberation is complete only after a proposal has been approved by the Board of Directors and, depending on the item, considered fully by the Family Council after the opinion of the Management

Department has been appended and evaluated by Counselor Inoue as well. This system is appropriate for Mitsui, given the use of the unlimited liability system in our large-scale enterprises.[38]

Perhaps due to criticism that this weighty, complicated structure hindered swift and effective decision-making within the Mitsui zaibatsu, one layer in the structure, the Board of Directors, was abolished in the December 1904 revision of the family constitution.

Despite Masuda's forceful leadership, the Management Department of the Family Council Secretariat retained the character of a conference of representatives of the bank, trading company, and mining company. "The harmful effects of each subsidiary's representative sticking to the point of view of his company and never giving way" remained a sore point,[39] and once again Mitsui confronted the problem of creating a strong central office. Inoue, Masuda, and the Mitsui family members were seeking a structure that would meet the social responsibilities of a wealthy family as well as the needs of modern management when they moved, in October 1909, to turn Mitsui into a multisubsidiary system.[40] At that point they would incorporate the Management Department of the Family Council Secretariat, establish Mitsui Gōmei, and reorganize the three unlimited partnership subsidiaries into joint-stock companies.

The Structure of Mitsubishi

The Mitsubishi enterprises were organized and run as operating divisions of Mitsubishi, Ltd. Thus, this management structure was in direct contrast to that of Mitsui, where the diversified enterprises had initially been independent firms. In the Mitsubishi Company era and in the early days after Mitsubishi, Ltd., was organized, the management structure had only one operating unit, the mining section, established in 1888. As diversified operations were developed, an appropriate management structure with separate operating divisions became necessary.

After Mitsubishi, Ltd., was founded, the corporation established a system for centrally organizing its diversified enterprises: several units (*basho*) were set up, including the metal mines, coal mines, bank and coal-distribution branches, shipyards, and real estate operations. The total of the fixed and liquid assets of each unit was defined as its capital. Depreciation of fixed assets was carried out for each unit, and all net profits were paid to the head office.[41] Mitsubishi had done nothing less than set the capital and institute independent accounting for each unit. Orders, proposals, and other communication flowed between the head office and the units.

The system of direct management became increasingly cumbersome as the units grew in number and diversification continued. Hence, it became necessary to organize the units by operational field. First, in October 1895, a banking division was established. It was followed in February 1896 by a coal sales division and that October by a mining division. (The coal sales division was renamed simply the sales division in 1899.)

Each division was headed by a manager (called variously the *fuku shihainin*, *shihainin*, or *buchō*), and the responsibility for integration and coordination among the several divisions was borne by the senior executive director in the head office. A general affairs division was also inaugurated in 1899. These operationally defined divisions were established as nothing more than a convenient way to group the units together. Apart from banking, the divisions were not separately capitalized, did not have independent accounting, and did not pay their profits into the head office.

Mitsubishi carried out a major reorganization in October 1908, changing the system of operationally defined divisions into a system of operating divisions in very nearly the same sense as the latter term is used today. There were three divisions, apart from general affairs: banking, mining (the sales and mining divisions having been merged two years earlier), and shipyard (newly established the year before). Direct communication between the head office and the operating units was now interrupted; orders and proposals flowed from the head office to the divisions and then to the units. The capital of the banking division was set at ¥1 million, that of the mining division ¥15 million, and that of the shipyard division ¥10 million, and each division adopted a self-supporting accounting system.[42] Moreover, the divisions absorbed their units' profits and paid them into the head office. The banking division had been delivering annually 10 percent of its capitalization, or ¥100,000, to the head office since 1897. The other divisions followed its lead in sending profits in an amount equal to 10 percent of their capital and in retaining earnings above that amount for their own reserves.[43]

Also under the reorganization of 1908, each division was authorized to establish its own regulations and accounting procedures and to handle its own personnel matters. From then on, only critical matters needed referral to the president.[44] In sum, Mitsubishi formed operating divisions that were remarkably decentralized.

The number of divisions gradually increased. A real estate division was founded in 1910, and separate mining and sales divisions were again set up; in 1912 the coal-mining unit within the mining division was made an independent division. The six Mitsubishi divisions with their number of employees as of 1913 are shown in Table 4.5.

TABLE 4.5   Size of the Mitsui and Mitsubishi Zaibatsu in 1913

Mitsui		Mitsubishi	
Subsidiary	Number of employees	Division	Number of employees
Bank	426[a]	Banking	132
Bussan	1,528	Mining	785 (15,073)[c]
Mining	1,856[b]	Coal mining	695 (29,238)[c]
Total	3,810	Sales	560 (1,752)[c]
		Shipyard	1,063 (13,841)[c]
		Real estate	45
		Total	3,280

SOURCES: *Mitsui Ginkō 80-nen shi* (80 Years of Mitsui Bank) (Tokyo: Mitsui Bank, 1957), p. 524; *Kōhon Mitsui Bussan Kabushiki Kaisha 100-nen shi* (100 Years of Mitsui Bussan) (Tokyo: Japan Business History Institute, 1978), vol. 1, p. 332; Kasuga Yutaka, "1910-nendai ni okeru Mitsui Kōzan no tenkai" (The Development of Mitsui Mining in the 1910s), *Mitsui Bunko ronsō*, 12 (1978):120; Mitsubishi Gōshi, *Mitsubishi sha-shi* (Records of Mitsubishi Company) (Tokyo: University of Tokyo Press, 1979–82), vol. 22, pp. 1986–89.
[a] Males only, January 1914.
[b] October 1914.
[c] Including workers hired and managed by labor bosses or subcontractors rather than by the enterprise itself.

According to Alfred D. Chandler, Jr., the first decentralized multi-divisional systems in the United States (and in the world) were instituted by Du Pont and General Motors in 1920–21.[45] Mitsubishi, Ltd., however, anticipated those firms by adopting a divisional system in 1908, although its system was not fully developed, lacking as it did a marketing function, for example. Why Mitsubishi adopted this structure at that time and what it used as a model remain unclear. It can only be assumed that the new structure was part of a program undertaken to counteract the 1908 slump and that Iwasaki Koyata's views must have contributed to the decision to reorganize in this way. Koyata, eldest son of Iwasaki Yanosuke and cousin of Mitsubishi, Ltd. President Iwasaki Hisaya, had been appointed vice president on his return from study in Great Britain just two years earlier.

Finally, there was a fascinating interplay between the organizational structures of the Mitsui and Mitsubishi zaibatsu. Inoue and some of the Mitsui family members proposed in 1906 that the system of organizing Mitsui's diversified enterprises as independent corporations be abandoned in favor of bringing them together into one corporation. They therefore recommended the founding of a new entity, Mitsui Gōmei Kaisha,[46] and expressed disapproval of the tendency toward decentralization of authority on the part of the independent enterprises. It is not clear what form was contemplated for pulling the separate enterprises under one corporate roof or if a system of operating divisions would have been used to organize them. Yet this proposal was clearly an attempt to bring the Mitsui management structure closer to that of Mitsubishi.

The idea of reorganizing Mitsui along the lines of Mitsubishi was of course opposed by the remarkably independent subsidiaries; opposition also appeared among the Mitsui family members and their advisers. The proposal never reached the stage of being formally considered by the Mitsui Family Council.[47] Interestingly enough, however, beginning in 1917 the Mitsubishi zaibatsu abandoned the operating division system and, like Mitsui, converted to a multisubsidiary system. In short, movement toward the other's system on the part of each zaibatsu took place.

THE ZAIBATSU FAMILY

A third set of factors affecting zaibatsu development involved the owner family, specifically the relations among zaibatsu family members as well as between the family members and the salaried managers.

The wealthy families that owned zaibatsu carefully maintained the family fortunes inherited from their forefathers. They exercised strict control over their assets, business, and lifestyle in order to be able to hand those fortunes to their descendants. To that end, it was common for a zaibatsu family to draw up and enforce house rules.

The rule-making tendency was evident in the earliest years of the old zaibatsu families, such as the Mitsui. House Mitsui founder Takatoshi and his sons established rules that set forth the principles of joint ownership of the family fortune and joint control of their enterprises as well as procedures for putting those principles into practice.[48] Those rules took the form of Takatoshi's last will, but they were supplemented and modified until they were finally codified in 1722 in his eldest son Takahira's will. Known as the Sōchiku Will (Sōchiku being Takahira's posthumous name), the document became the Mitsui family constitution, and its principles were fundamentally adhered to by house members even after the Meiji Restoration.[49] The Sumitomo family also had a family constitution. Thus such zaibatsu as Mitsui and Sumitomo with histories dating back to the Tokugawa period aimed for permanence by updating their family constitutions to suit the modern laws and institutions established after the Meiji Restoration. The zaibatsu that originated in the Meiji period used the Mitsui, Sumitomo, and the other old houses as models in instituting their own family constitutions to conserve their fortunes effectively.

Inoue at Mitsui cared most keenly about the Mitsui family constitution; he wanted the family to create a revised constitution that would not violate the new civil and commercial codes while remaining true to the principles of the Sōchiku Will. He persuaded the Mitsui to codify an updated version with the assistance of a legal scholar and oversaw the process. The result was the Mitsui Family Constitution, implemented in July 1900.[50]

The fundamentals of the Mitsui Family Constitution, comprised of ten chapters and 109 sections, faithfully carried on the principles of the earlier Sōchiku Will. It clearly delimited, for instance, the family members who had the right to participate in the joint ownership of house assets. Takatoshi's will and the Sochiku Will both similarly limited membership in order to avoid a dispersal of assets and loss of consensus within the family. The Sōchiku Will, however, designated the heads of nine families as members. Takahira's successor increased the membership to eleven family heads, who formed the apex of a pyramid. The Mitsui Family Constitution also designated the heads of eleven families as members of the House of Mitsui.

In addition, the Mitsui Family Constitution, like the Sōchiku Will, did not grant the members freedom to dispose of assets. Borrowing money or standing as guarantor for another's loans was also forbidden. A chance therefore was taken that such provisions would come into conflict with the Civil Code, which respected the property rights of individuals. To avoid such a problem, the Family Constitution itself took the character of a contract based on the Civil Code and was put into effect by the eleven members' signing of a contract recognizing that all the rules it specified held within the family.[51] For members to claim their rights as individuals or seek a legal settlement to intrafamilial questions was also prohibited by the constitution. As Section 14 stated, "No matter what disputes may occur between family members, taking a problem to court is forbidden." If disputes did break out, the constitution specified that they were to be settled by an arbitrator designated by the Family Council.[52]

The accommodation of the principles of the Sōchiku Will to the Civil Code's respect for private ownership of property can be seen in the Family Constitution's designation of common assets as well. The assets of the eleven families were divided into assets for business use, common assets for nonbusiness use (reserves used for the support of the eleven families), and family property. The first two categories were designated as common assets, whereas family property was defined as assets of which the various families could freely dispose.[53] According to the Sōchiku Will, each family received as income only a part of the profits of the joint enterprises. Private ownership of assets was not permitted. Therefore, the addition of a partial recognition of private ownership of assets was a clear sign of bending to the requirements of the new Civil Code.

The Family Constitution furthermore specified each family's share of the joint assets. The senior main family (that of the family head) had 23 percent of the joint assets, the junior branches (*honke*, those descended from Takatoshi's sons) had 11.5 percent each, and the associate families (*renke*, mostly families of the in-marrying sons-in-law of the founder and the second- and third-generation family heads) had 3.9 percent each. Although the percentages were called "shares," the joint assets were not actually distributed accordingly and represented nothing more than the percentage of profits each family received. The difference in size among the shares was a tradition inherited from the founder's will, but the Family Constitution simplified the system by grouping the shares into three classes; it also decreased the gaps between them.

The updating of the Sumitomo family constitution began in 1882 when the Sumitomo Family Bylaws (Sumitomo *kahō*), revised in 1891, were enacted. The nineteen chapters and 196 sections were detailed but almost exclusively concerned with the business—its ideals, organization, and personnel. They lacked complicated provisions for the distribution within the family of assets and management rights such as were found in the Mitsui Family Constitution.[54] Such provisions were not included because the Sumitomo zaibatsu was owned by a single family, the Sumitomo having practiced strict primogeniture. Although the bylaws did specify such terms as *makke* (junior family) and *jun makke* (associate junior family), they indicated honorary positions awarded to employees for long service. Such honors were a matter of courtesy and had nothing to do with rights to the assets of the Sumitomo family.

The owners of most of the zaibatsu that originated after the Meiji Restoration also drew up family constitutions. Yasuda is a typical case. When Yasuda Zenjirō established the Hozensha in 1887, he also drafted the Hozensha Regulations (Hozensha *kiyaku*), which formed the Yasuda Family Constitution. Unincorporated until 1912, the Hozensha functioned as a holding company to guarantee the capital of Yasuda Bank and the livelihood of the Yasuda family.[55]

Hozensha Regulations specified that half the shares of Yasuda Bank were to be held in the name of the Hozensha president and that the dividends on those shares were to be accumulated and increased through investments in government bonds, stocks, and real estate. The other half of the bank stock was parceled out among ten families,[56] their shares adjusted according to their ranking. Six main families (*dōke*) comprised the house: those of Zenjirō, his sons, and an in-marrying brother-in-law. Of these, the families of Zenjirō, one of his adopted sons, and his oldest son by birth ranked highest. After the six main families came two branch families (*bunke*), one descended from one of Zenjirō's sisters and one from another adopted son. Two associate families (*ruike*), those of Zenjirō's wife's sister and Zenjirō's sister, whose husband did not switch to Yasuda family membership, were the lowest ranked. The number of main families was fixed at six, but main family members could set up new branch families, just as branch and associate family members could establish new associate families. Thus, unlike Mitsui, Yasuda provided for an increase in the number of branch and associate families.[57]

The Yasuda regulations, of course, forbade the families to dispose freely of the stock distributed among them; they even prohibited the families from holding the certificates for their stocks. To receive their dividends, the families had to submit budgets for their living expenses to the Hozensha president every six months. After deducting the approved expenses, the families were required to keep the remainder of the dividends as reserves. When its reserve funds reached ¥10,000 a family could use them to buy stock owned by the Hozensha. The reserves and stocks were the assets of the individual families, but all were entrusted to Yasuda Bank. The families were also forbidden to borrow from outside the Yasuda zaibatsu.

Mitsubishi was a zaibatsu with post-Restoration origins that did not have an expressly stated family constitution. Two families, those of founder Iwasaki Yatarō and his brother Yanosuke, were the Mitsubishi zaibatsu owners. A 1907 document established that only the heads and heirs of those two families were to be investors in Mitsubishi, Ltd.[58] That rule was eliminated in 1920 by agreement of the heads of the families, Hisaya and Koyata; the change opened the way to capital participation in Mitsubishi, Ltd., by others.[59] Nonetheless, the Mitsubishi holding company remained owned exclusively by the two families until 1940, when stocks of Mitsubishi, Inc., which succeeded Mitsubishi, Ltd., in 1937, were sold outside the families. The unwritten rule that the presidency would rotate between the heads of the two families was upheld until the dissolution of the Mitsubishi zaibatsu. The ratios of capital participation in Mitsubishi, Ltd., by the two Iwasaki families were not fixed by a family constitution but, rather, determined by discussion at the time of each capital increase.

The Mitsubishi approach to deciding questions of joint investment and management rights without the existence of a written family constitution was unique among the zaibatsu owned by more than one family line.

The system derived from the form of ownership adopted by the two Iwasaki families. In the case of Mitsui, for instance, apart from the family property of each Mitsui family, the entire House of Mitsui fortune, for both business and nonbusiness use, was held as the common property of the eleven families; breaking up or freely disposing of the property was absolutely forbidden. In contrast, the two Iwasaki families divided their assets in 1893, forming Mitsubishi, Ltd., through joint capital investment based on their respective fortunes. Each of the Iwasaki families was free to invest its own assets, and each did found enterprises over which the family, and not Mitsubishi, had control. These included the Hisaya family's Koiwai Farm, Mitsubishi Paper Mill, and Inawashiro Hydroelectric and Koyata's Asahi Glass. Both families were also involved in joint ventures with nonfamily members, for example Kirin Brewery. Admittedly, due to such enterprises' common relationship with the Mitsubishi zaibatsu, they would not be operated without reference to the wishes of the other Iwasaki family members or of Mitsubishi, Ltd. Nonetheless, fundamental differences clearly obtained between the forms of asset ownership adopted by the two Iwasaki families and that adopted by the eleven Mitsui families.[60]

Relations between the zaibatsu family members and salaried managers also influenced the zaibatsu development process. In the zaibatsu with long histories, the authority to make top-level decisions had usually passed to the salaried managers. In the zaibatsu with post-Restoration origins, the founder and his family normally retained control of top management. The restraining power that the family had over its top managers, however, differed considerably among zaibatsu. In Sumitomo, for example, the single owner family entrusted the salaried managers with full authority to make top-level decisions. In Mitsui, comprised of eleven owner families, salaried managers were customarily, but not absolutely, entrusted with full authority. The possibility of owner participation in management, together with the large number of owners involved, made the relationship between owner and manager at Mitsui rather fluid. Mitsubishi's owner, by contrast, had a firm grip on top management. Yet even the Mitsubishi style of ownership-management relations could change over time with the aging and death of the founder, depending on the abilities and attitudes of his heirs.

SUMMARY

The zaibatsu's diversification strategies during the period 1893–1913 were shaped by factors including managerial resources, organizational structures, and personal relationships among owners and managers. Regarding the financial dimension of managerial resources, the zaibatsu tended to rely heavily on the capital accumulations of their owner families and subsidiary companies rather than on funds from their banks. As for human resources, the role of highly educated salaried managers was particularly vital to the development of the zaibatsu.

Generally one of two organizational structures was adopted by the zaibatsu in their pursuit of a form of organization suitable to the operation and control of diversified enterprises: a Mitsui-style multisubsidiary system or a Mitsubishi-style multidivisional system. Eventually the former type became dominant. Meanwhile, the zaibatsu families strove to preserve their fortunes in perpetuity, most doing so by enacting family constitutions. Mitsubishi was unique in that it did not draw up a family constitution nor employ the system of joint ownership of property.

These factors, then, helped set the parameters for zaibatsu growth and diversification during the two decades following 1893. But exactly how big had the zaibatsu become by the end of that period? Table 4.5 on the number of employees at Mitsui and Mitsubishi in 1913 gives some indication of the size of these two zaibatsu, the giants in the field. The figures are necessarily imprecise, given the shortcomings of statistical methods at the time, and only the number of direct employees can be ascertained for Mitsui. Such limitations notwithstanding, the data show that the scale of even the biggest zaibatsu enterprises was not unusually large compared to big businesses of that time in the United States. Mitsui had a total of 3,810 employees in its three designated subsidiaries, and Mitsubishi 3,280 in its six operating divisions. By contrast, in the fall of 1914 the total number of employees at E. I. Du Pont de Nemours & Co. was 5,300.[61] The comparison suggests that, in spite of the considerable expansion the zaibatsu had undergone prior to World War I, their growth during the fifteen years following the war enabled Mitsui and Mitsubishi to become probably the largest business empires in the world.

PART III

SHIFTING FORTUNES, 1914–29

World War I was a watershed not only for Japan's capitalist economy but also for the zaibatsu, which were provided by war conditions with remarkable opportunities to capture and develop huge new markets. The openings seemed almost unlimited, especially in such fields as foreign trade, shipping, manufacturing for export, and heavy industry aimed at import substitution. The positive environment was offset, however, by the postwar recession, which began suddenly in March 1920 as a reaction against the war boom. The postwar boom and recession that occurred immediately after the war's end dealt a severe blow to all zaibatsu, particularly those that had been rushing to overtake their competitors. Clear-cut differences in strength consequently appeared among the zaibatsu. Some failed to survive the postwar conditions, and others were obliged to scale down considerably owing to managerial failures stemming from poor judgment, reckless speculation, or lack of preparedness. The Mitsui zaibatsu emerged as the undisputed winner, with Mitsubishi the runner-up. The Yasuda and Sumitomo zaibatsu were at least able to keep up their pace of development, but Furukawa and Asano fell into decline while Fujita, Kuhara, and Suzuki went bankrupt.

Here we will trace the complicated processes of the rise and fall of the major zaibatsu. In addition, a comparative approach will be used to examine the multisubsidiary system adopted by each zaibatsu during or after World War I, taking the Mitsui structure, adopted earlier, as the model. The changing relations between the zaibatsu families and their salaried managers in the top levels of the multisubsidiary systems is the third theme taken up in this part.

CHAPTER 5

THE ZAIBATSU AND WORLD WAR I

During World War I, Japan, as a noncombatant nation well removed from the battlefields, was able to enjoy extraordinary economic advantages. The war cut off exports of manufactured goods by the European nations, an interruption that not only secured the domestic market for Japanese manufacturers but also made possible an expansion of their share of the Asian market. Japan's exports grew from ¥600 million in 1914 to ¥2,200 million in 1919, with a wide surplus of exports over imports. The value of industrial production quintupled in this period, soaring from ¥1.3 billion in 1914 to ¥6.5 billion in 1919. Freed from the pressure of imports, heavy industries in particular seized upon the opportunities for expansion. The growth of enterprises, in both numbers and scale, was also remarkable. Japan had 17,000 corporations with a total paid-in capital of ¥2.1 billion in 1914; by 1919, the number of corporations had risen to 26,000 with a total paid-in capital of ¥6 billion. During those same years, the number of large firms (those capitalized at ¥5 million or more) increased from 62 to 368.[1]

ZAIBATSU, OLD AND NEW

The zaibatsu already established during the Meiji period (1868–1912) were able to expand radically through their aggressive responses to the war boom. They grew quantitatively—for example, in terms of their capital (Table 5.1)—but also qualitatively, developing a full network of diversified enterprises by strengthening or establishing operations in the fields most favored by the opportunities presented by the war, particularly heavy industry and foreign trade.

The war also facilitated the emergence of new zaibatsu.[2] Several

TABLE 5.1   Authorized Capital of Zaibatsu Enterprises, 1913 and 1919 (in yen)

	Authorized capital	
Zaibatsu	1913	1919
Mitsui Gōmei	50,000,000	200,000,000
Mitsui Bank	20,000,000	100,000,000
Mitsui Bussan	20,000,000	100,000,000
Mitsui Mining	20,000,000	100,000,000
Mitsubishi, Ltd.	15,000,000	30,000,000[a]
Shipyard division	10,000,000	—
Sales division	3,000,000	—
Mining division	6,000,000	—
Coal-mining division	8,000,000	—
Banking division	1,000,000	—
Real estate division	3,000,000	—
Mitsubishi Shipbuilding and Engineering	—	50,000,000
Mitsubishi Iron and Steel	—	30,000,000
Mitsubishi Trading	—	15,000,000
Mitsubishi Mining	—	50,000,000
Mitsubishi Bank	—	50,000,000
Sumitomo Bank	15,000,000	30,000,000[b]
[Yasuda] Hozensha	10,000,000	10,000,000[c]
Yasuda Bank	10,000,000	25,000,000
Furukawa Gōmei	5,000,000	20,000,000
Tokyo Furukawa Bank	—	5,000,000
Furukawa Trading	—	10,000,000
Furukawa Mining	—	20,000,000
Ōkura-gumi	1,000,000	10,000,000[d]
Ōkura Mining	—	20,000,000
Ōkura Public Works	—	2,000,000
Ōkura & Co.	10,000,000	10,000,000
Fujita-gumi	6,000,000	6,000,000
Fujita Bank	—	10,000,000
Fujita Mining	—	30,000,000
Asano, Ltd.	3,000,000[e]	—
Asano Dōzoku Kaisha	—	35,000,000

SOURCE: Shōgyō Kōshinsho, *Nihon zenkoku shokaisha Yakuin roku* (Japanese Directory of Company Directors) (Tokyo: Shōgyō Kōshinsho, 1913–20).
[a] Increased to ¥80,000,000 in 1920.
[b] Increased to ¥70,000,000 in 1920.
[c] Increased to ¥30,000,000 in 1921.
[d] Increased to ¥50,000,000 in 1920.
[e] Figure for 1914, when Asano, Ltd. was established.

wealthy families took advantage of the boom to expand and diversify their enterprises, to form new zaibatsu and attempt to catch up with the older ones. Some tried to turn this unprecedented opportunity into a means of catapulting themselves into top positions in the business world. The newer zaibatsu included Kuhara, Suzuki, Iwai, Murai, Matsukata, and Nomura, of which Kuhara Mining and Suzuki Shōten were the most important examples. Kuhara's emergence from Fujita-gumi was discussed in chapter 3; here we will describe briefly the Iwai, Murai, Matsukata, and Nomura zaibatsu before treating the prewar history of Suzuki Shōten in detail.

The Iwai zaibatsu was formed through the diversification of Iwai Shōten, managed by Iwai Katsujirō. That firm had principally engaged in importing manufactured goods, during the course of which it ventured gradually into domestic production of such goods. The Iwai group of enterprises established or reorganized during the war included Osaka Teppan (Osaka Sheet Iron; now Nisshin Steel Co.), Nippon Soda Kōgyō (now Tokuyama Soda), Kansai Paint, and Chūō Keito Bōseki (Chūō Wool Yarn Spinning; now Tōa Wool Spinning & Weaving Co.). The head office of the zaibatsu, Gōshi Kaisha Iwai Honten, a limited partnership, was set up in 1916 and capitalized at ¥3 million.[3]

Murai Kichibei, the "cigarette king," created the Murai zaibatsu. After his tobacco operation was taken over by the government under the 1904 Tobacco Monopoly Law, Murai founded Murai Bank, Murai Nōjō (a farm operation in Korea), Murai Chochiku Bank (a savings bank), Murai Kōgyō (a firm involved principally in oil exploration), and Teikoku Seishi (Imperial Silk Reeling) and engaged in afforestation projects in Taiwan. He organized these units into the Murai zaibatsu before the war and during the war expanded operations further, founding Murai Kisen (shipping), Murai Sōko (warehousing), and Murai Bōeki (international trade). The failure of Murai Bōeki in 1920, however, triggered the collapse of the Murai zaibatsu. Murai Bank went out of business during the financial crisis of 1927.[4]

Whether the Matsukata zaibatsu can really be called a zaibatsu is debatable, but it was certainly a diversified enterprise group. It developed under the control of Matsukata Kōjirō, president of Kawasaki Shipbuilding Co., a company founded by Kawasaki Shōzō on the basis of a state enterprise he had bought in 1887 and reorganized as a joint-stock company in 1896. At that time, Kawasaki withdrew from its management, entrusting the presidency to Kōjirō, who was the third son of Kawasaki's patron and leading government figure Matsukata Masayoshi. The Kawasaki family thereafter concentrated on expanding its real estate holdings and reduced its share of Kawasaki Shipbuilding stock. The drop in the family's holdings was particularly pronounced after Shōzō's death in 1912. The Matsukata family, by contrast, increased its ownership of Kawasaki Shipbuilding stock, by 1921 its holdings surpassing those of the Kawasaki. Kawasaki Shipbuilding thus came under Matsukata family control.

Kawasaki Shipbuilding under Kōjirō steadily diversified into shipping (Kawasaki Kisen Kaisha), steelmaking, and the production of aircraft and railway rolling stock. Matsukata gained control of Kobe Gas, Kyushu Denki Kidō (Kyushu Electric Railway), and other firms by becoming their major stockholder. Gōshi Kaisha Matsu Shōkai, a holding company, acted as the head office of the group. Although it lacked the characteristic of exclusive family control, the Matsukata group shared enough features with other zaibatsu to warrant categorization as a zaibatsu.[5]

The Nomura zaibatsu was based on a fortune built up through spot transactions in stocks by the Nomura Tokushichi Shōten, which had its origins in an Osaka exchange shop. The securities business that was the main line of the Nomura house was organized as Nomura Shōten in 1917 and as Nomura Shōken in 1925. During and after the war, Nomura branched into a variety of other enterprises. A South Seas division to operate plantations in Borneo, Sumatra, and Brazil was established in 1917. Nomura Bank, capitalized at ¥10 million (now the Daiwa Bank), and Daitō Bussan, which engaged in foreign trade, were founded in 1918. Chōya Shatsu Seizōsho (Chōya Shirt Factory) was established in 1921 and Nomura Ringyō (Nomura Forestry) in 1924. The Nomura Sōhonten, set up in 1918 to control these diversified enterprises, was reorganized in 1921 as Nomura Gōmei Kaisha, an unlimited partnership capitalized at ¥20 million.

Nomura experienced a setback in 1920 when Daitō Bussan was dissolved with losses of about ¥1.5 million, but the failure did not prove too great a blow to the emergent zaibatsu. In the 1930s it went on to add such new companies as Nomura Shintaku (Nomura Trust) and Nomura Seimei (Nomura Life Insurance) and developed more fully as a zaibatsu. In its later development Nomura tended to specialize in finance; and its scale remained small, but it became an influential second-rank zaibatsu. At the time of the zaibatsu dissolution after World War II, Nomura was designated as one of the big ten zaibatsu, and the Nomura family as one of fifty-six zaibatsu families, along with the likes of the Mitsui and Iwasaki. Today the Nomura Group, which includes Nomura Securities, Daiwa Bank, Nomura Fudōsan (Nomura Real Estate), Tokyo Life Insurance, and Nomura Research Institute, is quite vigorous.[6]

Suzuki Shōten was a Kobe-based importer of sugar that began business in 1874. It also exported camphor and mint. At the time of the death of its founder, Suzuki Iwajirō, in 1894, it was doing ¥5 million in business annually. Two *bantō*, Yanagida Fujimatsu and Kaneko Naokichi, who had begun with Suzuki as shopboys, then took over the management of the firm with the general authorization of Suzuki's heirs. Kaneko in particular wielded overwhelming authority.

At the conclusion of the Sino-Japanese War, in 1895 the island of Taiwan became a Japanese colony. Kaneko became friendly with Gotō Shinpei, the minister responsible for economic affairs in the office of the Governor-General of Taiwan. Thanks to this connection, Suzuki Shōten acquired exclusive sales rights to 65 percent of the camphor oil produced under the Taiwan camphor monopoly system, which was instituted in 1899 according to Gotō's ideas. This coup was the first step in Suzuki Shōten's dramatic growth. With its near monopoly on the handling of camphor oil, the company's capital reserves grew rapidly.

Using those funds and borrowings from Mitsui Bank and the Bank of Taiwan, Suzuki Shōten began diversifying from around the time it reorganized as an unlimited partnership company, capitalized at ¥500,000, in 1902. It moved into camphor manufacturing, mint processing, sugar refining, and steel making. In 1903 it built a sugar mill for ¥2.5 million in Dairi, Fukuoka Prefecture, and in 1905 bought the Kobayashi Seikōsho, a steel mill it had financed, renaming it Kobe Seikōsho (Kobe Steel Works). Suzuki Shōten sold the Dairi sugar mill in 1907 to Dai Nippon Seitō (Dai Nippon Sugar Manufacturing) for ¥6.5 million plus exclusive rights to the sale of Dai Nippon Sugar's products in western Japan and Korea. The profit from that sale was invested in facilities to upgrade Kobe Steel so that it could secure orders from the navy. Suzuki Shōten spun off Kobe Steel in 1911 as a wholly owned joint-stock company capitalized at ¥1.4 million.

Suzuki Shōten diversified in several additional directions. It founded or bought a series of companies, including Azuma Leather (predecessor of Teijin), Nippon Celluloid Jinzō Kenshi (Nippon Celluloid and Rayon, founded jointly with the Iwasaki family and Iwai Shōten), Sapporo Seifun (Sapporo Flour Mill), Dairi Seifunsho (Dairi Flour Mill), and Teikoku Beer. Suzuki also moved into international trade and marine shipping with direct import-export and tramp steamer businesses. Those enterprises required highly educated personnel, which Suzuki secured by hiring, for the most part, graduates of the Kobe Commercial Higher School and dispatching them overseas. By the beginning of World War I, Suzuki Shōten was well on its way to becoming a zaibatsu.[7]

DIVERSIFICATION INTO HEAVY INDUSTRIES

During World War I, the zaibatsu developed operations in a wide range of heavy industries and made rapid progress in those fields. Among those operations were well-established enterprises that were reorganized into joint-stock companies during the war, including Sumitomo Chūkōsho (Sumitomo Steel Works) and Mitsubishi Zōsen (Mitsubishi Shipbuilding and Engineering). The majority of cases fell into one of two other categories, however. Some were enterprises that had been in a fledgling state before the war and then took advantage of the unprecedented market opportunity presented by the sharp wartime curtailment of imports to burst into growth. Others emerged when the zaibatsu, attracted by the sudden expansion in demand during the war, entered new heavy industrial fields by building or buying factories.

The first category, heavy industries that the zaibatsu had already begun to build up and that grew rapidly during the war, is typified by iron and steel making at Mitsui and Mitsubishi and Mitsui's coal chemical business. Mitsui's involvement in the iron and steel industry began in 1913 when it acquired control of the Hokkaido Tankō Kisen Company (Hokkaido Colliery and Steamship) with ownership of a third of its shares. That firm had changed its name from Hokkaido Tankō Tetsudō (Hokkaido Colliery and Railway) following the nationalization of its railroads in 1906. During the Nakamigawa era, Mitsui Bank had bought a large number of Hokkaido Colliery and Railway shares. In the reforms after Nakamigawa died, Mitsui made an effort to sell those shares, but before they could be unloaded, Hokkaido Colliery's performance worsened. Moreover, the government, concerned because the imperial family was the major shareholder, pressured Mitsui to keep the shares and put the firm's operations on a sounder basis.[8]

Hokkaido Colliery used the compensation it had received for the railroad nationalization to move into iron and steel production. With joint investment from two British firms, Armstrong and Vickers, and with a guarantee of orders from the navy, Hokkaido Colliery in 1907 founded the Nippon Seikōsho (Nippon Steel Works) to produce steel and armaments. It began operation of the Wanishi Iron Works in 1909, but within twenty days—when use of the iron sand mined in Hokkaido as ore proved to be technologically unfeasible—operations at the iron works were suspended and never resumed. Thus, by gaining control of Hokkaido Colliery in 1913, Mitsui had come indirectly to manage the Nippon Steel Works and Wanishi Iron Works.[9] Its involvement in iron and steel production expanded when Mitsui Mining purchased Tanaka Kōzan Co., capitalized at ¥20 million, in 1924. Tanaka Kōzan, which had managed the Kamaishi iron works, was renamed Kamaishi Kōzan Co.

Mitsubishi began its entry into iron and steel making when Mitsubishi, Ltd. purchased the Kyomip'o iron mine in what is now North Korea and immediately laid plans to construct an iron works close to the mine. Equipment for the works was ordered from the United States on the very eve of World War I.[10] To run the enterprise, in 1917 Mitsubishi founded an iron and steel company, Mitsubishi Seitetsu, (Mitsubishi Iron and Steel) capitalized at ¥30 million. The following year, the iron works went into operation.

The Mitsui coal chemical venture had its start in the late 1900s. The planner, Makita Tamaki, was an engineer at Mitsui Mining who had long asserted that burning coal for fuel was wasteful when the coal could be used as a raw material for the chemical industry. Makita was not only a trusted subordinate of Dan Takuma, top manager of Mitsui Mining, but also his son-in-law, and the Makita plan had Dan's support; the two men were agreed in their goal of industrializing Mitsui.[11]

Perhaps because the Miike coal mine was doing well, the top management of the Mitsui zaibatsu was favorably inclined to the idea of moving into the coal chemical industry. It approved in 1909 the introduction of a Kopper's-type by-product recovery coking furnace at the Miike coking plant; construction costs totaled ¥850,000. Operation of the Kopper's coke oven and distillation of the by-product, tar, began in 1912. Intermediate tests of coal tar dyes began in 1914. In 1915 domestic production of chemical dyes became commercially feasible as their supply started to diminish owing to the cutoff of imports. Mitsui's Miike-produced chemical dyes still had quality problems, but the wartime situation made them profitable.[12]

The second category of zaibatsu heavy industries centered on shipbuilding, a field into which several zaibatsu, stimulated by the rapid growth in demand for shipping, newly diversified during the war. This move was accompanied by entry into the iron and steel industry in order to produce the steel plate needed for shipbuilding.

The newcomers to shipbuilding among the zaibatsu were Suzuki, Mitsui, Kuhara, and Asano. Suzuki Shōten in 1916 bought Harima Zōsen, a shipyard in Aioi, Hyōgo Prefecture, capitalized at ¥500,000 and renamed Harima Zōsensho (Harima Shipyard). It also bought a shipyard at Toba in Mie Prefecture, which it renamed Toba Zōsensho. In the case of Mitsui, Mitsui Bussan, responding to strong demand from its shipping division, established a new shipbuilding division and began building a shipyard in Tama, Okayama Prefecture, in 1917.

Kuhara's Nippon Kisen (Nippon Steamship) came to control Osaka

Tekkōsho, a shipbuilding company founded in 1881 by Edward H. Hunter of Great Britain. When Osaka Tekkōsho was reorganized into a joint-stock company capitalized at ¥6 million in 1914, 70 percent of its stock was still owned by Hunter's family. Then in 1916, in order to take advantage of the wartime boom, the company devised an expansion plan and doubled its capitalization, carrying out a public stock offering. From then on, Nippon Steamship increased its ownership of Osaka Tekkōsho shares and in 1918 succeeded in controlling the majority.[13]

Asano Sōichirō had hoped to branch out from the operation of the Oriental Steamship Company into the shipbuilding field. He had already dispatched Oriental Steamship engineers to Europe in 1912 to study the industry there,[14] and in 1913 had unsuccessfully petitioned the city of Yokohama to allow him to reclaim land in the harbor for a shipyard.[15] With the outbreak of World War I, Asano hastened his entry into shipbuilding; in April 1916 he established Yokohama Zōsensho, a joint-stock company capitalized at ¥3.75 million, and the firm was renamed Asano Zōsensho (Asano Shipbuilding) by the end of the year. Since Asano did not have extensive capital reserves, in February 1916 he sold his Ishikari Coal stock to Mitsui Mining and applied the proceeds to the shipyard. The proposed site for the shipyard was switched to land reclaimed in Tsurumi by Asano's Tsurumi Reclamation, and the Tsurumi shipyard completed its first ship in July 1917. Asano Shipbuilding responded to the increased wartime demand by building standardized ships and reaped huge profits. In 1918 its capital was increased to ¥10 million, and in 1920 to ¥50 million, of which sum half was paid in. Its ambitious policies led to a merger with Asano Seitetsusho (Asano Steel Works), discussed below, and to the construction of dry docks.[16]

The new zaibatsu entries in the iron and steel industry were Matsukata and Asano. Matsukata Group's Kawasaki Shipbuilding Co. had begun in-house production of steel plate for ships in 1916; Asano began similar production in 1917. The steel mill built for Kawasaki Shipbuilding was the forerunner of the present Kawasaki Seitetsu (Kawasaki Steel Corporation). The Asano steel-making division in 1918 became an independent joint-stock company, Asano Steel Works, capitalized at ¥6 million. Facing difficulties after the war ended, it merged with Asano Shipbuilding in 1920.[17]

The Asano zaibatsu added one other steel company besides Asano Seitetsusho during World War I: Tokyo Seiko (Tokyo Rope Manufacturing Co.), of which Asano Sōichirō had been a large stockholder, had spent ¥7 million to build a steel mill in Kokura, Fukuoka Prefecture, that would produce the wire rod which was the rope factory's raw material. The steel mill was completed in May 1918, and Asano bought it for ¥9.36 million. The premium paid indicates how urgently he wanted to enter the iron and steel industry in order to capitalize on the wartime boom. A joint-stock company, Asano Kokura Steel, capitalized at ¥15 million, was founded in December 1918 to manage the mill.[18]

DEVELOPMENT OF OVERSEAS TRADE

In addition to expanding into heavy industries, many zaibatsu attempted to establish new trading companies or to strengthen existing ones in order to take advantage of the wartime trade boom. Mitsui Bussan was the model for the other zaibatsu in that effort, for it was the most developed general trading company. When Mitsui Bussan was organized into a joint-stock company in 1909 it was dealing in 120 items covering a wide range of products and had more than 1,200 employees.[19] Bussan instituted in 1911 a product-based divisional system and a set of regulations suitable for its diversified businesses and speculative dealings. The divisions included those for cotton, coal, lumber, sugar, and machinery, and an effort was made to tie the divisions and local branch offices into an effective structure.[20]

The other zaibatsu attempted to catch up with Mitsui Bussan by exploiting to the fullest the favorable trading conditions presented by the war. But Mitsui Bussan also responded positively to the wartime boom, its transaction volume jumping during the years 1914 to 1919 (Table 5.2). Bussan's growth was substantial: its exports increased nearly two and a half times, imports over threefold, domestic trade almost eightfold, and third-country trade over eleven times. The number of its staff also swelled from 1,676 to 3,827. About 40 percent of the employees worked at overseas branches, which likewise increased in number, from 35 in 1910 to 57 in 1919.[21] The new branches were located in cities throughout the world, ranging from Zhongqing, Haiphong, and Batavia to Melbourne, Dallas, and Marseilles.

The know-how built up at Mitsui Bussan was really effective less in furthering the wartime expansion than in keeping operations on a safe scale, based on management's early prediction of an end to the wartime boom. Even in 1916, when the boom was still in its initial phase, Bussan's top management warned at a meeting of branch managers that a drop in prices and shipping charges was inevitable after the war ended. Management therefore urged that everyone take care not to be caught by an unexpected blow.[22] Five months before the Armistice, in June 1918, top managers directed the branches to reduce transactions in

TABLE 5.2   Trading Volume and Profits of Mitsui Bussan during World War
I, 1914–19 (in million yen)

Year[a]	Trading volume					Profit
	Export	Import	Domestic	Third country	Total	
1914	168.62 (27.3)[b]	153.00 (23.9)	67.54	63.24	452.39	3.96
1915	152.18 (22.3)	109.40 (19.8)	76.11	100.48	438.17	7.05
1916	242.36 (22.8)	167.66 (22.6)	117.90	193.86	721.78	19.18
1917	334.36 (21.0)	200.90 (20.5)	245.82	313.96	1,095.04	32.19
1918	398.27 (20.6)	322.93 (19.5)	401.90	479.61	1,602.72	38.46
1919	403.91 (19.7)	490.85 (22.0)	521.53	713.98	2,130.27	19.86

SOURCE: *Kōhon Mitsui Bussan Kabushiki Kaisha 100-nen shi* (100 Years of Mitsui Bussan) (Tokyo: Japan Business History Institute, 1978), vol. 1, pp. 342, 410.
[a] For the fiscal year from November through October.
[b] The figures in parentheses are Mitsui Bussan exports or imports as a percentage of total customs clearings.

anticipation of the coming of peace.[23] The worldwide boom suffered a temporary setback due to the armistice but then rebounded even higher. Mitsui Bussan's top management, however, adhered to its policy of holding down transactions also in 1919, asserting that stability and soundness had to have priority, even if profits were small.[24] Such sound leadership was the factor that made the difference between the fates of Mitsui Bussan and the other trading companies.

Mitsui Bussan's top management was so much more farsighted than were its rivals because, in the course of its long history as a general trading company, the firm had developed a large body of skilled "Bussan men" through on-the-job training and an extensive intelligence network, together with an experienced team of top salaried managers who utilized these assets to the fullest in making strategic decisions.

In contrast to Mitsui Bussan, with its long history, most of the other zaibatsu trading companies in this period were newly established to take advantage of the wartime conditions. Only Ōkura Shōji and Suzuki Shōten dated from an earlier time, the first part of the Meiji period. The following is a list of Mitsui Bussan's competitors during the war years.

FURUKAWA TRADING. The trading department of Furukawa Gōmei, the body charged with marketing Furukawa products, was spun off as Furukawa Shōji (Furukawa Trading) in 1917. Capitalized at ¥10 million, it was intended to handle non-Furukawa products.

ŌKURA & CO., LTD. Ōkura-gumi Co. renamed itself Ōkura Shōji (Ōkura & Co., Ltd.) in 1918. It was capitalized at ¥10 million.

MITSUBISHI TRADING. The sales division of Mitsubishi, Ltd., was made independent as Mitsubishi Shōji (Mitsubishi Trading) in 1918. Its capital was set at ¥15 million.

MURAI BŌEKI. Murai Bōeki was established in 1918 and capitalized at ¥1 million.

DAITŌ BUSSAN. Founded in 1918, this Nomura zaibatsu trading company was capitalized at ¥500,000.

ASANO BUSSAN. Asano Bussan was founded in 1918 with a capital of ¥1 million. Half of that amount was provided by Asano and half by W. R. Grace & Co. of New York. Asano Bussan did not specialize in the import-export business but, rather, sold measuring instruments and contracted for construction work.[25]

KUHARA TRADING. The sales division of Kuhara Kōgyō was spun off as Kuhara Shōji (Kuhara Trading) in 1918 with a capitalization of ¥10 million, of which ¥2.5 million was paid in. Moving into overseas trade had been Kuhara Fusanosuke's long-held dream, and with the burgeoning of the wartime boom he had established overseas offices for the sales division. Also, while expanding the market for products of Kuhara Kōgyō, he had moved ahead with the preparations for setting up a trading company, Kuhara Trading. Fusanosuke drew in talented personnel from established trading companies for his new firm, which engaged in shipping, exclusive sales of Kuhara products, import and export of a variety of goods, and third-country trade. Clearly, it was intended from the outset to encompass a wide range of operations.[26]

The war years engendered another Kuhara commercial enterprise: in 1915 Kuhara and his elder brother Tamura Ichirō (who had been adopted into the Tamura family) put up the capital for Nippon Steamship, a limited partnership company that was set up to deal in ships in order to take advantage of the wartime shortage of shipping. The following year it was reorganized as a joint-stock company, capitalized at ¥5 million, of which ¥1.25 million was paid in. It purchased stock and secured control of Osaka Tekkōsho as part of its effort to secure a large volume of bottoms to put on sale.

SUZUKI SHŌTEN. Kaneko Naokichi succeeded in his plan to have Suzuki Shōten trade in large volumes on a global scale, and huge profits were recorded. The firm's performance during the war years was particularly remarkable: its trade volume for 1917 was ¥1.54 billion, surpassing even the ¥1.1 billion recorded by Mitsui Bussan that year. (See Table 5.2.) Kaneko exhorted his subordinates to take advantage of the wartime confusion in order to make a great deal of money and to outstrip Mitsui and Mitsubishi, or at least to reach parity with them.[27]

With the exception of Ōkura & Co., Mitsui Bussan's competitors failed to respond appropriately to the end of the boom that followed the war and during 1919 and 1920 went into the red in varying degrees. They also came under pressure from the postwar recession. Mitsubishi Trading Company, Suzuki Shōten, and Asano Bussan were able to overcome their difficulties despite sustaining losses. Asano Bussan, for example, lost ¥7 million in 1920, which prompted Grace & Co. to turn over its stock to Asano and withdraw from the firm. Though Asano Sōichirō at one point decided to dissolve the company, he changed his mind on the advice of his employees,[28] and Asano Bussan thereafter applied itself to reconstructing operations by performing commission transactions. Dividends to stockholders were resumed in 1925.[29] In contrast, Furukawa Trading, Kuhara Trading, Murai Bōeki, and Daitō Bussan all went bankrupt. The failure of these companies, with the exception of Daitō Bussan, dealt serious blows to the zaibatsu that owned them.

Kuhara Trading had embarked on handling types of goods that had engendered wariness in the existing trading companies, and it went on to engage in speculation of a kind that earned Kuhara the nickname "Wild Boar." Its pursuit of an expansionist policy even after the war ended resulted in losses of about ¥100 million during the panic of 1920. Having personally guaranteed those losses, Kuhara Fusanosuke put Kuhara Trading into liquidation in 1924.[30]

The case of Furukawa Trading offers the most dramatic instance of the adverse impact exerted by the collapse of a zaibatsu trading company on the zaibatsu as a whole. Furukawa and Sumitomo, though both based on copper production, had followed sharply contrasting diversification strategies prior to World War I. Their decisions about establishing trading companies during the war presented another striking contrast. Moreover, the trading company policy adopted by each zaibatsu made a significant difference in its later development.

Furukawa Trading performed extremely well initially, but the failure of its Dalian branch in speculative grain transactions led to losses of about ¥58 million in 1920 and ultimately to the company's bankruptcy. It was absorbed by Furukawa Mining Company in 1921.[31] The bankruptcy of Furukawa Trading cannot, however, be ascribed wholly to the actions of the Dalian branch. The Furukawa zaibatsu, in cleaving to founder Furukawa's copper-only policy, had avoided development of diversified businesses. The lack of unity within top management, due to long-term factional strife, prevented the zaibatsu from throwing off the copper-only policy and striking out in a new direction. Management did experience uneasiness over its delayed diversification, as compared with Sumitomo and other zaibatsu, and nurtured a pent-up desire to proceed with diversification. In the mid-1910s, however, several changes in top management enabled the zaibatsu to achieve a complete policy turnaround. Hara Kei in 1913 severed his relationship with the Furukawa family enterprise.[32] The same year Kimura Chōshichi and Okazaki Kunisuke resigned as senior executive director and director, respectively, of the head office. Kondō Rikusaburō replaced Kimura, but he died in 1917. And Inoue Kaoru died in 1915. Thus, the old-line top managers were cleared away, leaving the Furukawa zaibatsu in the hands of men eager to branch out in new directions just as the World War I boom arrived. The result was a number of start-ups in a variety of new fields. Furukawa in 1917 established the following enterprises: Asahi Denka (Asahi Electric), with joint investment from Tokyo Dentō (Tokyo Electric Light) and Katsuragawa Suiryoku (Katsuragawa Hydroelectric); Tokyo Furukawa Bank, capitalized at ¥5 million; Yokohama Gomu Seizō (Yokohama Rubber); and Furukawa Trading. In 1918 Furukawa invested in Teikoku Seimei (now Asahi Life Insurance). In 1919 it bought Tōa Paint and began negotiations to establish an electrical equipment manufacturing company as a joint venture with Siemens. Furukawa Trading thus started up amid this boom.

Furukawa Trading eventually failed, however. Kondō appears to have been strongly opposed to the founding of a trading company, and Inoue Kōji, who succeeded Kondō, was unable to withstand his subordinates' fervent demands for the formation of such a firm. In the end, he gave final approval for the establishment of Furukawa Trading without adequate assessments of conditions and training of personnel. The lack of preparation was the major reason for the failure of Furukawa Trading.[33]

The actions of Suzuki Masaya, senior executive director of the Sumitomo Sōhonten, were in direct contrast to those of the Furukawa top management. At Sumitomo also were strong calls for the boom-time establishment of a trading company. Suzuki avoided meeting those demands, however, and after the war gathered information from Sumitomo branches in the United States and Europe on the activities of Japanese trading companies, using this intelligence to make a calm decision on the matter. He refused to give his approval to the already worked-out plan for a trading company. His reasons included the long-term investment in preparations needed to establish a trading company (for example, the training of personnel and devising a code); the new wartime trading companies' unsatisfactory performance, which owed to their lack of experience; and the difficulties inherent in international trade, difficulties so great that even Mitsui Bussan, with its wealth of experience, made mistakes.[34]

A Sumitomo trading company would not necessarily have failed, but in view of a postwar start-up time and the poor performance of the new trading companies, it is reasonable to assume that such a firm could not have escaped huge losses. Under the circumstances Suzuki showed sound judgment in resisting his subordinates' enthusiasm for entering international trade. Even more important, though, were the cohesion among Sumitomo personnel that led them to accept Suzuki's decision and the composed outlook of Sumitomo, based on its long-term diversification strategy. As a result of their contrasting decisions regarding the establishment of a trading company, Furukawa fell to the ranks of the second-class zaibatsu while Sumitomo set aside huge wartime earnings in preparation for taking even greater strides. Today's Sumitomo Group trading company, Sumitomo Shōji (Sumitomo Corporation), grew out of the real estate firm Osaka Hokkō Kaisha (Osaka North Port Development) and developed into a trading company after World War II.

MOVEMENT INTO BANKING AND INSURANCE

Thanks to their high earnings during World War I, the zaibatsu accumulated considerable financial reserves. Some of these zaibatsu before the war had suffered from financial limitations because they had not operated their own banks, but during the war they were able to use their expanded reserves to move into banking. The new banks included the Asano Chūya, Furukawa, and Fujita banks.

Asano Chūya Bank

Asano's banking venture originated with a request to Asano Sōichirō from Hashimoto Umetarō, a member of the Asano faction among the stockholders of the Oriental Steamship Company. Hashimoto requested that Asano provide financial assistance to Daigo Ginkō (Fifth Bank), of which he was senior executive director. Asano agreed and as a result was able in 1916 to place the bank under his own control. The Daigo Bank, which had grown out of a small local bank in Kanagawa Prefecture and had no connection with Daigo Kokuritsu Ginkō (Fifth National Bank), operated as both an ordinary commercial bank and a savings bank. Asano renamed it Nippon Chūya Bank (*chūya* means "day and night") and appointed Shiraishi Motojirō to be president.

Asano had earlier brought Nippon Chūya Chochiku Ginkō (Nippon Chūya Savings Bank) under the Asano umbrella. That institution also engaged in both ordinary commercial banking and savings banking. In 1916, however, the Savings Bank Ordinance was modified, making it impossible for a bank to double as a commercial and a savings bank. Asano at that point made the former Daigo Bank strictly a commercial bank and Nippon Chūya Savings Bank a savings bank. The two banks shared the distinctive feature of operating day and night; indeed, Nippon Chūya Bank was the first commercial bank in Japan to adopt day and night operations, and the expanded hours led to a growing number of customers. Nippon Chūya Bank's capital, which stood at ¥1 million when Asano gained control of the bank, was raised to ¥5 million in 1917 and then to ¥10 million in 1920. With eight branches in Tokyo and two each in Kanagawa Prefecture, Kyoto, and Osaka, the bank was renamed Asano Chūya Bank in 1918; at the same time the Nippon Chūya Savings Bank was renamed Asano Chūya Savings Bank.[35]

Furukawa Bank

The Furukawa zaibatsu established its bank after a long period of preparation. The second president, Furukawa Junkichi, had been interested in banking, but the real champion of the bank idea was Nakajima Kumakichi, who worked in the secretariat of the House of Furukawa. A nephew of Mutsu Munemitsu, Nakajima had joined the House of Furukawa as a representative of the Mutsu family. Amid Furukawa's copper-only atmosphere, Nakajima set about planning a bank. As part of his preparations, he dispatched a Furukawa employee who had been educated at a commercial college to Europe and the United States to study the banking industry and to master banking practices there.[36]

Nakajima in 1916 submitted to the board of Furukawa Gōmei his plan for founding a bank, along with a report written by the employee who had been sent abroad. With the changed wartime circumstances, the atmosphere at Furukawa had become favorable to the establishment of a bank, and the Nakajima plan was accepted. Tokyo Furukawa Bank was established in 1917.[37] Initially it had ¥5 million in capital (half of which was paid in), ¥13.5 million in deposits, and ¥15.3 million in loans. In the same year Sumitomo Bank was capitalized at ¥30 million (¥18.8 million paid in), with ¥187.6 million in deposits and ¥120.1 million in loans. Tokyo Furukawa Bank, therefore, was a relatively small operation; the disadvantage of its late entry is clear. The bank nonetheless got off to a good start due to its connection to the Furukawa family enterprises.

Fujita Bank

Fujita Bank was also founded in 1917. The Fujita zaibatsu, like Asano and Furukawa, had envisioned establishing a bank that would function as its financial center based on the capital reserves accumulated during the wartime boom. The bank was capitalized at ¥10 million at its initiation.[38]

Despite promising starts, however, these new banks began under the handicap of late entry and went on to suffer the blows of the postwar recession and the 1927 financial panic. Ultimately, Asano, Furukawa, and Fujita all had to leave the banking industry. Rather than solving the problems of limited capital, the new banks ended up placing a heavy burden on their zaibatsu owners.

In contrast to these newcomers to the field, the four zaibatsu with long and rich experience in banking—Mitsui, Mitsubishi, Sumitomo, and Yasuda—followed sound banking policies and simply observed the situation during the war, thus avoiding risky expansionary moves. These banks managed to preserve themselves without being adversely affected by the drastic fluctuations during and after the war. The cautious policy of Mitsui Bank provides a good example of their behavior: despite the overseas shipping boom during the war, Mitsui Bank tightly restricted credit to the shipping industry and thereby escaped damage from the postwar reaction.[39]

On the other hand, during the years 1917–19 Sumitomo, Mitsui, and Mitsubishi did move into another finance-related field, the marine insurance business. Each of these zaibatsu founded a marine insurance company in response to the wartime growth in foreign trade and shipping by Japan.

First, Fusō Kaijō Kasai (Fusō Marine and Fire Insurance) was established in 1917 with the Sumitomo head office, Sōhonten, as the major shareholder at 18 percent of the shares. The new company was capitalized at ¥10 million, one-fourth of which was paid in. It became a designated subsidiary of Sumitomo, Ltd., in 1930 and was renamed Sumitomo Kaijō Kasai (Sumitomo Marine and Fire Insurance) in 1940.

Next came Taishō Kaijō Kasai Hoken (now Mitsui Marine and Fire

Insurance), founded in 1918 with Mitsui Bussan as the central investor but with the participation of outside financiers as well. Its initial capitalization was ¥5 million, one-fourth of which was paid in. Mitsui Bussan strongly requested the provision of capital and management know-how from Tokyo Kaijō Kasai Hoken (Tokio Marine and Fire Insurance), the leader in the field. As a result, Tokio Marine became a major stockholder of Taishō Marine with about 15 percent of its shares, while the executive director of Tokio Marine, Hirao Hachisaburō, also assumed the executive directorship of Taishō Marine.[40]

Finally, in 1919 the insurance department of Mitsubishi, Ltd., was spun off as an independent company, Mitsubishi Kaijō Kasai (Mitsubishi Marine and Fire Insurance). This firm was capitalized at ¥5 million, one-fourth of which was paid in. Tokio Marine and Fire Insurance, one of Mitsubishi's ordinary subsidiaries, contributed a fourth of the capital for the new company and maintained a close relationship with its management. Mitsubishi Marine merged with Tokio Marine in 1944.[41]

SUMMARY

The zaibatsu responded in a variety of ways to the World War I boom. During the war they stepped up their activities in the fields of heavy industry, foreign trade, and banking. The relative success of those activities depended heavily on the management of each zaibatsu and is reflected in the zaibatsu's postwar ranking in terms of financial resources and level of diversification. Judged by those terms, Mitsui clearly came out on top, followed first by Mitsubishi and then Sumitomo and Yasuda. These zaibatsu recorded solid business results during and after the war. Meanwhile, Furukawa, Ōkura, Fujita, Asano, and several newly emergent zaibatsu trailed far behind the big four.

CHAPTER 6

THE POST-WORLD WAR I ERA

The decade that stretched from the end of World War I to the onset of the Depression in 1929 was a period of drastic instability in Japan. The signing of the Armistice was followed by a brief recession, which was succeeded by an upturn and then a panic in 1920. The major industrialized area of Japan was devastated by the Great Kantō Earthquake in 1923. A banking crisis flared in 1927. Growth phases did occur during that decade, but they were shortlived and failed to develop much vigor.

Many factors were involved in this economic instability, but those pressing the Japanese economy included the worldwide slump in shipping and reduction in armaments spending, resumption of imports that had been interrupted by the war, decline in the rate of growth of Japanese exports, and global overproduction and the fall in the price of mineral products. On the other hand, urbanization, electrification, and the fixed capital formation accompanying those trends sustained Japanese economic growth during this period. For example, from 1919 to 1929 domestic consumption of electricity increased nearly fourfold, from 2.71 billion KwH to 10.26 billion KwH.[1]

Existing market conditions contributed to important changes in Japan's industrial structure. Production in the mining and shipbuilding industries declined while the iron, steel, and chemical dye industries struggled in the face of renewed imports. Although the cotton-spinning industry steadily expanded output, the silk-reeling industry stagnated. In contrast, such electricity-based industries as electric power, electric railways, electrical machinery, electric wire, and electrochemicals rapidly increased output. The growth of new heavy industries in such fields as synthetic ammonium sulphate and rayon manufacture was also remarkable.

During these ten years the relative strengths and weaknesses of the

TABLE 6.1   Paid-in Capital of Zaibatsu Subsidiaries, 1928 (in million yen)

Zaibatsu	Designated subsidiaries	Subsidiaries of designated subsidiaries	Ordinary subsidiaries
Mitsui	242.0	204.0	203.6
Mitsubishi	225.6	124.8	181.1
Yasuda	159.5	132.0	67.0
Sumitomo	132.1	8.1	47.0
Asano	82.1	97.6	71.4
Furukawa	42.7	9.7	16.6
Ōkura	33.7	12.5	97.5

SOURCE. Compiled from Takahashi Kamekichi, *Nihon zaibatsu no kaibo* (Analysis of the Japanese Zaibatsu) (Tokyo: Chūō Kōron Sha, 1930), various tables.

zaibatsu became clear. By the end of the decade, Mitsui and Mitsubishi had retained their preeminent positions among the zaibatsu. Yasuda and Sumitomo had strengthened their positions in the second rank after Mitsui and Mitsubishi and pulled ahead of Asano, Furukawa, and Ōkura. (See Table 6.1.) Meanwhile, three zaibatsu had been eliminated: Suzuki folded in 1927; Kuhara was removed from Kuhara family control in 1927; and Fujita came under the control of Bank of Japan upon the bankruptcy of Fujita Bank in 1928.

STRENGTHS AND WEAKNESSES OF THE ZAIBATSU

Several factors accounted for the major differences in performance among the zaibatsu. The World War I boom had provided all of them with extraordinary opportunities for growth. Those zaibatsu weaker than Mitsui and Mitsubishi attempted to catch up by actively moving into the new fields opened by the wartime market conditions. But in most cases, excluding Yasuda and Sumitomo, their zeal to reap unreasonably huge gains at once led them beyond the bounds of sound managerial practice. Their aggressive behavior proved, by and large, harmful to them after the wartime boom vanished.

The zaibatsu that attempted at one stroke to overtake Mitsui Bussan in trading not only saw their trading companies fail but also jeopardized their overall operations. The best example is the detrimental effect of the bankruptcy of Furukawa Trading on the Furukawa zaibatsu as a whole; the collapse dealt a huge blow to the Furukawa zaibatsu. From 1922 to 1930 Furukawa Gōmei recorded losses, the results of huge interest payments in almost every semester (Table 6.2), and the interest

TABLE 6.2   The Finances of Furukawa Gōmei, 1922–30

Year semester		Net profits (thousand yen)	Gross income (thousand yen)	Interest payments (thousand yen)	Notes payable as % of total funds in use
1922:	2nd	−771	—	—	56.9
1923:	1st	−2,326	532	1,306	52.0
	2nd	174	623	1,327	56.6
1924:	1st	−1,207	270	1,368	58.3
	2nd	826	2,365	1,409	58.7
1925:	1st	−223	1,241	1,419	58.5
	2nd	−178	1,288	1,405	59.1
1926:	1st	36	2,250	1,352	57.6
	2nd	−403	1,057	1,406	56.4
1927:	1st	−328	1,156	1,422	54.7
	2nd	−536	1,167	1,463	52.4
1928:	1st	−177	2,611	1,268	50.7
	2nd	35	1,558	1,187	47.2
1929:	1st	5	1,643	1,060	44.3
	2nd	103	1,440	968	46.1
1930:	1st	−159	1,286	964	44.1
	2nd	−179	1,063	979	44.2

SOURCES: Compiled from Furukawa Kōgyō, *Sōgyō 100-nen shi* (100 Years of Furukawa Mining) (Tokyo: Furukawa Kōgyō Kabushiki Kaisha, 1976), p. 403; Imuta Yoshimitsu, "Ryōtaisen kan ni okeru kigyō kin'yū" (The Finances of Enterprises in the Interwar Period), in *Keiei Shigaku*, vol. 12, no. 1 (April 1977):89.

payments exceeded its gross revenues in seven of the eleven losing semesters. Such huge interest payments were necessitated by accumulated loans in the form of notes payable from Furukawa Bank and Dai-ichi Bank amounting to about 50 percent of Gōmei's total funds in use throughout the 1920s. In the same period, the capitalization of Furukawa Gōmei remained constant at ¥20 million. That is, rather than drawing on the resources of the zaibatsu family to carry out a capital increase, the Furukawa zaibatsu became dependent on its bank and even on an outside bank for the supply of necessary funds to the parent company:

This dependency was anomalous among the zaibatsu. The Furukawa family had been forced to exhaust its fortune in order to deal with the losses and debts of Furukawa Trading. After World War I, the zaibatsu lost vigor and achieved nothing outstanding; in addition to the collapse of Furukawa Trading, the postwar stagnation in copper production affected Furukawa Mining, and the damage suffered by the electric wire division of Furukawa Denki Kōgyō (Furukawa Electric) and Yokohama Rubber in the Great Kantō Earthquake helped to ensure Furukawa's descent to the status of a second-class zaibatsu.

Another source of weakness for the zaibatsu in the postwar era was the stagnation of coal and copper mining as well as of shipbuilding, which all had earlier provided a strong industrial base. With competition from coal imported from Manchuria and elsewhere and declining demand due to the postwar slump, coal prices sagged. Domestic copper producers also suffered from a drop in copper prices brought on by imports of inexpensive copper, particularly from the United States, and by falling domestic demand. In addition, as domestic copper deposits were nearing exhaustion, production costs rose and exports declined. In shipbuilding, cuts in military spending and poor performance in the shipping industry produced a drastic decline in demand.

Despite the adverse conditions, some zaibatsu managed to find their way through these difficulties by forming cartels, upgrading technology, and rationalizing and diversifying operations. In fact, some not only survived but increased their market shares in the industrial fields in which they were engaged. That was the difference between the first-class zaibatsu, which managed to grow despite the long-term stagnation of the economy, and the second-class zaibatsu, which failed to overcome the slump.

The coal- and copper-mining industries offer a clear illustration of these trends. Both coal and copper mining had a high degree of production concentration, and zaibatsu-related mining companies accounted for a large proportion of the total output. Thus, at times those companies attempted market stabilization by forming cartels or having import duties raised. For instance, the first national coal-mining cartel, the Sekitan Kōgyō Rengōkai (Coal Mining Association), was formed in 1921 with the participation of zaibatsu companies. It succeeded in restricting coal shipments and limiting imports of Manchurian coal beginning 1926.[2] Partly as a result of these restrictions, the domestic market share of five zaibatsu companies, Mitsui Mining, Mitsubishi Mining, the Mitsui-affiliated Hokkaido Colliery and Steamship, Furukawa Mining, and Sumitomo Coal Mining, rose from about 40 percent in 1919 to 46 percent in 1929. If subsidiaries of those five companies are also included their total share was greater than 50 percent.[3]

Cartels were formed in the copper industry as well. Furukawa, Kuhara, Fujita, and Sumitomo in 1920 formed the Nippon Sandō Kumiai (Nippon Copper Production Association), and in 1921 Furukawa, Kuhara, Fujita, and Mitsubishi formed another copper cartel, the Suiyōkai. The four Suiyōkai members and Sumitomo succeeded in having import duties on copper raised substantially in 1922. The five zaibatsu copper companies had a 69.5 percent share of domestic copper production in 1917, but by 1929 their cartel activity had raised that share to 93.4 percent.[4]

The differences in performance among the zaibatsu, however, stemmed not from such oligopolistic activity but from plant modernization and rationalization. Mitsui Mining, Mitsubishi Mining, and Hokkaido Colliery, the coal companies that achieved the greatest increases in market share, did so by investing heavily in technological improvements and rationalization. In copper as well, Mitsubishi, Sumitomo, and Furukawa carried out forward and backward integration, using their own copper for the manufacture of electric wire and their own coal for fuel. Their performance during the twenties differed markedly from that of such zaibatsu copper producers as Kuhara and Fujita, who failed to invest in such integration.[5]

THE ZAIBATSU AND HEAVY INDUSTRIES AFTER WORLD WAR I

The war years' favorable market environment had encouraged the zaibatsu's activity in a range of heavy industries; new operations were started and existing ones expanded. The postwar slump, however, required the pursuit of various strategies in order to ensure the survival of the enterprises, including shipyards and chemical plants. The zaibatsu also took up the difficult challenge of developing new heavy industries, including synthetic ammonia, rayon, and automobile manufacturing, which had never before existed in Japan. By doing so they displayed a pattern of behavior that contradicts the conventional view of the zaibatsu as conservative and shy of risk.

Among the zaibatsu entering new fields of heavy industry after the war, Furukawa was exceptional in that it was the only one that failed to weather the postwar stagnation without major damage and yet founded subsidiaries in such fields.

Survival Strategies

SHIPBUILDING. Shipbuilding was one of the main heavy industries in which the zaibatsu devised strategies for survival after the war. The boom in shipping during World War I and naval plans for building a new fleet had led some to anticipate limitless demand in the market for new ships and brought many zaibatsu into the industry. At the beginning of the war, Mitsubishi and Kawasaki (Matsukata) were the only zaibatsu operating shipyards, but during the war they were joined by Mitsui (the shipbuilding division of Mitsui Bussan), Suzuki (Harima

TABLE 6.3   Major Shipbuilding Companies: Gross Tonnages Launched and Market Shares, 1919–26

Company	1919–20		1921–26	
	Gross tonnage launched	Market share (%)	Gross tonnage launched	Market share (%)
Kawasaki Shipbuilding	272,717	25.5	67,060	13.4
Osaka Tekkōsho	140,400	13.1	72,039	14.4
Asano Shipbuilding	128,700	12.0	30,840	6.2
Mitsubishi Shipbuilding and Engineering	128,288	12.0	110,826	22.1
Harima Shipyard	80,545	7.5	26,426	5.3
Uraga Dock	80,270	7.5	22,323	4.5
Yokohama Dock	51,040	4.8	60,534	12.1
Uchida Shipbuilding	29,400	2.8	5,700	1.1
Mitsui Bussan, shipbuilding division	24,100	2.3	35,180	7.0
Ishikawajima Shipbuilding	18,564	1.7	25,300	5.1
Subtotal	954,024	89.2	456,228	91.2

SOURCE: Kaneko Eiichi, *Zōsen* (Shipbuilding), vol. 9 of *Gendai Nihon sangyō-shi* (History of Modern Japanese Industries) (Tokyo: Kōjunsha, 1964), p. 190.

Shipyard), Asano, and Kuhara (Osaka Tekkōsho). The industry was additionally enlivened by active nonzaibatsu participants including Ishikawajima Zōsensho, Uraga Dock, Hakodate Dock, and Uchida Zōsensho. (Of the nonzaibatsu shipyards, only Uchida Zōsensho was founded during the war.) Yokohama Dock was another major shipbuilding company, but it was a subsidiary of NYK and had close ties to Mitsubishi. (It merged with Mitsubishi Heavy Industries in 1935.)

The postwar slump and disarmament, however, meant sharp market reductions and operating difficulties for the shipbuilding industry. Table 6.3 presents a comparison of tonnages launched in 1919–20, when the effects of the wartime prosperity were still felt, and in 1921–26, when the industry was stagnating. Production dropped precipitously overall, but the performances of individual zaibatsu shipyards differed significantly. Kawasaki Shipbuilding Co. (Matsukata), Osaka Tekkōsho (Kuhara), Asano Shipbuilding, and Harima Shipyard (Suzuki) all fell in terms of tonnage launched, and all but Osaka Tekkōsho did so in terms of share of total production. In contrast, Mitsubishi Shipbuilding and Engineering and Yokohama Dock experienced a slight decrease in production, but together with the shipbuilding division of Mitsui Bussan they increased their shares of total production.

Such differences reflect the varying postwar performances of these zaibatsu's shipping businesses. Compared to Matsukata's Kawasaki Steamship, Asano's Oriental Steamship Company, Suzuki's Teikoku Steamship, and Kuhara's Nippon Steamship, all of which barely limped along during the postwar slump, Mitsui Bussan's shipping division weathered the hard times with relative ease. The shipping division of Mitsubishi Trading Company, founded in 1912 as the shipping department of the company's sales division and promoted to divisional status in 1918, was small in scale during the postwar years, but its performance was sound. Meanwhile, the Mitsubishi zaibatsu continued to maintain its cooperative relationship with Japan's largest shipping company, NYK.

The orders and inside financial assistance enjoyed by Mitsubishi and Mitsui shipbuilding helped them to survive after the war, but the soundness cannot be attributed solely to guaranteed demand from shipping firms within their respective zaibatsu groups. Their solid performance was largely dependent on the fact that both made policy decisions appropriate to the postwar scene, and in this regard their experience contrasted sharply with that of Kawasaki Shipbuilding. Kawasaki, which had boasted the greatest tonnage of ships launched in Japan, could have supported its operations based on the demand from NYK, OSK, and other major shipping lines without depending on orders from its associated firm, Kawasaki Steamship—but the company dealt itself a blow when it decided during the war to produce stock boats to its own design on speculation. In fact, it specialized in such production to such an extent that it declined orders from OSK. Consequently, Kawasaki made a huge profit on stock boats, but at the price of alienating a major customer.[6]

Kawasaki Shipbuilding made a number of other mistakes in its policy decisions. It continued mass production of stock boats even as the postwar shipping crisis was approaching. To tide over the recession, it adopted aggressive policies and moved into new fields with low profitability, such as shipping, iron and steel production, and airplane manufacture. Consequently, it became dependent upon massive loans from the Jūgo Ginkō (Fifteenth Bank), of which the Matsukata family was a major shareholder and provider of the top management.[7] As a result, Kawasaki Shipbuilding's profits dried up (see Table 6.4), and it collapsed in April 1927.

In contrast, Mitsubishi Shipbuilding and Engineering did not engage in mass production of stock boats and therefore had wartime profits small compared to those of Kawasaki Shipbuilding. But thanks to its steadier policy Mitsubishi Shipbuilding suffered no great fluctua-

TABLE 6.4   Net Profits of Mitsubishi Shipbuilding and Engineering and
Kawasaki Shipping, 1919–27 (in thousand yen)

Year	Mitsubishi	Kawasaki
1919	9,921	22,492
1921	6,051	7,871
1924	7,369	5,632
1927	3,336	−35,300

SOURCES: Compiled from various company histories.

tions in its postwar profit trend. Moreover, it responded sensitively to the postwar shrinking market and excess capacity conditions, from 1920 on dismissing large numbers of shipyard workers; Kawasaki did not.

In devising a strategy for dealing with the postwar recession, the shipping division of Mitsui Bussan immediately after the war began to study the field and to gather information from ship captains. The result was a decision to use high-speed diesel-powered ships. Compared with contemporary steamships of the same tonnage, diesel ships demonstrated superiority in both speed and cargo capacity at lower cost. Mitsui Bussan's shipbuilding division bought diesel engines from a Danish firm, Burmeister & Wain, to install in its new ships. It launched Japan's first diesel-powered ship, the *Akagisan-maru*, in March 1924 and went on to meet the demand from its shipping division for diesel ships.[8] The shipbuilding division had studied Burmeister & Wain's diesel engines since 1920[9] and in 1926 secured from the Danish company the rights to manufacture and sell diesel engines of the Burmeister & Wain type. Embarking on internal production of the engines, Mitsui was able to respond well to a brisk market for diesel-ship construction.

CHEMICALS.   The chemical industry provides a classic case of the desperate efforts of one zaibatsu to ensure that its venture in a particular industry would survive the postwar crisis: synthetic dye production at Mitsui. In Japan's postwar climate, nurturing an infant industry was not an easy task even for a zaibatsu as powerful as Mitsui. No sooner had Mitsui initiated the first domestic production of synthetic dyestuffs at its Miike mine coking plant and delivered its first products to the market than World War I broke out. As a result of the war, imported dyes came to be in short supply and prices soared, and thus, despite quality problems, Mitsui was able to earn high profits on its synthetic dyes. The coking plant attached to the Miike mine was given the status of a separate division within Mitsui Mining as Miike Senryō Kōgyōsho (Miike Dyestuff Works) in 1918. The wartime bubble broke when imports were resumed after the war, and the situation was made even worse by the dumping of cheap German dyes.

The import offensive was felt by the domestic chemical dye industry as a whole, including such firms as Nippon Senryō (Nippon Dyestuff), which were established after Mitsui pioneered the field in Japan.

The effect, however, was particularly severe on Miike Dyestuff Works, which, unlike Nippon Dyestuff, did not receive government assistance. Miike had chosen a difficult production method in processing the by-products of the Kopper's-type coke oven without relying on imported technology, and moreover its range of products was small.[10] In the years 1919–25, it absorbed an investment of about ¥4 million and recorded losses totaling ¥2.3 million. Despite a downward trend in performance due to falling coal prices, Mitsui Mining continued to generate high profits, compared to which the Miike Dyestuff Works losses were relatively small (Table 6.5). That is, given the huge scale of the Mitsui zaibatsu and the oligopolistic position of Mitsui Mining in the coal industry, it was able to invest in such an unprofitable enterprise as the fledgling chemical dyestuff venture. That conclusion is based on hindsight, however. At the time, the sad plight of Miike Dyestuff Works made it the object of criticism within the Mitsui zaibatsu.

TABLE 6.5   Net Profits of Miike Senryō Kōgyōsho and Mitsui Mining, 1919–32 (in thousand yen)

Year	Miike Senryō Kōgyōsho	Mitsui Mining
1919	206	15,481
1920	−456	11,108
1921	−456	6,652
1922	−704	7,510
1923	7	7,721
1924	−146	5,821
1925	−724	4,625
1926	486	4,290
1927	846	5,837
1928	1,366	6,639
1929	1,211	6,751
1930	1,370	4,953
1931	872	3,747
1932	1,722	5,718

SOURCE: *Mitsui Kōzan 50-nen shi* (50 Years of Mitsui Mining), unpublished ms., vol. 5, appended table.

Investment in plant and equipment as well as in research and development at Miike Dyestuff Works was restricted, and some called for casting it off as an independent company or closing it down.

The credit for saving Miike Dyestuff Works goes to the efforts of its engineers, who succeeded in 1926 in creating the first domestically produced artificial indigo; to government protection in the form of a licensing system for imports of tar products instituted in 1924 and a 1925 dyestuff industry promotion law;[11] and to the commitment of the top-level Mitsui executives. Dan Takuma and Makita Tamaki, senior executive director of Mitsui Mining, had long been enthusiastic about the coal chemical industry. Dan's view was that "Mitsui Mining has the resources, so we'll accept the fact that dyestuffs production will go into the red and invest in it on an experimental basis. We'll end up contributing to the national welfare."

Consistently backed by Dan, Mitsui Mining protected Miike Dyestuff Works through its bad years.[12] The dyestuffs enterprise took a turn for the better in 1926 (Table 6.5) and by 1932 was performing so well that it accounted for 30 percent of the total profits of Mitsui Mining. During World War II, Miike Dyestuff Works, with a world-class technological level, grew into Japan's biggest dyestuffs manufacturer. In 1941 it was spun off from Mitsui Mining as Mitsui Kagaku Kōgyō (Mitsui Chemical Industries), capitalized at ¥80 million.

The ammonia-method soda plant of Asahi Glass offers another example of zaibatsu efforts in the postwar chemical industry. Founded by Iwasaki Toshiya, Koyata's younger brother, Asahi Glass was faced with interruptions in imports of the soda ash it needed for glass production. It therefore opened an ammonia-method soda ash factory in 1917, but technological inexperience and postwar competition from imports drove it into a hopeless state. It received enormous financial backing from the Mitsubishi zaibatsu and weathered losses of ¥4 million against investments of ¥2.91 million up to 1929. An ongoing conflict now afflicted the venture: Koyata demanded that production of soda ash by the ammonia-soda method be abandoned, and Toshiya resisted his brother's demand. Toshiya's determination was rewarded: due to the granting of ¥642,000 in government subsidies from 1929 to 1932, a halt in soda ash dumping by ICI in 1932, and the improvement of technology in use at Asahi Glass, the ammonia-method soda ash division was finally able to move into the black in 1932, when it recorded a profit of ¥92,000 (exclusive of the government subsidy).[13] Ensuring the firm's survival, however, inflicted years of strain on Toshiya, who died in 1930, before he was able to witness the full fruition of his efforts at Asahi Glass.

THE POSTWAR ADVANCE INTO NEW HEAVY INDUSTRIES

Zaibatsu Conservatism

In the course of their advance into heavy industry, the major zaibatsu, with their enormous financial resources, were in several cases more passive and dilatory than groups of firms that were clearly inferior in terms of available capital. The following factors have been concluded to be responsible for the zaibatsu's conservative entry into heavy industry. First, the increasing bureaucratization of the zaibatsu's structures acted as a brake on speedy decision making and dynamism. Second, the influence of the zaibatsu family, which tended to put preservation of the family fortune first, and the difficulty of harmonizing opinion among the subsidiaries charged with operating the diversified enterprises of the zaibatsu also hindered swift decision making and encouraged conservatism.

Production of synthetic ammonium sulphate is a good example. Noguchi Jun's Nippon Chisso Hiryō (Nippon Nitrogenous Fertilizer) in 1921 bought the Casale technology for synthesizing ammonia and put it into use at its Nobeoka factory, completed in 1923. Suzuki Shōten in 1920 bought the Claude process and in 1924 opened the Hikoshima plant of a subsidiary company, Claude-shiki Chisso Kōgyō (Claude-Process Nitrogen Industries). In contrast with these first-comers, Mitsui, Mitsubishi, and Sumitomo waited until the 1930s to move into the new field.

The manufacture of chemical fibers, particularly rayon, is another example. Mitsui Bussan established Tōyō Rayon, providing all of its capital of ¥10 million, and moved into viscose rayon production in 1926. Suzuki Shōten, however, had made the decision to enter the field as early as 1915. Suzuki Shōten took a subsidiary, Azuma Kōgyō (Azuma Industries), originally Azuma Leather, and reorganized it as the independent Teikoku Jinzō Kenshi (Imperial Artificial Silk; now Teijin, Ltd.), Japan's first viscose rayon maker, founded in 1918 with a capitalization of ¥10 million. The company, which used entirely domestic technology, was placed under the leadership of two engineers, each of whom later served as president: Kumura Seita and Hata Itsuzō. Assisted by the wartime shortages and cutoff of imports, the firm eventually was able to sell its products beginning in late 1916.

Teijin was followed in 1922 by Asahi Kenshoku (Asahi Silk Manufacturing), capitalized at ¥2 million and jointly founded by Nippon Menka (Nippon Cotton Trading) and Noguchi of Nippon Nitrogenous Fertilizer. Noguchi had entered into a contract for technological cooperation between himself as an individual and the German firm Glanzstoff and intended to institute viscose rayon production within Nippon Nitrogenous Fertilizer. He did not dominate that company, however, and its board of directors did not support his plan. Consequently, Noguchi on his own linked up with Nippon Cotton Trading, whose president, Kita Matazō, was also strongly interested in the rayon industry, and established Asahi Silk Manufacturing as a joint venture to produce rayon using the Glanzstoff technology.[14]

Mitsui Bussan's entry into rayon production clearly came late. In fact, while the pioneering firms were struggling to produce rayon domestically, Mitsui Bussan was a major rayon importer. By the mid-1920s, however, the development of the domestic market for rayon was well advanced, the competitive power of domestically produced rayon was rising thanks to the efforts of the pioneering firms, and an increase in the import duty on rayon was anticipated. (It finally came in 1926.) At that point Mitsui Bussan at last began planning for rayon production. It had hoped to cooperate with Courtaulds of Britain and Du Pont of the United States, but they could not agree on terms. Finally, with the assistance of Oscar Kohorn, a German firm, it imported the necessary technology and entered the rayon industry. Mitsui Gōmei had regarded Mitsui Bussan's rayon production plan as extremely risky and in the end approved the plan only after imposing a number of conditions, such as requiring that Bussan cut by half the production capacity it originally proposed and refrain from using the family name Mitsui in the new company name.[15]

A somewhat different type of zaibatsu conservatism with regard to new heavy industries can be seen in the automobile industry: in this case a major zaibatsu pioneered such an industry but then withdrew from it.

The course by which the Japanese automobile industry, led by Toyota and Nissan, has risen to its present level is well known. Toyota is now the world's number two automaker, and Nissan is number four. The firms that spawned these two automobile companies were not huge. Toyota grew out of Toyoda Jidō Shokki Seisakusho (Toyoda Automatic Loom Works), and Nissan out of Tobata Imono, a foundry. Both companies overcame technological difficulties and bore risks to open the way in the 1930s to domestic automobile production.[16]

The huge Mitsubishi zaibatsu, however, had first taken up the question of domestic automobile production some twenty years earlier. The shipbuilding division of Mitsubishi, Ltd., began research on the internal combustion engine before World War I. An internal combustion engine department was added to the Kobe Shipyard in 1916, and construction begun on a factory to manufacture the engines. The following year the factory's internal combustion engine unit, promoted from department to division, began trial production of the Mitsubishi Model A automobile, which was based on the Fiat Model A. Trial production of military trucks was also ordered in accordance with a law that promoted production of military vehicles. The performance of the resulting vehicles was highly praised. Soon after, the internal combustion engine division also began airplane production.

The division was spun off from Mitsubishi Shipbuilding as Mitsubishi Nainenki Seizō (Mitsubishi Internal Combustion Engine Works) in 1920; the new company built a factory in Nagoya and moved airplane and automobile production there. With the vast financial resources of the Mitsubishi zaibatsu behind it, the Nagoya works should have become the mecca of the Japanese automobile industry. It should have attained an insurmountable lead in the domestic production of automobiles with no rivalry from Toyota and Nissan. That, however, did not happen. In 1922 Mitsubishi Internal Combustion Engine withdrew from automobile production in order to concentrate on aircraft manufacture.

Several probable factors led Mitsubishi to decide against automobile production. First, in international terms the automobile industry in the 1920s had already established a mass production system; the aircraft industry had not. Consequently, domestic automakers would have to confront fierce competition from imports while domestic aircraft producers would not. Further, there was little prospect of growing domestic demand for automobiles, but aircraft production could expect military demand and generous protective policies. In addition, the military, as the consumer of Mitsubishi aircraft, may have demanded that Mitsubishi Internal Combustion Engine engage exclusively in aircraft production. And finally the losses sustained by Mitsubishi Trading Company in the postwar slump and the stagnation of the mining and shipbuilding industries may have meant that the money to effect a two-front strategy of automobile and airplane manufacture was simply not there. In any event, the result of Mitsubishi's decision was that it missed the chance to become the undisputed leader of the automobile industry in Japan.[17]

Zaibatsu Progressiveness: The Case of the Synthetic Ammonium Sulphate Industry

The above examples suggest that the zaibatsu always behaved conservatively with respect to heavy industries, but such a conclusion is mistaken. Zaibatsu actions that might be considered the result of conservatism often prove to have other explanations when the alternatives available at the time are considered. Even the huge zaibatsu did not have unlimited financial resources, and in diversifying they had to select which fields to enter. Naturally, prudent calculations of profit and loss would be performed at such times. Moreover, it must be recalled that by the end of the war the major zaibatsu had already invested managerial resources in several diversified subsidiaries; their resources, though vast, were largely tied up. It is all the more remarkable, then, that the zaibatsu did indeed display risk-taking and innovative behavior in advancing into certain new fields of heavy industry after the war.

Take, for example, the case of the synthetic ammonium sulphate industry. The major zaibatsu were undeniably tardy, compared with Nippon Nitrogenous Fertilizer and Suzuki Shōten, in entering this field, but given that Mitsui and Sumitomo had in the 1920s eagerly sought to enter, we cannot explain their lateness in terms of conservative behavior.

Sumitomo actually became interested in synthetic ammonium sulphate in the 1910s as part of its effort to clean up the pollution at the Besshi mine. It had set up a fertilizer factory to use sulphuric acid produced at the mine as the raw material for making superphosphate of lime in 1913. Furthermore, in order to consume a larger volume of the sulphuric acid, Sumitomo conceived of producing ammonium sulphate, and as a first step, in July 1915 the head office (Sōhonten) hired Takeuchi Isakichi, a graduate of Kyoto Imperial University who had studied the synthesis of ammonia.[18]

Sumitomo sought to acquire the technology for synthesizing ammonia in two ways. One was to introduce the American General Chemical Corporation process through a joint venture with the pharmaceuticals manufacturer Sankyō. The other was to adopt the Haber-Bosch process. The General Chemical process had proven successful only experimentally, but the Haber-Bosch process had been successfully applied in the only ammonia production factory in the world. However, use of the Haber-Bosch process by foreign manufacturers was prohibited. Sumitomo hesitated to introduce the fledgling General Chemical process, and in 1917 decided to send Takeuchi, Kajiura Kamajirō, and other Sumitomo engineers to the United States to study the method further. In July of that year the enactment of a wartime industrial property rights law made possible the adoption of the Haber-Bosch process after all. The United States study mission was postponed.[19]

Sumitomo then took the initiative in having the applicants for the Haber-Bosch process organize the Tōyō Chisso Kōgyō Kabushiki Kaisha Sōritsu Junbi Jimusho (Office to Prepare for the Establishment

of an Oriental Nitrogen Industry Joint-Stock Company). The applicants included Mitsui Gōmei and Mitsubishi, Ltd. Exclusive right to
the use of the Haber-Bosch process was granted to this office.[20]

It soon became clear, however, that serious obstacles blocked the
industrial application of the Haber-Bosch process. First, owing to the
war the required equipment could not be imported and technological
guidance was not available. Moreover, to achieve economies of scale
with that process, one had to produce 100,000 tons of ammonium
sulphate a year—and the annual domestic demand in Japan was only
60,000 tons.[21]

Sumitomo began to reconsider the General Chemical process. Since
the deficiencies of the process could be overcome by cooperation from
BASF, which owned the Haber-Bosch process, in the spring of 1919
Sumitomo proposed to General Chemical a joint Japanese-U.S.-
German venture, which General Chemical turned down.[22] Sumitomo
entered into negotiations with BASF in December 1919 for transfer of
patent rights to the Haber-Bosch process, but BASF insisted on the
following "prohibitive conditions":[23]

1. Construction of a factory with annual output of 100,000 tons
2. Payment of ¥5 million for supplying the plans for the factory
3. A fifteen-year limit on the rights to the process
4. Minimum payment of ¥25 million for use for the first ten years
5. Payment of a royalty of ¥25 per ton of ammonium sulphate
   produced[24]

Upon learning how much BASF was demanding, the other applicants for the Haber-Bosch process lost interest and merely went
through the motions of forming a Tōyō Chisso Kōgyō Kumiai (Oriental Nitrogen Industry Association) in 1921 in order to secure exclusive
rights to the use of the process. Sumitomo was actively interested in the
ammonia industry, but the price of over ¥30 million demanded by
BASF was much too high, compared with the ¥1 million paid
by Nippon Nitrogenous Fertilizer for the Casale process or the ¥5 million paid by Suzuki Shōten for the Claude process. The expense would
be a burden on the entire Sumitomo empire.

The prohibitively high price attached to the Haber-Bosch process
was a hindrance to Mitsui as well. Mitsui had made efforts to move into
synthetic ammonium sulphate production in the 1920s, based on Mitsui Mining's contact with the homemade technology, in the intermediate testing stage, of the Rinji Chisso Kenkyūjo (Special Nitrogen
Laboratory)[25] and Mitsui Bussan's contact with the English-modified
Haber-Bosch process[26] and the U.S. NEC process.[27] Nothing came of
those efforts until the 1930s.

Thus it is not fair to say that Mitsui and Sumitomo did nothing about entering the synthetic ammonium sulphate industry in the 1920s, or that their slowness was the result of a safety-first, conservative attitude. It was not that Mitsui and Sumitomo were conservative but that Nippon Nitrogenous Fertilizer was remarkably lucky in becoming involved with the trouble-free and inexpensive Casale process. (Suzuki Shōten's Claude process proved a source of endless difficulty for the zaibatsu.)

In the end, after studying a variety of technologies Sumitomo decided to adopt the NEC process. Sumitomo Hiryō Seizōsho (Sumitomo Fertilizer Manufacturing, a joint-stock company from 1925) in February 1928 sent a proposal to Sumitomo, Ltd., requesting approval to introduce the NEC process.[28] Mitsui Bussan also suggested the NEC process to Mitsui Mining, but the latter had already decided to introduce the Claude process.[29]

After the collapse of Suzuki Shōten in 1927, Mitsui Mining began considering requests that it adopt the Claude process, which Suzuki owned. The requests, which were routed to Mitsui Mining senior executive director Makita, came from two sources: Suzuki's synthetic ammonium sulphate company and the Bank of Taiwan, Suzuki's creditor.[30] Mitsui Mining conducted a thorough study of Suzuki's enterprise, including the management in trust that began in January 1928. Then it negotiated with the Bank of Taiwan and with the French firm L'Air Liquide, which owned the Claude-process patent, and succeeded in securing substantial concessions on the price of the factory and the size of the royalties.[31]

Mitsui Mining in January 1929 bought the two firms using the Claude process that Suzuki Shōten had owned and operated, Claude-shiki Chisso Kōgyō (Claude-Process Nitrogen Industries), which obtained exclusive rights to the Claude process, and the Daiichi Chisso Kōgyō (First Nitrogen Industries), which was founded in 1926 to implement the Claude-process patents and operated a factory at Hikoshima. Mitsui Mining had managed to acquire the Claude process, for which Suzuki Shōten had paid ¥5 million, and the Hikoshima factory, built by Suzuki at great expense, for a mere ¥1.5 million.[32]

The careful, frugal calculations that allowed Mitsui to make such a deal must be understood in terms of the considerable trouble that Suzuki Shōten had had with the Claude process in the past; Mitsui engineers evinced a lack of confidence in the process,[33] an uncertainty that had resulted in Sumitomo's decision not to introduce the process. Moreover, as Mitsui was also considering the construction of a new ammonia synthesis factory in Miike, using the hydrogen gas from the coking ovens of the Miike Dyestuff Works, Mitsui's need for the Hikoshima factory was not clear. In fact, in 1931 Miike Chisso (Miike Nitrogen), capitalized at ¥10 million, of which Mitsui Mining supplied about 55 percent, was established. Further, in 1933 Mitsui founded Tōyō Kōatsu (Oriental High Pressure), capitalized at ¥20 million and almost wholly owned by Mitsui Mining. This firm combined the Claude process with technology introduced from Du Pont to begin ammonia synthesis and ammonium sulphate production using coke as the raw material.[34] Tōyō High Pressure absorbed Claude-Process Nitrogen Industries in 1935 and Miike Nitrogen in 1937. The following year it absorbed Gōsei Kōgyō (Synthetic Industries), which Mitsui Mining had formed to produce methanol in 1932 with a capital of ¥500,000. Thus, Tōyō High Pressure came to subsume all the ammonia and methanol-related coal chemical industries within the Mitsui zaibatsu.

Heavy Industries at Furukawa

Furukawa joined Mitsui, Mitsubishi, and Sumitomo in entering new heavy industries after World War I. Furukawa Denki Kōgyō (Furukawa Electric Company) was the source of heavy industry within the Furukawa zaibatsu. Furukawa had controlled Japan's largest manufacturer of electric wire and cable, Yokohama Electric Wire Manufacturing. Yokohama Electric Wire had made use of its rubber-related facilities set up for coating electric wire toa lso begin manufacturing hose, packing, and other industrial rubber products; in 1917 it had founded Yokohama Gomu Seizō (Yokohama Rubber) as a joint venture capitalized at ¥2.5 million with the U.S. firm B. F. Goodrich. Then in 1920 Furukawa renamed the wire company Furukawa electric and transferred to it the zaibutsu's Nikkō electrolytic copper and iwre works and Honjo refinery in Tokyo.

That same year Furukawa Trading went bankrupt. Inoue Kōji, senior executive director at Furukawa Gōmei, took responsibility for the failure and resigned in 1921. He was succeeded by Konda Bunjirō, assisted by Suzuki Tsunesaburō, who had left his position as head of the Nikkō refinery to become factory manager of Mitsui's Kanegafuchi Cotton Spinning and then returned to Furukawa in 1920 as an adviser to Furukawa Gōmei. Suzuki, who had guided Furukawa Toranosuke, president of Furukawa Gōmei, during his studies at Keiō University and in the United States, had gained Toranosuke's confidence, and so Toranosuke asked Suzuki to return to Furukawa to solve its crisis. Suzuki became senior executive director of Furukawa Gōmei after Konda's death in 1927.

In the Konda-Suzuki era, Furukawa Gōmei's top management decided upon an unqualified policy of retrenchment, cutting back on the diversified operations pursued during World War I. For example, the planned joint venture with Germany's Siemens to manufacture electrical machinery in Japan was cancelled. Yamaguchi Kisaburō, executive director of Furukawa Electric and a proponent of expanding the zaibatsu's industrial activities, came into conflict with the reduction policy and resigned in 1921.[35] He was replaced by Nakagawa Suekichi, a member of the Furukawa family and formerly executive director of Tokyo Furukawa Bank. Nakagawa used both his forceful personality and his authority as a Furukawa family member to push ahead with the zaibatsu's industrialization, which caused him to clash head on with the retrenchment policy sworn by Furukawa Gōmei's top management.[36]

The top management, faced with a series of disasters—including the collapse of Furukawa Trading, the poor performance of Furukawa Bank, the financial panic of 1920, the managerial difficulties of copper production, and the devastation of the Yokohama and Honjo factories of Furukawa Electric in the Great Kantō Earthquake of 1923—was at first unwilling to accept the establishment of new heavy industries. But under Nakagawa's leadership, Furukawa Electric succeeded in disarming Furukawa Gōmei's opposition. Furukawa Electric president Nakajima Kumakichi was a member of the Mutsu group. When other members of that group, including Hara and Okazaki, left Furukawa, he found himself in a less favorable position. As a result, Nakajima entrusted the top management of Furukawa Electric to Yamaguchi and Nakagawa and devoted himself to activities in the business community, such as participating in the Japan Industrial Club. Nakagawa eventually succeeded Nakajima as president in 1925.[37]

The best examples of the new heavy industries developed at Furukawa Electric are the electric machinery and aluminum-refining operations. The electric machinery business began after Furukawa Electric took over the negotiations that Furukawa Trading had been conducting for a cooperative arrangement with Germany's Siemens. In September 1923, Fuji Denki Seizō (Fuji Electric Company) was founded as a joint venture of Furukawa Electric and Siemens (actually, three Siemens companies, Siemens Schuckert, Siemens Halske, and a Japanese-registered corporation, Siemens Schuckert Electric); it was capitalized at ¥10 million, one-fourth of which was paid in. Siemens owned 30 percent of the stock.[38] Furukawa Gōmei stipulated that no financial help at all be expected from Furukawa in the formation of Fuji Electric. Consequently, the latter was forced to use what was, for a zaibatsu venture, an abnormal method of financing: it made a public offering of its shares and also depended on credit from Siemens and several banks other than the Furukawa bank, including those of Mitsubishi and Mitsui.[39] The name Fuji (as in "Mount Fuji") was derived from the *fu* of Furukawa and the *ji* of Siemens (according to the Japanese pronunciation of the German name).

Fuji Electric had an inauspicious beginning: the Great Kantō Earthquake struck on the day of its founding, September 1, 1923. Construction of its Kawasaki factory was delayed, and overall production did not begin until late 1925. Fuji Electric supplied Japan with heavy electrical equipment, beginning with switchboards, but given the financial crisis within the Furukawa zaibatsu it was not able to expand production capacity and thus until the 1930s depended on the importation and sale of Siemens products.[40]

With the coming of more prosperous conditions in the mid-1930s, Fuji Electric was finally able to adopt a more aggressive policy, central to which was mass production of motors and start-up production of telephone equipment. The telephone unit was spun off in June 1935 as Fuji Tsūshinki Seizō (Fuji Communications Equipment Manufacturing, capitalized at ¥3 million), the forerunner of Fujitsū (FACOM). One reason for making that unit independent was that the technical and labor conditions as well as markets for telephone equipment and those for motors and other heavy electrical equipment were different. Another was that in 1935 Fuji Electric and Tokyo Electric reached an agreement to divide the communications field, with Fuji Electric specializing in wired telecommunications and Tokyo Electric in wireless; they also agreed to establish separate companies to produce their respective communications devices.[41]

Furukawa Electric began producing aluminum electric wire in 1920. That was the stimulus for its moving into aluminum refining despite fierce opposition from Furukawa Gōmei. Furukawa Electric added duralumin production to its operations in 1928 and in 1934, in cooperation with Tōkai Denkyoku (Tōkai Electrode) and Taisei Kagaku Kōgyō (Taisei Chemical Industries), acquired exclusive rights to purchase bauxite produced on the island of Bintan off the coast of the Malay Peninsula, then Dutch territory. The next year those three companies joined Mitsui Mining and Mitsubishi Mining to found Nippon Aluminum, which refined the Bintan bauxite into alumina by the Bayer process and produced aluminum by the Hall-Héroult electrolysis process at a factory in Gaoxiong, Taiwan, then a Japanese colony. The new aluminum refining operation recorded excellent results, demonstrating the profitability of the aluminum industry and prompting Furukawa Electric to establish Nippon Keikinzoku (Nippon Light Metal Company) in 1939 as a joint venture with Tokyo Dentō (Tokyo Electric Light.)

Nippon Light Metal's goal was the mass production of aluminum. Furukawa chose Tokyo Electric Light as its partner in this venture in order to secure the huge supply of electric power needed for aluminum refining. Nippon Light Metal was capitalized at ¥100 million; Furukawa Electric held 25 percent of the shares, Tokyo Electric Light 27 percent, and the remaining shares were sold to the public.[42] Furukawa's restricted financial resources thus forced it to employ financial methods abnormal for a zaibatsu. In this regard as well, Furukawa was exceptional among the zaibatsu that ventured into new heavy industries after World War II.

EXPANSION OF FINANCIAL ENTERPRISES

In the decade after World War I, the four major zaibatsu—Mitsui, Mitsubishi, Sumitomo, and Yasuda—poured energy into expanding their financial businesses and came to exert an overwhelming influence on the Japanese economy. One aspect of this development was the growing power of the major zaibatsu banks (Table 6.6). Another was the movement of the zaibatsu into other financial fields, including trust services and insurance.

Growing Influence of the Four Major Zaibatsu Banks

Table 6.6 shows the rapid gains made by the banks of the four major zaibatsu in terms of deposits, loans, and securities owned. The increases recorded in those areas resulted in part from their own positive policies. The problems besetting smaller banks, such as bankruptcy, shaky management, and lowered public confidence, represented an additional factor that eased the way for the major banks to increase their weight in the industry. The growth of Yasuda Bank was particularly striking.

THE GREAT YASUDA BANK MERGER. During the twenties the Yasuda zaibatsu retreated from nonfinancial areas of business and strengthened its banking, insurance, and trust enterprises. It established itself as a uniquely specialized financial zaibatsu, and Yasuda Bank, which in 1919 had been far behind the other three big zaibatsu banks, thereby managed by 1924 to become the most powerful of all. (See Table 6.6.)

From the very beginning, Yasuda Bank had rescued other banks that had fallen into difficulties, turning them into its subsidiaries or merging them with itself or its subsidiaries. In 1923 Yasuda Bank had twenty-two subsidiary banks.[43] After the death of Yasuda Zenjirō in 1921, Yūki Toyotarō led the Yasuda Hozensha in a deliberate policy of strengthening Yasuda Bank by having it merge with ten of the subsidiary banks. The first step, in May 1923, was the establishment of Hozen Bank, capitalized at ¥150 million (¥92.5 million paid in). That

TABLE 6.6   The Four Major Zaibatsu Banks: Deposits, Loans, and Securities Owned, 1919–29 (in million yen)

Bank	1919		1924		1929	
Mitsui						
Deposits	351		409		660	
Loans	298		324		454	
Securities	38	(7)	118	(40)	234	(87)
Mitsubishi						
Deposits	234		303		600	
Loans	209		189		279	
Securities	27	(2)	83	(10)	361	(168)
Sumitomo						
Deposits	348		377		663	
Loans	262		253		409	
Securities	45		109	(17)	233	(95)
Yasuda						
Deposits	129		573		658	
Loans	119		506		485	
Securities	30		160	(44)	246	(75)
Subtotal (A)						
Deposits	1,062		1,662		2,581	
Loans	888		1,272		1,627	
Securities	139		470	(111)	1,074	(425)
All banks in Japan (B)						
Deposits	9,918		11,066		12,523	
Loans	9,952		12,489		11,802	
Securities	848	(138)	1,880	(422)	4,219	(1,479)
A/B (%)						
Deposits	10.7		15.0		20.6	
Loans	8.9		10.2		13.8	
Securities	16.3		25.0	(26.3)	25.5	(28.7)

SOURCES: Compiled and calculated from histories of the various banks.
NOTE: Figures in parentheses denote domestic corporate bonds.

November, Hozen Bank absorbed Yasuda Bank and the ten subsidiaries; the resulting entity was named Yasuda Bank.[44]

The merger of the eleven banks was the Yasuda zaibatsu's ambitious response to the marked postwar trend among major banks towards a larger scale. The 1920 revision of the banking laws, which facilitated mergers between banks with the goal of helping them to strengthen operations, was an additional factor. The Hozensha also sought through the merger to begin to unify the management of Yasuda Bank's subsidiaries. The merger of the eleven banks was the first step in that direction. Additional mergers to consolidate all the subsidiary banks into a single bank were considered but not fully carried out. The new Yasuda Bank took on almost all the offices of the banks it had absorbed as branches and sub-branches; they totaled 209. In terms of deposits, loans, and securities owned, Yasuda Bank shot to the top of the Japanese banking world.

AGGRESSIVE POLICIES OF THE BANKS OF MITSUI, MITSUBISHI, AND SUMITOMO. The other three big zaibatsu banks did not simply sit back and watch Yasuda's dramatic rise. Mitsui Bank, for instance, had anticipated the slackening of economic growth and intensifying of competition after the war and in July 1919 had increased its capital from ¥20 million to ¥100 million in an effort to strengthen itself. Of the 800,000 new shares, the bank had offered 300,000 to the public. Sumitomo Bank had carried out a capital increase even earlier, raising its capitalization from ¥15 million to ¥30 million in June 1917. Of the 150,000 new shares, 30,000 had been sold in a public offering. Mitsubishi Bank was a late entrant, having been founded in 1919. It did not carry out a capital increase until 1929, when it hiked its capitalization from ¥50 million to ¥100 million, offering 235,000 of the 500,000 new shares to the public.[45]

The decisions of the three major zaibatsu banks to carry out huge capital increases are understandable, but why they chose to offer shares to the public is more difficult to explain. Undoubtedly one important reason was the insistence of the top salaried managers at each zaibatsu that the zaibatsu eliminate the common impression that its bank was the private possession of the zaibatsu or zaibatsu family. Among the major zaibatsu the top salaried managers won this point over the opposition of the family.

The Mitsui, Mitsubishi, and Sumitomo banks also worked to increase the number of overseas branches and to strengthen their foreign exchange operations. Table 6.7 makes clear the enormous expansion and scale of the Mitsui and Mitsubishi banks' foreign exchange business and highlights Sumitomo Bank's stagnation in this area. Sumitomo

TABLE 6.7   Total Volume of Foreign Exchange Transactions of Three Major Zaibatsu Banks, 1919, 1925, and 1931 (in million yen)

Year	Mitsui Bank	Mitsubishi Bank	Sumitomo Bank
1919	442	65*	534
1925	2,852	983	814
1931	2,873	1,400	486

SOURCE: Compiled from histories of the various banks.
* For the second half of the year only.

Bank's failure to expand its foreign exchange dealings is attributable to the lack of a trading company within the Sumitomo zaibatsu.

The three banks also invested energy in expanding the underwriting of corporate bonds. The dramatic increase in the total value of corporate bonds held by Mitsubishi Bank is particularly impressive (Table 6.6.). The banks of the huge zaibatsu held vast sums on deposit from the zaibatsu head office and its subsidiaries, laying aside sums from outside customers. Zaibatsu policy, however, discouraged lending within the zaibatsu. Moreover, some subsidiaries had grown so powerful that they no longer needed to borrow from banks, for instance, Mitsui Mining after the mid-1900s and Mitsui Bussan after World War I. Thus, in the postwar stagnation period the major zaibatsu banks suffered an embarrassment of idle funds and a shortage of ways to invest them. Underwriting corporate bonds was developed as a profitable alternative. Initially the banks handled domestic corporate bonds but later moved increasingly into foreign bonds. In the case of Mitsui Bank, the overwhelming majority of its long-term borrowers and the companies for which it underwrote corporate bonds were electric power companies; electric railways were next in importance. It also underwrote many local government bonds.[46]

The Mitsubishi and Sumitomo banks had the same problem of idle funds, but they did not stop increasing the number of their branches or welcoming deposits from the public. Mitsubishi Bank in 1919 had eight branches within Japan; in 1929 it had twenty. In the same period, Sumitomo Bank increased the number of its branches from twenty-eight to sixty-nine. Yasuda Bank was exceptional in this regard; through its huge merger, the number of branches grew in the same period from 22 to 153. Mitsui Bank was alone in not expanding the number of its domestic branches, adding only one new branch during these years, for a total of nineteen.[47] Mitsui Bank's relatively poor performance in the post-World War II period of economic recovery and growth (a trend based on popular savings) as compared with the Fuji (formerly Yasuda), Mitsubishi, and Sumitomo banks stemmed in part from its prewar refusal to court deposits from the public.

Asano, Furukawa, and Fujita Zaibatsu Banks

Compared with the rapid expansion of the banking operations of the four major zaibatsu, the lesser zaibatsu that had rushed to enter banking during World War I ended with wretched results. As the postwar slump began, Asano Chūya Bank found its deposits declining and its assets tied up in loans to the Asano subsidiaries. The resultant squeeze produced a sharp drop in returns. Yasuda Zenjirō had lectured Asano

Sōichirō on the dangers of combining the running of a bank with that of other businesses, and Sōichirō had determined to hand the Asano Chūya Bank to the Yasuda family. Zenjirō's death in 1921, however, interrupted the transfer negotiations. Finally, through the mediation of the Bank of Japan, the Asano zaibatsu turned its bank over to the Hozensha in 1922.[48]

The Furukawa Bank also suffered worsening business results owing to the postwar slump and the collapse of Furukawa Trading. Even after surviving the crisis with the aid of the Daiichi Ginkō (First Bank), operations continued to stagnate. Although the bank increased its capital in 1924 from ¥5 million to ¥10 million (of which ¥6.25 million was paid in), loans never exceeded the 1919 figure and deposits did only once, in the latter half of 1926. In the financial panic of 1927, Furukawa Bank, with the cooperation of the entire Furukawa zaibatsu, barely managed to avert a suspension of operations. Finally the Furukawa zaibatsu decided to withdraw from the banking business. After its bank failed to reach a merger agreement with the Daiichi Bank in 1931, the zaibatsu dissolved Furukawa Bank, leaving the head office, five branches, and the deposits and loans of two other branches to the Daiichi Bank and five branches to the Tokyo Chochiku Bank.[49]

Fujita Bank was also hard hit by the postwar recession and went bankrupt in 1928 immediately after the financial panic. Fujita Bank was a joint-stock company with limited liability, but Fujita-gumi had repeatedly stated that it bore unlimited liability toward its bank. Accordingly, Fujita-gumi put up its entire business assets as security for ¥90 million in special credit from the Bank of Japan, used those funds to cancel the loss to depositors, and then liquidated the bank. The deposits and loans were taken over by several banks, including the 34th Bank and Yamaguchi Bank, both forerunners of the present-day Sanwa Bank. The huge loans taken out by the Fujita zaibatsu resulted in its being placed under the control of the Bank of Japan.[50]

Entering New Fields of Finance

THE TRUST BUSINESS. Besides expanding their banking operations, the four major zaibatsu also moved into new financial fields, particularly the trust and life insurance businesses. Under the 1922 Trust Law and Trust Business Law, the government instituted a licensing system for the trust industry and set a minimum of ¥1 million in capital for trust companies with an eye to cleaning up the many shaky and small-scale trust enterprises then in operation. While the government was in the process of preparing the two laws, the four major zaibatsu began research with the idea of setting up trust companies and concluded that larger firms would be in a position of strength. After the two laws went into effect the four zaibatsu moved into the trust industry, each setting up a trust company by spinning off the trust department of its bank and receiving government licensing.[51] Mitsui established its trust company in 1924, Yasuda and Sumitomo in 1925, and Mitsubishi in 1927.

Among the big four the Yasuda zaibatsu displayed idiosyncratic behavior. Initially, Yūki Toyotarō, executive director of the Hozensha, approved of a plan for all the zaibatsu to set up a single trust company by merger, as proposed by Shidachi Tetsujirō, president of Nippon Kōgyō Bank (Nippon Industrial Bank) and a former Sumitomo officer. Consequently, Yasuda at first did not attempt to set up its own trust company. In response to the actions of the other zaibatsu, however, it finally did establish such a company, but without using the Yasuda name. The new firm, Kyōsai Shintaku (Kyōsai Trust), had its head office in Osaka, and Hamazaki Sadakichi, who had been a Sumitomo executive, became the top manager. Yūki disliked the narrow point of view that stressed Yasuda's profits alone, an attitude that earned him opposition from within the Yasuda zaibatsu. Probably due to internal zaibatsu demands the name of the trust company was changed in less than a year from Kyōsai Trust to Yasuda Trust, and its headquarters were moved to Tokyo in 1933.

In each of the new trust companies set up by the big zaibatsu banks, the top management consisted of bank officers. Among them, Yoneyama Umekichi, executive director of Mitsui Bank, had been devoted to the idea of starting a trust business. He became Mitsui Trust's leading light, serving as president until 1934 and then as chairman until 1936. The trust companies of the four major zaibatsu developed rapidly and soon had a secure lead in the trust industry (Table 6.8). Among them, Mitsui Trust stood preeminent.

LIFE INSURANCE. The Yasuda and Mitsubishi zaibatsu were early entrants into the life insurance field. Yasuda had Kyōsai Seimei (Kyōsai Life, renamed Yasuda Seimei in 1929), and Mitsubishi had Meiji Seimei, founded as an ordinary subsidiary with capital participation from the Iwasaki family. In the postwar period, Sumitomo and Mitsui also entered the field by buying existing life insurance companies that had been adversely affected by the postwar slump. Sumitomo, Ltd., acquired Hinode Seimei (Sunrise Life Insurance, founded in 1907) in 1925 and renamed it Sumitomo Seimei (Sumitomo Life Insurance) the following year. Mitsui Gōmei bought Takasago Seimei (founded in 1914) in 1926 and changed its name to Mitsui Seimei (Mitsui Life Insurance) the following year. The two companies were simply put under the zaibatsu umbrella without significant reorganization, and they continued to do poorly.[52]

TABLE 6.8 Capital and Business Results of the Four Major Trust Companies, November 1931

Trust company	Authorized capital (thousand yen)	Paid-in capital (thousand yen)	Reserves (thousand yen)	Net profits (first semester) (thousand yen)	Profit rate (%)	Dividend rate (%)
Mitsui	30,000	7,500	7,439	705	18.8	7.0
Mitsubishi	30,000	7,500	1,864	266	7.1	5.0
Yasuda	30,000	7,500	2,775	301	8.0	5.0
Sumitomo	20,000	5,000	2,965	277	11.1	5.0
Subtotal (A)	110,000	27,500	15,043	1,549		
All trust companies (B)	288,500	81,450	23,148	3,004		
A/B	38.1%	33.8%	65.0%	51.6%		

SOURCE: *Mitsui Shintaku Ginkō 50-nen shi* (50 Years of Mitsui Trust Company) (Tokyo: Mitsui Trust Bank, 1974), p. 26.

Two other zaibatsu life insurance companies were Teikoku Seimei of Furukawa and Kyōho Seimei, which originated within the old Kuhara zaibatsu before being transferred to the Tokyo Fujita family and then to the Nomura family. Data on the six life insurance companies described are presented in Table 6.9. The contract figures for Mitsui Life and Sumitomo Life, both latecomers in the insurance industry, show these two companies lagging far behind Meiji and Kyōsai.

Significance of the Zaibatsu Financial Enterprises

The major zaibatsu had stringent restraints on zaibatsu use of funds on deposit in their banks from outside sources. Initially, such restraints existed as policy only and were difficult to put into practice, but from around 1905 the zaibatsu began to observe the policy. In the case of the Mitsui-designated subsidiaries (corporations in which Mitsui Gōmei owned almost all the stock), Mitsui Mining ceased from the late 1900s to receive long-term lending from Mitsui Bank.[53] Mitsui Bussan greatly reduced its dependency on loans from Mitsui Bank after World War I.[54] The Mitsui ordinary subsidiaries (corporations in which Mitsui Gōmei owned large amounts of stock) also reduced their borrowings from Mitsui Bank, as did the subsidiaries of the Mitsui-designated subsidiaries. Data from 1934 are available for nine Mitsui affiliates that were either subsidiaries of designated subsidiaries or ordinary subsidiaries: Hokkaido Colliery, Denki Kagaku (Electrochemical), Dai Nippon Celluloid, Ōji Paper, Onoda Cement, Tōyō Cotton Trading, Kanegafuchi Cotton Spinning, Taiwan Sugar, and Mitsukoshi, Ltd. Of these, only Ōji Paper and Tōyō Cotton had loans from Mitsui Bank. Moreover, Mitsui Bank loans accounted for only 4.3 percent of the total borrowings of Ōji Paper and only 0.3 percent of those of Tōyō Cotton.[55] This meant not that Mitsui Bussan and the ordinary subsidiaries did not need to borrow but rather that they depended on loans from banks other than Mitsui.

Similarly, both Mitsubishi and Sumitomo closely limited internal use of their banks' deposits. In the 1920s and 1930s Mitsubishi did have some enterprises, such as Mitsubishi Trading Company, with a high degree of dependency on Mitsubishi Bank loans. But the Mitsubishi head office adopted a policy of minimizing lending by its bank to Mitsubishi subsidiaries.[56] Consequently, the Mitsubishi subsidiaries generally did not have a high degree of dependency on Mitsubishi Bank until about 1937, when heavy demand for capital was generated by the expansion of production capacity to supply the military.

Mitsubishi Bank underwrote corporate bonds for only two Mitsubishi subsidiaries, Mitsubishi Shipbuilding and Engineering (¥10 mil-

TABLE 6.9 Zaibatsu Life Insurance Companies in 1928

Company	Paid-in capital (thousand yen)	Total value of contracts (thousand yen)	Reserves (thousand yen)	Number of branches	Zaibatsu capital participation as % of total capital
Meiji Life	2,000 (all)	638,008	114,519	15	36.8, Iwasaki Hisaya family
Kyōsai (Yasuda) Life	300 (75)	302,101	56,930	16	Almost 100, Yasuda Hozensha and Yasuda families
Mitsui Life	2,000 (500)	80,025	7,306	37	52, Mitsui Gōmei
Sumitomo Life	1,500 (217)	74,441	10,118	13	Almost 100, Sumitomo, Ltd. and Sumitomo family
Teikoku Life	1,000 (all)	426,073	93,296	23	42.2, Furukawa Gōmei
Kyōho Seimei	1,000 (400)	170,798	34,289	20	52.8, Fujita Masasuke family
All life insurance companies	48,700 (23,217)	6,540,095			

SOURCE: Compiled from Jitsugyō no Seikai-sha, *Meiji Taishō-shi* (History of Meiji and Taishō) (Tokyo, 1930) vol. 10.
NOTE: Parentheses indicate paid-in capital.

TABLE 6.10   Borrowing by Mitsubishi Subsidiaries, 1918–36 (in thousand yen)

Year	Loans	Notes payable	Overdrafts	Bills discounted
1918	24,849	24,190	1,512	—
1919	24,900	46,784	2,244	—
1920	19,709	43,948	1,079	—
1921	25,320	48,776	205	—
1922	13,415	48,533	595	—
1923	3,871	59,465	4,827	—
1924	6,323	83,594	7,363	—
1925	6,666	73,198	10,804	44
1926	5,629	69,928	8,449	73
1927	5,837	75,848	17,930	105
1928	1,275	61,961	12,683	62
1929	14,357	56,089	7,447	10,253
1930	15,819	55,316	1,859	9,810
1931	13,549	57,357	602	7,336
1932	18,864	64,596	1,274	9,461
1933	18,855	69,645	730	12,181
1934	8,504	72,438	979	7,287
1935	8,652	100,547	1,164	11,797
1936	11,368	106,208	1,998	14,908

SOURCE: Asajima Shōichi, "Daiichiji taisen go no Mitsubishi zaibatsu no kin'yū" (The Finances of the Mitsubishi Zaibatsu after World War I), in *Shakai Kagaku Nenpō* (1985): 98, 101, 103.

lion, issued between 1918 and 1927) and Mitsubishi Warehouse and Transportation (¥5 million, issued between 1928 and 1936). Borrowings by Mitsubishi subsidiaries peaked in 1921, then declined until 1929, when they began to rise again but without reaching the earlier peak. (See Table 6.10.) Even if these sums could have all been borrowed from Mitsubishi Bank and Mitsubishi Trust, "loans did not play a great role among the funding methods of the Mitsubishi zaibatsu as a whole."[57]

Notes payable, overdrafts, and discounted bills rather than loans served as principal means of debt financing at Mitsubishi. Again, these were not all credit facilities extended by Mitsubishi Bank and Mitsubishi Trust, but even if we suppose that most of them were, only Mitsubishi Trading Company relied heavily on any of these methods, with Mitsubishi Iron and Steel having a somewhat smaller dependence on notes payable. Utilization of these instruments by the other Mitsubishi subsidiaries was negligible.[58] In other words, in the Mitsubishi zaibatsu of the interwar period, Mitsubishi Trading Company and Mitsubishi

Iron and Steel were financial encumbrances for which Mitsubishi Bank and Mitsubishi Trust were forced to use a part of their funds within the zaibatsu.

Most of Sumitomo's diversified enterprises were reorganized into joint-stock companies and began to receive financing from Sumitomo Bank and Sumitomo Trust in the 1920s. Until then, the funds required by each enterprise had been provided by Sumitomo Sōhonten.[59] The Sumitomo subsidiaries were rather more dependent upon loans from their own zaibatsu bank and trust company than were their counterparts at either Mitsui or Mitsubishi.[60] Nonetheless, Sumitomo as well observed a policy of keeping lending by Sumitomo Bank within the zaibatsu below a certain level. As Kawada Jun, top manager at the Sumitomo head office, recalled, "People might wonder whether Sumitomo Bank gave a great deal of credit to the Sumitomo enterprises. It certainly did not. The bank would not readily lend to other Sumitomo subsidiaries even if they provided sound security. There were strict limits setting the percentage of total lending that could go to Sumitomo-related firms, and those were firmly adhered to. That is why people had such trust in the bank."[61]

VICISSITUDES OF THE ZAIBATSU TRADING COMPANIES

Many trading companies went bankrupt in the recession that followed World War I, among them such zaibatsu-related firms as Furukawa Trading, Kuhara Trading, Murai Bōeki, and Daitō Bussan. Some non-zaibatsu family-owned enterprises also failed, including the Mogi, Masuda, Abe, and Yuasa trading companies, and, after the Great Kantō Earthquake, Takada Shōkai.

Table 6.11 presents a comparison of the financial strength of the major trading companies in the latter half of 1925, after they had survived the immediate postwar slump. The overwhelming strength of Mitsui Bussan is obvious; its net worth far exceeded that of any of its competitors and surpassed its indebtedness. Suzuki Shōten and Nippon Cotton Trading followed Mitsui Bussan in terms of net worth, but their excess indebtedness is striking. Mitsubishi Trading Company's small scale and large indebtedness are also noteworthy. The trading companies continued to experience a variety of ups and downs. Mitsui Bussan went on to increase its strength even further while Mitsubishi Trading Company tried to catch up with it. On the other hand, Suzuki Shōten collapsed in the financial panic of 1927.

TABLE 6.11 Net Worth and Indebtedness of the Major Trading Companies, second half of 1925 (in thousand yen)

Company	Paid-in capital	Reserves	Net profits[a]	Total (net worth)	Indebtedness[b]
Mitsui Bussan	100,000	32,800	8,835	141,635	127,589
Suzuki Shōten	50,000	9,690	6,240	65,930	98,282
Nippon Cotton Trading	26,000	20,600	3,084	49,684	85,768
Gōshō	20,000	1,300	1,200	22,500	NA
Tōyō Cotton Trading	15,000	4,250	3,574	22,824	NA
Mitsubishi Trading	15,000	4,025	589	19,614	51,528
Ōkura & Co.	8,000	3,155	654	11,809	2,211
Iwai Trading	7,000	566	1,325	8,891	14,132
C. Itoh & Co.	7,000	—	1,137	8,137	7,605
Itoman & Co.	5,000	1,657	1,185	7,842	1,483

SOURCE: *Kōhon Mitsui Bussan Kabushiki Kaisha 100-nen shi* (100 Years of Mitsui Bussan) (Tokyo: Japan Business History Institute, 1978) vol. 1, p. 427.
[a] Brought forward and for the current period.
[b] Loans, notes payable, etc.

Mitsui Bussan and Mitsubishi Trading

Mitsui Bussan spun off its cotton-trading division in 1920 as Tōyō Cotton Trading, capitalized at ¥25 million, half of which was paid in. Mitsui Bussan held 90 percent of the stock, with the remaining 10 percent distributed among employees and others. The long-established cotton-trading division had handled the largest of Bussan's commodity specialties, namely, raw cotton and cotton textiles. Cotton transactions were speculative and remarkably large volumes were dealt in—thus independence helped the enterprise to retain its maneuverability.

Mitsui Bussan's trading volume temporarily declined after World War I, due to the postwar recession and the spin-off of Tōyō Cotton Trading (Table 6.12). It bottomed out, however, at ¥814 million in 1921 and recovered steadily from then on. Volume fell again at the height of the depression in 1930–31, but Mitsui Bussan did not incur losses. Remarkably, during that period the ratio of profits to paid-in capital was consistently on the order of 10 percent. Mitsui Bussan was the only one of the major trading companies to enjoy such stability; the others suffered drastic fluctuations in their profit ratios.[62]

The wealth of funds that Mitsui Bussan had been able to accumulate

TABLE 6.12   Trading Volumes and Net Profits of Mitsui Bussan and Mitsubishi Trading Company, 1919–31 (in thousand yen)

Year	Mitsui Bussan		Mitsubishi Trading Company	
	Transaction volume	Net profits	Transaction volume	Net profits
1919	2,130,270	19,864	100,123	876
1920	1,921,010	16,395	89,529	964
1921	813,970	6,718	118,592	−1,629
1922	865,162	11,121	202,329	1,791
1923	882,934	10,164	250,140	1,963
1924	1,035,510	14,177	309,244	1,988
1925	1,141,729	16,226	341,071	953
1926	1,181,824	20,766	315,034	1,230
1927	1,167,520	15,573	401,881	1,836
1928	1,265,045	17,652	462,285	2,923
1929	1,323,980	17,558	439,145	386
1930	1,080,547	13,582	347,044	389
1931	841,731	11,637	278,164	−1,794

SOURCES: Compiled from *Kōhon Mitsui Bussan Kabushiki Kaisha 100-nen shi* (100 Years of Mitsui Bussan) (Tokyo: Japan Business History Institute, 1978), vol. 1, pp. 449, 544; *Ritsugyō bōeki roku* (Records of the Enterprises and Trade of the Mitsubishi Trading Co.) (Tokyo: Mitsubishi Shōji Kabushiki Kaisha, 1958), p. 947.

by successfully applying the brakes toward the end of the war, in order to avoid losses in the postwar slump, was partly responsible for the firm's steady development. The know-how built up through years of experience in international trade was another factor, but the appropriateness of its postwar managerial strategies also played a very large part. The top management in June 1921 instructed branch managers in sound but aggressive business strategies, and the next year the management called for "moderate activism." Yamazaki Hiroaki has summarized the content of this program as follows: to stress new inventions and projects and invest in facilities; to advance into regional markets within Japan and work together with cooperative associations there; and to engage in trade between foreign countries or in third-country trade.[63] Such policies fitted well the changes in the economic environment and took advantage of Mitsui Bussan's distinctive trading knowledge and skills. Moreover, they were extremely effective in enabling Mitsui Bussan to win out in the fierce competition among trading companies without resorting to speculative measures.

The first policy, that calling for new projects and investments, represented a response to the development of heavy industries after the war and led to such actions as the direct management of the shipbuilding division and of Tōyō Rayon, as well as the search for technology to produce synthetic ammonium sulphate. Another result was the signing of exclusive sales contracts with carefully selected manufacturers in several promising but not yet mature heavy industries, such as Nakajima Hikōki Seisakusho (Nakajima Aircraft Company),[64] with which a contract was signed in 1923.

The best example of Mitsui Bussan's policy to enter domestic regional markets was its program of trade in chicken eggs and bulk sales of imported chicken feed, based on organizing the poultry farmers beginning in 1925.[65] Mitsui Bussan has since been accused of profiting by exploiting poultry farmers, a criticism that deliberately ignores Bussan's contribution to the development of poultry farming and farm incomes. Bussan also advanced into regional markets through the woolen textile industry in western Aichi Prefecture, where it dealt in woolen yarn. By providing capital and technical information to the weavers, Bussan built up many of the area's manufacturers of high-quality men's suiting.[66]

With regard to the third policy, the percentage of Mitsui Bussan's total trading volume accounted for by third-country trade reached a postwar peak of 33.5 percent in 1919, then gradually declined to 20.2 percent in 1929. The decline stemmed from the trading company's growing involvement in regional markets within Japan and the consequent increase in the share of Bussan's total trade held by domestic business. From 1919 to 1929 domestic trade rose from 24.5 to 35.2 percent of Mitsui Bussan's total trading volume.[67] Despite its relative decline in overall foreign trade, however, Mitsui Bussan's distinctive strategic weapon was third-country trade. Mitsui Bussan accounted for 40 percent of all third-country trade conducted by Japanese trading companies in 1930. If cotton-related transactions are excluded, Mitsui Bussan had a 55 percent share.[68]

Such activist, innovative policies ultimately resulted in the remarkable business performance shown in Table 6.12. Mitsui Bussan's ability to minimize the adverse impact of the depression in 1929–31 was particularly significant. Although lower in those years, its performance was still amazing: the company maintained a trading volume of about ¥1 billion and recorded annual profits of more than ¥10 million.

The interwar experience of Mitsubishi Trading Company presents a sharp contrast to that of Mitsui Bussan. As a later entrant, Mitsubishi Trading grew by trying to catch up with Mitsui Bussan. In the period from World War I to 1935, however, Mitsubishi Trading was characterized by a limited range and scale of operations, low profitability, and unstable performance. The relatively limited scope of its operations can be seen, for instance, in the number of product-defined divisions and overseas branches existing as of 1926: seven product divisions specialized respectively in metals, machinery, fuels, general merchandise, foodstuffs, fertilizers and cereals, and shipping,[69] and overseas three branches, eleven sub-branches, and eight agents had been established (branches: Shanghai, Hong Kong, and London; sub-branches: Hankou, Beijing, Qingdao, Seoul, Singapore, Surabaya, Paris, Berlin, Seattle, San Francisco, and New York; agents: Jinan, Fengtian, Tianjin, Dalian, Harbin, Taibei, Calcutta, and Sydney[70]). In the same year Mitsui Bussan had nine product divisions handling respectively sugar, coal, machinery, metals, lumber, fertilizers and cereals, raw silk, shipping, and sales, with the sales division covering general merchandise, wool, pharmaceuticals, and foodstuffs. Bussan also had seventeen overseas branches, ten sub-branches, eight agents, and twenty-one substations.[71]

An additional gap between Mitsubishi Trading Company and Mitsui Bussan existed in terms of scale of operations, as the trading columns presented in Table 6.12 make clear. The trading volume of Mitsubishi Trading did not reach even half that of Mitsui Bussan until 1936. The disparity in profits was even greater; Mitsubishi Trading Company's profits failed to amount to 20 percent those of Mitsui Bussan at any time during these years.

The instability of Mitsubishi Trading Company's performance is reflected in its frequent suspension of dividend payments. It did not pay a dividend in seventeen of the thirty semesters from its founding to the first half of 1932. (Suspensions occurred from the latter half of 1919 to the first half of 1922, in both semesters of 1925, in the latter half of 1926, and from the latter half of 1928 to the first half of 1932.) Moreover, except for the years during World War I, the dividend never reached 10 percent. By contrast, Mitsui Bussan failed to pay a dividend only once in this period (in the latter half of 1921), and the dividends were usually on the order of 10 percent.

The situation would begin to change, however, in the 1930s. Mitsubishi Trading had since its founding emphasized dealings in machinery and imports of foreign technology; machinery transactions accounted for about the same proportion of its total trading volume as they did at Mitsui Bussan. This expertise would enable Mitsubishi Trading to compete effectively with Mitsui Bussan during the wartime period beginning in the early 1930s.

Ups and Downs in the Zaibatsu Shipping Business

During World War I the zaibatsu were stimulated by the shortage of bottoms and high shipping rates to strengthen their shipping enterprises by buying vessels or building new ones. The consequently serious blow dealt by the postwar recession cast into sharp relief the strength of the Mitsui Bussan shipping division, which succeeded in weathering the slump, and the Asano, Suzuki, Matsukata, and Kuhara shipping operations, which could not overcome the damage caused by the recession.

The vigorous activities of Mitsui Bussan's shipping division were striking even in comparison with the trading company's other postwar operations. Moreover, it is of great interest that the shipping division's innovative and expansionary activities were supported, as were Mitsui Bussan's operations as a whole, by sound strategies based on anticipation of changes in the business climate. The shipping division became the war's largest ship operator by chartering bottoms. Quickly anticipating a postwar shipping slump, however, it reduced the number of its regular charters, a prudent decision that enabled Mitsui Bussan to avoid the damage suffered by the other zaibatsu's shipping enterprises. The shipping division was more than just prudent, however. It recognized that, with the recession-related reduction in cargoes, business would be limited should reliance be placed solely on the unscheduled lines, which typically carried cargoes for Mitsui Bussan. Thus, the division boldly initiated scheduled lines, opening routes to Seattle and Bangkok.[72]

The success of this venture was assured because Mitsui Bussan seized the lead over its competitors in the use of large, high-speed diesel-powered ships. Bussan aggressively acquired a series of the ships through the Mitsui Bussan shipbuilding division or importation.[73] Between 1919 and 1929 its operating tonnage jumped from 2,690,000 tons gross, including chartered vessels (its own vessels totaling 810,000 tons), to 5,390,000 tons gross (own vessels, 1,140,000 tons).[74] By the mid-1930s its strength rivaled that of NYK and OSK. The successful shipping division was spun off as Mitsui Senpaku (Mitsui Shipping) in 1942.

The Oriental Steamship Company of the Asano zaibatsu, on the other hand, suffered a major failure. The fatal blow was delivered by Asano Sōichirō's erroneous decision to build eleven new large ships in the midst of the postwar drop in shipping rates. The burden of loans from the Yasuda Bank totaling some ¥32 million in 1926 for the construction of the new ships compounded the problem of the drop in rates, and the company ran in the red from 1922 to 1926. The losses brought forward had reached about ¥17 million by 1926, when the operation of the firm's San Francisco and South American scheduled routes and the nine ships that sailed them were transferred to NYK. The company then shifted to operating cargo ships and oil tankers. Of the dividends on the NYK stock it had received in the deal, and of the profits earned by its ten remaining ships, half went for debt repayment to Yasuda Bank. Moreover, to wipe out its losses brought forward it was forced to reduce its capital from ¥32.5 million to ¥8.125 million.[75]

The shipping operations of Suzuki Shōten and the Matsukata family's Kawasaki group were also hard hit by the postwar recession. At the end of the war Suzuki Shōten, Kawasaki Shipbuilding Company, and Kawasaki Steamship Company, which Kawasaki Shipbuilding had founded to operate the stock boats it mass-produced, were left with an excess of ships. They (as the central actors) and other owners of excess tonnage (including Asano Shipbuilding and Nippon Steamship of the Kuhara zaibatsu) therefore joined in 1919 to form Kokusai Kisen Kaisha (International Steamship Company), to which they transferred surplus ships totaling about 500,000 tons. The new company also received financing from the government and was capitalized at ¥100 million. Kokusai Kisen began operating shipping lines between other countries, but it suffered from poor business results and was finally absorbed by OSK in 1937.

The Failure of Suzuki Shōten

Before Suzuki Shōten had recovered from the postwar recession, it was confronted with a downturn in business at two of its subsidiaries, Kobe Steel and Harima Zōsen (Harima Shipyard), owing to disarmament and the shipping slump. The persistent poor performance of Suzuki's manufacturing sector, which the firm had long worked to expand and diversify, presented a difficult burden. Then Suzuki Shōten was hit by a series of disasters: the Great Kantō Earthquake, the recording of huge losses by its Dalian branch in soybean transactions, and the 1924 collapse of the foreign exchange rate.[76]

Suzuki Shōten became increasingly dependent on credit from the Bank of Taiwan to find a way out of its predicament. After the Sino-Japanese War of 1894–95 Taiwan had become a Japanese colony under the rule of a governor-general, with whose support Suzuki Shōten began to trade in Taiwanese camphor oil and entered into an intimate financial relationship with the Bank of Taiwan. The bank stepped up financing of Suzuki Shōten in the early 1920s but also intervened in its management by such means as assigning directors. The 1923 reorganization of Suzuki Shōten, whereby its trading business was spun off as a joint-stock company, was the result of Bank of Taiwan intervention.

The Bank of Taiwan loans continued to swell ominously (Table 6.13), eventually totaling ¥378 million, more than seven times Suzuki Shōten's paid-in capital of ¥50 million. Far from escaping its difficulties, Suzuki Shōten was hard-pressed to make interest payments. On its side, the Bank of Taiwan had tied up two-thirds of its total loans in advances to Suzuki Shōten and was suffering a deterioration of its liquidity position. To make matters worse, financial panic broke out in March 1927. The Bank of Taiwan found its supply of call money from Mitsui and other major banks cut off; an appeal to the Bank of Japan for emergency funds was refused. On the brink of failure, the bank took

TABLE 6.13   Suzuki Shōten: Loans Outstanding from the Bank of Taiwan, 1920–27 (in thousand yen)

Year*	Loans outstanding
1920	80,811
1921	123,719
1922	179,036
1923	226,906
1924	276,051
1925	313,275
1926	356,857
1927	378,859

SOURCE: *Taiwan Ginkō-shi* (History of the Bank of Taiwan) (Tokyo: Nihon Bōeki Shinyō Kabushiki Kaisha, 1964).
*End of year except as of March for 1927.

steps to terminate lending to Suzuki Shōten, and the collapse of the zaibatsu was precipitated.

The eventual downfall of Suzuki Shōten does not in any way negate its achievements. Its fierce entrepreneurial spirit in attempting to overtake Mitsui and Mitsubishi and the passion it poured into developing diversified industries contribute a forceful page in Japanese business history. Furthermore, its subsidiary firms continued at the forefront of Japanese industry, and many are major corporations today: Kobe Steel; Teijin; Hōnen Oil; Nippon Flour Mills; Harima Shipyard, now part of Ishikawajima-Harima Heavy Industries; Claude-Process Nitrogen Industries, absorbed by Tōyō High Pressure; Asahi Petroleum, which merged into what is now Shōwa Shell Petroleum, and Nisshō, a trading company founded in 1928 by former employees of Suzuki Shōten in order to inherit its trading rights, now merged into Nisshō-Iwai.

SUMMARY

The earnings records of the zaibatsu head offices in the interwar period are shown in Table 6.14. Among these, the enormous profits and stable performance of Mitsui's head office were remarkable. With effective investment of the great financial resources it had built up during the war, Mitsui established a highly competitive position in a wide range of new fields, including chemicals, rayon, shipbuilding, shipping, and insurance, in addition to its standbys of banking, trading, and mining. Mitsui thereby retained the number one position among zaibatsu.

Mitsubishi suffered much greater constraints on its interwar development than did Mitsui. The losses posted by Mitsubishi Trading Company during the postwar recession and stagnation of mining and shipbuilding meant that, when the capital increases for Mitsubishi Mining and Mitsubishi Bank were carried out, the head office was unable to take on all the new shares. Nonetheless, advantaged by a diversified business base built up over many years, Mitsubishi managed to maintain the number two position.

The Yasuda head office performed relatively well during the interwar years while pursuing a strategy that was unique among the zaibatsu. After World War I Yasuda abandoned its nonfinancial enterprises—sulphur mining, warehousing, fertilizer production, machinery manufacture, and shipping. Instead, based on its bank mergers it developed into a huge zaibatsu with a distinctive financial specialization. As a result of the great merger of 1923, the profits of Yasuda Bank rose from ¥2.6 million at the end of 1922 to ¥11.8 million at the end of 1923. The merger gave Yasuda a strengthened source of revenues and helped

TABLE 6.14　Net Profits of the Zaibatsu Head Offices, 1919–31 (in thousand yen)

Year	Mitsui Gōmei	Mitsubishi, Ltd.	Sumitomo, Ltd. (est. in 1921)	Yasuda Hozensha	Furukawa Gōmei	Gōmei Kaisha Ōkura-gumi	Asano Dōzoku
1919	71,971	25,367	—	2,012	1,218	NA	NA
1920	24,324	1,550	—	1,629	414	NA	104
1921	15,923	1,095	-913	1,024	1,100	NA	NA
1922	22,313	3,996	105	365	-771	NA	NA
1923	12,920	-2,354	-1,411	-2,808	174	20	NA
1924	21,837	7,004	317	3,718	828	964	-162
1925	21,422	7,687	-126	638	-178	892	-277
1926	24,686	6,517	-1,061	673	-403	892	-151
1927	22,142	7,041	1,112	969	-536	898	-1,527
1928	22,664	10,974	1,180	968	35	691	NA
1929	22,787	14,413	3,088	991	103	2	232
1930	18,052	6,438	-441	381	-179	534	NA
1931	14,890	2,344	-388	-76	-1,303	512	NA

SOURCES: Compiled from Matsumoto Hiroshi, *Mitsui zaibatsu no kenkyū* (Studies of Mitsui Zaibatsu) (Tokyo: Yoshikawa Kōbunkan, 1979), pp. 173, 219; Mitsubishi Gōshi Kaisha, ed., *Mitsubishi Sha-shi* (Records of Mitsubishi Company) (Tokyo: University of Tokyo Press, 1981), vols. 30–36; Asajima Shōichi, *Senkan-ki Sumitomo zaibatsu keiei-shi* (Business History of the Sumitomo Zaibatsu during the Interwar Period) (Tokyo: University of Tokyo Press, 1983), p. 434; *Yasuda Hozensha to sono kankei jigyō shi* (History of Yasuda Hozensha and Its Affiliated Enterprises) (Tokyo: Yasuda Fudōsan Kabushiki Kaisha, 1974), pp. 404, 697; Furukawa Kōgyō, *Sōgyō 100-nen shi* (100 Years since the Founding of Furukawa Mining) (Tokyo: Furukawa Kōgyō Kabushiki Kaisha, 1976), pp. 402–403; Nakamura Seishi, "Taishō Shōwa shoki no Ōkura zaibatsu" (Ōkura Zaibatsu in the Taishō and Early Shōwa Eras), in *Keiei Shigaku*, vol. 15, no. 3:65; Kohayagawa Yoichi, "Asano zaibatsu no takakuka to keiei soshiki" (The Diversification and Management Structure of Asano Zaibatsu), in *Keiei Shigaku*, vol. 16, no. 1:59.

secure for it the number three spot among the zaibatsu during the 1920s.

Sumitomo, Furukawa, Fujita, and Kuhara were all zaibatsu that got their start in mining and earned huge profits during the war. A remarkably wide gap opened, however, between Sumitomo, which refrained from moving into international trade during the war, and Furukawa, Fujita, and Kuhara, which unsuccessfully tried their hand at trading and banking. Unlike the other three, Sumitomo also managed to hold on to the huge reserves it had built up during the war, investing them in expansion of its heavy industries and financial division to make up for the stagnation of its mining operations. These differences made Sumitomo's postwar performance decisively superior.

Nonetheless, the profit and loss record of the Sumitomo head office points to a marked instability, compared, for instance, with Yasuda or Ōkura. In particular, from 1921 to 1926 Sumitomo, Ltd., recorded losses in all but two years; in terms of net profits, it surpassed the Yasuda and Ōkura head offices only in 1927–29. Sumitomo, Ltd., directly managed its gold mining, forestry, and sales operations, and so its profit and loss account did not directly reflect the performance of the other Sumitomo enterprises, which were organized as subsidiaries of the head office. Still, the figures suggest that the diversified enterprises built by Sumitomo through investment of its wartime windfall did not demonstrate much profit potential until after 1926.

Among the factors that accounted for the relatively poor performance of Sumitomo in the 1920s as compared to, say, Mitsui or Yasuda were the smaller scale or less developed state of its enterprises. As Asajima Shōichi has noted, "Sumitomo had no trading company comparable to Mitsui Bussan, and its mining enterprises did not have the scale or yield the profits of Mitsui Mining. Apart from Sumitomo Bank, it had no large enterprises that could correspond to Mitsui Bussan, Mitsui Mining, or Mitsui Bank."[77] Sumitomo Bank was outdistanced in financial power by Yasuda Bank starting in 1923. In addition, Sumitomo's subsidiaries included many heavy industrial firms that were still developing and as yet manifested only low profitability, putting Sumitomo at a disadvantage in comparison to Yasuda or Ōkura. Among these firms were Sumitomo Shindō Kōkan (Sumitomo Copper and Steel), Sumitomo Seikōsho (Sumitomo Steel Works), Sumitomo Densen Seizōsho (Sumitomo Electrical Wire), Sumitomo Hiryō Seizōsho (Sumitomo Fertilizer Manufacturing), and Nichibei Ita Glass (Nichibei Sheet Glass). The situation began to change in 1927 owing to Sumitomo's entry into the trust and life insurance businesses and to the increasing vigor of its formerly unstable heavy industries. Sumitomo became number three after Mitsui and Mitsubishi only after surviv-

TABLE 6.15   Net Profits of Ōkura Mining, 1920–32 (in thousand yen)

Year	Total	From domestic coal mining
1920	−23	NA
1921	−24	NA
1922	−170	NA
1923	140	NA
1924	77	64
1925	3	43
1926	−14	51
1927	5	108
1928	−22	−597
1929	−235	−263
1930	−753	−660
1931	−1,027	−551
1932	−1,937	−1,576

SOURCE: Nakamura Seishi, "Taishō Shōwa shoki no Ōkura zaibatsu," (Ōkura Zaibatsu in the Taishō and Early Shōwa Eras), *Keiei Shigaku*, vol. 15, no. 3:58–59.

ing the 1930–31 depression, which was followed by an expanding market for heavy industrial products.

Ōkura zaibatsu's steady performance was meanwhile more apparent than real. Ōkura's trading enterprise escaped damage in the postwar recession and therefore continued to post stable profits. In the head office, however, the ratio of profits to total assets peaked at approximately 3 percent in 1925–28, but in most other years the ratio did not reach even 1 percent.[78] The low profit ratio was the result of Ōkura's investment in a variety of enterprises that fared poorly after the war, including coal mining (see Table 6.15), and of the huge losses run up by its operations on the Asian mainland.[79]

The remaining zaibatsu were hit hard by the postwar recession. Furukawa was hurt by the collapse of its trading company and continued to suffer from the mining slump and its bank's operational difficulties. Yet, as the examples of Fuji Electric and Nippon Light Metal show, Furukawa Electric was making a determined effort even in the face of opposition from the head office to develop heavy industries. Despite the failure of its bank, the Furukawa zaibatsu gained stature in the industrial world. The Asano zaibatsu's development was braked by the temporary losses of its trading firm, the failure of its bank, and the slump in the shipping and shipbuilding industries. For instance, Asano founded Naigai Sekiyu (Naigai Petroleum) in 1921 in an attempt to carry out a long-held plan to refine imported oil, but insufficient funds kept the company from becoming a petroleum industry leader. Asano Bussan eventually recovered from the postwar recession, however, and its cement enterprise remained a stable source of earnings that saved the Asano zaibatsu from collapse.[80] The Fujita zaibatsu received ¥90 million in credit from the Bank of Japan upon the liquidation of its bank, came under the control of the Bank of Japan, and for all intents and purposes collapsed. Similarly the Kuhara family abandoned control of the Kuhara zaibatsu enterprises, and Suzuki Shōten crashed.

CHAPTER 7

THE FAMILY MULTISUBSIDIARY SYSTEM

During the turbulent period spanning World War I and the 1920s, the zaibatsu either adopted or solidified the family multisubsidiary, or *Konzern*, system. Although all of the zaibatsu took on that system, to believe that they became zaibatsu only after doing so is incorrect.[1] The timing of the system's adoption varied; Mitsui and Yasuda instituted it before World War I, the others followed suit during or immediately after the war.

The study of the zaibatsu multisubsidiary system has flourished since before the Second World War,[2] but almost all works have focused on the financial ties among the constituent enterprises or on the concentration of capital and oligopolization. They have not treated such important management-related issues as the nature and degree of control exercised by the head office over the subsidiaries or by the owner family over the salaried managers. Here I will attempt to redress this neglect by surveying the formation of the family multisubsidiary system at each of the ten subject zaibatsu, presenting arguments as to why they all adopted the system, and addressing the issues of control concerning the head office and owner family that accompanied the system's development.

FORMATION OF THE MULTISUBSIDIARY SYSTEM

Mitsui, Mitsubishi, and Sumitomo

MITSUI. Mitsui was the first zaibatsu to convert to the family multi-subsidiary system. The system took shape at Mitsui from 1909 to 1911, but opinions favoring a structural change along those lines had been heard among Mitsui family members and top salaried managers as early as 1893, when the Commercial Code was enacted. Proponents of such change had called for incorporating the department responsible for controlling the zaibatsu subsidiary companies, namely, the Management Department of the Secretariat of the Mitsui Family Council, and for reorganizing the operating subsidiaries into joint-stock companies with limited liability.

The position supporting the proposed changes did not become dominant, however, until a group of family members and salaried managers embarked on a study tour of Europe and the United States from June to November 1906. Led by Masuda Takashi, the group sought advice from members of long-established wealthy families, top managers of corporations and banks, and lawyers. They learned that the limited liability system was in widespread use outside of Japan, and they were advised to turn their enterprises into joint-stock companies and to open stock ownership to the public to obtain earnings from the sale of stock.[3]

Based on these recommendations, in 1908 Masuda presented a written proposal for organizational reform to the Mitsui Family Council. It called for incorporation of the council as an unlimited partnership and for conversion of the Mitsui operating subsidiaries into joint-stock companies. Among the reasons Masuda gave for reorganizing the subsidiaries as joint-stock companies was the advantage to be gained in terms of the Tax Code and the foil it would provide for public criticism of the zaibatsu as closed enterprises.[4] Masuda's proposal received the approval of the Mitsui houses and of Inoue Kaoru; also no objections came from the subsidiaries. The Mitsui zaibatsu thus was launched on an extensive reform of its organization. The resulting structure was to become the model of the family multisubsidiary system in Japan.

As the first step in the reform, on October 11, 1909, the Mitsui houses abolished the Management Department of the Secretariat of the Mitsui Family Council and established Mitsui Gōmei Kaisha, capitalized at ¥50 million, to take over the Management Department's function of controlling the joint enterprises. The heads of the eleven Mitsui houses were the partners in Mitsui Gōmei. Their shares of the total capital were fixed by the Mitsui Family Constitution as follows: the house of Mitsui Hachirōemon Takamine (senior main family), 23 percent; the houses of Mitsui Motonosuke, Mitsui Gen'emon, Mitsui Takayasu, Mitsui Hachirōjirō, and Mitsui Saburōsuke (the five junior branches of the main family), 11.5 percent each; the houses of Mitsui Kiyoko, Mitsui Morinosuke, Mitsui Takenosuke, Mitsui Yōnosuke, and Mitsui Tokuemon (the five associate families), 3.9 percent each.

While the capital participation of each house was set in this manner, the capital of Mitsui Gōmei in fact consisted of the common assets of the House of Mitsui; the heads of the houses could not freely dispose of their shares. Hence, the capital participation figures were merely nominal. Their actual significance was only to serve as the basis for the distribution of Mitsui Gōmei's profits to the eleven houses.

On the same day that Mitsui Gōmei Kaisha was established, Mitsui Bank and Mitsui Bussan, both unlimited partnerships, were reorganized as joint-stock companies capitalized at ¥20 million each. Mitsui Bank's warehouse operation was simultaneously spun off as Tōshin Sōko (Tōshin Warehousing) with a capital of ¥2 million. Mitsui Mining, also an unlimited partnership, became the Mining Division of Mitsui Gōmei.[5]

The decision to locate the mining enterprise within Mitsui Gōmei was based on a plan to have mining, along with forestry and other operations, form a sound resource base for Mitsui Gōmei. It was later judged advantageous, however, to make the mining division independent, and in December 1911 it was accordingly spun off as the joint-stock company Mitsui Kōzan (Mitsui Mining), capitalized at ¥20 million.

These four Mitsui Gōmei subsidiaries—Mitsui Bank, Mitsui Bussan, Mitsui Mining, and Tōshin Warehousing—were joint-stock companies in form, but because their articles of incorporation forbade the free transfer of stock, they were abnormal joint-stock companies. Although, in accordance with the regulations of the Commercial Code, promoters and directors other than Mitsui Gōmei had to be included among the shareholders, the entire stock was the de facto possession of Mitsui Gōmei. Non-Mitsui Gōmei ownership was strictly nominal and resulted from nothing but a name change on Mitsui Gōmei's stock.

Besides owning all the shares in these four subsidiaries, Mitsui Gōmei also exercised overall control over them. To do so effectively, it established an inspection division in May 1912 to carry out uniform inspections of the four companies. The inspections differed from the usual financial auditing by covering a broad range of such matters as management ethics, personnel affairs, employee morale, and discipline.[6] The inspection division was focused on ensuring that the actions of each company would not harm the good name of Mitsui through internal trouble or external conflict.

The Mitsui Family Council and its Secretariat continued to exist even after the Management Department of the Secretariat of the Mitsui Family Council had been abolished and its functions taken over by Mitsui Gōmei, but their functions were limited to handling purely internal matters of the Mitsui families. These included distributing Mitsui Gōmei dividends to the families, amassing a part of the dividends as reserves, directly controlling the families' nonbusiness common assets, such as their villas in Kyoto and their Tokyo cemetery, conducting religious services for their ancestors, and seeing to the education of the sons and daughters of all the houses.[7]

Mitsui Hachirōemon Takamine, head of the senior main house, was appointed president of the newly formed Mitsui Gōmei. The active partners were Takamine and the heads of three of the five branches of the main family, Takayasu, Hachirōjirō, and Saburōsuke. The latter three were also appointed presidents of the three main Mitsui subsidiaries, Takayasu of Mitsui Bank, Hachirōjirō of Mitsui Bussan, and Saburōsuke of Mitsui Mining. The four were the older and more capable of the Mitsui men.[8]

Although Mitsui family members held the top management positions, their roles were nominal. They attended board of directors meetings, but the salaried managers exercised the business decision-making power. The heads of houses who were the presidents confined their participation to approving decisions and asking questions.

At the same time, the House of Mitsui regarded its salaried managers as mere employees working for the owners. The family moreover demanded from them the loyalty of a retainer to his master. For instance, at the founding of Mitsui Bank, president Takayasu admonished the salaried managers who were the directors, "Never forget this basic concept: you must do everything in your power to serve the House of Mitsui."[9] The salaried managers were of course conscious of their position as employees and did not forget the proper courtesies due the family, but such deference did not prevent these men, with their high-level managerial abilities, from exercising actual control over the zaibatsu's top management.

Masuda Takashi directed the newly established Mitsui Gōmei's top management in his capacity as adviser (*komon*) and was effectively the paramount leader of the Mitsui zaibatsu.

In each of the direct subsidiaries—Mitsui Bank, Mitsui Bussan, Mitsui Mining, Tōshin Warehousing, and, after 1924, Mitsui Trust—three to five executive directors (*jōmu torishimariyaku*) (rather than the Mitsui family members who served as presidents and the part-time director who represented the Mitsui families, Mitsui Gōmei, and the other zaibatsu companies) held effective power. From the founding of Mitsui Gōmei to the dissolution of the Mitsui zaibatsu after World War II, the executive directors were without exception all salaried managers who had risen through the ranks of their companies. At each of the subsidiaries, the most senior of the executive directors, the *hittō jōmu torishimariyaku* (senior executive director) held great authority and served in effect as de facto president.[10]

The first major turnover in Mitsui's top management following the establishment of the multisubsidiary system came in the wake of the

Siemens Scandal of 1914. In January of that year, the German firm Siemens & Schuckert was disclosed to have bribed Japanese naval officers in order to win contracts with the Japanese navy. That led to the discovery that Mitsui Bussan, the Japanese agent for the British firm Vickers, had also bribed high Japanese naval officials to secure for its client the order to construct the high-speed battleship *Kongō*. Three Bussan executive directors, Yamamoto Jōtarō, Iida Giichi, and Iwahara Kenzō, were found guilty and sentenced to jail. They and other responsible parties resigned their positions, including Mitsui Hachirōjirō and Masuda.[11]

As a result, it was necessary to select someone to replace Masuda as the leader of Mitsui Gōmei. Mitsui Bussan, the culprit in the bribery incident, was not in a position to suggest a candidate to replace Masuda. Since Mitsui Bank executive director Hayakawa (who might otherwise have been a natural replacement) was not highly regarded, Dan Takuma, whose record as top manager of Mitsui Mining was respected and who was trusted by Takamine, was chosen. He took the newly established position of senior executive director (*rijichō*) in August 1914 and continued to lead the zaibatsu until his assassination by a right-wing terrorist in March 1932.

With Dan's appointment, the top management of Mitsui Gōmei then consisted of the president; the other active partners who were Mitsui family members; Dan; Ariga Nagafumi, director (*riji*); and six councilors (*sanji*). Dan and Ariga held concurrent posts as councilors, as did Hayakawa and Watanabe Senjirō, Bussan senior executive director. The remaining two councilors, Mitsui Morinosuke, chairman of Shibaura Engineering Works and head of one of the associate houses, and Hatano Shōgorō, a former director of Mitsui Bank, were not allowed to attend the meetings of the active partners.[12] Thus Dan and Ariga were the only full-time top salaried managers at Mitsui Gōmei.

The situation changed in 1918 when Hayakawa left the bank to become vice senior executive director (*fuku rijichō*) of Mitsui Gōmei, and Fukui Kikusaburō resigned from his position as executive director of Mitsui Bussan and was appointed a director of Mitsui Gōmei. Hayakawa resigned from his new position after serving for two years.[13] From that time, Dan, senior executive director, and Ariga and Fukui, directors (called *jōmu riji* or "executive directors" beginning in 1922) were for many years the salaried managers who formed Mitsui Gōmei's top management.

In practice, then, six salaried managers (senior executive director of Mitsui Gōmei, its two executive directors, and the senior executive directors of the three main Mitsui subsidiaries) constituted the top management of the entire Mitsui zaibatsu from 1918 to 1924. In 1924

Yoneyama Umekichi was appointed president of Mitsui Trust, whose establishment he had directed. He had the same degree of influence as that held by the senior executive directors of the three older subsidiaries. From 1924 until Dan's assassination in 1932, the top management of the Mitsui zaibatsu consisted of Dan, Ariga, and Fukui of Mitsui Gōmei; the senior executive directors of the bank (Ikeda Seihin), the trading company (Yasukawa Yūnosuke), and the mining company (Makita Tamaki) and Yoneyama of the trust company.

With its new multisubsidiary system in place, the Mitsui zaibatsu underwent rapid growth after the opening of World War I. Mitsui Bank, Mitsui Bussan, and Mitsui Mining, the designated subsidiaries (*chokkei kaisha*) that were directly controlled and almost entirely owned by Mitsui Gōmei, steadily increased their capital. Their subsidiaries also grew, in number as well as size. Furthermore, Gōmei owned a large share of the stock in other enterprises that were referred to as ordinary subsidiaries (*bōkei kaisha*) of the zaibatsu, including concerns that might be described as the legacy of the Nakamigawa industrialization policy—Ōji Paper Company, Kanegafuchi Cotton Spinning Company, Hokkaido Colliery & Steamship Company, and Shibaura Engineering Works, all of which had become independent. Also included among the ordinary subsidiaries were the following firms in which the Mitsui Family Council or its successor Mitsui Gōmei had purchased blocks of shares: Nippon Seikōsho (Japan Steel Works), Sakai Celluloid, Onoda Cement, and Denki Kagaku Kōgyō (Electrochemical Industries). Mitsui Gōmei sent representatives into the top managements of these companies and exercised considerable influence over them. The ordinary subsidiaries and the other Mitsui enterprises by 1930 had achieved enormous scale under the family multisubsidiary system. (See Tables 7.1–7.3.)

TABLE 7.1   Mitsui Head Office and Designated Subsidiaries as of 1930 (in million yen)

Company		Authorized capital	Paid-in capital
Head office	Mitsui Gōmei	300	300
Designated sub-sidiaries	Mitsui Bank	100	60
	Mitsui Bussan	100	100
	Mitsui Mining	100	62.5
	Tōshin Warehousing	15	12.5
	Mitsui Trust	30	7.5
	Mitsui Life Insurance	2	0.5

SOURCE: Compiled from Shōgyō Kōshinsho, *Nihon zenkoku shokaisha yakuin roku, 1930* (Japanese Directory of Company Directors) (Tokyo: Shōgyō Kōshinsho, 1930).

TABLE 7.2   Subsidiaries of Mitsui-designated Subsidiaries (in million yen)

Company	Authorized capital	Paid-in capital
Taiheiyō Colliery[a]	11	5.5
Kamaishi Mining[a]	20	20
Claude-Process Nitrogen Industries	10	10
Tōyō Cotton Trading[b]	25	15
Tōyō Rayon[b]	10	10

SOURCE: Same as Table 7.1.
[a] Subsidiary of Mitsui Mining.
[b] Subsidiary of Mitsui Bussan.

TABLE 7.3   Mitsui Ordinary Subsidiaries, 1930

Company	Authorized capital (million yen)	Paid-in capital (million yen)	% owned by Mitsui Gōmei
Ōji Paper	65.91	48.68	24.0
Shibaura Engineering Works	20	20	56.4
Hokkaido Colliery & Steamship	70	43.68	19.7[a]
Nippon Steel Works	30	30	12.5
Dai Nippon Celluloid	10	10	27.9
Kanegafuchi Cotton Spinning	60	28.6	5.3
Onoda Cement	31	21.82	9.6
Denki Kagaku Kōgyō (Electrochemical Industries)	18	17.5	6.9
Mitsukoshi Department Store (department stores)	15	15	0

SOURCES: Same as Table 7.1 and company histories.
[a] Also 20.7 percent owned by Mitsui Mining.

MITSUBISHI. Mitsubishi began to adopt the multisubsidiary system in 1917 when Iwasaki Koyata, who had succeeded Hisaya as president of Mitsubishi, Ltd., the previous year, initiated the restructuring, including the spin-off of the operating divisions as independent joint-stock companies. He thereby converted Mitsubishi, Ltd., from a multidivisional operating enterprise into a holding company retaining nearly complete ownership as well as overall control of the joint-stock companies. It was not, however, a pure holding company, for it did have a directly managed real estate division that was not made independent, as Mitsubishi Jisho (Mitsubishi Estate Co.), until 1937. The conversion of its operating divisions into subsidiaries that were independent joint-stock companies marked the transformation of the Mitsubishi zaibatsu into a family multisubsidiary system.

Just as the reasons for Mitsubishi's adoption of the operating divisional system are unclear, so are the reasons for its shift to the multisubsidiary structure. Since the two systems differed little in terms of the authority and communication ties between the head office and the divisions or subsidiaries, it is unlikely that managerial efficiency was a motivating factor. Unlike Mitsui, Mitsubishi had already incorporated its head office, having reorganized it as a limited partnership in 1893, so that tax advantages would not have prompted the change. One reason may have been Koyata's feeling that sole ownership of the Mitsubishi enterprises by the Iwasaki exposed the family to criticism, so he turned the enterprises into joint-stock companies in order to make possible stock ownership by the general public.[14] Second, by converting the divisions into joint-stock concerns, Mitsubishi would be able to use the stocks it held in those firms as collateral for bank loans, thereby expanding its financial power. A third reason may have had to do with the internal needs of Mitsubishi's management structure. Under the old system Mitsubishi, Ltd., and its operating divisions had only a small number of top management positions, that is, the presidency, the senior executive directorship (*kanji*), and the division heads. By establishing joint-stock companies, Koyata created a large number of top positions for the promotion of senior managers in the various firms: chairmanships, presidencies, executive directorships, and so on. The move therefore may have been aimed at fostering an emotional attachment to the firm on the part of management.

The capital of Mitsubishi, Ltd., came solely from the two branches of the Iwasaki family (Hisaya-Hikoyata and Yanosuke-Koyata). Their shares of the total capital as they changed over the years are illustrated in Table 7.4. The changes were partly a product of variations in the capital accumulation of the two Iwasaki branches and also a function of the delicate interrelationships between the two.

Apart from their investment in Mitsubishi, Ltd., both branches held large amounts of stock in enterprises not under the direct control of Mitsubishi, Ltd., and controlled those enterprises separately. By the time Mitsubishi had completed its transition to the multisubsidiary system with the reorganization of its bank as a joint-stock company in December 1919, the management structure of Mitsubishi, Ltd., was firmly in place, comprising a board of directors with a senior executive director (*sōriji*), executive directors (*jōmu riji*), and appointees from among the directors of the subsidiary companies; and as staff divisions within Mitsubishi, Ltd., departments for general affairs, personnel, research, and inspection.[15] The members of the board, including the senior executive director and executive directors, were all salaried managers.

TABLE 7.4   Ownership of Mitsubishi, Ltd., 1893–1926

Year	Capitalization (million yen)	Iwasaki family member	Participation share (million yen)
1893	5	Hisaya	2.5
		Yanosuke	2.5
1907	15	Hisaya	12.5
		Yanosuke	1.5
		Koyata	1.0
1908	15	Hisaya	12.5
		Koyata	2.5
1918	30	Hisaya	25.0
		Koyata	5.0
1920	80	Hisaya	50.0
		Koyata	30.0
1922	120	Hisaya	90.0
		Koyata	30.0
1926	120	Hikoyata[a]	50.0
		Hisaya	40.0
		Koyata	30.0

SOURCE: Compiled from Mitsubishi Gōshi Kaisha, ed., *Mitsubishi Sha-shi* (Records of Mitsubishi Company) (Tokyo: University of Tokyo Press, 1980–82), vols. 18, 21, 29, 30, 32, 34.
[a] Hikoyata was the eldest son of Hisaya. He was appointed vice president of Mitsubishi, Ltd., in 1934, but Koyata held the position of president continuously until his death in December 1945.

Under the regulations established for Mitsubishi, Ltd., important matters concerning the zaibatsu were to be discussed by the board of directors, after which the president was to approve and implement the board's decisions. If a matter was urgent or otherwise unavoidable, then the president could make and implement a decision without referring the matter to the board. Similarly, if the president was unable to make a decision, the board could deliberate by itself and reach and implement a decision.[16] These provisions make clear that under Mitsubishi's system top-level decision-making was carried out cooperatively by the holding company president, who was a member of the owner family, and the board of directors, composed of salaried managers.

The structure of Mitsubishi, Ltd.'s top management was occasionally altered. In 1926, for example, the board was expanded to include directors other than those of subsidiaries. In addition, the regulations concerning the relationship between the president and the board of directors were revised in 1922, with the board's function being redefined to include the discussion of important matters at the president's request and coordination between Mitsubishi, Ltd., and its subsidiaries and among the subsidiaries themselves.[17] Despite such adjustments, however, the system of cooperative decision-making by the president and the directors did not change.

Iwasaki Koyata served as Mitsubishi, Ltd. president from 1916 to 1945. A graduate of the prestigious First Higher School in Tokyo and enrolled in the Law Faculty of Tokyo Imperial University for about a year, Koyata went on to study in Britain and was graduated from Pembroke College, Cambridge University. His good education enhanced his natural endowments of a discerning mind and forceful personality; all in all he was well suited for leading the Mitsubishi zaibatsu.

Unlike the heads of the Mitsui houses, Koyata was not a nominal leader but actively contributed to strategic decision-making in the zaibatsu. He was not a despot; rather, he cooperated with salaried managers on the board of directors. It is likely, however, that if Koyata had not been the able man he was, the system of cooperation between the president and board would not have functioned in practical terms, and the president's role would have shifted toward a nominal one. Without Koyata, the cooperative system might not even have been established in the first place.

Tables 7.5 and 7.6 present data on the subsidiaries and important affiliates of the Mitsubishi zaibatsu as of 1930. The chief executive officers of the subsidiaries were distinguished from the head of the holding company by title. The president of a subsidiary was called

TABLE 7.5 Mitsubishi Subsidiaries, 1930

Company	Date founded	Authorized capital (million yen)	Paid-in capital (million yen)
Mitsubishi Shipbuilding and Engineering	October 1917	50	30
Mitsubishi Iron and Steel	October 1917	25	25
Mitsubishi Warehousing and Transportation	March 1918[a]	10	10
Mitsubishi Trading	April 1918	15	15
Mitsubishi Mining	April 1918	100	62.5
Mitsubishi Bank	August 1919	100	62.5
Mitsubishi Aircraft[b]	May 1920	5	5
Mitsubishi Electric[c]	January 1921	15	10.5
Mitsubishi Trust	April 1927	30	7.5

SOURCE: Same as Table 7.1.
[a] Date when name was changed from Tokyo Sōko (Tokyo Warehousing).
[b] Formerly Mitsubishi Nainenki (Mitsubishi Internal Combustion Engine).
[c] Formerly the electrical manufacturing unit at the Kobo works of Mitsubishi Shipbuilding and Engineering.

TABLE 7.6   Major Affiliates of the Mitsubishi Zaibatsu, 1930

Company	Paid-in capital (million yen)	% Owned by Mitsubishi, Ltd., and by Iwasaki-related stockholders
Tokio Marine & Fire Insurance	30	18.1
Meiji Mutual Life Insurance	2	3.7
NYK	64.25	11.1
Kirin Brewery	8.3	16.3
Mitsubishi Paper Mills	8	100
Asahi Glass	6.87	87.1

SOURCES: Same as Table 7.1 and company histories.

kaichō (chairman), whereas only the chief executive officer of Mitsubishi, Ltd., was designated *shachō* (president). When the subsidiaries were initially spun off as independent firms, Koyata had served as *kaichō* of several of the subsidiaries, including Mitsubishi Shipbuilding and Engineering, Mitsubishi Trading, and Mitsubishi Bank. He soon gave up those positions but joined Iwasaki Hisaya and Kimura Kusuyata, the senior executive director, and Miyoshi Shigemichi, an executive director of Mitsubishi, Ltd., as director (*hira torishimariyaku*) of the subsidiaries. They represented the owners of the Mitsubishi zaibatsu and participated in the top management of the subsidiaries, but they attended only the regular directors' meetings and were not full-time managers of those firms. At each subsidiary, the full-time top management consisted of the chairman and one to three executive directors (*jōmu torishimariyaku*), all of whom were salaried managers.

In short, the top management of the Mitsubishi zaibatsu, with marked contrast to that of Mitsui, took the form of cooperative decision-making by the president of Mitsubishi, Ltd., who represented the two branches of the Iwasaki family; the top salaried managers, including the senior executive director and executive directors of Mitsubishi, Ltd.; and the chairmen and executive directors of the subsidiaries. Direct participation in strategic decision-making by the representative of the zaibatsu family, and, perhaps as a corollary to that point, the absence of dominant leaders among Mitsubishi's top salaried managers are also elements in the contrast to the situation at Mitsui.

LIMITS OF THE FAMILY MULTISUBSIDIARY SYSTEM AT MITSUI AND MITSUBISHI.   By providing an optimal combination of flexibility and control, the family multisubsidiary system facilitated the expansion and diversification of the Mitsui and Mitsubishi zaibatsu, but in so doing brought the zaibatsu to the limits of their ability to finance growth without relying on outside funds. In fact, after World War I both Mitsui and Mitsubishi made public offerings of portions of their subsidiaries' stock.

Mitsui offered the stock in 1919 when it increased the capital of Mitsui Bank from ¥20 million to ¥100 million, marketing 300,000 of the 800,000 newly issued shares to the public at a premium. It was compelled to take this step because the bank's capital increase, added to the ¥163 million in capital increases of the other Mitsui-designated subsidiaries during and immediately after World War I, was beyond the means of Mitsui Gōmei, despite a ¥140 million increase in the capitalization of Mitsui Gōmei itself and the absorption of the subsidiaries' ample internal reserves.[18]

The Mitsubishi public offering followed in 1920 when, in doubling the capital of Mitsubishi Mining Company, Mitsubishi, Ltd. not only allocated some of the new stock to employees and associates (*enkosha*) but also opened a portion to public subscription, reducing its share of Mitsubishi Mining stock to 60.8 percent of the total.[19] In doubling the capital of Mitsubishi Bank in 1929 it again allocated stock to employees and associates and made a public offering. The move reduced Mitsubishi, Ltd.'s share to 70 percent of the bank's stock.

A number of reasons may be suggested for Mitsubishi, Ltd.'s decision to let go of some of the shares of its mining company and bank through allocation and public subscription. First, President Koyata had long desired to open Mitsubishi to part ownership by the general public. Another reason may have been the urge to keep step with Mitsui once Mitsui Bank had offered part of its stock to the public. Most critical, however, was that the financial resources of Mitsubishi, Ltd., were not sufficient to meet the need for major capital expansion of its designated subsidiaries. Two factors were behind the limited funding capacity of the holding company. One was the poor performance of some of the designated subsidiaries during the postwar slump and their resultant inability to pay Mitsubishi, Ltd., much in the way of dividends. The second was the inability of the Iwasaki family to continue increasing the capital of the holding company.

The basis for the public offering of Mitsubishi Mining stock in 1920 was not the Iwasaki family's wish to avoid the burden of providing needed funds. After all, the family increased the capital of Mitsubishi, Ltd. by ¥50 million that year and by another ¥40 million in 1922. Rather, the explanation is to be found mainly in the postwar slump, particularly in the exhaustion of Mitsubishi, Ltd.'s financial reserves owing to losses at Mitsubishi Trading and Mitsubishi Iron and Steel.

The public offering of Mitsubishi Bank stock in 1929, in contrast, must be explained in terms of the Iwasaki family's limited funding power. Once Mitsubishi, Ltd.'s capital was raised to ¥120 million in 1922, no further changes in capitalization were made: the Iwasaki simply lacked the resources to carry out subsequent capital increases. This interpretation is supported by the fact that after Mitsubishi, Ltd. was reorganized into the joint-stock company Kabushiki Kaisha Mitsubishi Sha (Mitsubishi, Inc.) the capital of the holding company was doubled in 1940 but the newly issued shares were offered entirely to the public. That is, the Iwasaki family could no longer finance the expansion of the diversified enterprises of the Mitsubishi zaibatsu. Under the multisubsidiary system, then, the closed family ownership of the zaibatsu finally reached its limits. Nonetheless, apart from the 1920 offering of Mitsubishi Mining stock, the shares of Mitsubishi-designated subsidiaries were not sold on the stock market. The "public offerings" were actually restricted to Mitsubishi-designated and ordinary subsidiaries and their employees and to associates of Iwasaki family members. In this manner the substance, if not the form, of closed ownership was preserved.

SUMITOMO. The Sumitomo Honten or head office renamed itself Sumitomo Sōhonten in January 1909, a year after Mitsubishi had instituted its operating divisional system and the same year in which Mitsui adopted the multisubsidiary form. The name change did not reflect a change in structure; rather, the addition of *sō*, meaning "general," simply signified that the Sumitomo head office exercised overall control of diversified business activities.

Sumitomo Sōhonten went on to reorganize the various Sumitomo enterprises into joint-stock companies, beginning with the bank in 1912. Sumitomo Sōhonten itself by 1921 had been reorganized as Sumitomo Gōshi Kaisha (Sumitomo, Ltd.), a holding company capitalized at ¥150 million that owned the stock and exercised control of the various Sumitomo joint-stock corporations and was wholly owned by the Sumitomo family. Some of the top salaried managers were allowed to become partners through in-service contribution (*rōmu shusshi*). The partners with unlimited liability were the head of the House of Sumitomo, Sumitomo Kichizaemon Tomoito, and his adopted son-in-law Sumitomo Tadateru, as well as salaried managers Suzuki Masaya, Nakada Kinkichi, and Yukawa Kankichi. Tomoito's three sons were the limited liability partners.

Tomoito's eldest son Kan'ichi was a neurotic personality, not suited to become head of the Sumitomo zaibatsu, and consequently was relieved of the right to succession in 1916. The next son, Atsushi, was named heir in his place, but as Atsushi was only twelve when Sumitomo, Ltd., was founded, Tadateru was selected as partner with unlimited liability. Tadateru died in 1923 and Tomoito in 1926, at which time Atsushi succeeded Tomoito as the sixteenth-generation head of the Sumitomo house.[20]

The lineup of partners in the holding company reflected the Sumitomo house tradition of giving great authority to its salaried managers. Suzuki Masaya was the first senior executive director (*sōriji*) of Sumitomo, Ltd.; Nakada Kinkichi its first executive director (*jōmu riji*); and Yukawa Kankichi Sumitomo Bank's senior executive director (*hittō jōmu torishimariyaku*). Tomoito and his successors as head of the House of Sumitomo held the presidency of Sumitomo, Ltd., but the authority to make strategic decisions was left entirely in the hands of the top salaried managers.

When Suzuki retired in 1922, Nakada replaced him as senior executive director of Sumitomo, Ltd., serving until 1925. Yukawa was senior executive director from 1925 to 1930, Ogura Masatsune from 1930 to 1941, and Furuta Toshinosuke from 1941 to 1946. All except Furuta were former civil servants—Sumitomo was unique among the zaibatsu in its preference for ex-civil servants as salaried managers.

Data on the joint-stock companies that were members of the Sumitomo zaibatsu as of 1930 are presented in Table 7.7. In addition to these, Sumitomo exercised control over several other joint enterprises, including Tosa Yoshinogawa Suiryoku Denki, a hydroelectric power company founded in February 1919, to which the Besshi electricity-generating facilities were transferred in 1927. Tosa Yoshinogawa was capitalized as of 1930 at ¥5 million, and ¥3 million was paid in. Another such operation was Osaka Hokkō (Osaka North Port Development), founded in December 1919 and capitalized at ¥35 million.

In comparison with Mitsui Gōmei and Mitsubishi, Ltd., Sumitomo, Ltd.'s share of the total stock of each of its subsidiaries was relatively low. For example, it held interests of about 60 percent in Sumitomo Electrical Wire and Osaka Hokkō, about 50 percent in Sumitomo Building and Sumitomo Bank, and about 25 percent in Sumitomo Trust.[21] The small percentages in the cases of the bank and trust company resulted from Sumitomo's opening share ownership to subscribers other than the holding company, as Mitsui and Mitsubishi did, but distinctive to Sumitomo's case were the high ratio of stockholding by the bank (in Sumitomo Building and Sumitomo Trust) and capital participation by external investors (Nippon Electric Co. in Sumitomo Electrical Wire and Kansai financiers in Osaka Hokkō), which reduced the holding company's share in the subsidiaries it directly controlled. These phenomena were not to be seen at Mitsubishi or Mitsui.

Sumitomo was also a joint investor in two critical heavy industrial

TABLE 7.7   Sumitomo, Ltd., Subsidiaries as of 1930

Company	Date founded	Authorized capital (million yen)	Paid-in capital (million yen)
Sumitomo Bank	February 1912[a]	70	50
Sumitomo Steel	December 1915	12	9
Sumitomo Electrical Wire[b]	December 1920	10	10
Sumitomo Warehousing	August 1923	15	15
Sumitomo Building[c]	August 1923	6.5	6.5
Sumitomo Ban Colliery[d,e]	November 1924		
Sumitomo Fertilizer Manufacturing	June 1925	3	1.8
Sumitomo Life Insurance[f]	July 1925[g]	1.5	0.75
Sumitomo Trust	July 1925	20	5
Sumitomo Copper and Steel	July 1926	15	12
Sumitomo Besshi Mining[h]	June 1927	15	15
Sumitomo Kyushu Colliery[i,j]	July 1928		
Fuso Marine & Fire Insurance[k]	March 1931[l]	10	10
Sumitomo Coal Mining	April 1930	15	11

SOURCE: Same as Table 7.1.
[a] Date reorganized.
[b] Renamed Sumitomo Electric Industries in 1939.
[c] Real estate, leasing.
[d] Name changed from Ban Colliery in 1925.
[e] Merged with Sumitomo Coal Mining.
[f] Name changed from Hinode Life Insurance in 1926.
[g] Date when operations were taken over by Sumitomo.
[h] Formerly Besshi Copper Mine.
[i] Formerly Wakamatsu Colliery.
[j] Merged with Sumitomo Coal Mining.
[k] Renamed Sumitomo Marine & Fire Insurance in 1940.
[l] Date when operations were taken over by Sumitomo.

enterprises in which Sumitomo-related shareholders owned less than half the stock and over which Sumitomo, Ltd. did not exercise single-handed control: Nippon Sheet Glass Co., Ltd., and Nippon Electric Co. (now NEC). Nippon Sheet Glass was a joint venture involving the U.S. firm Libbey, Owens Sheet Glass Company, Ltd., Asahi Glass Co., Ltd., the Sumitomo family, and other Japanese investors. Initially named Nichibei Ita Garasu (Japan-American Sheet Glass), it was founded in June 1918 and capitalized at ¥3 million, of which one-fourth was paid in.

Nippon Sheet Glass almost immediately fell into management difficulties. The Sumitomo zaibatsu ultimately took over its operation in 1922 because of the large debts owed by the company to Sumitomo Bank. Officers were dispatched from Sumitomo, Ltd., and the bank to take responsibility for the firm's top management. The ratio of capital provided by sources within the Sumitomo zaibatsu rose from 11.3 percent at the time the firm was founded to 34 percent when its capital was increased in 1928. Taking the name Nippon Sheet Glass Co., Ltd., in January 1931, the company from then on shared sheet glass manufacturing in Japan with Asahi Glass, a Mitsubishi ordinary subsidiary.[22]

Nippon Electric Co. was founded in 1899 with capital participation from the U.S. firm Western Electric to produce, import, and sell electrical equipment. Sumitomo Electrical Wire in 1920 introduced electric wire and cable technology from Western Electric and was reorganized as a joint-stock company capitalized at ¥10 million. One-fourth of its stock was held by Nippon Electric Co. on behalf of Western Electric. At the same time, Nippon Electric Co. increased its capital to ¥10 million, about two-thirds of which was provided by Western Electric, and transferred 5 percent of its stock to Sumitomo Electrical Wire. Thus originated the connection between Nippon Electric Co. and the Sumitomo zaibatsu.[23]

In the atmosphere of growing political pressure to exclude foreign enterprises from Japan, in June 1932 Nippon Electric Co. and its parent company ISE (Western Electric, having been bought by ITT in 1925, had become ISE) decided to entrust their operation to Sumitomo, Ltd. At that point, the percentage of Nippon Electric stock held by Sumitomo, Ltd. and Sumitomo Electrical Wire combined stood at 14.1 percent compared to the 50 percent held by ISE. Thus Sumitomo, Ltd. still had to share high-level decision making with ISE. Not until after the U.S. entry into World War II in 1941 was the Sumitomo head office able to surpass ISE in the ratio of stock held in Nippon Electric and to exercise sole control over it.[24]

These cases show that, while the Sumitomo zaibatsu developed in a number of different fields, particularly in heavy industry, it was unable to achieve full control of its enterprises due to its weaker capital accumulation compared with that of Mitsui and Mitsubishi.

Just as the top management of Sumitomo, Ltd., was in the hands of salaried managers, so was this the case at the subsidiaries. Initially the subsidiaries were classified into those in which the head of the House of Sumitomo, in his capacity as president of Sumitomo, Ltd., held the post of president (including the bank, trust company, warehouse company, wire and cable company, and steel works); those in which the senior executive director or executive director of Sumitomo, Ltd., served as chairman; and those without a president or chairman. After

Tomoito's death, however, a uniform system was adopted whereby the senior executive director of Sumitomo, Ltd., also served as chairman of all the subsidiaries, with two exceptions. The chairman at Sumitomo Trust Company was Yoshida Shin'ichi, the salaried manager responsible for the company's establishment, and Sumitomo Building had no chairman. But in general, the chairman or president held concurrent appointments and did not serve full time at the subsidiary.

The top management functions thus usually devolved upon the subsidiary's senior executive director (*senmu torishimariyaku*) and executive director (*jōmu torishimariyaku*). Such positions were almost all filled by full-time salaried managers, except at Sumitomo Steel Works and Sumitomo Shindō Kōkan (Sumitomo Copper and Steel), for both of which Sumitomo, Ltd., executive director Ogura Masatsune served long terms as executive director. Ogura was a Sumitomo salaried manager, but from the point of view of the salaried managers of the subsidiaries he represented the owner, Sumitomo, Ltd. As he participated in the highest level of decision making, they did not regard him as one of their own. These are the only cases in which the director of the holding

TABLE 7.8   Mitsui Top Management, 1930

	Head office (Mitsui Gōmei) Type (number)		
President[a]	F (1)		
Active partners	F (2)		
Senior executive director[b]	S (1)		
Excutive directors[b]	S (2)		
Directors	S (2)		

	Major subsidiaries		
	Bank	Trading	Mining
President	F (1)	F (1)	F (1)
Representative director		F (1)	
Executive directors[b]	S (4)	S (4)	S (3)
Directors (total)	6	7	8
Family members	1	1	1
Mitsui Gōmei directors	1	1	2
Directors of other subsidiaries	1	1	0
Salaried managers of each subsidiary	2	4	5
Outsiders	1	0	0

SOURCE: Same as Table 7.1.
NOTE: F = zaibatsu family member; S = salaried manager.
[a] Also an active partner.
[b] Full-time top manager.

company doubled as executive director of a subsidiary, and the situation was unique to Sumitomo.

TOP MANAGEMENT OF THE THREE MAJOR ZAIBATSU. Tables 7.8–7.10 indicate the composition of the top management of the three major zaibatsu in 1930, after they had all introduced the family multisubsidiary system. Although at first glance the managements exhibit a marked resemblance in organization, on closer examination important differences are found. First, the decision-making system in the Mitsui and Sumitomo holding companies differed from that of the Mitsubishi counterpart. At Mitsui and Sumitomo, strategic decision making in the holding company was left to the salaried managers—the senior executive director and executive director(s), whereas at Mitsubishi such decision making was a cooperative affair between the family head, as president of the holding company, and the salaried senior executive director and executive directors. Second, considerable variety existed in the systems for appointing presidents or chairmen of the subsidiaries. At Mitsui, different members of the zaibatsu family were selected to serve in

TABLE 7.9   Mitsubishi Top Management, 1930

	Head office (Mitsubishi, Ltd.) Type (number)			
President[a]	F (1)			
Senior executive director[a]	S (1)			
Executive directors[a]	S (2)			
Directors	S (2)			

	Major subsidiaries			
	Bank	Shipbuilding	Trading	Mining
Chairman[a]	S (1)	S (1)	S (1)	S (1)
Executive directors[a]	S (1)	S (1)	S (3)	S (3)
Directors (total)	4	8	5	6
Family members	2	1	1	1
Mitsubishi, Ltd. directors	1	0	1	1
Directors of other subsidiaries	0	2	0	1
Salaried managers of each subsidiary	1	5	3	3

SOURCE: Same as Table 7.1.
NOTE: F = zaibatsu family member; S = salaried manager.
[a] Full-time top manager.

TABLE 7.10   Sumitomo Top Management 1930

	Head office (Sumitomo, Ltd.) Type (number)
President	F (1)
Senior executive director[a]	S (1)
Executive directors[a]	S (1)
Auditor	S (1)
Directors	S (1)

	Major subsidiaries		
	Bank	Electrical Wire	Copper and Steel
Chairman (Sumitomo, Ltd. senior executive director)	1	1	1
Senior executive director	S 1	0	0
Executive directors* (total)	2	1	2
Sumitomo, Ltd. executive director	0	0	1
Salaried managers of each subsidiary	2	1	1
Directors (total)	5	6	3
Family members	1	0	0
Sumitomo, Ltd. directors	0	2	1
Salaried managers of each subsidiary	3	2	2
Outsiders	1	2	0

SOURCE: Same as Table 7.1.
NOTE: F = zaibatsu family member; S = salaried manager.
* Full-time top manager.

such capacities at each subsidiary; at Mitsubishi, a different salaried manager filled each such position; and at Sumitomo, a single officer of the holding company was appointed to serve as chairman of several subsidiaries. Third, at all three zaibatsu the substantive strategic decision making in the subsidiaries was consistently carried out by the full-time executive directors, who were salaried managers, but Sumitomo does offer the one exception of Ogura Masatsune.

Finally, in the case of Mitsui, family members other than the president of the holding company were appointed as directors of the subsidiaries, but at Mitsubishi and Sumitomo the same family member was both president of the holding company and a director of the subsidiaries. The difference between Mitsubishi and Sumitomo on this point was that at Mitsubishi the holding company president served as a director of all the directly controlled subsidiaries except the aircraft and electrical equipment enterprises, while at Sumitomo the holding company president served as a director of only four subsidiaries (the bank, warehousing, trust, and life insurance companies).

Other Zaibatsu Groups

YASUDA. Of the seven other zaibatsu, Yasuda adopted the family multisubsidiary system earlier than did Mitsubishi or Sumitomo, and it did so in two stages. First, in 1911 Yasuda established two joint-stock companies, Yasuda Ginkō (Yasuda Bank) and Yasuda Shōji (Yasuda Trading). The latter was merely a managerial device to organize Yasuda's stagnating nonfinancial enterprises, which were proving to be a burden on the zaibatsu.[25] The bank was capitalized at ¥10 million, Yasuda Shōji at ¥500,000. Then in 1912 Yasuda's existing unlimited liability companies, Gōmei Kaisha Yasuda Bank and Yasuda Shōji (Trading) Gōmei Kaisha, were merged with their corresponding joint-stock companies, and the capitalization of Yasuda Trading was increased by ¥1 million. At the same time, Gōmei Kaisha Hozensha, an unlimited liability partnership, was established as the central office in order to fulfill the functions of holding the two joint-stock companies' stock and exercising general control over them.[26]

At its founding the Hozensha had a total capital of ¥10 million provided by the House of Yasuda according to the fixed percentages shown in Table 7.11.

The active partners, Zenjirō and Zenzaburō, were also president and vice president of the Hozensha. In addition, Zenjirō served as adviser and Zenzaburō as supervisor for Yasuda Bank and Yasuda Shōji. Yasuda Zennosuke (Zenjirō's eldest son) was named president of the bank and Yasuda Yoshie of Yasuda Trading. Hoping to develop more complete managerial functions within the central office, Zenzaburō arranged for forty-nine employees to be transferred from Yasuda Bank to the Hozensha in 1917.[27] This move, however, was unsuccessful, as were Zenzaburō's other experimental reforms.

Zenjirō, who had expressed his intention to retire from active leadership in 1909, did so in 1911; in the ensuing reorganization the zaibatsu's leadership nominally passed to Zenzaburō. Zenzaburō then succeeded to the family headship in 1913, with an increase in his share of the Hozensha capital to 18.5 percent. (Zenjirō's share was reduced correspondingly to 2.5 percent.) Zenjirō actually retained effective authority over Yasuda's top management, and the incident in which he overruled Zenzaburō's decision to invest in Nippon Kōkan (NKK) illustrates this reality.

Zenzaburō, a graduate of Tokyo Imperial University, had preten-

TABLE 7.11   Family Ownership of Yasuda Hozensha (%)

Families and family members	Ownership
Main families (*Dōke*)	
Zenjirō (the founder)	5.0
Zenzaburō (Zenjirō's son-in-law)	16.0
Zennosuke (Zenjirō's eldest son)	14.5
Zenshirō II (son of Zenshirō I, Zenjirō's adopted son)	14.5
Zengorō (Zenjirō's third son)	12.5
Yoshio (Zenjirō's fourth son)	12.5
Yoshie (Zenjirō's sister's son)	11.5
Branch families (*Bunke*)	
Zensuke II (son of Zensuke I, another adopted son of Zenjirō)	4.0
Hikotarō (Zenjirō's grandnephew)	2.5
Zenhachirō (Zenjirō's sister's son-in-law)	1.0
Associate families (*Ruike*)	
Zenbei (Zenjirō's wife's sister's grandson)	3.0
Zen'ya II (son of Zen'ya I, Zenjirō's cousin)	2.0
Tamezō (son of Zenjirō's other cousin)	1.0

SOURCE: Compiled from *Yasuda Hozensha to sono kankei jigyō shi* (History of Yasuda Hozensha and Its Affiliated Enterprises) (Tokyo: Yasuda Fudōsan Kabushiki Kaisha, 1974), p. 400.

sions to being a highly educated manager, which contributed to the continuing friction between himself, on the one hand, and Zenjirō and Zenjirō's natural children, on the other. Ultimately Zenzaburō in 1919 resigned his position as vice president and heir apparent and left the Yasuda family. In order to resolve the family confusion that accompanied Zenzaburō's departure, Zenjirō took such measures as instituting a family constitution and a director system for the Hozensha.[28] He increased the capitalization of the Hozensha to ¥30 million in 1921.

Zenjirō was assassinated in September 1921 by a deranged man who had come to demand money from him.[29] The day after the murder Zennosuke, forty-two years old, became the second president of the Hozensha and took the name Zenjirō II. It was decided that his brothers Zengorō and Yoshio and his aunt's grandson Zenbei would assist him as directors of the Hozensha, but they proved to lack the requisite managerial ability, and so a vacuum appeared in the Hozensha top management. The Hozensha then called upon Takahashi Korekiyo, the minister of finance, and Inoue Junnosuke, president of the Bank of Japan, to recommend potential managerial personnel. With their help, Yasuda was able to bring in Yūki Toyotarō, a director of the Bank of

Japan and manager of its Osaka branch. Yūki was appointed executive director of the Hozensha and vice president of Yasuda Bank toward the end of 1921.[30]

The position of Hozensha executive director had just been instituted when Yūki joined Yasuda. At that time the House of Yasuda changed its articles of incorporation and regulations so that directors could now be chosen from outside, rather than only from within, the family. The term executive director was chosen to apply to a director who was not a family member and who also exercised managerial authority.[31] Zenjirō II promised in Takahashi and Inoue's presence to leave everything up to Yūki.[32]

Exercising the enormous authority guaranteed him under the new structure, Yūki carried out a series of ambitious strategic moves, including the big Yasuda Bank merger and the founding of Yasuda Trust Company. The Yasuda zaibatsu had preserved outmoded traditions under Zenjirō I's dictatorial leadership, and Yūki now pushed ahead with modernization of its management practices. He rationalized the organization of the Hozensha, built up its research and planning functions, and employed and promoted many highly educated personnel.

Under Yūki, Yasuda in fact hired scores of highly educated men: 30 in 1922, 50 in 1923, 180 in 1924, and about a hundred a year thereafter.[33] Their presence changed the face of the Yasuda zaibatsu. It is true that Zenzaburō had also worked to bring such men into the zaibatsu, but because Zenjirō I had not recognized the value of higher education, Zenzaburō's efforts were ineffective and most of the men he attracted to Yasuda left.

Yūki's aggressive policies, however, proved to be too radical, too inclined to centralize power, and too high-handed. Resistance developed not only among Yasuda family members and old-style *bantō* but also among the highly educated middle managers whom Yūki himself brought in.[34] At the initiative of some twenty executives in the Hozensha and subsidiaries, the Yasuda Hozensha (its name was changed from Hozensha to Yasuda Hozensha in 1925) was reorganized in 1928. The number of directors was increased, the board of directors made the ultimate decision-making body, and Yūki placed under the authority of the family members, thereby eliminating his ability to act arbitrarily on his own authority.[35] Yūki responded by indicating his intention to resign, which he did formally in March 1929.

At this time Yasuda again turned to Takahashi's good offices in order to find outside managerial talent. Takahashi this time recommended Mori Kōzō, who had served in the Yokohama Specie Bank and presided over the Bank of Taiwan; he was named a director of the Yasuda Hozensha in January 1929. In the April following Yūki's departure

Mori succeeded to the vice-presidency of Yasuda Bank. In the same month, Takahashi also recommended Shijō Takahide, a former vice minister in the Ministry of Commerce and Industry; he became a Yasuda Hozensha director and assistant to Mori.[36]

Mori and Shijō together continued Yūki's aggressive strategy and management modernization policy but were able to eliminate his arbitrary, authoritative style. They sought the cooperation of Yasuda family members and the old-fashioned *bantō*, treated the mutual consultation system with respect, simplified the structure of the head office, and transferred authority to lower-ranking personnel. Thus they were able to bring off the strategic and structural revolution that Yūki had attempted.[37]

FURUKAWA. Furukawa converted to the family multisubsidiary system with the rapid diversification of its enterprises during World War I. Furukawa Gōmei Kaisha, an unlimited partnership originally founded as Furukawa Mining Company in 1905 and renamed in 1911, was in November 1917 again renamed, this time as Gōmei Kaisha Furukawa Kōgyō (Mining). It was directed to specialize in mining.

A new Furukawa Gōmei Kaisha was then established to act as the zaibatsu's head office. Capitalized at ¥20 million, it owned the stock of the several joint-stock companies operating Furukawa's diversified enterprises and exercising general control over them. The trading department of the earlier Furukawa Gōmei was reorganized into a joint-stock company, Furukawa Shōji (Furukawa Trading). And in April of the following year the mining division of Gōmei Kaisha Furukawa Kōgyō was also made independent as the joint-stock company Furukawa Kōgyō (Furukawa Mining), today's Furukawa Co., Ltd.

Along with such structural changes, Furukawa founded a variety of enterprises, including Asahi Denka (Asahi Electrochemical), Tokyo Furukawa Bank, Yokohama Rubber, Osaka Seiren (Osaka Refining), Furukawa Electric, and Fuji Electric. It also purchased Tōa Paint and increased its stockholdings in Teikoku Seimei Hoken (today's Asahi Life Insurance). The new enterprises were not uniformly successful: Furukawa Trading folded and was merged with Furukawa Mining in 1921; Furukawa Bank (Tokyo Furukawa Bank until 1922) closed its doors in 1931. The year before the bank closed, the Furukawa family multisubsidiary system included the companies shown in Table 7.12. Furukawa was indeed diversified, but owing to the effects of Furukawa Trading's collapse, the scale of its enterprises was small.

Of the three partners in Furukawa Gōmei at the time of its founding, Furukawa Toranosuke, head of the family and founder Ichibei's natural son, owned 99 percent. The remaining 1 percent was divided equally

TABLE 7.12   Companies in the Furukawa Zaibatsu, 1930

Company	Date founded	Authorized capital (million yen)	Paid-in capital (million yen)
Furukawa Gōmei	November 1917	20	20
Asahi Electric Chemical	January 1917	2	2
Furukawa Bank	June 1917	10	6.25
Yokohama Rubber	October 1917	1.6	1.6
Furukawa Mining	April 1918	22.5	22.5
Tōa Paint	October 1919	0.5	0.395
Osaka Refining	October 1919	1.5	1.5
Furukawa Electric	April 1920	20	12.5
Fuji Electric	September 1923	10	8.3
Teikoku Life Insurance	1927[a]	1	1

SOURCE: Same as Table 7.1.
[a] Came under Furukawa control.

between long-serving *bantō* Kimura Chōshichi and Yoshimura Man-jirō.[38]

Yoshimura was the fourth son of Kimura Chōbei, who in turn was Ichibei's nephew and appointed by Ichibei to be manager of the Ashio copper mine. After Chōbei's death, his son was adopted into the Yoshi-mura, the natal family of Ichibei's wife. Yoshimura, who also married one of Toranosuke's sister's, had multiple ties to the House of Furuka-wa. Yoshimura assisted Toranosuke as a relative of the family, as did Nakagawa Suekichi, who had already emerged as the leader of the Furukawa heavy industrial enterprises. Yoshimura's sister was Nakaga-wa's wife and also Ichibei's adopted daughter.[39]

Toranosuke was appointed president of Furukawa Gōmei, Furukawa Mining, Furukawa Trading, and Furukawa Bank. He was backed up by Yoshimura as vice president of the mining and trading companies and by Nakagawa, who was executive director of Tokyo Furukawa Bank and, beginning in 1921, of Furukawa Electric. Nakagawa in 1924 be-came president of Furukawa Electric as well as of Yokohama Rubber. The Furukawa family was thus represented by Toranosuke, Yoshimura, and Nakagawa in the top management of the zaibatsu, and the trio shared strategic decision making with the highest ranking salaried man-agers.

The senior executive director of Furukawa Gōmei acted as the central top salaried manager. It had been agreed that the first to hold the post would be Kondō Rikusaburō, but he died suddenly just before Furu-kawa Gōmei was set up. Instead Inoue Kōji became the first senior executive director, but following the collapse of Furukawa Trading he was succeeded by Konda Bunjirō and Suzuki Tsunesaburō. These conservative directors, Suzuki in particular, crushed the hopes of those salaried managers attempting to expand the Furukawa zaibatsu. Nakagawa Suekichi developed heavy industries within Furukawa despite Suzuki's opposition. Furukawa thus is an interesting case of a zaibatsu with progressive family members and a conservative salaried senior executive director.

ŌKURA. Ōkura also became a family multisubsidiary business during World War I. The Ōkura family in 1911 had merged the trading and mining businesses of Gōmei Kaisha Ōkura-gumi with Ōkura Dobokugumi (Ōkura Construction) to form Kabushiki Kaisha Ōkura-gumi, a joint-stock company capitalized at ¥10 million. That move had made Gōmei Kaisha Ōkura-gumi (capitalized at ¥1 million) a holding company. But Gōmei Kaisha held stock in one single subsidiary, Kabushiki Kaisha Ōkura-gumi. And Gōmei Kaisha devoted itself to clearing off the huge debts, about ¥0.8 million that came from the failure of the Tianjin branch in 1908.[40] Thus at that point Ōkura had not yet met the "multisubsidiary" criterion of the family multisubsidiary system. It finally did so in 1917, when Ōkura Kōgyō (Ōkura Mining) and Ōkura Construction were established as independent joint-stock companies. Ōkura Construction was the predecessor of today's Taisei Kensetsu (Taisei Corporation). Kabushiki Kaisha Ōkura-gumi then took the name Ōkura Shōji (Ōkura Trading, now Ōkura and Co., Ltd.) in 1918, and also in that year increased its capitalization from ¥1 million to ¥10 million. Its capitalization was again raised in 1920, to ¥50 million. As of 1930, the member firms of the Ōkura zaibatsu were as shown in Table 7.13.

TABLE 7.13   Companies in the Ōkura Zaibatsu, 1930

Company	Date founded	Capitalization (yen)
Gōmei Kaisha Ōkura-gumi	November 1893	50 million
Ōkura & Co.	November 1911	10 million (8 million paid-in)
Ōkura Mining	December 1917	10 million
Ōkura Construction	December 1917	2 million
Ōkura Fire and Marine Insurance	1927 (by purchasing Nisshin Kasai)	2 million (500,000 paid-in)

SOURCE: Same as Table 7.1.

The presidencies of Gōmei Kaisha Ōkura-gumi and its operating subsidiaries were all held by Ōkura Kihachirō, who exercised a strong leadership. At his retirement in 1924, his eldest son, Ōkura Kishichirō, succeeded to the holding company presidency, but the chairmanships of the three subsidiaries, Ōkura & Co., Ōkura Mining, and Ōkura Construction were given to Kadono Chōkurō, a top salaried manager within the zaibatsu. Kadono played a highly important role in Ōkura's top management, representing the entire Ōkura zaibatsu,[41] and he was also a partner in Gōmei Kaisha Ōkura-gumi. When Kihachirō died in 1928, Kishichirō held 95 percent of Gōmei Kaisha Ōkura-gumi's capital, Ōkura Kumema 3 percent, and Kadono 2 percent.[42] That Kadono acquired a share in the holding company indicates how great was his influence as a salaried manger in the top management.

ASANO. Asano was anomalous among the zaibatsu in its incomplete familial control. As a result, it was relatively slow to develop a full-fledged family multisubsidiary structure with a holding company to manage the family properties and provide overall control over the zaibatsu's diversified enterprises. As a first step in setting up a head office, the Asano family established Asano, Ltd. (Asano Gōshi Kaisha) in June 1914, which did not function as a pure holding company.[43] When Asano Dōzoku (Family), a joint-stock company, was founded in August 1918 with a capitalization of ¥10 million, it promptly merged with Asano, Ltd., which by that time also had ¥10 million in capital. As a result of the merger, Asano Dōzoku's capitalization increased to ¥35 million, which was fully paid-in by the end of 1920.[44]

Investment in Asano, Ltd. and Asano Dōzoku was restricted to members of the Asano families. In the case of Asano Dōzoku, the investors were Asano Sōichirō and his wife; the eldest son, Taijirō (who was to become Asano Sōichirō II), his wife, and their son; the second son, Ryōzō, his wife, and their eldest son; the third son, Hachirō; the fourth son, Yoshio; the second daughter and her husband, Shiraishi Motojirō, the in-marrying son-in-law of Sōichirō I; the fourth daughter, her husband, Suzuki Monjirō, and their eldest son; the eldest daughter, who was married to the legal scholar Hozumi Yatsuka, and their eldest son; the fifth daughter, Masugi Keiko; and the third daughter, Shimizu Kō and her son. Of the 35,000 shares, Sōichirō and his wife owned 49.6 percent, or 17,360 shares, with the remainder divided among their children. That Asano divided the remaining shares equally among the nine families established by his children (1,960 shares each) rather than by sex or birth order distinctions is very unusual.[45]

Unlike other zaibatsu, Asano adopted a joint-stock company format for its head office. The reason for this lay in Asano's relationship with one of Sōichirō's major supporters, Shibusawa Eiichi, who commanded Sōichirō's great respect. Shibusawa also had a family connection; his daughter had married the legal scholar Hozumi Nobushige, brother of Sōichirō's son-in-law Hozumi Yatsuka. Shibusawa in 1915 had established a joint-stock company, Shibusawa Dōzoku, to serve as a holding company, and that firm became the model for Asano Dōzoku. Nevertheless Sōichirō never considered offering Asano Dōzoku stock to the public. Family members were strictly forbidden under the articles of incorporation to dispose freely of their stock.[46]

Asano Dōzoku, like Asano, Ltd., did not function as a pure holding company. Rather, it directly managed a wide variety of business activities: coal sales, shipping between Tokyo and Yokohama, dealing in bottoms, overseas trade, gunpowder manufacture, dredging, construction with reinforced concrete, life and other insurance, and the import, processing, and sale of marble. These enterprises were organized as departmental units within Asano Dōzoku. Most were eventually either spun off, transferred to the operating subsidiaries within the Asano zaibatsu, or abolished, but the coal, dredging, and insurance departments remained under Asano Dōzoku's direct management for a long time.[47]

Among the subsidiary enterprises within the zaibatsu were Asano Zōsensho (shipbuilding), Asano Kokura Seikōsho (steel), Asano Bussan (trading), Nippon Kōkan (steel), Tokyo Wan Umetate (reclamation), and Iwaki Tankō (coal). The Asano subsidiaries also included the Oriental Steamship Company and Asano Chūya Bank, which retrenched and merged with other companies in the 1920s. Apart from these firms, all of which have been described earlier, the zaibatsu controlled several other major companies such as Oki Denki (electrical equipment) and Dai Nippon Kōgyō (mining).

The composition of the Asano zaibatsu as of 1930 is presented in Table 7.14. Given the difficulties faced by Oriental Steamship and the poor performance of Asano's other heavy industries, Asano Cement was by far the largest corporation in the combine. Sōichirō was president of all the subsidiaries except Nippon Kōkan (NKK). He abstained from serving even as a director of the latter, probably because he regarded it as his son-in-law Shiraishi's firm.

FUJITA. Fujita took on the family multisubsidiary form in 1917, when the Fujita family established Fujita Bank, capitalized at ¥10 million, and turned the mining division of Gōmei Kaisha Fujita-gumi into an independent joint-stock company, Fujita Kōgyō (Fujita Mining), capitalized at ¥30 million. At that point Fujita-gumi had a capitalization of ¥6 million. Its partners were the three sons of Fujita Denzaburō (who died in 1912): Heitarō, the president; Tokujirō, the vice president; and

TABLE 7.14 Companies in the Asano Zaibatsu, 1930

Company	Date founded	Paid-in capital (million yen)	% Owned by Asano Dōzoku	% Owned by Asano Dōzoku plus Asano family members
Iwaki Colliery	February 1894	9.1	NA	NA
Oriental Steamship	October 1896	5.68	NA	NA
Asano Cement	February 1898[a]	53.98	30.1	31.0
Oki Denki	May 1907[b]	3.5	17[c]	NA
Nippon Kōkan (NKK)	June 1912	15.22	NA	9.8[d]
Dai Nippon Mining	November 1915	5.0	8[c]	NA
Asano Trading	March 1918	1.0	NA	NA
Asano Kokura Steel	December 1918	6.3	34.7	47.6
Asano Shipbuilding	March 1920	26.5	NA	NA
Tokyo Bay Reclamation	March 1920	12.5	31.7	NA

SOURCES: Same as Table 7.1 and company histories.

[a] As a limited partnership.
[b] As a limited partnership with capital participation by Asano.
[c] Figure for 1925.
[d] Figure for Shiraishi Dōzoku and Shiraishi Motojirō.

Hikosaburō, the executive director. Fujita-gumi functioned as a holding company for the two designated subsidiaries, Fujita Bank and Fujita Mining, and exercised general control over them, but it also managed directly a wide range of operating units, including those for the reclamation of Kojima Bay and for the cultivation of flax and coconut palms in Davao, the Philippines.[48]

KUHARA. The Kuhara zaibatsu converted to the family multisubsidiary system in 1920 when it founded Gōmei Kaisha Kuhara Honten to act as the head office of the combine. Kuhara from early in its history had established or controlled joint-stock companies in a variety of fields, thus pursuing a strategy of diversification. During World War I, however, it had been content to reap the high profits resulting from the wartime boom and had not demonstrated concern for the overall coordination and control of its companies. In view of the postwar slump and the 1920 tax reform, Kuhara finally did move to achieve overall control and preserve the family fortune by hurriedly setting up a holding company, Kuhara Honten.[49] When the holding company came to be fully occupied in dealing with the aftermath of the failure of Kuhara Trading in 1920, overall control of the Kuhara enterprises was exercised through Kuhara Mining instead.[50]

The ratio of Kuhara enterprise stock held by Kuhara Honten was relatively low, and there was little of the familial exclusiveness characteristic of zaibatsu. At the time that Kuhara Honten was set up the largest share it held in any subsidiary was its 50 percent interest in Kuhara Shōji (Trading); it held only 23 percent of Kuhara Mining's stock. The small share in the latter was due in part to the two capital increases that Kuhara Mining carried out in 1916–17 (from ¥10 million to ¥30 million and then to ¥75 million), at which time it sold new shares on the stock market at a premium and earned huge profits.

The zaibatsu suffered through the financial difficulties caused by the collapse of Kuhara Trading only to be burdened further by the deteriorating performance of Kuhara Mining, which had failed to respond effectively to the recession in the copper industry. By late 1926 Kuhara was on the verge of collapse. Kuhara Fusanosuke was forced to step down, entrusting the reconstruction of the zaibatsu to his wife's elder brother, Aikawa Yoshisuke. Aikawa, who was ten years younger than Fusanosuke, succeeded in rebuilding the enterprises, which he then tied into his own business to form the Nissan multisubsidiary system.[51]

The subsidiaries directly controlled by Kuhara, together with their capitalizations as of 1926, when the zaibatsu stalled, are listed in Table 7.15. Osaka Tekkōsho (with a paid-in capital of ¥12.5 million), a subsidiary of Nippon Steamship, and Hitachi Seisakusho (¥10 million

TABLE 7.15   Companies in the Kuhara Zaibatsu, 1926

Company	Date founded	Authorized capital (million yen)	Paid-in capital (million yen)
Kuhara Mining	September 1912	75	41.25
Nippon Steamship	December 1915	10	10
Kyōho Life Insurance	November 1916	1	0.40
Kuhara Real Estate	June 1921	10	10

SOURCE: Same as Table 7.1.

paid-in capital), a Kuhara Mining subsidiary, were not directly managed by the Kuhara zaibatsu. Hitachi was an electrical equipment manufacturer started in 1911 by Odaira Namihei, an electrical engineer with Kuhara Mining, on the basis of the electrical equipment repair shop at Kuhara Mining's Hitachi mine. Permission to begin the venture had to be forced out of Kuhara Fusanosuke, who had little interest in running the new company. Accordingly, Odaira was named executive director of Hitachi and became president in 1929. Kuhara Mining owned three-fourths of Hitachi's stock.[52]

SUZUKI. Prior to assuming the family multisubsidiary form, the unlimited partnership Gōmei Kaisha Suzuki Shōten in 1920 increased its capital a hundredfold, to ¥50 million. The partners were Suzuki Yone (with 40 percent of the capital), Suzuki Iwajirō II (30 percent), his brother Iwazō (20 percent), Kaneko Naokichi (5 percent), and Yanagida Fujimatsu (5 percent). The trading division was spun off in 1923 as Suzuki Shōten, a joint-stock company capitalized at ¥80 million. Gōmei Kaisha Suzuki Shōten thereafter functioned as a holding company for Suzuki Shōten and the other subsidiaries, controlling them and conserving the Suzuki family assets.[53] Suzuki had so many subsidiaries that only the important ones can be listed in Table 7.16. The capitalization figures are for 1927, the year in which Suzuki Shōten, both unlimited partnership and joint-stock company, collapsed.

RATIONALE FOR ADOPTING THE FAMILY MULTISUBSIDIARY SYSTEM

Under the family multisubsidiary system, which was adopted by all the major zaibatsu, the diversified enterprises were organized as joint-stock companies, and the head office that exercised general control over these

TABLE 7.16   Major Companies in the Suzuki Zaibatsu, 1927

Company	Date founded	Capital (million yen)
Kobe Steel	September 1905	20
Harima Shipyard	April 1916[a]	5
Teikoku Steamship	October 1916	1
Teijin	February 1918	12.5
Claude-Process Nitrogen Industries[b]	April 1922	10
Hōnen Oil[c]	April 1922	10
Suzuki Shōten[d]	March 1923	80

SOURCE: Same as Table 7.1.
[a] Date purchased.
[b] Producer of ammonium sulphate.
[c] Producer of edible oils.
[d] Joint-stock company.

companies by holding their shares took the form of an unlimited or limited partnership (*gōmei* or *gōshi kaisha*) owned exclusively by the zaibatsu family. (Asano was exceptional in setting up its head office as a joint-stock company.) The leading zaibatsu all turned to this system in order to profit from the advantages it held over other systems. First, it was more beneficial to organize diversified enterprises as companies rather than as divisions because incorporation of the subsidiaries enabled them to raise capital from the public, strengthened the zaibatsu's financial power, and boosted the morale of the officers by increasing the number of directorships. This was plainly indicated by Mitsubishi's decision to switch from a multidivisional system to a multisubsidiary one and by the refusal of the other zaibatsu to follow Mitsubishi's prior example in assuming a multidivisional form.

Second, by bearing limited rather than unlimited liability, as would have been the case under either of the partnership formats, the enterprises were able to avoid the risk that the failure of any one would prove catastrophic for the combine as a whole. Furthermore, the joint-stock company was subject to a lower tax rate than were the partnerships, an advantage that became even more pronounced after the tax reforms of 1913 and 1920.[54]

Third, being a corporation was better for the zaibatsu head office than remaining a personal organ of the zaibatsu family, in which case employees would be regarded as family servants, a situation in which talented individuals would be unwilling to place themselves. Further, it was anticipated that the arbitrary wishes of the owner family would get in the way of rational management. In addition to such problems, under the Commercial Code (which required that a stockholder be either an individual or a corporation) unincorporated bodies established jointly by zaibatsu family members (for example, the Mitsui Family Council) could not hold the shares of the joint-stock companies operating the zaibatsu's diversified enterprises. Moreover, the individual stockholder's dividends were taxed as personal income, whereas a corporation could retain dividends as internal reserves and enjoyed a lower tax rate, another advantage magnified by the 1913 and 1920 tax reforms.

Finally, with the exception of Asano, a limited or unlimited partnership was not legally obliged to disclose the company's financial and managerial affairs. This outweighed the disadvantages that obtained in terms of taxation and risk (and because the head office was a holding company, the risk was actually reduced). For these reasons, then, by the early 1920s all the zaibatsu had opted for the family multisubsidiary system.

ISSUES OF CONTROL IN THE MULTISUBSIDIARY SYSTEM

An examination of two issues that concern the extent of the power to control within the zaibatsu multisubsidiary system will provide a closer view of the zaibatsu's actual operation. One issue has to do with the degree of control exercised by the holding company as the head office over the subsidiaries; the second involves the degree of control held by the zaibatsu family over the salaried managers.

Control by the Holding Company

The first issue will be examined by studying the decision-making process within the top management of a holding company, using the Mitsui zaibatsu as a case study. Here I want to emphasize that the role of the holding company in almost all the zaibatsu was not one of directing from above but rather of providing informal coordination. The holding company concentrated on providing coordination between itself and the subsidiaries, between the zaibatsu family and the subsidiaries, and among the subsidiaries themselves.

The Mitsui zaibatsu provides an excellent example of this function. Prior to Mitsui's conversion to the multisubsidiary system, the Mitsui subsidiaries displayed a strong centrifugal tendency. The zaibatsu consequently sought to create a powerful central office that would unify the subsidiaries. Mitsui Gōmei, the culmination of repeated control office reorganizations, was established in 1909, with the multisubsidiary system formed around it.

Mitsui Gōmei, as well as serving as the zaibatsu's holding company, also acted as the head office, in which capacity it functioned to control and integrate a number of subsidiaries within one system. But it cannot be assumed that Mitsui Gōmei was the zaibatsu's centralized policy-making and command unit. The method of control exercised by the head office within the multisubsidiary system was more sophisticated than that.

In fact, Mitsui Gōmei cooperated with the designated and ordinary subsidiaries in making strategic decisions. First, the subsidiary's board of directors would decide on a strategy. Such decisions would then be presented for approval to the Mitsui Gōmei board of directors. Since Mitsui Gōmei owned all or a majority of the subsidiaries' shares, subsidiary directors could not establish policies without Mitsui Gōmei's approval. Moreover, Mitsui Gōmei held huge monetary resources accumulated by absorbing the subsidiaries' profits as dividends, and such funds were allocated to the subsidiaries only after assessment and coordination of their proposals.

Mitsui Gōmei did not, however, command the subsidiaries from above. True, it often opposed their proposals and could reject them, but it avoided imposing a veto unless the subsidiaries were being too selfish. According to the minutes of the Mitsui Gōmei board of directors, between 1923 and 1932 the board did not once exercise its power of veto over proposals by subsidiaries.[55] For instance, the company history of Tōyō Rayon, a subsidiary of Mitsui Bussan, shows that before Tōyō Rayon's establishment in 1926, Mitsui Gōmei hesitated to approve the plans of the trading company to enter the rayon industry, arguing that lack of experience would make it too risky.[56] But the records of the Mitsui Gōmei board of directors indicate nothing of this problem. If a conflict between Mitsui Gōmei and Mitsui Bussan flared over this issue, it was undoubtedly resolved through informal negotiation. Thus, for Mitsui Gōmei, control over the subsidiaries meant checking, revising, and approving proposals originated by the subsidiaries on the basis of negotiation.

Mitsui Gōmei's method of controlling the subsidiaries retained this character throughout its existence. Consequently the holding company did not need an extensive research and planning section and had only a small central staff. The number of Mitsui Gōmei officers, apart from employees who handled simple routine tasks, ranged from 115 in 1923 to a maximum of 153 in 1929. These figures include the staffs of operating departments in charge of real estate and colonial agricultural enterprises and such auxiliary departments as secretarial, accounting, and

TABLE 7.17 Officers of Major Designated Subsidiaries of Mitsui and Mitsubishi

Zaibatsu subsidiary	1920	1925	1930	1935
Mitsui				
Bank[a]	697	988	1,227	1,187
Trading[b]	3,749	2,867	3,192	2,926
Mining	3,441	3,373	3,035	2,771
Mitsubishi				
Bank	380	841	1,164	1,395
Trading	1,199	952	1,426	1,547
Mining	2,435	2,265	2,418	3,133
Shipbuilding	2,941	1,932	2,113	c
Aircraft	157	273	293	c
Heavy Industries	—	—	—	2,750[c]

SOURCES: Compiled from various company histories.
[a] Males only.
[b] Excluding females and subofficers.
[c] The shipbuilding and aircraft subsidiaries merged to form Mitsubishi Heavy Industries in 1934.

maintenance services. Probably no more than twenty officers worked in research and planning.[57] Compared to the staffs of the Mitsui subsidiaries, that number was remarkably small indeed (Table 7.17).

A small head office planning staff was common to the other zaibatsu as well. The Mitsubishi zaibatsu head office, Mitsubishi, Ltd., in 1941 had only 104 employees, including typists, nurses, and doorkeepers, a tiny number compared to the staffs of the Mitsubishi subsidiaries (Table 7.17).[58]

Thus, almost every zaibatsu's holding company lacked a centralized authority to decide strategy for the subsidiary enterprises. Its function was rather to coordinate policy among the subsidiaries and to unify the zaibatsu as a whole. In that role, the holding companies performed top managerial functions and proved to be useful. Even in Japan today, the top management of most large corporations behaves in a similar fashion, not often directing from the top down. Instead, management collects proposals from below and, rarely exercising a straight veto, coordinates their implementation through informal negotiations, thus preserving the unity of the company.

Two points with regard to control by the holding company should be emphasized: First, in each case the zaibatsu multisubsidiary system formed around a holding company, but such companies should not be confused with the many large enterprises of pre-World War II Britain that likewise took the holding company form. In contrast to the zaibatsu holding company, which was a device whereby a single family controlled diversified businesses, the British holding company emerged through the federation of several enterprises and was the organ through which the participating enterprises cooperated and coordinated strategies (H-form). Though both organizations were holding companies, their functions were fundamentally different.

Second, one must distinguish between the loose control exercised by the holding company under the zaibatsu multisubsidiary system and that under the business federations of the British system. In the latter, the light control was dictated by the fact that the holding company had emerged as the result of the coming together of several enterprises; but in the Japanese case the holding company opted for loose control in order to permit the subsidiary companies to operate their diversified enterprises in an active and autonomous fashion within the zaibatsu framework. The same logic was at work here as that in the case of the U.S. multidivisional system that resulted from the diversification strategies of American business in the 1920s (M-form).

Changes in Zaibatsu Family Control

The second issue regarding the power to control will be approached through a consideration of the transformations in the relationship between the zaibatsu family and its top salaried managers on the basis of examples taken from Mitsui and other zaibatsu. Changes in the degree of control exercised by the owner families over their zaibatsu accompanied the conversion of the zaibatsu to the family multisubsidiary system. By 1930 the top managements of nearly all the zaibatsu had come to be based on cooperation between members of the zaibatsu family and salaried managers (Table 7.18). Within this cooperative framework, however, was a considerable range among the zaibatsu top managements both in the ratio of family members to salaried managers and in the relative influence exerted by each group. Among managements with a larger proportion of salaried managers, the Mitsui top salaried managers held greater authority than their relative number— five salaried managers to three family members—would indicate. Conversely, at Mitsubishi, President Iwasaki Koyata wielded greater power than the composition of the head office top management—one family member and five salaried managers—would suggest.

Ōkura presents the case of a zaibatsu head office with equal representation by family members and salaried managers. Although founder Ōkura Kihachirō retired in 1924 and entrusted the business to his eldest son Kishichirō, a cooperative management structure prevailed because Kihachirō had greatly trusted vice president Kadono Chōkurō,

TABLE 7.18 The Top Managements of the Major Zaibatsu Head Offices, 1930

	Composition of top management	
Head office	Family member(s)	Salaried manager(s)
Mitsubishi, Ltd.[a]	President (Koyata)	1 senior executive director 2 executive directors 2 directors
Yasuda Hozensha[b]	President (Zenjirō II) 4 directors	3 directors
Furukawa Gōmei[b]	President (Toranosuke) 1 active partner and director 1 director	1 senior executive director 2 executive directors 4 directors
Ōkura-gumi[b]	President (Kishichirō)	1 vice president
Asano Dōzoku[c,d]	President (Sōichirō II) 5 directors	
Fujita-gumi[b]	President (Heitarō) 1 vice president 1 director	2 directors
Mitsui Gōmei[b]	President (Hachirōemon) 2 active partners	1 senior executive director 2 executive directors 2 directors
Sumitomo, Ltd.[a]	President (Kichizaemon)	1 senior executive director 1 executive director 1 director

SOURCE: Same as Table 7.1.
[a] Limited partnership.
[b] Unlimited partnership.
[c] Joint-stock company.
[d] Data as of 1931, founder Sōichirō I having died in 1930.

a salaried manager. The two had been together since 1911, when Kihachirō was in Ōkura-gumi with Kadono as his chief assistant.

Family members outnumbered salaried managers in the top managements of two other zaibatsu head offices with a cooperative management structure, Fujita-gumi and Yasuda Hozensha. At Fujita-gumi, though, one salaried manager (actually, two men serving in succession) was in charge as executive director from 1916 to 1929. Yasuda Hozensha, on the other hand, placed only family members in the top management during founder Yasuda Zenjirō's lifetime. Yūki Toyotarō did not join the high command from outside the zaibatsu until after the founder's death in 1921. Yūki was the cause of discord at Yasuda, and he eventually quit, an outcome that undoubtedly reflected the high proportion of family members in the top management.

Asano was the exception to the cooperative management pattern: Asano Dōzoku's top management was filled entirely by Asano family members. The president was Sōichirō II; the directors were Shiraishi Motojirō and Suzuki Monjirō (both brothers-in-law of Sōichirō II) and Asano Ryōzō, Hachirō, and Yoshio (Sōichirō II's brothers). Asano still retained exclusive family control in 1931 because its autocratic founder had died only the year before. None of the other zaibatsu founders survived to 1930.

As in Yasuda's case, the usual pattern among the zaibatsu included a strong and autocratic founder. Once he left the scene—and as the business abilities and interest of the succeeding generations of family members declined and the salaried managers acquired greater management know-how—the zaibatsu top management tended to adopt a system of shared responsibility between the family members and salaried managers. Moreover, in such a cooperative structure the family members' position tended to become increasingly nominal, a merely symbolic dominance based on their ownership rights.

Although the zaibatsu family owned the enterprises and the salaried managers were the family's employees—and constrained by rule and custom to respect and show loyalty to their masters, the family members—the zaibatsu's stable management and successful growth depended on the salaried managers. The family members lacked the managerial knowledge and experience to take their place. Salaried managers therefore came to wield greater influence than the family members within the cooperative management structure.

Their influence, moreover, tended to increase over time: the older the zaibatsu, the greater the salaried managers' command, a trend accounted for by several factors. First, as the scale, complexity, and diversity of the zaibatsu enterprises grew, so did the degree of dependency on the skills of the salaried managers grow. Also, increase in the scale and diversity of a zaibatsu was accompanied by growth in the number of its salaried managers. Such growth in turn led to the formation of a managerial hierarchy, which tended to reinforce the influence of the salaried managers. Their increasing power was fostered by trends within the zaibatsu family as well. The energetic founder would age, retire, and die, and his heirs would often lack managerial skills and be uninterested in business. As a result, their authority within the zaibatsu would wane. Together these factors suggest a tendency on the part of the zaibatsu to make the transition from what was formally a family enterprise to a managerial enterprise.[59]

In many zaibatsu, the shift in control within the top management was clearly reflected in the process of decision making with regard to the zaibatsu enterprises. In the Mitsui zaibatsu, for example, Mitsui Gōmei's top management consisted of the board of directors and the active partners. The two groups would hold successive meetings on the same day, twice a week. The board of directors, composed of salaried managers, would first meet to make decisions concerning the designated and ordinary subsidiaries. Then, the active partners, composed of representatives of the eleven Mitsui families, would meet the directors in order to approve their decisions.[60] But family members were often absent from their meetings. For instance, Mitsui Hachirōemon Takamine, Mitsui Gōmei president and head of the senior main family, attended less than half of the active partners' meetings each year.[61] Even when they did attend, family members would usually simply ask questions of the top salaried managers.

Occasionally family members would oppose a decision made by the directors, but they would invariably yield to persuasion. An example of this occurred in 1919 when Mitsui Bank offered part of its stock to the public. Ikeda Seihin, the bank's senior executive director, had requested the public offering, and the bank president, a member of the Mitsui family, agreed. Ikeda's plan was opposed, however, by Mitsui Hachirōemon Takamine. Dan Takuma, the highest positioned manager, supported Ikeda and tried, unsuccessfully, to convince Hachirōemon Takamine to change his mind. Takamine was not averse to a public offering if it were confined to the bank, but he feared that such a move would have repercussions on Mitsui Bussan and the other subsidiaries and thus cause the exclusive family ownership of the zaibatsu as a whole to break down. At a later meeting in person, Ikeda presented his arguments to Takamine and succeeded in obtaining his permission to proceed with the public offering.[62]

Such examples show that just as the standard view that the zaibatsu holding company exercised tight control over the subsidiary enterprises needs to be revised, so too does the notion that exclusive ownership by the zaibatsu family meant a firm grip on strategic decision making by family members.

PART IV

DEPRESSION, WAR, AND DISSOLUTION, 1930–48

CHAPTER 8

TRANSFORMATION, COLLAPSE, AND POSTWAR DISSOLUTION

Over time the zaibatsu families tended not only to yield control over strategic decision-making to their salaried managers but also to lose exclusive ownership of their main enterprise. In fact, the zaibatsu, which had come to dominate the Japanese economy as the leading representatives of the closed system of business ownership, were unable to survive the tumultuous period that began with the Great Depression and ended with the postwar American Occupation of Japan.

Although individual zaibatsu enterprises, particularly heavy industrial firms, flourished during the 1930s and early 1940s, the zaibatsu as closed family businesses started to crumble in the political and economic crisis that followed the onset of the Depression in 1930. The final demise of the zaibatsu occurred in two successive phases. The first took place after the outbreak of war with China in 1937, when, in the attempt to reorganize themselves in order to raise capital from the public and thereby meet the growing military demand for expanded investment in heavy industry, they further undermined their exclusive family ownership. The second phase was the dissolution of the zaibatsu under the direction of Occupation forces immediately after World War II. The Occupation in effect completed what the depression and war had begun by forcing the zaibatsu formally to dissolve.

The collapse of the zaibatsu can therefore be explained in terms of a combination of political and economic factors. On the one hand, a series of political movements, ranging from antizaibatsu attacks during the Depression to military pressure after 1937 to forced dissolution under the U.S. Occupation, was in operation. On the other hand, an economic process that made the basic character of the zaibatsu untenable—that is, exclusive ownership of diversified enterprises by a single wealthy family—was also at work. Under single-family ownership, the zaibatsu could not respond successfully to the trend toward expansion of heavy industry that was brought on by the post-Depression wartime boom.

If the zaibatsu clung to the closed system and tried to rely solely on self-financing, they would run short of capital and have to abandon diversification that centered on heavy industry. The contradiction between exclusive family ownership and diversified management, which had already manifested itself in the 1920s, became even clearer and limited the continued growth and existence of the zaibatsu after 1930.

THE ZAIBATSU "CONVERSION"

The zaibatsu started on the road to collapse in 1930 when the Japanese economy fell into the so-called Shōwa Depression, which for the industrial sector lasted until 1932. Two main factors triggered the depression: first, the effects of the Wall Street Crash of 1929 began to reach Japan at that time; second, a shock was caused by the disastrous lifting of the gold embargo by the Japanese government in early 1930.[1] The depression itself was not the blow that brought down the majority of the zaibatsu, because their enormous power enabled them to survive the economic cataclysm with ease. That very power, however, became the object of critical attacks during the depression years. Furthermore, anger over the ineffectiveness and corruption of the party cabinets that governed Japan until 1932 intensified criticism of the zaibatsu, which were major financial contributors to the political parties. Such criticism put the zaibatsu on the route to demise.

The antizaibatsu movement of the early 1930s did not represent a spontaneous response by the Japanese people to the hardships imposed by the depression, but rather resulted from skillful maneuvering by anticapitalist forces on the political left as well as right. The press, especially the major newspapers, served as the medium for their ideas. Demagoguery has always been the most effective means of influencing public opinion on any given issue, and so the formation of antizaibatsu opinion among the Japanese public in the early 1930s depended heavily on demagoguery, specifically the spreading of false rumors concerning dollar buying by the zaibatsu.

Mitsui Bank and Mitsui Bussan in particular came under virulent attack for their allegedly treasonous behavior in buying dollars with yen just before Japan went off the gold standard in late 1931, thereby earning huge profits in spite of the depression. In fact, such dollar buying was a normal contingency measure taken to protect overseas investments, in this case in response to Great Britain's departure from the gold standard and the steep drop in the pound earlier that year. Mitsui Bank, far from reaping windfall profits, actually recorded losses of ¥12 million in the latter half of 1931.[2] Mitsui Bussan likewise suffered a decline in profits. Furthermore, these two companies were not alone in buying dollars at the time.[3] But the public, stirred up by attacks on Mitsui, was not about to consider such facts, nor did Mitsui's top management attempt to vindicate itself.[4]

The antizaibatsu movement turned violent in March 1932 when a right-wing terrorist assassinated Mitsui Gōmei senior executive director Dan. Faced with the threat of further terrorist attacks, Mitsui family members and top managers decided to carry out a program of reform as a means of allaying public antagonism. Thus was initiated what has come to be known as the "conversion of the zaibatsu" (*zaibatsu no tenkō*). As the first step in the process, Mitsui Takamine, head of the Mitsui family, president of Mitsui Gōmei, and chairman of the Mitsui Family Council, resigned in March 1933, handing over his positions to his heir, thirty-eight-year-old Takakimi.

Since Dan's assassination strategic decisions at Mitsui Gōmei had been made by consultation among six executives: the two executive directors of Mitsui Gōmei, Ariga Nagafumi and Fukui Kikusaburō; the senior executive directors of the bank, mining company, and trading company, Ikeda Seihin, Makita Tamaki, and Yasukawa Yūnosuke; and the chairman of Mitsui Trust Company, Yoneyama Umekichi. The latter four had retained their positions in the designated subsidiaries while also serving as directors of Mitsui Gōmei. Takakimi, however, believed that Mitsui needed the leadership of a single top management figure. At the recommendation of retired senior Mitsui manager Masuda Takashi, he asked Ikeda Seihin to accept the office of senior executive director.[5] Ikeda agreed and resigned from Mitsui Bank in September 1933 to take up the Mitsui Gōmei post.

The new regime implemented its conversion policy in a number of steps. First, all Mitsui family members except Takakimi resigned their offices in Mitsui-related enterprises. The holding company then sold shares of Mitsui subsidiaries on the stock market. The main goal of the public offering was to dampen criticism of the zaibatsu, but it was also hoped that operating capital as well as funds for charitable contributions would be generated. Next, Takakimi and Ikeda had Mitsui contribute vast sums to charities and community organizations, a strategy exemplified by the establishment in April 1934 of the Mitsui Hō'onkai (Repayment of Kindness Society), a charitable foundation with ¥30 million in capital.[6] And finally, in January 1934 they forced the resignation of Mitsui Bussan's top manager, Yasukawa, who had been widely criticized for his profits-first mentality.[7]

The conversion measures proved effective, as public censure of Mitsui gradually abated. Other zaibatsu escaped becoming direct targets of organized antizaibatsu attacks but nevertheless imitated Mitsui in offering stock to the public and making charitable contributions. Such moves in essence stemmed from a desire to avoid the impression that the zaibatsu families monopolized wealth and economic influence. But by opening ownership to the public it followed that the conversion dealt a serious blow to the familial exclusiveness that was one of the defining characteristics of the zaibatsu.

Another measure that served to deflect public criticism was cooperation with the military and the "revisionist" bureaucrats who were collaborating with military planners in an effort to change the political and economic status quo. The Japanese army was steadily expanding its encroachment on China with the invasion of Manchuria in 1931 and the establishment of Manchukuo as a puppet state the following year. The military and its bureaucratic allies supported the expansion by promoting the development at home of both heavy industry and state control of the economy. That the zaibatsu adopted a management strategy conforming to these trends was not simply a matter of seeking to gain profits by supplying military demand. They were also clearly motivated by the need to demonstrate their patriotism in order to redeem themselves in the public eye.

Adding to the zaibatsu's difficulties in the early 1930s, a powerful rival emerged in the form of industrial groups commonly called the "new zaibatsu." These groups were not really zaibatsu, but the largest of them, Nippon Sangyō zaibatsu (Nissan Konzern), did have some zaibatsu-like features, for it was a group of firms rebuilt from the struggling Kuhara zaibatsu by Kuhara Fusanosuke's brother-in-law, Aikawa Yoshisuke, with financial assistance from relatives.

Under Aikawa, Kuhara Kōgyō's mining operations were transferred to the newly established Nippon Kōgyō (Japan Mining) in 1928. Aikawa thereupon converted Kuhara Mining into a holding company, renamed Nippon Sangyō, which made public stock offerings. The Nissan group therefore lacked the familial exclusiveness characteristic of the zaibatsu. Aikawa and his relatives owned about 40 percent of Nippon Sangyō's stock in 1928, a figure that plummeted to about 5 percent by 1937.[8] Nippon Sangyō came to control a multisubsidiary empire that encompassed such leading manufacturers as Nissan Jidōsha (Nissan Motor Co.), Hitachi Seisakusho (Hitachi, Ltd.), Osaka Tekkōsho (Osaka Shipyard, renamed Hitachi Zōsen or Hitachi Shipbuilding in 1943), and Nissan Kagaku Kōgyō (Nissan Chemical Industries).

The scale of Nippon Sangyō's operations required such huge investments that Nissan was unable to maintain a zaibatsu-style system of exclusive family ownership. All the other "new zaibatsu," including Nitchitsu (developed from Nippon Nitrogenous Fertilizer), Nissō, Mori, and Riken, from the outset lacked family-based exclusiveness. Thus the term "new zaibatsu" is plainly a misnomer.[9] Perhaps "new industrial group" is a more appropriate designation, for these more widely held and loosely controlled combines generally got their start in manufacturing industries, especially the heavy industries, whereas the zaibatsu tended to have originated in mining industries or in such services as banking, shipping, and commerce.

Because these new groups were for the most part actively entering new fields of heavy industry, they were praised by the military and revisionist bureaucrats, who were dissatisfied with the more cautious zaibatsu. Such officials tended in their economic planning to favor the new industrial groups over the zaibatsu. For instance, the military obstructed efforts by Mitsui and Mitsubishi to found or expand enterprises in Korea and Manchukuo while granting monopolistic rights there to Nissan and Nitchitsu. The new groups grew rapidly with such military and bureaucratic support.

In the long run, the new industrial groups could not equal the major zaibatsu in economic power, given the latter's vast financial resources. When the government in 1940 began to intensify wartime control of the economy, the performance of some of the new groups deteriorated, their overambitious policies having brought them to a standstill for lack of funds. At that point, those relying mainly on the Nippon Kōgyō Ginkō (Japan Industrial Bank) for capital fell under the control of that semiofficial organ.

The new industrial groups were an active party to Japanese military expansion during the 1930s. The comparative role of the zaibatsu in this trend is ambiguous. Some scholars claim that the zaibatsu actually spearheaded Japan's war of aggression beginning with the Manchurian invasion,[10] a view that is totally unfounded. The driving force behind Japanese aggression was the military, in particular the army. The zaibatsu did nothing more than follow the military. They may be accused of having acquiesced in the army's unilateral actions on the continent, which culminated in the Sino-Japanese War of 1937–45 and the Pacific War of 1941–45, but the zaibatsu could not be expected to have had the power to halt the runaway army when the emperor and navy had failed to do so. Once hostilities broke out, the zaibatsu simply had to adjust to the growing wartime situation.

The zaibatsu did indeed cooperate with the military to the extent that they accepted orders from it. They took advantage of the burgeoning military demand as well as concessions in conquered territories in order to earn huge profits. Nevertheless, the real preference of the zaibatsu was to avoid war—not because they were pacifists, but because they wanted to protect their interests. The zaibatsu reasoned that, as Japan depended so heavily on the resources and technology of the dollar-pound community, the nation could not afford to make enemies of the United States and Great Britain, which would be the inevitable result of continued Japanese aggression against China.[11] The zaibatsu moreover perceived that escalation of the conflict would entail greater economic controls, higher taxes, and compulsory investment, and such an eventuality would threaten the zaibatsu's ability to survive in a free enterprise system.

Despite the conversion of the zaibatsu, the military and right-wing groups remained hostile toward them. For example, it was feared that the military would force Mitsui Bussan to dissolve as a corporation as a result of the 1943 Sansei Incident, in which Bussan's Taiyuan branch was accused of breaking military regulations by dealing in the black market.[12] Military actions that were not aimed at eliminating the zaibatsu could still threaten their existence—for instance, the army compelled the zaibatsu to make a series of nonremunerative investments in such semicolonial ventures as Kita Shina Kaihatsu (North China Development) and Naka Shina Shinkō (Central China Promotion). The zaibatsu-military relationship was at best an uneasy one, and zaibatsu support of Japanese military expansion was more a matter of necessity than choice.

WARTIME GROWTH OF THE ZAIBATSU IN HEAVY INDUSTRY

While antizaibatsu attacks and military demands were the political factors driving the zaibatsu system to collapse, the wartime expansion of heavy industry was the main economic factor. As Japan slid deeper into war after 1937, the zaibatsu began to suffer from a lack of funds for their growing heavy industries and were finally forced to abandon exclusive family ownership in a reorganization that permitted the introduction of outside capital.

This was not the first time that the zaibatsu were compelled by a shortage of capital to reconsider the principle of familial exclusiveness. In the decade after World War I Mitsui and Mitsubishi had opened some of the stock in their subsidiaries to public subscription. At least in the case of Mitsubishi Bank, the public offering was clearly dictated by the zaibatsu's confrontation with the limits of the capital that could be supplied by the two branches of the Iwasaki family. Thus the family exclusiveness of the zaibatsu had started to break down well before the late 1930s, as the capital demand generated by diversification into heavy industry exceeded the owner families' financial resources, forcing the zaibatsu to seek partial funding for their subsidiaries from extrafamilial sources.

Although the zaibatsu's closed ownership system began to crumble, their heavy industrial subsidiaries thrived in the 1930s. Japan's heavy industries as a whole had suffered in the postwar recession and ensuing decade of economic stagnation, but they had nevertheless strengthened their competitiveness through rationalization and technological improvements. In the thirties they took advantage of the drop in imports that owed to the reimposition of the gold embargo and the resulting depreciation of the yen as well as to the increase in military demand after the Manchurian invasion. Heavy industries accounted for 32 percent of Japanese factory production in 1929; by 1937 the figure had risen to 61 percent.[13] Not surprisingly, the heavy industrial firms built by the zaibatsu over the years led in that expansion. In the mid-1930s the zaibatsu enjoyed a continuance of self-financing as they actively invested in heavy industry the high profits earned by their mining enterprises. The mining operations, both coal and nonferric metal, were able to reap the necessary profits thanks to the renewal of the gold embargo, and the reinvestment of those earnings led the zaibatsu to dominate Japan's heavy industrial sector.

Zaibatsu activity in heavy industry during the 1930s consisted almost entirely of reorganizing and strengthening existing operations. This was particularly true of Mitsui and Sumitomo, which took very little initiative in new fields of heavy industry at the time. In Mitsui's case, such movement was confined to developing its chemical companies, Tōyō High Pressure and Miike Dyestuff Works (the latter was made independent in 1941 as Mitsui Kagaku Kōgyō or Mitsui Chemical Industries); spinning off the shipbuilding division of Mitsui Bussan as Tama Zōsensho (Tama Shipyard), capitalized at ¥10 million and renamed Mitsui Zōsen (Mitsui Shipbuilding) in 1942; and bringing into the Mitsui Bussan fold such machinery manufacturers as Ushio Seisakusho, Kayaba, and Tokyo Keiki (Tokyo Gauge).

Sumitomo actively upgraded and restructured its heavy industrial enterprises during this period. Sumitomo Fertilizer Manufacturing Co., for example, increased its technological capabilities after taking on Nakao Shinroku and other engineers from the old Suzuki Shōten and in 1934 renamed itself Sumitomo Kagaku Kōgyō (Sumitomo Chemical Industries). Sumitomo Copper and Steel and Sumitomo Steel Works merged in 1935 to form Sumitomo Kinzoku Kōgyō (Sumitomo Metal Industries), capitalized at ¥40 million. In addition, Sumitomo began to participate in the management of NEC (Nippon Denki) in 1932. Still, Sumitomo did not move vigorously into new heavy industries; in fact, the only venture it started in this period was Sumitomo Aluminum Seiren (Sumitomo Aluminum Refining), founded in 1934 with a capital of ¥10 million.

Compared to Mitsui and Sumitomo, Mitsubishi had a much bolder and perhaps exceptional record of entering new fields of heavy industry in the 1930s. Mitsubishi's enormous resources enabled it to succeed as a latecomer in several heavy industries, including the oil-refining and coal chemical industries. Mitsubishi Sekiyu (Mitsubishi Oil) was founded in 1931. Mitsubishi Trading Company had set up a fuel division in 1924 aiming to import and refine crude oil and to establish a joint-venture refinery with its customer Associated Oil and Associated's parent company, Tidewater Oil. After extended negotiations beginning in 1928 over capital participation ratios, Mitsubishi Oil was finally established, with the Mitsubishi zaibatsu and Associated Oil each contributing half its total capital of ¥5 million.[14]

The basis for Mitsubishi's coal chemical industry was laid with the purchase of the Makiyama coke factory in 1898, but not until August 1934, when Mitsubishi Mining and Asahi Glass founded Nippon Tar Kōgyō (Nippon Tar Industries), capitalized at ¥5 million, did Mitsubishi seriously enter the field.[15] Mitsubishi intended through Nippon Tar Industries to catch up with Mitsui in the coal chemical industry in the manufacture of synthetic chemicals, including tar chemicals, which Mitsui Mining had been producing since the 1910s, and ammonia chemicals, produced by Mitsui Mining since the early 1930s. Nippon Tar Industries in 1936 purchased a technology for the synthesis of ammonia and production of ammonium sulphate from the German firm I. G. Farben at a cost of ¥4.13 million;[16] at that time Nippon Tar Industries's capital was increased sixfold to ¥30 million, and the firm was renamed Nippon Kasei Kōgyō (Nippon Chemical Industries). The following year Nippon Kasei bought large amounts of stock in Shinko Jinken (Shinko Rayon), and in 1942 took over the company. Mitsubishi Kasei Kōgyō (Mitsubishi Chemical Industries) was formed in 1944 by a merger of Nippon Kasei and Asahi Glass, but after World War II it was broken up into the present Mitsubishi Chemical Industries, Asahi Glass, and Mitsubishi Rayon.

The exceptional case of the withdrawal of the leading zaibatsu from a heavy industry, that of iron and steel, occurred during the mid-1930s. The state-owned Yawata Iron Works and private iron and steel companies merged in 1934 to form Nippon Seitetsu (Nippon Iron and Steel, the predecessor of today's Nippon Steel Corporation). Among the private firms were Mitsui's Wanishi Seitetsu (the successor to the Wanishi Iron Works of Hokkaido Colliery), Kamaishi Kōzan, and Mitsubishi Iron and Steel. Initially, it appeared that Asano's Nippon Kōkan (NKK), Asano Kokura Steel, and the steel-making division of Asano Shipbuilding would also take part in the new venture, but when the three Asano firms bounced back from their doldrums after the reimposition of the gold embargo, they declined to participate, using as their excuse a difference of opinion on the method of asset evaluation to be employed in the merger.

Because Wanishi Seitetsu, Kamaishi Kōzan, and Mitsubishi Iron and Steel had maintained iron production as their core divisions, they had long run heavily in the red owing to pressure from imports of inexpensive Indian iron. Hence, the standard view is that Mitsui and Mitsubishi transferred their iron and steel companies to Nippon Iron and Steel in order to unload unprofitable operations on favorable terms. In fact, like Asano, Mitsui and Mitsubishi had hoped to retain their iron and steel enterprises after seeing the Mitsui and Mitsubishi companies turn around in the more favorable economic climate after 1932. Once the state and private firms began to move ahead with plans for Nippon Iron and Steel, however, the top two zaibatsu, striving to demonstrate their patriotic "conversion" at the time, were unable to pull out.[17]

With the exception of iron and steel, then, the three major zaibatsu had greatly expanded their heavy industrial capacities by 1937; thereafter, as the wartime situation intensified, their involvement in heavy industries grew dramatically. As Table 8.1 indicates, from 1937 to 1945 the total paid-in capital of Mitsui's heavy industrial subsidiaries increased over tenfold, and that of Mitsubishi and Sumitomo tenfold; at the same time, within each zaibatsu, the heavy industries' share of the paid-in capital of all subsidiaries rose from less than half to between three- and four-fifths. The biggest gains were made in machinery and metallurgy, with the zaibatsu not only increasing the productivity and capitalization of their existing enterprises but also bringing many other firms, in particular machinery manufacturers, under their control.

Much of this wartime expansion in zaibatsu heavy industries of course involved military-related enterprises. The most successful of these was Mitsubishi Jūkōgyō (Mitsubishi Heavy Industries), which was the new name given to Mitsubishi Shipbuilding and Engineering in April 1934, a month before it absorbed Mitsubishi Aircraft. The company had an immense wartime role, producing the warships and airplanes that spearheaded Japanese military expansion. During the war years it consistently accounted for more than 30 percent of Japan's total airplane production (fuselages and engines). Mitsubishi Heavy Industries is especially renowned for having built the battleship *Musashi* and the Zero fighter plane, both perfected in 1940. Sumitomo Metal Indus-

TABLE 8.1   Industrial Distribution of the Subsidiaries of the Top Three Zaibatsu, 1937 and 1945 (million yen)

Industry of Subsidiaries	Mitsui 1937 Paid-in capital		Mitsui 1945 Paid-in capital		Mitsubishi 1937 Paid-in capital		Mitsubishi 1945 Paid-in capital		Sumitomo 1937 Paid-in capital		Sumitomo 1945 Paid-in capital	
Heavy industry	136	(22.2%)	1,732	(56.6%)	156	(27.2%)	1,590	(58.9%)	136	(35.3%)	1,338	(81.3%)
Mining	162	(26.4)	481	(15.7)	106	(18.5)	274	(10.1)	34	(8.8)	111	(6.7)
Light industry	84	(13.9)	273	(9.0)	66	(11.5)	73	(2.7)	36	(9.4)	29	(1.8)
Finance	70	(11.5)	169	(5.5)	127	(22.1)	159	(5.9)	58	(15.1)	65	(3.9)
Other	159	(25.9)	403	(13.2)	118	(20.6)	604	(22.4)	121	(31.4)	102	(6.2)
Total	612	(100.0)	3,061	(100.0)	574	(100.0)	2,700	(100.0)	385	(100.0)	1,646	(100.0)

SOURCE: *Nihon Kōgyō Ginkō 50-nen shi* (50 Years of Japan Industrial Bank) (Tokyo: Nihon Kōgyō Ginkō, 1957), p. 425.

tries, which manufactured steel, rolled copper, and light metal alloys, also played a key part in the war; for example, it developed the extra strong duraluminum (ESD) used in the Zero fighter.

The Mitsui zaibatsu likewise built up heavy industries with military applications, including Mitsui Shipbuilding under Mitsui Bussan; Tōyō High Pressure and Mitsui Chemical Industries under Mitsui Mining; and the affiliated firms Nippon Steel Works, Tokyo Shibaura Denki (Tokyo Shibaura Electrical Machinery), and Shōwa Hikōki (Shōwa Aircraft). In addition, in 1943 Mitsui founded Miike Sekiyu Gōsei (Miike Petroleum Synthesis) in order to produce synthetic petroleum from liquified coal. Its work attracted considerable interest within the military, but the war ended before the operation had become profitable. Though Mitsui developed such war-related industries, its advance into the munitions field was relatively restrained compared to that of Mitsubishi and Sumitomo.

WARTIME REORGANIZATION AND COLLAPSE

The enormous wartime expansion of zaibatsu heavy industries (Table 8.2) dealt a severe blow to the closed system of the zaibatsu by taking them well beyond the limits of their own financial resources. In the wake of the zaibatsu conversion, the owner families could no longer claim a legitimate right to exclusive ownership, even had they been able to exercise it. The large charitable contributions made by the zaibatsu as part of their conversion programs and the oppressive wartime taxes imposed by the state had greatly eroded the financial reserves of the owner families just when the zaibatsu needed huge capital increases to expand their heavy industries. It was no longer possible for a zaibatsu family to operate a diversified set of heavy industrial enterprises by relying only upon its own wealth, and with the gradual collapse of the one-family ownership system, the zaibatsu had no choice but to move toward a system suitable for mobilizing capital from society at large. The zaibatsu then not only opened their subsidiaries' stock to public ownership but also proceeded to turn their head offices into joint-stock companies and to make public stock offerings of them as well.

Sumitomo was the first of the three major zaibatsu to reorganize its head office into a joint-stock company, converting Sumitomo, Ltd. into Kabushiki Kaisha Sumitomo Honsha (Sumitomo Head Office, Inc.) in March 1937. The new head office, like its predecessor, was capitalized at ¥150 million, and stock ownership was restricted to members of the Sumitomo family. When Sumitomo Honsha doubled its capitalization in March 1945 it offered 50,000 of the 300,000 new shares to the

Depression, War, and Dissolution

TABLE 8.2 Concentration of Fourteen Zaibatsu Subsidiaries in Heavy Industries (paid-in capital, thousand yen)

	1937		1947*	
	14 zaibatsu subsidiaries	Total companies (within Japan)	14 zaibatsu subsidiaries	Total companies (within Japan)
Manufacturing and mining	2,039.348 (25.3%)	8,056.601 (100%)	10,440.200 (47.2%)	22,089.231 (100%)
Heavy industries	985.504 (27.3)	3,612.502 (100)	7,919.585 (54.9)	14,430.619 (100)
Metal	174.478 (19.1)	911.752 (100)	1,655.406 (43.2)	3,829.681 (100)
Machinery	385.312 (29.4)	1,311.471 (100)	4,302.777 (56.4)	7,632.409 (100)
Chemical	425.714 (30.6)	1,389.279 (100)	1,961.402 (66.1)	2,968.529 (100)

SOURCE: Yamazaki Hiroaki, "Senjika no sangyō kōzō to dokusen soshiki," in *Senji Nihon Keizai* (Japan's Wartime Economy), ed., University of Tokyo Institute of Social Science (Tokyo: University of Tokyo Press, 1979), p. 252.

*1947 was the year that SCAP ordered the freezing of assets of zaibatsu family members and the sale to the public of their stockholdings.

NOTE: The fourteen zaibatsu are Mitsui, Mitsubishi, Sumitomo, Furukawa, Asano, Ōkura, Yasuda, Nomura, Aikawa (Nissan), Nitchitsu, Nissō, Mori, Riken, and Nakajima (aircraft manufacturer). Not all of these were zaibatsu in the strict sense.

public. This "public" offering, however, was limited to three Sumitomo subsidiaries: Sumitomo Bank, Sumitomo Trust, and Sumitomo Life Insurance.[18]

The next of the major zaibatsu to restructure its head office was Mitsubishi; it turned Mitsubishi, Ltd., into Kabushiki Kaisha Mitsubishi Sha in December 1937. As in Sumitomo's case, the capitalization of the head office remained unchanged at ¥120 million, and stock ownership was limited to members of the two branches of the Iwasaki family. When Mitsubishi Sha doubled its capitalization in 1940, new stock was offered to the public—but the "public" was defined somewhat narrowly to include only major shareholders, apart from Iwasaki family members, of Mitsubishi designated subsidiaries; employees of those subsidiaries; and those who had rendered distinguished service to Mitsubishi. Still, 20,000 individuals were eligible to acquire the stock. As a result of the public offering, the Iwasaki family's interest in Mitsubishi Sha fell to 50 percent. Mitsubishi Sha was renamed Mitsubishi Honsha in 1943.[19]

Mitsui converted its head office, Mitsui Gōmei, to the joint-stock company format in August 1940, but it did not do so directly. The direct approach would have required the liquidation of Mitsui Gōmei, with a resultant enormous tax assessment—some ¥300 million, based on Gōmei's income at that time.[20] Mitsui instead merged Gōmei with one of its designated subsidiaries, Mitsui Bussan, and was able to avoid the taxation. Mitsui chose Bussan rather than Mitsui Bank or Mitsui Mining as the merger partner because both the bank and mining companies had already made partial public offerings of their stock (the bank in 1919, and the mining company in 1938).[21] Thus Bussan became both a joint-stock company capitalized at about ¥300,000 and the zaibatsu's head office. Its accounts were then made public for the first time.

With its elevation to head office, Mitsui Bussan acquired the authority to control Mitsui Bank and Mitsui Mining, which as fellow designated subsidiaries were, however, ranked on the same level as Bussan in the zaibatsu hierarchy. To correct this abnormal situation, the zaibatsu limited Bussan's functions to those of a holding company as well as an operating company while entrusting control functions to the newly established Mitsui Sōmotokata (General Family Council). The formal members of this council were the heads of the eleven Mitsui houses, the directors, and the top salaried managers. The General Family Council thus became the zaibatsu's de facto head office and Bussan the nominal head office.[22]

Bussan did not make a public stock offering until November 1942, two years after its merger with Mitsui Gōmei. The 150,000 shares offered to the public amounted to 25 percent of Bussan's total stock. Of these, 140,000 were made available to Mitsui-designated subsidiaries and their employees and the remaining 10,000 to Mitsui's customers and other business connections. Compared to the public stock offerings of Sumitomo and Mitsubishi, this was a genuinely public offering that netted the General Family Council a huge sum with which to sustain itself through the tight wartime situation. Significantly, however, the measure ran counter to the tradition of common ownership of assets by the Mitsui family members and represented a major crack in the Mitsui zaibatsu's bastion of familial exclusiveness.

Under the new setup, Mitsui Bussan was functioning as both a trading firm and a holding company, while actual control was exercised by the unincorporated General Family Council. This abnormal situation gave rise to a number of inconveniences, which Mitsui leaders decided to prevent by the formation of a new head office. Accordingly, in March 1944 Mitsui Bussan was reorganized as a pure holding company and head office and renamed Mitsui Honsha. The General Family Council transferred its control functions to Mitsui Honsha and dissolved. At the same time the zaibatsu established a new Mitsui Bussan to act as a pure trading company.[23]

Most of the other zaibatsu also turned their head offices into joint-stock companies, using the same method as Mitsui had. The Fujita zaibatsu, for example, merged its head office, Gōmei Kaisha Fujita-gumi, with Fujita Mining in 1937 to form Kabushiki Kaisha Fujita-gumi, a joint-stock company. The new head office did not make a public stock offering, but when it increased its capital from ¥50 million to ¥70 million in 1942, it allowed two state corporations, Teikoku Kōhatsu and Tōhoku Shinkō, to acquire the new shares. The government pushed this acquisition with the aim of enabling the weakened Fujita-gumi, then under the control of the Bank of Japan, to contribute to the national program of expanding wartime industrial capacity. The decline of Fujita family control had progressed so far that in 1943 the Fujita family transferred its Fujita-gumi shares to Teikoku Kōhatsu.[24]

Similarly, in the Furukawa zaibatsu Furukawa Sekitan Kōgyō (Furukawa Coal Mining), a joint-stock company established in 1934, absorbed Furukawa Gōmei, the head office and metal-mining division, in 1941; the resulting firm was named Furukawa Kōgyō (Furukawa Mining). The following year Furukawa Mining increased its capital from ¥30.14 to ¥50 million and offered 300,000 of the 397,200 new shares to the public; of these, 270,000 were divided among banks, insurance companies, and the shareholders and employees of Furukawa subsidiaries, and the remaining 30,000 were put on the market.[25]

In the Ōkura zaibatsu as well, Ōkura Mining, a joint-stock company, absorbed the head office, Gōmei Kaisha Ōkura-gumi, in 1942. When the zaibatsu were finally dissolved after World War II, however, the Ōkura family still held 93 percent of the Ōkura Mining shares. Ōkura thus appears to have given a low priority to making public offerings of its head office stock.[26] Additionally, the Yasuda zaibatsu toward the end of the war was considering the reorganization of its head office, Yasuda Hozensha, into a joint-stock company, but the change never came about. Yasuda perhaps held back because as a financial zaibatsu it did not have as pressing a need to introduce capital from society at large as did the other more industrially oriented zaibatsu.[27]

END OF THE ROAD: FORCED DISSOLUTION

The zaibatsu dissolution program carried out under the postwar Occupation delivered the final blow to the zaibatsu system. After Japan's surrender on August 15, 1945, the Allies began to implement Occupation policies that were designed to demilitarize and democratize the country. Zaibatsu-busting was a major item on their agenda, for the Occupation authorities regarded the zaibatsu as having been the main economic support of Japanese militarism and "feudalism."

The United States, which as the leading Allied power had almost total control over the Occupation, declared in its "Initial Post-Surrender Policy for Japan" of August 29, 1945, that it would liquidate Japan's large industrial and financial combines. Some of the zaibatsu responded by submitting plans for reforming themselves, but the Americans rejected these as inadequate and ordered the Japanese government to take steps to dissolve the zaibatsu.[28]

The dissolution program began in September 1945 with the designation of five corporations as holding companies: Mitsui Honsha, Mitsubishi Honsha, Sumitomo Honsha, Yasuda Hozensha, and Fuji Sangyō. The list of firms was subsequently expanded to include eighty-three concerns, all of which turned over their stockholdings to the Holding Company Liquidation Commission (HCLC) and were dissolved. Among the liquidated companies, Fuji Sangyō (formerly Nakajima Aircraft Co.) may not fit the criteria that would allow it to be regarded as a zaibatsu head office; but because the firm received all of its capital from the family of Nakajima Chikuhei, and because it controlled a number of subsidiaries and cooperated in the war effort, it was subject to dissolution as a zaibatsu holding company.

The next step came in March 1947, when fifty-six "designated persons" from ten zaibatsu (note that not all were zaibatsu in the strict sense) families—Mitsui, Iwasaki, Sumitomo, Yasuda, Nakajima, Asano, Ōkura, Furukawa, Nomura, and Aikawa—were ordered to freeze their assets and transfer their stockholdings to the HCLC. These individuals were forbidden to hold office in any of the zaibatsu-related enterprises.

The Japanese government in 1948 enacted the Law for the Termination of Zaibatsu Family Control, under which the families were compensated for their holdings but only within an official limit—and payment was made in government bonds. The postwar runaway inflation and the resultant drop in the bond market meant that the family holdings were all but confiscated. The HCLC gradually sold on the stock market the shares taken over from the former zaibatsu head offices and families, and thus those shares came to be widely dispersed. The system of exclusive family ownership that had been the distinctive feature of the zaibatsu was now completely destroyed.

The dissolution program targeted some of the operating companies as well as the zaibatsu head offices and families. Mitsui Bussan and Mitsubishi Trading Company in particular were singled out for dissolution, with their breakup ordered by Occupation authorities in July 1947. Perhaps these two companies were regarded as having played a central role in their respective zaibatsu, or perhaps their global trading power was seen as having contributed to Japanese military expansion. Then, too, Mitsui Bussan and Mitsubishi Trading had been conspicuously active in the maneuvering by major zaibatsu firms to avoid the anticipated breakup measures—such as the December 1947 Law for the Elimination of Excessive Concentrations of Economic Power— and that activity may have attracted the wrath of the Occupation authorities.[29] Whatever the reasons, the two trading companies were subjected to drastic dissolution measures, including restrictions on their middle and top managers that prohibited them from forming a new company and that forbid two or more of them from being employed by the same company. The same prohibitions applied as well to over a hundred of the lower-level managers and nonmanagerial employees.[30] The companies were then each split into approximately two hundred firms.

As the Cold War between the United States and Soviet Union intensified after 1947, Occupation policy toward Japan shifted from the reformation of a past enemy to the rehabilitation of a present ally. A number of zaibatsu dissolution measures were therefore reversed or dropped, a process that continued after the Occupation ended in 1952. The originally forbidden practice of using the old zaibatsu names in the names of new companies was now allowed to revive. Employment restrictions on holding company officers were removed, and the company groupings that had been broken up during the early phase of the Occupation began to reassemble. The regrouping included those special targets of the dissolution program, Mitsui Bussan (now Mitsui & Co.) and Mitsubishi Trading Company (now Mitsubishi Corporation). In addition, the former subsidiaries of a zaibatsu were permitted to communicate and consult among themselves, activities that had been forbidden (although secretly engaged in) before the reversal of Occupation policy. The upshot of these changes was the reemergence of powerful groups of former zaibatsu corporations.

Despite claims by many critics to the contrary, this process did not signify a "zaibatsu revival," because the key factor that was not revived was exclusive ownership by the zaibatsu families. Instead, the family fortunes were lost by way of the virtual confiscation of their stockholdings and the heavy postwar property tax. The families no longer were able to become major stockholders in the corporations that had made up the former zaibatsu, no longer had the power to intervene in the appointment of top managers, and no longer had the prerequisites to become top managers themselves.

Zaibatsu family members did receive respectful treatment and financial assistance from the top management of the zaibatsu-descended corporate groupings, but all control, even nominal, had passed to their former employees, the salaried managers. Once entrusted with managerial authority by the owner family, the managers had now seized that authority in name as well as fact and would impart it to their junior colleagues. Exclusive family ownership and control vanished without a trace, and the zaibatsu were indeed dissolved.

EPILOGUE

REVIEW OF THE HISTORY OF THE ZAIBATSU

The zaibatsu were founded by wealthy individuals who through government purveying or mining or both amassed great fortunes during the period of political and economic change that followed the Meiji Restoration of 1868. On the basis of their wealth, these entrepreneurs embarked on strategies of business diversification, which until about 1890 encompassed the fields of banking, mining, trading, shipping, and construction. The sale of state enterprises beginning in the early 1880s played a big part in the diversification process undertaken by the nascent zaibatsu, but the advantages of continuing to rely on government patronage were outweighed by such disadvantages as the unpredictability of state policy and restrictions on managerial autonomy. Between the late 1880s and early 1890s both Mitsui and Mitsubishi therefore distanced themselves from the government, abandoning their role as "political merchants."

With the implementation of the Commercial Code in 1893, many of the emergent zaibatsu adopted the corporate form, a change that coincided with the takeoff period of the Japanese economy. The various zaibatsu expanded the range of their diversified enterprises and advanced into manufacturing industries. Mitsui moved into paper manufacturing, cotton spinning, silk reeling, and electrical machinery production; Mitsubishi into shipbuilding; Sumitomo into steel and electric wire manufacturing; Furukawa into electric wire production; and Asano into cement making and oil refining.

In each case, the nature of the advance into manufacturing was determined by the particular pattern of strategic decision making within the zaibatsu. The result was a variety of developmental experiences. Mitsui switched its emphasis from industry to commerce and then back to industry. Mitsubishi displayed a special zeal for the modern shipbuilding industry and stationed its top manager at its Nagasaki Shipyard. Sumitomo and Furukawa contrasted with each other sharply in the extent to which they branched out from copper-related industries, and Asano pursued an aggressive strategy of diversification but exercised limited control over its subsidiary enterprises.

The zaibatsu stepped up their diversification programs with the expansion of economic opportunities during World War I. In an effort to catch up with the leading Mitsui, the other zaibatsu strove to implement such programs in one stroke. The subjects of their activity included trading and shipping companies, banks, shipyards, and iron and steel works. During this time the multisubsidiary system became the common organizational structure of the zaibatsu, and Mitsui and Yasuda, which had adopted that system before the war, served as the model for its introduction within the other zaibatsu.

The zaibatsu differed in their abilities to cope with the end of the wartime boom and the onset of the postwar recession. At one extreme, some zaibatsu went under, especially those that had expanded recklessly beyond the limits of their managerial resources or had failed to make plans on the basis of careful market projections. At the other extreme were zaibatsu like Mitsui, which rather than collapsing actually increased their power under the unstable postwar economic conditions.

Whereas most of the zaibatsu trading companies failed during the recession, in some cases bringing the zaibatsu down with them, Mitsui Bussan alone continued to show excellent business results. Through a management strategy suited to the changing economic environment, Bussan continued to pull away from the pack and developed into a huge general trading company.

Additionally during this difficult period, several zaibatsu poured managerial resources into the development of heavy industries while withstanding the pressure of renewed Western imports. Among these industries were relatively established ones like shipbuilding and iron and steel but also new ones that had been introduced into Japan around 1910, such as electrical machinery, dye, synthetic ammonium sulphate, rayon, aircraft, and automobile manufacturing. Zaibatsu behavior in the field of heavy industries was by no means conservative and involved a good measure of innovation and risk.

Yasuda alone liquidated its industrial operations (except for nail making) and devoted itself to the diversification of financial enterprises. Mitsui, Mitsubishi, and Sumitomo, while expanding their industrial interests, also sought to diversify their financial businesses. Thus in the field of finance competition among the big four zaibatsu intensified.

The zaibatsu system started on the road to collapse with the coming of the Depression and militarism in the 1930s. In the wake of World

War I, some zaibatsu had already found that their growth was restricted by an inability to make full use of outside capital owing to the principle of exclusive family ownership. After 1930 and during World War II the zaibatsu increasingly came up against the obstacles presented by family exclusiveness and faced a shortage of funds. At the same time they made huge charitable contributions to allay public criticism of their profit levels, met heavy wartime taxes, and expanded their heavy industrial investments. In the end, the zaibatsu made public offerings of stock first within their operating firms and then within their head offices after the latter had been reorganized into joint-stock companies. Thus did the zaibatsu modify the principle of family exclusiveness while giving greater weight to heavy industries during the war. That principle and the entire zaibatsu system came to a decisive end under the zaibatsu dissolution program of the Allied Occupation.

CLOSED AND OPEN SYSTEMS OF OWNERSHIP

Until the implementation of the dissolution program, the private businesses that spearheaded Japanese economic development were either "open" enterprises characterized by joint investment and public stock offerings or "closed" enterprises that featured exclusive ownership by a single family or an extended family. The zaibatsu were the chief representatives of the closed form of business ownership. Inasmuch as this book has treated the history of the zaibatsu, it has largely omitted a discussion of the open form of ownership, but to conclude that up to 1945 the Japanese economy grew solely on the basis of closed enterprises led by the zaibatsu would be a mistake.

In order to comprehend fully the extremely complex business history of the zaibatsu, one must avoid preconceptions based on Western experience. For example, to regard joint-stock companies and "managerial" enterprises as elements peculiar to the open system of ownership would make difficult an understanding of the phenomenon whereby the zaibatsu organized their enterprises as joint-stock companies but restricted the public offering of their shares—whereby, with the exception of Yasuda and Asano, salaried managers came to hold all or part of the top management positions in the zaibatsu.

I have tried to explain the success of zaibatsu growth and diversification in terms of such internal factors as managerial resources and business strategy and organization, but the role of external forces, including Japan's overall economic growth and changes in the industrial structure, must not be denied. Insofar as that external environment equally affected both closed and open enterprises, however, a detailed analysis of it would serve little to distinguish the development of the zaibatsu from that of other businesses. I have instead stressed diversification strategy in particular.

Within the closed system the zaibatsu were more devoted to strategies of diversification than were nonzaibatsu family enterprises. By definition, following such a strategy is what separated the zaibatsu from other family businesses. In addition, the zaibatsu preceded joint-stock companies of the open system in carrying out diversification strategies. For example, nonzaibatsu cotton-spinning firms did not branch out into rayon, woolen yarn, and silk thread until the 1920s; moreover, their diversification was limited to fields within the textile industry.

Why did the zaibatsu precede other businesses in diversifying their interests? Certainly an important factor was the zaibatsu's adoption of the multisubsidiary system, a management structure suited to diversification, but because they took on that system *in response to* their diversification strategies, it did not serve as the motive force. Rather, I have emphasized the comparatively more abundant managerial resources possessed by the zaibatsu—that is, their greater supplies of capital and managerial talent. I have stressed in particular the role of highly educated salaried managers who rose through the ranks to the high command, where they devised both diversification strategies and an organizational structure to match.

Why in fact did the zaibatsu fare better than businesses of the open system or of the nonzaibatsu closed system in terms of the accumulation of capital and availability of managerial resources? With respect to capital, first of all the zaibatsu as closed businesses did not have to pay out their profits as dividends but could accumulate them internally. Second, mining, which until World War I was a highly profitable industry, for the most part came under the closed system, especially of the zaibatsu variety, and served to increase the owned capital of the zaibatsu. Third, once a zaibatsu had formed a diversified business structure based on its ample reserves, it was able to concentrate the earnings of its diversified enterprises in the zaibatsu head office and to use them systematically to promote established operations or to found new ones. Finally, a zaibatsu could reap much higher returns by having its subsidiaries provide each other with raw materials and markets, share technology and information, and jointly invest in affiliated enterprises than by carrying out such activities with outside companies. In other words, the combine was able to increase profits through internalization. Successful internalization required only well-organized diversified enterprises, but their organization could take the form of either a multidivisional or multisubsidiary system. The multisubsidiary system, however, has been seen to be the structure most suited to the diversification strategies of the zaibatsu.

As for highly educated managerial personnel, first, the zaibatsu possessed sufficient funds to employ such staff on a large scale. Second, in open businesses a number of major stockholders competed for top management posts, thus limiting the chances for qualified salaried managers to advance beyond the level of middle management. By contrast, the ownership of a zaibatsu consisted of just a single family, and—insofar as the family recognized that salaried managers were indispensable to the growth of the enterprise and displayed a measure of progressiveness and flexibility, such that family members did not insist on monopolizing the top management positions—salaried managers in the zaibatsu had far more opportunities to participate in the high command than did their open-system counterparts. This not only contributed directly to strengthening the top management of the zaibatsu but also indirectly caused highly educated personnel to gravitate toward zaibatsu.

EXCLUSIVE OWNERSHIP, PROGRESSIVE MANAGEMENT

It may appear that I am emphasizing the advantages that accrued to the zaibatsu from their closed nature. To be sure, compared to open enterprises, the zaibatsu enjoyed conditions in the areas of finance and personnel that favored the pursuit of diversification strategies, and those conditions did result from the closed system of the combines. Yet that system did not automatically bring about the diversification of the zaibatsu. In fact, it had great potential for *impeding* the growth of the zaibatsu—for example, by restricting their access to outside funds. The conclusion, therefore, is that the zaibatsu managed to minimize the drawbacks of the closed system while giving full play to its advantages.

Family businesses in general possess an ambivalent character. Scholars often point to the positive aspects of such businesses in order to explain their longevity or economic importance. In the business histories of Europe and the United States many examples of exclusively family-owned enterprises that continued to grow over long periods of time can be found. It has been argued that successful family businesses were aided by such favorable conditions as loyalty based on blood ties, freedom from outside interference in decision making, and ability to groom the next generation of top managers early and systematically. Moreover, in developing countries today the overwhelming majority of the private enterprises spearheading economic development is comprised of businesses owned exclusively by families. From this perspective, it would not be surprising if my discussion of the remarkable growth of the zaibatsu, whose basic characteristics included family exclusiveness, should lead some to misinterpret my view as a conclusion that family exclusiveness itself was the responsible element.

The experience of Western countries and present-day developing nations, however, also indicates the shortcomings of family businesses, many examples of which have been raised by scholars: limited access to funds owing to the avoidance of capital from outside the family; a conservative policy of eschewing new, risky enterprises in order to meet the company's highest obligation, preservation of the family fortune; a tendency for the founding family to lose the ability and desire to engage in strategic management; a loss of drive on the part of salaried managers owing to the monopolization of top management posts by family members; and a tendency for the private interests of the family to get in the way of rational management.

How were the zaibatsu families able to maximize the strengths of family exclusiveness while minimizing its weaknesses? They did so by avoiding a narrow fixation on immediate profits and instead taking the long view; in other words, they displayed progressiveness and flexibility. Those attributes made it possible for the families both to approve the use of their fortunes to carry out diversification strategies and to accept the participation of numerous salaried managers in the high command. While noting that a few zaibatsu, such as Yasuda and Asano, did remain cool to the promotion of salaried managers, it is safe to say that in general the qualities of progressiveness and flexibility were to be found widely among zaibatsu families and became even more pronounced as the founders gave way to succeeding generations.

Those qualities were not always the products of thorough deliberation by the zaibatsu families. Sometimes they resulted from the families' instinctive realization that economic danger lay in uncompromising adherence to traditional kinship customs. In the challenging international and domestic situations confronted by Japan after 1868, a family business that was ruled by blood ties and family traditions and that refused to develop new enterprises or employ new talent put its very survival in jeopardy. Other times they were a passive response to the urgings of patrons who possessed a strong voice in family matters, as in the case of Inoue Kaoru and the Mitsui family.

Several other factors help to explain the zaibatsu families' progressiveness and flexibility. In the course of the political and social revolution following the Meiji Restoration, authorities in a wide range of fields selected men of talent for leadership positions regardless of class or status and invested them with broad decision-making powers. The amateur practice of giving command posts to members of the old ruling class irrespective of their ability did not take root in either the government bureaucracy or the military.

Finally, Japan had just emerged from a long period of seclusion and was subject to the impact of Western culture; therefore, for the Japanese at this time "men of talent" meant above all those who possessed knowledge of the West. Such knowledge was believed to be acquired only through higher education. Modern Japan's characteristic fixation on educational qualifications, something that has continued to this day, was at work here. Thus bringing in highly educated personnel was considered to be in the interest of zaibatsu families. Because such personnel were in short supply, the families competed for their services and, in order to attract and retain such men, ultimately promoted them to top management positions.

THE ZAIBATSU AND POSTWAR JAPANESE BUSINESS

Several years after the post-World War II dissolution of the zaibatsu, groups of major enterprises once belonging to the same zaibatsu emerged, and they continue to be active today. But these enterprise groups are not zaibatsu, because they lack the fundamental zaibatsu characteristic of family exclusiveness. The zaibatsu and the present-day business groups are not only separated historically but also completely differ in their structure and function. Therefore, a study of the prewar zaibatsu, such as this one—although it may serve to elucidate the history of contemporary individual big businesses of zaibatsu descent— is of no use in clarifying the actual conditions and activities of the present-day groups of formerly zaibatsu affiliates.

Rather, I would hope that in reading this book one might discover something of the origins of the managerial intensiveness and vitality of contemporary Japanese business. Even the zaibatsu, with their extremely closed ownership, did not make the preservation and safe expansion of family assets their only objective but, in a harsh environment that included competition from foreign enterprises, also took risks in their drive to develop industries at the forefront of Japanese economic development.

In few instances did family members regardless of their managerial ability occupy top management positions or wield dictatorial power. In many cases, highly educated salaried managers participated in strategic decision making to a greater or lesser degree. In addition, the intense competition among the zaibatsu, with Mitsui in the lead and the others in pursuit, encouraged them to embrace aggressive policies of expansion and diversification. Thus a lively picture of prewar Japanese business can be drawn by taking into account only the extremely closed enterprises of the zaibatsu variety. By filling out the picture with a study of enterprises of the open system of ownership, one ought to have little difficulty in finding the roots of the intense management and vitality that characterizes Japanese business today.

NOTES

Most company histories and businessmen's biographies in Japan are written and published by editorial or publishing committees established on an ad hoc basis. The committees are organized by the companies or individuals concerned and are disbanded once a book is published. And it is very often the case that the editor, book title, and publisher have the same name: for example, *The 100-Year History of Company A* will be edited and published by the Committee for the Publication of the 100-Year History of Company A.

In order to avoid tedious repetition and in the interest of a simplified bibliographical style, I have used the following rules for the citation of company histories and biographies in the endnotes.

1. When the editor of a book is a committee or a company and the name of the company or businessman is given in the book title, the editor's name is omitted.

2. When the publisher of a company history is an ad hoc committee within the company itself, only the company's name is given as the publisher. In the case of a biography published by an ad hoc committee, the publisher's name is omitted.

3. When the publisher of a book is a company or a committee with a specific name, e.g., Itsukakai in the biographies of the Furukawa zaibatsu presidents, the publisher's name is given.

Introduction

1. William W. Lockwood, *The Economic Development of Japan: Growth and Structural Change, 1868–1937* (Princeton, N.J.: Princeton University Press, 1954).

2. Kanno Watarō, *Kaisha kigyō hasseishi no kenkyū* (Studies in the History of the Growth of Corporate Enterprise) (Tokyo: Iwanami Shoten, 1932). The Meiji Restoration, an idiomatic expression, refers to the transfer of political power from the Tokugawa regime to the new Meiji regime and the commencement of the large-scale reforms for Japan's modernization.

3. For more on the smaller and local zaibatsu, see my book *Chihō zaibatsu* (The Local Zaibatsu) (Tokyo: Nihon Keizai Shinbunsha, 1985). For convenience I refer to the ten zaibatsu covered in this book simply as "the zaibatsu," but it should be understood that these ten do not represent all the zaibatsu.

4. "A zaibatsu was a business group in which one parent company (holding company) owned by a family or an extended family controlled subsidiaries operating in various industries, with large subsidiaries occupying oligopolistic positions in their respective industries," according to Yasuoka Shigeaki, "Nihon zaibatsu no rekishiteki ichi" (The Historical Situation of Japanese Zaibatsu), in *Nihon no zaibatsu* (Japanese Zaibatsu), ed., Yasuoka Shigeaki (Tokyo: Nihon Keizai Shinbunsha, 1976), p. 14. The multisubsidiary system is similar to the multidivisional system, another type of organizational structure suited to the diversification of big business enterprises. The latter system organizes the diversified operations of a business in the form of internal divisions, whereas the former organizes them as subsidiary companies.

5. Mark Fruin adopts this definition of zaibatsu in his *Kikkoman: Clan and Community* (Cambridge, Mass.: Harvard University Press, 1983). "Zaibatsu means literally 'financial clique' and was the word used to describe large industrial and financial combines that formed in Japan around the turn of the twentieth century" (p. 127). Fruin, however, in setting the starting point for zaibatsu at the turn of the century overlooks the history of zaibatsu prior to that point.

6. Morikawa Hidemasa, "Multi-Industrial Concentration: One Aspect of the Concentration Process in Japan's Economy," a paper presented at a workshop organized by Hans Pohl at the International Economic History Congress, Berne, 1986.

7. Morikawa Hidemasa, "Prerequisites for the Development of Managerial Capitalism: On the Basis of Cases in Prewar Japan," in *The Development of Managerial Enterprise*, ed., Kobayashi Kesaji and Morikawa Hidemasa (Tokyo: University of Tokyo Press, 1986), pp. 13–14.

8. According to the Chandler model for the evolution of modern business corporations, "managerial enterprises" are "firms in which representatives of the founding families or of financial interests no longer make top-level management decisions—where such decisions are made by salaried managers who own little of the companies' stock." Alfred D. Chandler, Jr., "The United States: Seedbed of Managerial Capitalism," in *Managerial Hierarchies*, ed., Alfred D. Chandler, Jr., and Herman Daems (Cambridge, Mass.: Harvard University Press, 1980), p. 14.

Chapter 1 Zaibatsu Origins

1. The following description is based on Mitsui Bank, *Mitsui ryōgaedana* (The Mitsui Exchange Shops) (Tokyo: Japan Business History Institute, 1983), ch. 1.

2. Mitsui Bunko (Mitsui Research Institute for Social and Economic History), *Mitsui jigyō-shi* (History of the Mitsui Enterprises) (Tokyo: Mitsui Bunko, 1980), vol. 1, pp. 378–79, 500–501.

3. Mitsui Bank, *Mitsui ryōgaedana*, pp. 328–29.

4. Ibid., pp. 372–73; Mitsui Bunko, *Mitsui jigyō-shi*, vol. 1, pp. 639, 646.

5. Minomura Seiichirō, *Minomura Rizaemon den* (Biography of Rizaemon Minomura) (Tokyo: Minomura Gōmei Kaisha, 1969), pp. 7–10.

6. Mitsui Bank, *Mitsui ryōgaedana*, p. 331.

7. Minomura, *Minomura Rizaemon den*, pp. 23–24.

8. Mitsui Bank, *Mitsui ryōgaedana*, pp. 377–79.

9. Ibid., p. 442.

10. Mitsui Bunko, *Mitsui jigyō-shi*, vol. 2, pp. 58–59.

11. Ibid., pp. 60–61.

12. Yasuoka Shigeaki, *Zaibatsu keisei shi no kenkyū* (History of the Formation of the Zaibatsu) (Kyoto: Minerva Shobō, 1970), pp. 260–62. *Bekke* families were not part of the House of Mitsui. They did not have a share in the jointly held fortune of the Mitsui House or the right to participate in the joint management of the Mitsui enterprises. Many branch families established by members of the House of Mitsui became *bekke* because the number of families within the House was limited to eleven. Normally, a *bekke* could not use the Mitsui surname.

13. Mitsui Bunko, *Mitsui jigyō shi*, vol. 2, pp. 98–103, 126.

14. Sugiyama Kazuo, "Kin'yū seido no sōsetsu" (The Establishment of the Financial System), in *Nihon keizai shi taikei* (Outline of Japanese Economic History), ed., Kajinishi Mitsuhaya (Tokyo: University of Tokyo Press, 1965), vol. 5, pp. 187–92.

15. Mitsui Bunko, *Mitsui jigyō shi*, vol. 2, pp. 126–37. Daiichi Kokuritsu Bank was not allowed to act as a true central bank. Japan had no central banking facility until the Bank of Japan was founded in 1882. In the meantime, national banks proliferated, especially after 1876 when the government relaxed the regulations governing them, so that by 1879 they had reached a total of 153. Thereafter the government refused to permit the establishment of any more national banks.

16. *Daiichi Ginkō shi* (History of Daiichi Bank) (Tokyo: Daiichi Bank, 1957), vol. 1, pp. 112, 176–77. For more on Shibusawa's life, see Johannes Hirschmeier, "Shibusawa Eiichi: Industrial Pioneer," in *The State and Economic Enterprise in Japan*, ed., William W. Lockwood (Princeton, N.J.: Princeton University Press, 1965), pp. 209–47.

17. Mitsui Bank, *Mitsui ryōgaedana*, p. 442.

18. Miyamoto Mataji, *Ono-gumi no kenkyu* (A Study of Ono-gumi) (Nishinomiya, 1970), vol. 4, pp. 679–718.

19. Ibid., pp. 673–74, 697–98; Mitsui Bank, *Mitsui ryōgaedana*, p. 461.

20. *Mitsui Ginkō 80-nen shi* (80 Years of Mitsui Bank) (Tokyo: Mitsui Bank, 1957), p. 371.

21. Ishii Kanji, *Nihon keizai shi* (Japanese Economic History) (Tokyo: University of Tokyo Press, 1976), p. 83.

22. *Daiichi Ginkō shi*, vol. 1, pp. 198–99, 205.

23. *Yasuda Hozensha to sono kankei jigyō shi* (History of Yasuda Hozensha and Its Affiliated Enterprises) (Tokyo: Yasuda Fudōsan Kabushiki Kaisha, 1974), pp. 4–17.

24. Yui Tsunehiko, ed., *Yasuda zaibatsu* (The Yasuda Zaibatsu) (Tokyo: Nihon Keizai Shinbunsha, 1986), p. 38.

25. *Fuji Ginkō 100-nen shi* (100 Years of Fuji Bank) (Tokyo: Fuji Bank Research Department, 1982), pp. 28–29.

26. *Ōkura Tsuruhiko-ō* (Biography of Ōkura Kihachirō) (Tokyo: Kakuyūkai, 1924), pp. 11–54.

27. Ōkura Zaibatsu Kenkyū-kai, ed., *Ōkura zaibatsu no kenkyū* (Studies of the Ōkura Zaibatsu) (Tokyo: Kondō Shuppansha, 1982), pp. 24–29; *Taisei Kensetsu Sha-shi* (History of Taisei Corporation) (Tokyo: Taisei Kensetsu Kabushiki Kaisha, 1963), pp. 43–65.

28. *Kuhara Fusanosuke* (Biography of Kuhara Fusanosuke) (Tokyo: Nihon Kōgyō Co., Ltd., 1970), pp. 20–28, 49.

29. *Iwasaki Yatarō den* (Biography of Iwasaki Yatarō) (Tokyo: University of Tokyo Press, 1967), vol. 1, pp. 215, 311–15, 352–53.

30. Ibid., pp. 565, 574, 589–600.

31. Ibid., p. 664; vol. 2, pp. 10–11, 16–17.

32. Ibid., vol. 2, pp. 25, 30–31.

33. Ibid., quotation on p. 34; pp. 47–48.

34. Ibid., p. 689.

35. William D. Wray, *Mitsubishi and the N.Y.K., 1870–1914: Business Strategy in the Japanese Shipping Industry* (Cambridge, Mass.: Council on East Asian Studies, Harvard University, 1984), pp. 33–39.

36. Ibid., pp. 42–44.

37. Mitsubishi Gōshi Kaisha, ed., *Mitsubishi Sha-shi* (Records of Mitsubishi Company) (Tokyo: University of Tokyo Press, 1980), vol. 3–10, *saimatsu zassai* in each volume.

38. *Iwasaki Yatarō den*, vol. 2, p. 452.

39. The following discussion of the origin of the Sumitomo family is based on Sakudō Yōtarō, *Sumitomo zaibatsu* (The Sumitomo Zaibatsu) (Tokyo: Nihon Keizai Shinbunsha, 1982), pp. 37–42.

40. *Izumiya sōkō* (Kobe: Sumitomo Shūshi Shitsu, 1956), vol. 8, pp. 7–9, 58; Hatakeyama Hideki, *Sumitomo zaibatsu seiritsu shi no kenkyū* (History of the Formation of the Sumitomo Zaibatsu) (Tokyo: Dōbunkan Shuppan, 1988), p. 7.

41. Hiratsuka Masatoshi, *Besshi kaikō 250-nen shiwa* (250 Years of the Besshi Copper Mine) (Osaka: Sumitomo Honsha, 1941), p. 168; Hatakeyama, *Sumitomo zaibatsu seiritsu shi*, pp. 11–13.

42. Sakudō, *Sumitomo zaibatsu*, pp. 77–80.

43. Hatakeyama, *Sumitomo zaibatsu seiritsu shi*, pp. 104–6; Hirose Saihei, *Hansei Monogatari* (My Years with Sumitomo) (Osaka: By the author, 1895), vol. 1, pp. 7–8, 20, 25–26.

44. Hiratsuka, *Besshi kaikō*, pp. 282–83, 305, 318.

45. *Sumitomo Kinzoku Kōzan 20-nen shi* (20 Years of Sumitomo Metal Mining) (Osaka: Sumitomo Kinzoku Kōzan Kabushiki Kaisha, 1970), appended table.

46. *Furukawa Ichibei-ō den* (Biography of Furukawa Ichibei) (Tokyo: Itsukakai, 1926), pp. 60–61, 89–92.

47. Ibid., pp. 67–68

48. Furukawa Kōgyō Kabushiki Kaisha, *Sōgyō 100-nen shi* (100 Years Since the Founding of Furukawa Mining) (Tokyo: Furukawa Kōgyō, 1976), pp. 25–36.

49. Ibid., pp. 36–39.

50. Ibid., pp. 47–66.

51. Ibid., pp. 90, 92.

52. Ibid., pp. 95–100.

53. Japan's first hydroelectric plant was located at a linen-spinning mill in the same prefecture containing the Ashio mine. At 65 horsepower, this plant

had a much smaller output than that of the 400-horsepower Ashio generating plant. It was built only to provide electric light, not to power the mill. Ibid., pp. 152–53; *Meiji kōgyō shi denki hen* (History of Meiji Industry, Volume on Electricity), ed., Nippon Kōgakkai (Tokyo: Nippon Kōgakkai, 1928), p. 334.

54. Furukawa Kōgyō, *Sōgyō 100-nen shi*, pp. 85–88.

55. Asano Sōichirō, *Asano Sōichirō* (Tokyo: Asano Bunko, 1923), chaps. 6–7.

56. Ibid., pp. 420–54.

57. Mitsui Bunko, *Mitsui jigyō-shi*, vol. 2, pp. 338–39, 446.

58. Ibid., pp. 436–41.

59. Minomura Risuke left Mitsui Bank to become a director of the Bank of Japan in 1882. He will be discussed in greater detail subsequently.

60. Ibid., pp. 445–46; *Mitsui Ginkō 80-nen shi*, p. 121; Japan Business History Institute, ed. *Nakamigawa Hikojirō denki shiryō* (Biographical Materials on Nakamigawa Hikojirō) (Tokyo: Tōyō Keizai Shinpōsha, 1969), p. 250.

61. Mitsui Bunko, *Mitsui jigyō-shi*, vol. 2, p. 468.

62. Ibid., p. 469.

63. See *Nakamigawa Hikojirō denki shiryō*, ch. 5.

64. *Iwasaki Yatarō den*, vol. 2, pp. 453–55.

65. Ibid., pp. 457–62.

66. This was the third directive issued by the government to Mitsubishi. The first was issued in 1875 and the second in 1876. Each prescribed the nature of Mitsubishi's services to the government and the state's support of Mitsubishi.

67. Wray, *Mitsubishi and the N.Y.K.*, p. 186.

68. Ibid., p. 193.

69. *Iwasaki Yatarō den*, vol. 2, p. 554.

70. Ibid., p. 607.

71. Ibid., p. 55.

72. The losses sustained by Mitsubishi and the KUK cannot easily be compared owing to differences in their methods of computation, such as their amortization systems. It is unlikely, however, that their losses differed significantly in amount.

73. Wray, *Mitsubishi and the N.Y.K.*, pp. 193–200.

74. *Iwasaki Yatarō den*, vol. 2, p. 581.

75. *Nippon Yūsen Kabushiki Kaisha 50-nen shi* (50 Years of the N.Y.K.) (Tokyo: N.Y.K., 1935), p. 548.

76. Ibid., p. 58.

Chapter 2 Emergence of the Zaibatsu

1. On the sale of state enterprises, see Kobayashi Masaaki, *Nihon no kōgyōka to kangyō haraisage* (Japan's Industrialization and the Sale of State Enterprises) (Tokyo: Tōyō Keizai Shinpōsha, 1977).

2. Imuta Yoshimitsu, *Meiji-ki kabushiki kaisha-shi josetsu* (Introduction to the History of the Joint-Stock Company in the Meiji Era) (Tokyo: Hōsei University Press, 1976), pp. 7–10.

3. *Iwasaki Yatarō den* (Biography of Iwasaki Yatarō) (Tokyo: University of Tokyo Press, 1967) vol. 2, p. 146.

4. Ibid., pp. 289–95.

5. Ibid., pp. 305–8.
6. Ibid., p. 312.
7. Ibid., pp. 200–201; Mitsubishi Gōshi Kaisha, ed., *Mitsubishi Sha-shi* (Records of Mitsubishi Company) (Tokyo: University of Tokyo Press, 1979), vol. 2, p. 485.
8. *Iwasaki Yatarō den*, vol. 2, pp. 321–22.
9. *Mitsubishi Ginkō-shi* (History of Mitsubishi Bank) (Tokyo: Mitsubishi Bank, 1954), p. 21; *Iwasaki Yatarō den*, vol. 2, pp. 322–28.
10. *Iwasaki Yatarō den*, vol. 2, p. 322.
11. Ibid., p. 328; Mitsubishi Gōshi, *Mitsubishi Sha-shi*, vol. 12, pp. 364–67.
12. On the Takashima Coal Mine, see *Mitsubishi Kōgyō Sha-shi* (History of Mitsubishi Mining Company) (Tokyo: Mitsubishi Kōgyō-Cement, 1976), pp. 36–45.
13. Mitsubishi Gōshi, *Mitsubishi Sha-shi*, vol. 12, pp. 142–52.
14. *Iwasaki Yatarō den*, vol. 2, pp. 387–95.
15. *Mitsubishi Ginkō-shi*, pp. 45–49; Mitsubishi Gōshi, *Mitsubishi Sha-shi*, vol. 13, pp. 165–66, 210–12.
16. *Iwasaki Yatarō den*, vol. 2, pp. 344–45.
17. Ibid., pp. 331–37; *Yokohama shi-shi* (History of the City of Yokohama) (Yokohama: Yokohama City, 1963), vol. 3, no. 1, pp. 656–62; Ōnishi Rihei, ed., *Asabuki Eiji-kun den* (Biography of Asabuki Eiji) (Tokyo, 1928), pp. 81–82.
18. Ōnishi, *Asabuki Eiji-kun den*, p. 97.
19. Mitsubishi Gōshi, *Mitsubishi Sha-shi*, vol. 15, pp. 27–29.
20. Ibid., p. 30.
21. Ibid., vol. 16, p. 244.
22. *Mitsubishi Kōgyō Sha-shi*, pp. 73–75.
23. *Asō Takichi-ō den* (Biography of Asō Takichi) (Iizuka, 1935), p. 87.
24. *Mitsubishi Kōgyō Sha-shi*, p. 70.
25. Ibid., pp. 81–82.
26. Ibid., pp. 88–89.
27. *Mitsubishi Ginkō-shi*, pp. 66–67.
28. *Iwasaki Yatarō den*, vol. 2, p. 395; Mitsubishi Gōshi, *Mitsubishi Sha-shi*, vol. 15, no. 2, pp. 27–28.
29. *Shin Mitsubishi Kobe Zōsensho 50-nen shi* (50 Years of the New Mitsubishi Kobe Shipyard) (Kobe: Mitsubishi Jūkōgyō Kabushiki Kaisha, Kobe Zōsensho, 1957), p. 3.
30. Morikawa Hidemasa, "Iwasaki Yanosuke jidai no Mitsubishi no top management" (Mitsubishi's Top Management in Iwasaki Yanosuke's Time), in *Kigyōsha katsudō no shiteki kenkyū* (Historical Approaches to Entrepreneurship), ed., Tsuchiya Moriaki and Morikawa Hidemasa (Tokyo: Nihon Keizai Shinbunsha, 1981), pp. 54–56.
31. *Iwasaki Yatarō den*, vol. 2, pp. 403–10.
32. Ibid., pp. 410–13.
33. Ibid., p. 436.
34. Ibid., p. 442.
35. Ibid., p. 439.
36. Ibid., p. 448.
37. Japan Business History Institute, ed. *Nakamigawa Hikojirō denki shiryō* (Biographical Materials on Nakamigawa Hikojirō), (Tokyo: Tōyō Keizai Shinpōsha, 1969), p. 170.

38. Fumoto Saburō, *Koiwai Nōjō 70-nen shi* (70 Years of Koiwai Farm) (Tokyo: Koiwai Nōboku Co., 1986), pp. 35–45.

39. *Kōhon Mitsui Bussan Kabushiki Kaisha 100-nen shi* (100 Years of Mitsui Bussan) (Tokyo: Japan Business History Institute, 1978), vol. 1, pp. 17–18; Mitsui Bunko, *Mitsui jigyō-shi* (History of the Mitsui Enterprises) (Tokyo: Mitsui Bunko, 1980), vol. 2, pp. 225–29.

40. Shibusawa Eiichi also had left the Finance Ministry at that time.

41. Mitsui Bunko, *Mitsui jigyō-shi*, vol. 2, pp. 217–20.

42. Ibid., pp. 221–22.

43. On *bekke*, see ch. 1, note 12.

44. *Kōhon Mitsui Bussan 100-nen shi*, pp. 48–49, 53–56.

45. Shinomiya Toshiyuki, *Kan'ei Miike Tankō no haraisage o megutte* (On the Disposal of the Miike Mine by the Government), *Energy shi kenkyū note* (Studies in Energy History) (Fukuoka: Nishi Nihon Bunka Kyōkai, 1977), p. 6.

46. *Mitsui Kōzan 100-nen shi kōhon* (100 Years of Mitsui Mining), unpublished ms.

47. Ibid.

48. *Danshaku Dan Takuma den* (Biography of Baron Dan Takuma) (Tokyo, 1938), vol. 1, ch. 25.

49. *Kamioka Kōzan shi* (History of Kamioka Mine) (Tokyo: Mitsui Metal Mining Co., 1970), pp. 539–53, 612–21.

50. Hatakeyama Hideki, *Sumitomo zaibatsu seiritsu shi no kenkyū* (History of the Formation of the Sumitomo Zaibatsu) (Tokyo: Dōbunkan Shuppan, 1988), pp. 111–12.

51. *Osaka Shōsen Kabushiki Kaisha 50-nen shi* (50 Years of Osaka Merchant Marine Company, Ltd.) (Osaka: Osaka Shōsen, 1934), pp. 37, 359–60.

52. *Sumitomo Ginkō 80-nen shi* (80 Years of Sumitomo Bank) (Osaka: Sumitomo Bank, 1979), pp. 87–92.

53. Hatakeyama, *Sumitomo zaibatsu seiritsu shi*, pp. 117–18.

54. Hiratsuka Masatoshi, *Besshi Kaikō 250-nen shiwa* (250 Years of Besshi Copper Mine) (Osaka: Sumitomo Honsha, 1941), pp. 347–62.

55. Hatakeyama, *Sumitomo zaibatsu seiritsu shi*, pp. 444–47.

56. Yui Tsunehiko, "Meiji-ki ni okeru Yasuda zaibatsu no takakuka" (The Diversification of Yasuda Zaibatsu in the Meiji Era), in *Kigyōsha katsudō no shiteki kenkyū*, ed., Tsuchiya and Morikawa, pp. 27–28.

57. Ibid., pp. 28–34.

58. Asai Yoshio, "Yasuda kin'yū zaibatsu no keisei" (Formation of the Yasuda financial zaibatsu), *Seijō Daigaku Keizai Kenkyū* (Seijō University Economic Papers), no. 84 (March 1984): 121, 126, 129.

59. Dōwa Kōgyō Kabushiki Kaisha, *Sōgyō 100-nen shi* (100 years of Dōwa Mining) (Tokyo: Dōwa Kōgyō, 1985), p. 91.

60. Ibid., pp. 59–60, 68–70, 85.

61. Takeda Haruhito, "Meiji zenki no Fujita-gumi to Mōrike yūshi" (Fujita-gumi and Financing by the Mōri Family in Early Meiji), *Keizaigaku Ronshū*, vol. 48, no. 3 (1982): 6.

62. Ibid.: 21.

63. Ōkura Zaibatsu Kenkyū-kai, ed., *Ōkura Zaibatsu no kenkyū* (Studies of the Ōkura Zaibatsu) (Tokyo: Kondō Shuppansha, 1982), p. 116.

64. Shōgyō Kōshinsho, *Nihon zenkoku shokaisha yakuin roku, 1905* (Japanese Directory of Company Directors) (Tokyo: Shōgyō Kōshinsho, 1905).

65. Mitsui Bunko, *Mitsui jigyō-shi*, vol. 2, pp. 439–40, 447–53.

66. *Mitsui Hachirōemon Takamine den* (Biography of Mitsui Hachirōemon Takamine) (Tokyo: Mitsui Bunko, University of Tokyo Press, 1988), p. 167.

67. Ibid.

68. Mitsui Bunko, *Mitsui jigyō-shi*, vol. 2, pp. 496–97, 506–9, 511–15.

69. *Mitsui Hachirōemon Takamine den*, pp. 183–84.

70. Ibid., pp. 185–86.

71. Ibid., pp. 186–87.

72. Ibid., pp. 188–91.

73. Mitsui Bunko, *Mitsui jigyō-shi shiryō-hen* (Historical Materials for the History of the Mitsui Enterprises) (Tokyo: Mitsui Bunko, 1974), vol. 3, p. 254.

74. Yasuoka Shigeaki, "Nihon zaibatsu no rekishiteki ichi," in *Nihon no zaibatsu* (Japanese Zaibatsu), ed., Yasuoka Shigeaki (Tokyo: Nihon Keizai Shinbunsha, 1976), p. 140.

75. Ibid., p. 141.

76. Mitsui Bunko, *Mitsui jigyō-shi*, vol. 2, p. 538.

77. Ibid., pp. 539–40.

78. Ibid., p. 541.

79. Under the 1899 Commercial Code revision, some partners in a limited partnership had both limited liability and some unlimited liability, but in limited partnership companies established before 1899 all partners continued to be regarded as having limited liability.

80. Mitsui Bunko, *Mitsui jigyō-shi*, vol. 2, pp. 169–72, 197–210.

81. Ibid., p. 196; *Mitsui Ginkō 80-nen shi* (80 Years of Mitsui Bank) (Tokyo: Mitsui Bank, 1957), pp. 84–85.

82. Mitsui Bunko, *Mitsui jigyō-shi*, vol. 2, pp. 389–97.

83. *Zaikai bukkoketsubutsu den* (Lives of Deceased Business Leaders) (Tokyo: Jitsugyō no Sekaisha, 1936), vol. 2, pp. 203–6.

84. *Nakamigawa Hikojirō denki shiryō*, p. 250.

85. *Mitsui Ginkō 80-nen shi*, p. 110.

86. *Sumitomo Shunsui* (Biography of Sumitomo Tomoito) (Kyoto, 1955), pp. 173–75, 178–82, 207.

87. Hirose Saihei, *Hansei monogatari* (My Years with Sumitomo) (Osaka: By the author, 1895), vol. 2, pp. 5–6, 22; Hatakeyama, *Sumitomo zaibatsu seiritsu shi*, p. 176.

88. *Sumitomo Shunsui*, pp. 246–47, 278–79.

89. Ibid., pp. 241–46.

90. Hiratsuka, *Besshi*, pp. 394–97.

91. *Sumitomo Shunsui*, pp. 254–55.

92. Nishikawa Shōjirō, ed., *Yū-ō* (Tokyo: Buseisha, 1933), pp. 191–92.

93. *Sumitomo Ginkō 80-nen shi*, pp. 107–27.

94. *Furukawa Ichibei-ō den* (Biography of Furukawa Ichibei) (Tokyo: Itsu-kakai, 1926), pp. 261, 266.

95. *Taisei Kensetsu Sha-shi* (History of Taisei Corporation) (Tokyo: Taisei Kensetsu Kabushiki Kaisha, 1963), pp. 44, 116–17, 121.

96. *Tekkō kyojin den Shiraishi Motojirō* (Biography of Shiraishi Motojirō) (Tokyo: Tekkō Shinbunsha, 1967), pp. 131, 139–40, 144.

97. *Yasuda Hozen-sha to sono kankei jigyō shi* (History of Yasuda Hozensha and Its Affiliated Enterprises) (Tokyo: Yasuda Fudōsan Kabushiki Kaisha, 1974), pp. 270–71.

98. See *Shōin Motoyama Hikoichi-ō* (Biography of Motoyama Hikoichi) (Osaka: Osaka Mainichi Shinbunsha, 1937).

99. Yukichi Fukuzawa, "Jitsugyō ron" (On Business), in *Fukuzawa Yukichi zenshū* (Collected Works of Yukichi Fukuzawa), ed., Keiō Gijuku (Tokyo: Iwanami Shoten, 1959), vol. 6, pp. 155–56.

100. *Iwasaki Yatarō den*, vol. 2, p. 163.

101. On Toyokawa Ryōhei, see Uzaki Kumakichi, *Toyokawa Ryōhei* (Tokyo, 1922).

102. On Hasegawa Yoshinosuke, see Yamaguchi Shōichirō, *Hakushi Hasegawa Yoshinosuke* (Dr. Hasegawa Yoshinosuke) (Tokyo: Seikyōsha, 1913).

103. On Kondō Renpei, see Suehiro Kazuo, *Danshaku Kondō Renpei den narabi ikō* (The Life and Posthumous Papers of Baron Kondō Renpei) (Tokyo: By the author, 1926).

104. *Iwasaki Yatarō den*, vol. 2, pp. 415–18.

105. Takekoshi Yosaburō, *Isono Hakaru-kun den* (Biography of Isono Hakaru) (Tokyo: Meidi-ya, 1935), pp. 34–35.

106. Morikawa, "Iwasaki Yanosuke jidai no Mitsubishi no top management," p. 53.

Part II Development of the Zaibatsu, 1893–1913

1. Nihon Tōkei Kenkyūsho, ed., *Nihon keizai tōkei shū* (Collected Statistics on the Japanese Economy) (Tokyo: Nihon Hyōronsha, 1958), pp. 55, 340.

2. Takamura Naosuke, *Nihon bōsekigyō-shi josetsu* (Introduction to the History of the Japanese Spinning Industry) (Tokyo: Hanawa Shobō, 1971), vol. 1, p. 183; vol. 2, p. 82.

3. *Nippon keizai tōkei sōkan* (Statistical Survey of the Japanese Economy) (Tokyo: Asahi Shimbunsha, 1930), pp. 548–49.

Chapter 3 Diversification Strategies

1. *Mitsui Ginkō 80-nen shi* (80 Years of Mitsui Bank) (Tokyo: Mitsui Bank, 1957), p. 144; Japan Business History Institute, ed., *Nakamigawa Hikojirō denki shiryō* (Biographical Materials on Nakamigawa Hikojirō) (Tokyo: Tōyō Keizai Shinpōsha, 1969), pp. 280–82.

2. *Kōhon Mitsui Bussan Kabushiki Kaisha 100-nen shi* (100 Years of Mitsui Bussan) (Tokyo: Japan Business History Institute, 1978), vol. 1, p. 207.

3. Ibid., pp. 221–25.

4. Ibid., pp. 208, 214–16.

5. Mitsui Bunko, *Mitsui jigyō-shi* (History of the Mitsui Enterprises) (Tokyo: Mitsui Bunko, 1980), vol. 2, p. 708.

6. *Danshaku Dan Takuma den* (Biography of Baron Dan Takuma) (Tokyo, 1938), vol. 1, p. 206.

7. Ibid., pp. 291–98.

8. Mitsui Bunko, *Mitsui jigyō-shi*, vol. 2, p. 629.

9. Ibid., p. 708.

10. Morikawa Hidemasa, *Zaibatsu no keieishi-teki kenkyū* (Studies in the Business History of the Zaibatsu) (Tokyo: Tōyō Keizai Shinpōsha, 1980), pp. 43–57.

11. Ibid., p. 44.

12. *Nakamigawa Hikojirō denki shiryō*, p. 289.

13. Narita Kiyohide, *Ōji Seishi sha-shi* (History of Ōji Paper Company) (Tokyo: Ōji Seishi Co., 1957), vol. 2, pp. 72–85.

14. *Mitsui Ginkō 80-nen shi*, pp. 144–45.

15. Mitsui Bunko, *Mitsui jigyō-shi*, vol. 2, p. 575.

16. *Nakamigawa Hikojirō denki shiryō*, pp. 262, 529; Sugiyama Kazuo, "Gōmei Kaisha Mitsui Ginkō no kikanginkō-teki seikaku" (The Organ Bank Character of Mitsui Bank, Unlimited), in *Gendai shihonshugi no zaisei kin'yū* (Finance in Modern Capitalism), ed., Ōuchi Tsutomu (Tokyo: University of Tokyo Press, 1976), vol. 3, pp. 248–51.

17. *Mitsui Ginkō 80-nen shi*, p. 146.

18. *Nakamigawa Hikojirō denki shiryō*, chs. 4–5.

19. Mitsui Bunko, *Mitsui jigyō-shi*, vol. 2, pp. 681–90, 724.

20. Morikawa, *Zaibatsu no keieishi-teki kenkyū*, pp. 54–57.

21. Ibid., pp. 61–69.

22. *Kōhon Mitsui Bussan 100-nen shi*, vol. 1, pp. 222–23.

23. Ibid., p. 333.

24. Ibid., p. 299.

25. Ibid., pp. 287, 298.

26. *Mitsui Kōzan 100-nen shi kōhon* (100 Years of Mitsui Mining), unpublished ms.

27. Mitsui Bunko, *Mitsui jigyō-shi*, vol. 2, pp. 711–15.

28. *Mitsubishi Kōgyō Sha-shi* (History of Mitsubishi Mining) (Tokyo: Mitsubishi Kōgyō-Cement, 1976), pp. 146–65.

29. Kobayashi Masaaki, *Nihon no kōgyōka to kangyō haraisage* (Japan's Industrialization and the Sale of State Enterprises) (Tokyo: Tōyō Keizai Shinpōsha, 1977), ch. 12.

30. *Meiji kōgyō-shi: kōgyō hen* (History of Meiji Industry: Mining) (Tokyo: Nippon Kōgakkai, 1930), pp. 126–29.

31. *Mitsubishi Ginkō-shi* (History of the Mitsubishi Bank) (Tokyo: Mitsubishi Bank, 1954), pp. 76–83.

32. Mishima Yasuo, ed., *Mitsubishi zaibatsu* (Tokyo: Nihon Keizai Shinbunsha, 1981), p. 240.

33. *Mitsubishi Sōko 75-nen shi* (75 Years of Mitsubishi Warehouse) (Tokyo: Mitsubishi Warehouse, 1962), pp. 186–89, 254–77.

34. *Iwasaki Hisaya den* (Biography of Iwasaki Hisaya) (Tokyo: University of Tokyo Press, 1961), pp. 425–26.

35. William D. Wray, *Mitsubishi and the N.Y.K., 1870–1914: Business Strategy in the Japanese Shipping Industry* (Cambridge, Mass.: Council on East Asian Studies, Harvard University, 1984), pp. 308–9.

36. *Nihon Yūsen Kabushiki Kaisha 50-nen shi* (50 Years of the N.Y.K.) (Tokyo: N.Y.K., 1935), p. 137.

37. Shukuri Jūichi, *Shōda Heigorō* (Biography of Shōda Heigorō) (Tokyo: Taikyōsha, 1932), pp. 502–3.

38. Mishima, *Mitsubishi zaibatsu*, p. 195.

39. Shioda Taisuke, *Jijoden* (Autobiography) (By the author, 1938), p. 190.

40. Mitsubishi Gōshi Kaisha, ed., *Mitsubishi Sha-shi* (Records of Mitsubishi Company) (Tokyo: University of Tokyo Press, 1981), vol. 19, p. 109.

41. Mishima, *Mitsubishi zaibatsu*, p. 195.

42. *Nippon Yūsen Kabushiki Kaisha 50-nen shi*, pp. 642–44.

43. Shukuri, *Shōda Heigorō*, pp. 106–8.

44. Morikawa Hidemasa, "Iwasaki Yanosuke jidai no Mitsubishi no top management" (Mitsubishi's Top Management in Iwasaki Yanosuke's Time), in *Kigyōsha katsudō no shiteki kenkyū* (Historical Approaches to Entrepreneurship), ed., Tsuchiya Moriaki and Morikawa Hidemasa (Tokyo: Nihon Keizai Shinbunsha, 1981), p. 59.

45. *Iwasaki Hisaya den*, p. 437.

46. Mitsubishi Shōji Kabushiki Kaisha, *Ritsugyō bōeki roku* (Records of Mitsubishi Trading Company) (Tokyo: Mitsubishi Shōji, 1958), pp. 732–33.

47. Fumoto Saburō, *Koiwai Nōjō 70-nen shi* (70 Years of Koiwai Farm) (Tokyo: Koiwai Nōboku Co., 1986), pp. 92, 97, 174–82.

48. *Mitsubishi Seishi 60-nen shi* (60 Years of Mitsubishi Paper Making Co.) (Tokyo: Mitsubishi Paper Making, 1962), chs. 2, 3, 6.

49. *Kirin Biiru Kabushiki Kaisha 50-nen shi* (50 Years of Kirin Brewery Co., Ltd.) (Tokyo: Kirin Brewery, 1957), pp. 21–64.

50. Not only the Iwasaki family but also shareholders in the railway companies were favored with good compensatory conditions. Noda Masaho, "Tetsudō kokuyūka to shōken shijō no kōzō henka" (The Railway Nationalization and the Structural Change of the Stock Market) (1), *Keiei Shirin*, vol. 8, no. 2 (1971): 9.

It is not certain how many railway shares the Iwasaki family held at the time of the nationalization, but in 1905, among major railroad companies the Iwasaki had 44,103 shares in the San'yō Railway or 6.1 percent of the total stock and 123,277 shares in the Kyushu Railway or 9.9 percent of the total stock. From these figures, one can easily infer the enormous size of Mitsubishi's overall railroad investment. Sugiyama Kazuo, "Kigyō no zaimu-tōshi katsudō to bunkateki haikei" (The Financial and Investment Activities of Enterprises and Their Cultural Environment), *Keiei Shigaku*, vol. 10, no. 1 (1975):67, 79.

51. Furukawa Kōgyō Kabushiki Kaisha, *Sōgyō 100-nen shi* (100 Years since the Founding of Furukawa Mining) (Tokyo: Furukawa Kōgyō, 1976), pp. 117–18.

52. *Furukawa Ichibei-ō den* (Biography of Furukawa Ichibei) (Tokyo: Itsukakai, 1926), pp. 215–17, 275–79.

53. Ibid., p. 277.

54. Ibid., p. 219.

55. Furukawa Kōgyō, *Sōgyō 100-nen shi*, pp. 163–79.

56. Ibid., p. 176.

57. Ibid., p. 82.

58. Ibid., p. 193.

59. Ibid., p. 115.

60. Ibid., pp. 243–44.

61. *Sha-shi Sumitomo Denki Kōgyō Kabushiki Kaisha* (History of Sumitomo Electric Co.) (Osaka: Sumitomo Electric, 1961), pp. 174–75.

62. *Furukawa Junkichi-kun den* (Biography of Furukawa Junkichi) (Tokyo: Itsukakai, 1926), pp. 104–9; *Furukawa Toranosuke-kun den* (Biography of Furukawa Toranosuke) (Tokyo, 1953), p. 167.

63. Morikawa, *Zaibatsu no keieishi-teki kenkyū*, pp. 142–49.

64. *Sumitomo Ginkō 80-nen shi* (80 Years of Sumitomo Bank) (Osaka: Sumitomo Bank, 1979), pp. 134–46, 168–69.

65. Sakudō Yōtarō, *Sumitomo zaibatsu* (Tokyo: Nihon Keizai Shinbunsha, 1982), p. 142.

66. These engineers were Yamazaki Kyutarō and Hamuro Yōnosuke. They were among the engineers sent to Germany to study steel-casting techniques in preparation for the founding of Yawata Iron Works. Both resigned from government service in order to set up the independent Nippon Steel Works before Yawata Iron Works' founding in 1901. *Sumitomo Kinzoku Kōgyō 60-nen shōshi* (Short History of the 60 Years of Sumitomo Metal Industries Co.) (Osaka: Sumitomo Kinzoku Kabushiki Kaisha, 1957), p. 75.

67. Ibid., p. 76.

68. Ibid., pp. 75–76.

69. Hatakeyama Hideki, *Sumitomo zaibatsu seiritsu shi no kenkyū* (History of the Formation of the Sumitomo Zaibatsu) (Tokyo: Dōbunkan Shuppan, 1988), pp. 198–201.

70. Ibid., pp. 201–3.

71. *Sumitomo Kagaku Kōgyō Kabushiki Kaisha-shi* (History of Sumitomo Chemical Co.) (Osaka: Sumitomo Kagaku Kōgyō, 1981), pp. 16–21.

72. Takeda Haruhito, "Nichiro sengo no Furukawa zaibatsu" (Furukawa Zaibatsu after the Russo-Japanese War), *Keizaigaku kenkyū*, no. 21 (1978): 25–26.

73. Furukawa Kōgyō, *Sōgyō 100-nen shi*, p. 227.

74. Sakudō, *Sumitomo zaibatsu*, pp. 136–38.

75. In 1899 Sumitomo absorbed the Osaka Seidō Kabushiki Kaisha (Osaka Copper), in which it had previously been an investor. The firm was reorganized as the Nakanoshima branch factory of Sumitomo Shindōjo, which expanded its business largely through supplying the military. In 1912 it received a navy order for the first seamless steel pipe produced in Japan. *Sumitomo Kinzoku Kōgyō 60-nen shōshi*, pp. 7–10, 18.

76. *Sha-shi Sumitomo Denki-Kōgyō*, pp. 68–71, 92–95, 98–124, 129.

77. Wada Hisajirō, ed., *Asano Cement enkaku shi* (History of Asano Cement Co.) (Tokyo: Asano Cement, 1940), p. 194.

78. Ibid., pp. 233–35, appended Table 2; *Onoda Cement 100-nen shi* (100 Years of Onoda Cement Co.) (Tokyo: Onoda Cement, 1981), p. 195.

79. Nakano Hideo, ed., *64-nen no ayumi* (64 Years) (Tokyo: Tōyō Kisen Kabushiki Kaisha, 1964), pp. 9, 27, 32–34.

80. Ibid., pp. 75, 121.

81. Ibid., pp. 97–98.

82. *Tekkō kyojin den Shiraishi Motojirō* (Biography of Shiraishi Motojirō) (Tokyo: Tekkō Shinbunsha, 1967), pp. 281–83.

83. Nakano, *64-nen no ayumi*, pp. 107–11, 117–20.

84. Majima Sanji, ed., *Kondō Kaijirō den* (Biography of Kondō Kaijirō) (Yokohama: By the editor, 1933), pp. 46–48, 70–71, 74–76, 83, 93.

85. Ibid., pp. 96–98; Abe Sei, "Kindai Nihon sekiyu sangyō no seisei hatten to Asano Sōichirō" (The Formation and Development of the Japanese Modern Petroleum Industry and Asano Sōichirō), *Chūō Daigaku Kigyō Kenkyūsho Nenpō*, no. 9 (1988):165–66.

86. Majima, *Kondō Kaijirō den*, pp. 99–104.

87. Ibid., pp. 126–27.

88. Ibid., pp. 114–24; Abe, "Kindai Nihon sekiyu sangyō," p. 175.

89. Majima, *Kondō Kaijirō den*, pp. 125–27.

90. Based on the list of stockholders.
91. *Tekkō kyojin den Shiraishi Motojirō*, pp. 291–327.
92. Kohayagawa Yōichi, "Asano zaibatsu no takakuka to keiei soshiki" (The Diversification and Management Structure of the Asano zaibatsu), *Keiei Shigaku*, vol. 16, no. 1 (1981): 43.
93. Ibid.
94. *Yasuda Ginkō 60-nen shi* (60 Years of Yasuda Bank) (Tokyo: Yasuda Bank, 1940), appendix, p. 7.
95. Ibid., pp. 208–12.
96. Yui Tsunehiko, ed., *Yasuda zaibatsu* (Tokyo: Nihon Keizai Shinbunsha, 1986), pp. 141–43, 219–46.
97. Ibid., pp. 213–16.
98. Ibid., pp. 235–40.
99. Ibid., pp. 196–200.
100. Ibid., pp. 229–32.
101. Ibid., pp. 245–46.
102. Ibid., pp. 224–29, 249, 395–96; Noyori Shūichi, *Meiji Taishō-shi* (History of the Meiji and Taishō Eras) (Tokyo: Jitsugyō no Sekaisha, 1930), vol. 11, pp. 114, 119, 131–33.
103. Asai Yoshio, "Yasuda kin'yū zaibatsu no keisei" (Formation of the Yasuda Financial zaibatsu), *Seijō Daigaku Keizai Kenkyū*, no. 84 (March): 144.
104. Ibid.: 154.
105. Kakuyūkai, *Ōkura Tsuruhiko-ō* (Biography of Ōkura Kihachirō) (Tokyo: Kakuyūkai, 1924), pp. 149, 160.
106. Yamazaki Hiroaki, "The Logic of the Formation of General Trading Companies in Japan", in *Business History of General Trading Companies*, ed., Shin'ichi Yonekawa and Hideki Yoshihara (Tokyo: University of Tokyo Press, 1987), pp. 52–53.
107. Kakuyūkai, *Ōkura Tsuruhiko-ō*, pp. 207, 211.
108. Ōkura Zaibatsu Kenkyū-kai, *Ōkura zaibatsu no kenkyū* (Studies on the Ōkura Zaibatsu) (Tokyo: Kondō Shuppansha, 1982), pp. 424–26.
109. Ibid., pp. 427–29, 435–42.
110. Ibid., pp. 443–44.
111. Ibid., pp. 479–82.
112. Nakamura Seishi, "Taishō-Shōwa ki no Ōkura zaibatsu" (The Ōkura Zaibatsu in the Taishō and Shōwa Eras), *Keiei Shigaku*, vol. 15, no. 3 (1980): 51, 72.
113. Dōwa Kōgyō Kabushiki Kaisha, *70-nen no kaiko* (70 Years of Dōwa Kōgyō) (Tokyo: Dōwa Kōgyō, 1955), p. 41.
114. Ibid., pp. 36–38.
115. Udagawa Masaru, "Kuhara Fusanosuke," in *Nihon no kigyōka (2): Taishōhen* (Japanese Entrepreneurs (2): The Taishō Era), ed., Tsunehiko Yui et al. (Tokyo: Yūhikaku, 1978), pp. 158–59.
116. Ibid., pp. 159–60.
117. *Kuhara Fusanosuke* (Biography of Kuhara Fusanosuke) (Tokyo: Nihon Kōgyō Co., Ltd., 1970), pp. 85–87.
118. Kaya Minoru, ed., *Hitachi Kōzan-shi* (History of the Hitachi Mine) (Hitachi: Nihon Kōgyō Kabushiki Kaisha, Office of the Hitachi Mine, 1952), pp. 69–70, 77.
119. *Nihon Kōgyō Kabushiki Kaisha 50-nen shi* (50 Years of Nihon Mining Company) (Tokyo: Nihon Kōgyō Kabushiki Kaisha, 1957), pp. 25–43.

Chapter 4 Factors Affecting Zaibatsu Development

1. The Kōnoike family of Osaka is a very good example. The Kōnoike, who formed an extremely wealthy money-lending and land-owning family in the Tokugawa period, were not willing to diversify their interests in response to the changed situation after the Meiji Restoration. The family confined itself to such fields as banking, warehousing, and real estate. See Yasuoka Shigeaki, *Zaibatsu keisei-shi no kenkyū* (History of the Formation of the Zaibatsu) (Kyoto: Minerva Shobō, 1970), Part I, and Miyamoto Matao and Hiroyama Kensuke, "The Retreat from Diversification and the Desire for Specialization in Kōnoike, Late Meiji to Early Shōwa," in *Japanese Yearbook on Business History*, no. 1 (1984): 104–28.

2. The Fujita family had invested in Kitahama Bank at the time of its founding, and Kuhara Shōzaburō of Fujita had served as its first president. The Fujita gradually bought up the bank's stock in order to gain control, but the bank's failure in 1914 prevented their success. Imuta Yoshimitsu, "Iwashita Seishū to Kitahama Ginkō," in *Shihonshugi no keisei to hatten* (Formation and Development of Capitalism), ed., Ōtsuka Hisao et al. (Tokyo: University of Tokyo Press, 1968) pp. 326–28, 334–35.

3. Mitsubishi Gōshi Kaisha, ed., *Mitsubishi Sha-shi* (Records of Mitsubishi Company) (Tokyo: University of Tokyo Press, 1977–82), vol. 19, p. 40; vol. 21, p. 925.

4. Ibid., vol. 21, p. 1100.

5. Mitsui Bunko, *Mitsui jigyō-shi* (History of the Mitsui Enterprises) (Tokyo: Mitsui Bunko, 1980), vol. 2, p. 575.

6. *Mitsui Ginkō shiryō* (Historical Materials on Mitsui Bank) (Tokyo: Japan Business History Institute, 1977), vol. 2, p. 83–85.

7. Yagi Yoshio, "Mitsui Ginkō shuyō shiten to yokin sōdatsu-sen" (Main Branches of the Mitsui Bank and the Competition on Deposit Acquisition), *Chihō Kin'yūshi Kenkyū*, no. 20 (1989):52–53.

8. Mitsui Bunko, *Mitsui jigyō-shi*, vol. 2, p. 567; *Mitsui Ginkō 80-nen shi* (80 Years of Mitsui Bank) (Tokyo: Mitsui Bank, 1957), p. 745.

9. *Mitsubishi Ginkō-shi* (History of the Mitsubishi Bank) (Tokyo: Mitsubishi Bank, 1954), p. 753.

10. *Sumitomo Ginkō 80-nen shi* (80 Years of Sumitomo Bank) (Osaka: Sumitomo Bank, 1979), Appendix, p. 45.

11. Leslie Hannah, "Introduction," in *From Family Firm to Professional Management: Structure and Performance of Business Enterprise*, ed., L. Hannah (Budapest: Eighth International Economic History Congress, B9, 1982), p. 3.

12. Japan Business History Institute, ed., *Nakamigawa Hikojirō denki shiryō*, (Biographical Materials on Nakamigawa Hikojirō) (Tokyo: Tōyō Keizai Shinpōsha, 1969), chapter 2.

13. Ibid., pp. 187–93.

14. Ibid., p. 220.

15. Fukuzawa Yukichi, "Jitsugyō ron" (On Business), in *Fukuzawa Yukichi Zenshū* (Collected Works of Fukuzawa Yukichi), ed., Keiō Gijuku (Tokyo: Iwanami Shoten, 1959), vol. 6, pp. 190–94.

16. On Fujiyama Raita, see Nishihara Yūjirō, ed., *Fujiyama Raita den* (Biography of Fujiyama Raita) (Tokyo: Fujiyama Aiichirō, 1939).

17. On Mutō Sanji, see Mutō Sanji, *Watakushi no minoue banashi* (My Life Story) (Sumiyoshi, Hyōgo Prefecture: Mutō Kinta, 1934).

18. On Hibi Ōsuke, see Hoshino Kojirō, *Mitsukoshi sōshisha Hibi Ōsuke* (Biography of Hibi Ōsuke, Founder of Mitsukoshi) (Tokyo, 1951).

19. For instance, in response to the high-handed behavior of foreign trading companies in Yokohama that were monopolizing the export trade, Japan's traders banded together, with Masuda Takashi taking a leading role in the efforts of the Japanese Silk Merchant Association from 1880 to 1881 in particular. *Yokohama shi-shi* (History of the City of Yokohama), vol. 3-II (Yokohama: Yokohama City, 1963), pp. 106–23.

20. *Nakamigawa Hikojirō denki shiryō*, p. 220.

21. On Masuda Takashi's career, see Nagai Minoru, *Jijo Masuda Takashi-ō den* (Biography of Takashi Masuda) (Kamakura: By the author, 1939).

22. *Kōhon Mitsui Bussan Kabushiki Kaisha 100-nen shi*, (100 years of Mitsui Bussan) (Tokyo: Japan Business History Institute, 1979), vol. 1, p. 60.

23. On Ueda Yasusaburō, see Ueda Jushirō, "Ueda Yasusaburō Nenpu" (Chronological Personal History of Ueda Yasusaburō), *Mitsui Bunko Ronsō*, 7 (1973):301–16.

24. On Yamamoto Jōtarō, see *Yamamoto Jōtarō denki* (Biography of Yamamoto Jōtarō) (Tokyo, 1942). After resigning from Mitsui in 1914 over the Siemens Scandal, in which Bussan was implicated in bribing navy officials to win government contracts, Yamamoto served as a Diet member beginning 1920 and as president of the South Manchuria Railway Company from 1927 to 1929. His uncle, the Yokohama merchant, was the adoptive father of Yoshida Shigeru, who became prime minister after World War II.

25. On Shōda Heigorō, see Shukuri Jūichi, *Shōda Heigorō* (Biography of Shōda Heigorō) (Tokyo: Taikyōsha, 1932).

26. *Sumitomo Shunsui* (Biography of Sumitomo Tomoito) (Kyoto, 1955), p. 350.

27. On Suzuki Masaya, see *Suzuki Masaya* (Biography of Suzuki Masaya) (Osaka, 1961).

28. Majima Sanji, ed., *Kondō Kaijirō den* (Biography of Kondō Kaijirō) (Yokohama: By the editor, 1933), p. 45.

29. On Itō Takuma, see *Itō Takuma-ō* (Biography of Itō Takuma) (Tokyo, 1956).

30. *Tekkō kyojin den Shiraishi Motojirō* (Biography of Shiraishi Motojirō) (Tokyo: Tekkō Shinbunsha, 1967), pp. 339, 347, 356–57.

31. Mitsui Bunko, *Mitsui jigyō-shi*, vol. 2, p. 603.

32. Morikawa Hidemasa, *Zaibatsu no keieishi-teki kenkyū* (Studies in the Business History of the Zaibatsu) (Tokyo: Tōyō Keizai Shinpōsha, 1980), pp. 232–35.

33. Ibid., pp. 234–38.

34. Mitsui Bunko, *Mitsui jigyō-shi*, vol. 2, p. 604.

35. Ibid., p. 651.

36. Ibid., p. 661.

37. Ibid., pp. 669–70.

38. Morikawa, *Zaibatsu no keieishi-teki kenkyū*, p. 242.

39. Ibid., p. 227.

40. See Introduction, note 4.

41. Mishima Yasuo, ed., *Mitsubishi zaibatsu* (Tokyo: Nihon Keizai Shinbunsha, 1981), p. 165.

42. Mitsubishi Gōshi, *Mitsubishi Sha-shi*, vol. 21, p. 1096. It was decided that operating expenses, labor costs, entertainment expenditures, and contribu-

tions were to be borne by each division, while special bonuses, pensions, and annuities were to be borne by the head office.

43. Mishima, *Mitsubishi zaibatsu*, p. 131. In 1911 the system was changed so that the units handed over to the divisions all of their profits before depreciation, and the divisions could retain not only the profits above 10 percent of their capital but also the amount calculated for depreciation. Mitsubishi Gōshi, *Mitsubishi Sha-shi*, vol. 21, pp. 1352–53.

44. Ibid., pp. 1096–98.

45. Alfred D. Chandler, Jr., *The Visible Hand* (Cambridge: Harvard University Press, 1977), pp. 457–63.

46. *Mitsui Hachirōemon Takamine den* (Biography of Mitsui Hachirōemon Takamine) (Tokyo: Mitsui Bunko, University of Tokyo Press, 1988), pp. 252–53.

47. Ibid., p. 254.

48. Nakada Yasunao, *Mitsui Takatoshi* (Tokyo: Yoshikawa Kōbunkan, 1959), pp. 245–50.

49. Ibid., pp. 266–80.

50. Mitsui Bunko, *Mitsui jigyō-shi*, vol. 2, pp. 635–38.

51. Ibid., p. 642.

52. Ibid., pp. 644–45.

53. Ibid., p. 647.

54. Suga Toshio, "Sumitomo-ke no kōin no tōkyū-sei to ie seido ni tsuite" ("On the Employees' Ranking System and Family Structure of the House of Sumitomo"), in *Sumitomo no keieishi-teki kenkyū* (Studies in the Business History of Sumitomo), ed., Miyamoto Mataji and Sakudō Yōtarō (Tokyo: Jitsukyō Shuppan, 1979), pp. 146–55.

55. *Yasuda Hozensha to sono kankei jigyō shi* (History of Yasuda Hozensha and Its Affiliated Enterprises) (Tokyo: Yasuda Fudōsan Kabushiki Kaisha 1974), pp. 114–21.

56. Ibid., p. 117.

57. Ibid., p. 115.

58. *Iwasaki Hisaya den* (Biography of Iwasaki Hisaya) (Tokyo: University of Tokyo Press, 1961), pp. 308–9.

59. Ibid., p. 309.

60. Yasuoka Shigeaki has stressed this point in distinguishing the *sōyū* (general ownership) or *Gesamteigentum* of Mitsui from the *kyōyū* (joint ownership) or *Miteigentum* of Mitsubishi. Yasuoka Shigeaki, "Capital Ownership in Family Companies: Japanese Firms Compared with Those in Other Countries," in *Family Business in the Era of Industrial Growth: Its Ownership and Management*, ed., Ōkōchi Akio and Yasuoka Shigeaki, (Tokyo: University of Tokyo Press, 1984), pp. 9–10.

61. Alfred D. Chandler, Jr., *Strategy and Structure* (Cambridge: The M.I.T. Press, 1962), p. 102.

Chapter 5 *The Zaibatsu and World War I*

1. The data are from *Nihon keizai tōkei sōkan* (Statistical Survey of the Japanese Economy) (Tokyo: Asahi Shinbunsha, 1930), pp. 239, 548, 724.

2. These are to be distinguished from the so-called *shinkō zaibatsu* (newly

risen zaibatsu), Nissan, Nichitsu, Mori, Nihon Sōda, and Riken, the publicly held industrial groups that emerged during the interwar period.

3. On the Iwai zaibatsu, see *Iwai 100-nen shi* (100 Years of Iwai) (Osaka: Iwai Sangyō, 1964).

4. On the Murai zaibatsu, see Ōtani Motochiyo, *Tabako-ō Murai Kichibei* (Murai Kichibei, The Tobacco King) (Tokyo: Sekai Bunko, 1964).

5. On the Matsukata zaibatsu, see Mishima Yasuo, "Satsu-shū zaibatsu no seiritsu to hōkai" (The Formation and Collapse of a Kagoshima-related Zaibatsu), *Keiei Shigaku*, vol. 15, no. 1 (1980):1–27.

6. On the Nomura zaibatsu, see Mishima Yasuo, *Hanshin zaibatsu* (Zaibatsu of the Osaka-Kobe Region) (Tokyo: Nihon Keizai Shinbunsha, 1984), part 1.

7. On Suzuki Shōten, see Katsura Yoshio, *Sōgō shōsha no genryū Suzuki Shōten* (Suzuki Shōten, Origin of the Sōgō Shōsha) (Tokyo: Nihon Keizai Shinbunsha, 1977).

8. *Danshaku Dan Takuma den* (Biography of Baron Dan Takuma) (Tokyo, 1938), vol. 1, pp. 315–22.

9. Kashiwamura Toshio, *Muroran Seitetsusho 50-nen shi* (50 Years of Muroran Iron Works) (Muroran: Fuji Seitetsu Co., 1958), pp. 47–77.

10. *Mitsubishi Kōgyō sha-shi* (History of Mitsubishi Mining Company) (Tokyo: Mitsubishi Kōgyō-Cement, 1976), pp. 232–34.

11. On Makita Tamaki, see Morikawa Hidemasa, *Makita Tamaki denki shiryō* (Biographical Materials on Makita Tamaki) (Tokyo: Japan Business History Institute, 1982).

12. Morikawa Hidemasa, *Zaibatsu no keieishi-teki kenkyū* (Studies in the Business History of the Zaibatsu) (Tokyo: Tōyō Keizai Shinpōsha, 1980), pp. 61–69.

13. *Hitachi Zōsen Kabushiki Kaisha 70-nen shi* (70 Years of Hitachi Shipbuilding Co., Ltd.) (Osaka: Hitachi Zōsen, 1955), pp. 101–3.

14. Hara Masamiki, *Wagasha no oitachi* (The Birth of Our Company) (Yokohama: Asano Zōsensho Co., 1935), p. 5.

15. Kohayagawa Yōichi, "Asano zaibatsu no takakuka to keiei soshiki" (The Diversification and Management Structure of the Asano zaibatsu), *Keiei Shigaku*, vol. 16, no. 1 (1981):44.

16. Hara, *Wagasha no oitachi*, pp. 10, 57–61, 83.

17. Ibid., pp. 38, 70–71.

18. Kohayagawa, "Asano zaibatsu," p. 45.

19. *Kōhon Mitsui Bussan Kabushiki Kaisha 100-nen shi* (100 Years of Mitsui Bussan) (Tokyo: Japan Business History Institute, 1978), vol. 1, p. 297.

20. Hiroaki Yamazaki, "The Logic of the Formation of General Trading Companies in Japan," in *Business History of General Trading Companies*, ed., Shin'ichi Yonekawa and Hideki Yoshihara (Tokyo: University of Tokyo Press, 1987), pp. 41–44; Morikawa Hidemasa, "Taishō-ki Mitsui Bussan no keiei soshiki" (The Management Structure of Mitsui Bussan in the Taishō Era), *Keiei Shirin*, vol. 10, no. 1 (1974):1–15.

21. *Kōhon Mitsui Bussan 100-nen shi*, vol. 1, pp. 340–41.

22. Ibid., p. 311.

23. Ibid., p. 429.

24. Ibid.

25. Kohayagawa, "Asano zaibatsu," p. 49.

26. *Kuhara Fusanosuke* (Biography of Kuhara Fusanosuke) (Tokyo: Nihon Kōgyō Co., Ltd., 1970), pp. 223–26.

27. Katsura, *Sōgō shōsha no genryū Suzuki Shōten*, pp. 75–76.
28. Kohayagawa, "Asano zaibatsu," p. 49.
29. Ibid.
30. *Kuhara Fusanosuke*, pp. 285–90, 297, 310.
31. Takeda Haruhito, "Furukawa Shōji to Dairen Jiken" (Furukawa Trading and the Dalian Incident), in *Shakai Kagaku Kenkyū* (Studies in the Social Sciences), vol. 32, no. 2 (1970):1–61.
32. Hara Kei had been a prominent party politician since the turn of the century, serving as a minister in several cabinets. In 1918, he became prime minister and while serving his term was assassinated in 1921. Hara was one of the two or three most able politicians in prewar Japan and exerted a major impact on Japanese political history.
33. Morikawa, *Zaibatsu no keieishi-teki kenkyū*, pp. 118–23.
34. Ibid., pp. 123–25.
35. Ōta Kakuji, ed., *Hashimoto Umetarō* (Tokyo, 1939), pp. 102–9; *Yasuda Hozensha to sono kankei jigyō shi* (History of Yasuda Hozensha and Its Affiliated Enterprises) (Tokyo: Yasuda Fudōsan Kabushiki Kaisha, 1974), pp. 566–67.
36. *Furukawa Toranosuke-kun den* (Biography of Toranosuke Furukawa) (Tokyo, 1953), pp. 167–68.
37. It was not named Furukawa Bank because another bank existed in Ibaraki Prefecture whose name was written with the same characters, though read "Koga" rather than "Furukawa." When Koga Bank merged with Shimotsuke Bank in 1922, the Furukawa zaibatsu bank was finally named Furukawa Bank.
38. Dōwa Kōgyō Kabushiki Kaisha, *Sōgyō 100-nen shi* (100 years of Dōwa Mining) (Tokyo: Dōwa Kōgyō, 1985), pp. 193–94.
39. *Mitsui Ginkō 80-nen shi* (80 years of Mitsui Bank) (Tokyo: Mitsui Bank, 1957), pp. 207–8.
40. *Kōhon Mitsui Bussan 100-nen shi*, vol. 1, pp. 389–91.
41. Mishima Yasuo, ed., *Mitsubishi zaibatsu* (Tokyo: Nihon Keizai Shinbunsha, 1981), pp. 254–55.

Chapter 6 The Post-World War I Era

1. Minami Ryōshin, *Tetsudō to denryoku* (Railroads and Electric Power), vol. 12 of *Chōki keizaikai tōkei* (Long-term Economic Statistics) (Tokyo: Tōyō Keizai Shinpōsha, 1965), p. 198.
2. Matsuo Sumihiro, "Sekitan Kōgyō Rengōkai to Shōwa Sekitan Kabushiki Kaisha" (The Coal Mining Association and the Shōwa Colliery Company, Ltd.), in *Ryōtaisenkan-ki Nihon no cartel* (Cartels in Interwar Japan), ed., Hashimoto Jurō and Takeda Haruhito (Tokyo: Ochanomizu Shobō, 1985), pp. 223, 225.
3. Calculated from government statistical sources and company histories.
4. Hayashi Takehisa, Yamazaki Hiroaki, and Shibagaki Kazuo, *Nihon shihonshugi* (Japanese Capitalism), vol. 6 of *Teikokushugi no kenkyū* (Studies on Imperialism) (Tokyo: Aoki Shoten, 1973), p. 146.
5. Ibid.
6. Takao Shiba, "Succeeding Against Odds, Courting Collapse: How Mitsubishi Shipbuilding and Kawasaki Dockyard Managed the Post-WWI Slump," in *Japanese Yearbook on Business History*, no. 2 (1985):103.
7. Ibid.: 109–10.

8. Nakagawa Keiichirō, *Ryōtaisenkan no Nihon kaiungyō* (The Shipping Industry in Interwar Japan) (Tokyo: Nihon Keizai Shinbunsha, 1980), pp. 144–45.

9. Mitsui Zōsen Kabushiki Kaisha, *35-nen shi* (35-Year History of Mitsui Shipbuilding) (Tokyo: Mitsui Zōsen, 1953), pp. 44–45.

10. Morikawa Hidemasa, *Zaibatsu no keieishi-teki kenkyū* (Studies in the Business History of the Zaibatsu) (Tokyo: Tōyō Keizai Shinpōsha, 1980), pp. 188–91.

11. Ibid., pp. 194–95.

12. Ibid., pp. 193–94.

13. Asahi Glass Co., Ltd., *Sha-shi* (Company History of Asahi Glass) (Tokyo: Asahi Glass, 1967), pp. 146–47, 156, 176, 180.

14. Yamazaki Hiroaki, *Nihon kasen sangyō hattatsu-shi ron* (History of the Japanese Rayon Industry) (Tokyo: University of Tokyo Press, 1975), pp. 65–67.

15. *Tōyō Rayon sha-shi* (Company History of Tōyō Rayon) (Tokyo: Tōyō Rayon Kabushiki Kaisha, 1954), p. 67.

16. For more on the history of Toyota and Nissan, see Michael A. Cusumano, *The Japanese Automobile Industry* (Cambridge, Mass.: Council on East Asian Studies, Harvard University, 1985).

17. Morikawa, *Zaibatsu no keieishi-teki kenkyū*, pp. 178–80.

18. Suzuki Tsuneo, "Nihon ryūan kōgyō-shi ron" (On the History of the Japanese Ammonium Sulphate Industry), *Bulletin of Kurume University*, 14 (1985):82.

19. Ibid.: 83.

20. Ibid.: pp. 83, 106.

21. *Suzuki Masaya* (Biography of Suzuki Masaya) (Osaka, 1961), p. 206.

22. Ibid., p. 207.

23. Suzuki, "Nihon ryūan kōgyō-shi ron," p. 15.

24. *Suzuki Masaya*, p. 208.

25. Morikawa Hidemasa, *Makita Tamaki denki shiryō* (Biographical Materials on Makita Tamaki) (Tokyo: Japan Business History Institute, 1982), p. 285.

26. *Kōhon Mitsui Bussan Kabushiki Kaisha 100-nen shi* (100 years of Mitsui Bussan) (Tokyo: Japan Business History Institute, 1978), vol. 1, p. 493.

27. Suzuki, "Nihon ryūan kōgyō-shi ron," p. 93.

28. Ibid., p. 84.

29. Ibid., p. 93.

30. Morikawa, *Makita Tamaki denki shiryō*, p. 285.

31. Ibid., p. 286.

32. Ibid.

33. Morikawa, *Zaibatsu no keieishi-teki kenkyū*, pp. 206–8.

34. Suzuki, "Nihon ryūan kōgyō-shi ron," pp. 94–101.

35. *Yamaguchi Kisaburō den* (Biography of Yamaguchi Kisaburō) (Kawasaki: Tokyo Shibaura Denki Co., 1950), pp. 38–40. Yamaguchi was invited to become executive director of Tokyo Electric (Tokyo Denki), where his father-in-law was president. When Tokyo Electric merged with Shibaura Engineering Works, a Mitsui corporation, to become Tokyo Shibaura Denki (Toshiba), Yamaguchi became its first president. Ibid., pp. 41, 63.

36. On Nakagawa Suekichi, see *Nakagawa Suekichi-ō* (Biography of Nakagawa Suekichi) (Tokyo, 1965).

37. On Nakajima Kumakichi, see Nakajima Kumakichi, *Seikai zaikai 50 nen* (50 Years in the World of Politics and Business) (Tokyo: Kōdansha, 1951).
38. Hisashi Watanabe, "History of the Process Leading to the Formation of Fuji Electric," in *Japanese Yearbook on Business History*, no. 1 (1984): 47–71.
39. *Fuji Denki sha-shi* (Company History of Fuji Denki) (Tokyo: Fuji Electric Co., 1957), p. 6.
40. Ibid., pp. 21–22.
41. Fuji Tsūshinki Seizō Kabushiki Kaisha, *Sha-shi* (Company History of Fuji Tsūshinki) (Tokyo, 1964), pp. 23–24.
42. *Nihon Keikinzoku 20-nen shi* (20 Years of Nippon Light Metal) (Tokyo: Nihon Keikinzoku, 1959), pp. 3–11, 23–24, 29.
43. Yui Tsunehiko, ed., *Yasuda Zaibatsu* (Tokyo: Nihon Keizai Shinbunsha, 1986), p. 327.
44. Ibid., pp. 327–31.
45. Based on the self-published histories of the banks.
46. *Mitsui Ginkō 80-nen shi* (80 Years of Mitsui Bank) (Tokyo: Mitsui Bank, 1957), pp. 421–22, 450–51.
47. Based on the self-published histories of the banks.

Change in number of branches (including sub-branches) of four zaibatsu banks:

	Mitsui	Mitsubishi	Sumitomo	Yasuda
1909	14	4	17	20
1919	18	8	28	22

48. Yui, *Yasuda zaibatsu*, pp. 366–67.
49. *Daiichi Ginkō-shi* (History of Daiichi Bank) (Tokyo: Daiichi Bank, 1959), vol. 2, pp. 113–19, 121–22.
50. Dōwa Kōgyō Kabushiki Kaisha, *Sōgyō 100-nen shi* (100 years of Dōwa Mining) (Tokyo: Dōwa Kōgyō, 1985), pp. 239–42.
51. *Sumitomo Shintaku Ginkō 50-nen shi* (50 Years of Sumitomo Trust Bank) (Osaka: Sumitomo Shintaku Ginkō, 1976), pp. 61–89.
52. Noyori Shūichi, *Meiji Taishō-shi* (History of the Meiji and Taishō Eras) (Tokyo: Jitsugyō no Sekaisha, 1929), vol. 10, pp. 292–93, 297–98.
53. Asai Yoshio, "1920-nendai ni okeru Mitsui Ginkō to Mitsui zaibatsu" (Mitsui Bank and the Mitsui zaibatsu in the 1920s), in *Mitsui Bunko Ronsō* 11 (1977): 254–60.
54. Ibid.: 263; *Kōhon Mitsui Bussan 100-nen shi*, vol. 1, pp. 639–40.
55. *Mitsui Ginkō shiryō* (Historical Materials on Mitsui Bank) (Tokyo: Japan Business History Institute, 1977), vol. 5, p. 491.
56. *Mitsubishi Jūkōgyō Kabushiki Kaisha-shi* (History of Mitsubishi Heavy Industries) (Tokyo: Mitsubishi Jūkōgyō, 1956), p. 69.
57. Asajima Shōichi, "Daiichiji taisen go no Mitsubishi zaibatsu no kin'yū" (The Finances of the Mitsubishi Zaibatsu after World War I), in *Shakai Kagaku Nenpō* (1985):100.
58. Ibid.: 101, 103.
59. Shōichi Asajima, "Flow-of-Funds Analysis of the Sumitomo Zaibatsu," in *Japanese Yearbook on Business History*, no. 1 (1984):74.
60. Morikawa, *Zaibatsu no keieishi-teki kenkyū*, p. 219.
61. Kawada Jun, *Sumitomo kaisō ki* (Memories of the Sumitomo Zaibatsu) (Tokyo: Chūō Kōron Sha, 1951), pp. 138–39.
62. *Kōhon Mitsui Bussan 100-nen shi*, vol. 1, p. 428.
63. Yamazaki Hiroaki, "1920-nendai no Mitsui Bussan" (Mitsui Bussan in

the 1920s), in *Senkan-ki no Nihon keizai bunseki* (Analysis of the Japanese Economy during the Interwar Period), ed., Nakamura Takafusa (Tokyo: Yamakawa Shuppansha, 1981), p. 311.

64. *Kōhon Mitsui Bussan 100-nen shi*, vol. 1, p. 487.

65. Ibid., p. 581; Yamazaki, "1920-nendai no Mitsui Bussan," pp. 316–17.

66. *Ito hitosuji* (One Thread) (Tokyo: Daidō Keori Kabushiki Kaisha, 1960), pp. 627–28.

67. *Kōhon Mitsui Bussan 100-nen shi*, vol. 1, p. 449.

68. Yamazaki, "1920-nendai no Mitsui Bussan," p. 321.

69. *Ritsugyō bōeki roku* (Records of the Enterprises and Trade of the Mitsubishi Trading Co.) (Tokyo: Mitsubishi Shōji Kabushiki Kaisha, 1958), pp. 932–35.

70. Kawabe Nobuo, *Sōgō shōsha no kenkyū: Senzen Mitsubishi Shōji no zaibei katsudō* (A Study of a General Trading Company: The Prewar Activities of Mitsubishi Trading Company in the United States) (Tokyo: Jitsukyō Shuppan, 1982), p. 36.

71. *Mitsui Bussan Kabushiki Kaisha shokuin roku* (List of the Staff of Mitsui & Co., Ltd. each year, unpublished).

72. Nakagawa, *Ryōtaisenkan no Nihon kaiungyō*, pp. 143–46.

73. Mitsui Senpaku Kabushiki Kaisha, *Sōgyō 80-nen shi* (80 Years of Mitsui Shipping) (Tokyo: Mitsui Senpaku, 1958), pp. 135–37; Shin Gotō, "The Progress of Shipping Operators Belonging to Trading Companies: The Scheduled Services to North America of the Shipping Division of Mitsui Trading Company Between the Two World Wars," in *Japanese Yearbook on Business History*, no. 3 (1986):52–81.

74. Mitsui Senpaku, *Sōgyō 80-nen shi*, pp. 536–50.

75. Nakano Hideo, ed., *64-nen no ayumi* (64 Years) (Tokyo: Tōyō Kisen Kabushiki Kaisha, 1964), pp. 171–73, 226–29.

76. On the collapse of Suzuki Shōten, see Katsura Yoshio, *Sōgō shōsha no genryū Suzuki Shōten* (Suzuki Shōten, Origins of the Sōgō Shōsha) (Tokyo: Nihon Keizai Shinbunsha, 1977).

77. Asajima Shōichi, *Senkan-ki Sumitomo zaibatsu keiei-shi* (Business History of the Sumitomo Zaibatsu during the Interwar Period) (Tokyo: University of Tokyo Press, 1983), p. 578.

78. Nakamura Seishi, "Taishō Shōwa shoki no Ōkura zaibatsu" ("The Ōkura Zaibatsu in the Taishō and Shōwa Eras"), *Keiei Shigaku*, vol. 15, no. 3 (1980):65.

79. Ibid.: 66.

80. Wada Hisajirō, ed., *Asano Cement enkaku-shi* (History of Asano Cement Co.) (Tokyo: Asano Cement, 1940), appendix.

Chapter 7 The Family Multisubsidiary System

1. For more on the term "multisubsidiary system," see Introduction, note 4 .

2. Representative of such zaibatsu studies are Takahashi Kamekichi, *Nippon zaibatsu no kaibō* (An Analysis of Japanese Zaibatsu) (Tokyo: Chūō Kōron Sha, 1930); *Nihon konzern zensho* (Complete Works on Japanese Konzern), 19 vols. (Tokyo Shunshūsha, 1937–38); and Shibagaki Kazuo, *Nihon Kin'yūshihon bunseki* (An Analysis of Japanese Financial Capital) (Tokyo: University of Tokyo Press, 1965).

3. Mitsui Bunko, *Mitsui jigyō-shi* (History of the Mitsui Enterprises) (Tokyo: Mitsui Bunko, 1980), vol. 2, pp. 742–45.

4. Ibid., pp. 745–49.

5. The disposition of Mitsui Mining was actually somewhat more complicated. Mitsui Mining changed its name to Mitsui Gōmei Kaisha and took over the Management Department's function, whereupon the operations that had been the substance of Mitsui Mining were carried out by the Mining Division of Mitsui Gōmei, ibid., p. 751.

6. *Mitsui Hachirōemon Takamine den* (Biography of Mitsui Hachirōemon Takamine) (Tokyo: Mitsui Bunko, University of Tokyo Press, 1988).

7. Ibid., pp. 374–76.

8. Mitsui Bunko, *Mitsui jigyō-shi*, vol. 3-1, p. 7.

9. Ibid., p. 11.

10. At Mitsui Mining, however, the practice of appointing executive directors did not actually begin until 1918.

11. Ibid., pp. 242–49.

12. Ibid., pp. 262–64.

13. Ibid., p. 288.

14. *Iwasaki Koyata den* (Biography of Koyata Iwasaki) (Tokyo: University of Tokyo Press, 1957), pp. 218–19.

15. Mishima Yasuo, ed., *Mitsubishi zaibatsu* (Tokyo: Nihon Keizai Shinbunsha, 1981), p. 88.

16. Mitsubishi Gōshi Kaisha, ed., *Mitsubishi Sha-shi* (Records of Mitsubishi Company) (Tokyo: University of Tokyo Press, 1980), vol. 11, pp. 4965–66.

17. Mishima, *Mitsubishi zaibatsu*, p. 90.

18. Takeda Haruhito, "Shihon chikuseki (3): Zaibatsu" (Capital Accumulation (3): The Zaibatsu), in *Nihon teikokushugi-shi* (History of Japanese Imperialism), ed., Ōishi Kaichirō (Tokyo: University of Tokyo Press, 1985), pp. 252–54.

19. *Mitsubishi Kōgyō sha-shi* (History of Mitsubishi Mining Company) (Tokyo: Mitsubishi Kōgyō-Cement, 1976), pp. 272–74.

20. Asajima Shōichi, *Senkan-ki Sumitomo zaibatsu keiei-shi* (Business History of the Sumitomo Zaibatsu during the Interwar period) (Tokyo: University of Tokyo Press, 1983), pp. 21–22.

21. Sakudō Yōtarō, *Sumitomo zaibatsu* (Tokyo: Nihon Keizai Shinbunsha, 1982), p. 240.

22. *Nippon Ita-Garasu Kabushiki Kaisha 50-nen shi* (50 Years of Nippon Sheet Glass Co., Ltd.) (Osaka: Nippon Ita-Garasu, 1968), pp. 46, 54, 97–101, 130, 144.

23. *Nippon Denki Kabushiki Kaisha 70-nen shi* (70 Years of NEC) (Tokyo: Nippon Denki, 1972), pp. 100–8.

24. Ibid., pp. 152–58, 189–90.

25. Yui Tsunehiko, "Meiji-ki ni okeru Yasuda zaibatsu no takakuka," (The Diversification of Yasuda Zaibatsu in the Meiji Era), in *Kigyōsha katsudō no shiteki kenkyū* (Historical Approaches to Entrepreneurship), ed., Tsuchiya Moriaki and Morikawa Hidemasa (Tokyo: Nihon Keizai Shinbunsha, 1981), p. 45.

26. Yui Tsunehiko (ed.), *Yasuda zaibatsu* (Tokyo: Nihon Keizai Shinbunsha, 1986), pp. 290–91.

27. Asai Yoshio, "Yasuda kin'yū zaibatsu no keisei" (Formation of the

Yasuda Financial Zaibatsu), *Seijō Daigaku Keizai Kenkyū* (Seijō University Economic Papers) no. 84 (1984):154.

28. *Yasuda Hozensha to sono kankei jigyō shi* (History of Yasuda Hozensha and Its Affiliated Enterprises) (Tokyo: Yasuda Fudōsan Kabushiki Kaisha, 1974), pp. 442–62.

29. Ibid., pp. 522–23.

30. Ibid., pp. 530–32.

31. Kohayagawa Yōichi, "Yasuda Zenjirō shigo no Yasuda zaibatsu no saihensei" (The Reorganization of the Yasuda Zaibatsu after Yasuda Zenjirō's Death), in *Keiei-jōhō Gakubu Ronshū*, vol. 1, no. 1 (1985):29.

32. Ibid.

33. Ibid.: 28–34.

34. Ibid.: 37.

35. Ibid.: 38–39.

36. *Yasuda Hozensha,* pp. 677–80.

37. Kohayagawa, "Yasuda Zenjirō shigo," pp. 40–41.

38. *Furukawa Toranosuke-kun den* (Biography of Furukawa Toranosuke) (Tokyo, 1953), p. 155.

39. *Yoshimura Manjirō san o shinobite* (Remembering Yoshimura Manjirō) (Tokyo, 1972), pp. 4, 12; *Nakagawa Suekichi-ō* (Biography of Nakagawa Suekichi) (Tokyo, 1965), pp. 12–13.

40. Nakamura Seishi, "Ōkura zaibatsu no Meiji-matsu no kaiso o meguru ichi kōsatsu" (The Organization of Ōkura Zaibatsu in the Late Meiji), in *Kigyōsha katsudō no shiteki kenkyū*, ed., Tsuchiya and Morikawa, pp. 89, 92–95.

41. Nakamura Seishi, "Taishō-Shōwa ki no Ōkura zaibatsu" (The Ōkura Zaibatsu in the Taishō and Shōwa Eras), *Keiei Shigaku*, vol. 15, no. 3 (1980):74.

42. Noyori Shūichi, *Meiji Taishō-shi* (History of the Meiji and Taishō Eras) (Tokyo: Jitsugyō no Sekaisha, 1929), vol. 12, p. 329.

43. Kohayagawa Yōichi, "Asano zaibatsu no takakuka to keiei soshiki" (The Diversification and Management Structure of the Asano Zaibatsu), *Keiei Shigaku*, vol. 16, no. 1 (1981):51–53.

44. Ibid.: 53.

45. Ibid.: 54.

46. Ibid.: 53–54.

47. Ibid.: 57–58.

48. Dōwa Kōgyō Kabushiki Kaisha, *Sōgyō 100-nen shi* (100 years of Dōwa Mining) (Tokyo: Dōwa Kōgyō, 1985), pp. 197–202.

49. The tax reforms of 1913 and 1920, the latter in particular, put the personal stockholder at a disadvantage as compared to the corporation. Takeda, "Shihon chikuseki (3): Zaibatsu," pp. 248–51.

50. Udagawa Masaru, "Kuhara Fusanosuke," in *Nihon no kigyōka (2): Taishōhen* (Japanese Entrepreneurs (2): The Taishō Era) ed. Yui Tsunehiko et al. (Tokyo: Yūhikaku, 1978), pp. 190–91.

51. Udagawa Masaru, *Shinkō zaibatsu* (New Zaibatsu) (Tokyo: Nihon Keizai Shinbunsha, 1984), ch. 1.

52. *Hitachi Seisakusho-shi* (History of Hitachi, Ltd.) (Tokyo: Hitachi Hyōronsha, 1949), pp. 18–20.

53. Katsura Yoshio, *Sōgō shōsha no genryū Suzuki Shōten* (Suzuki Shōten,

Origins of the Sōgō Shōsha) (Tokyo: Nihon Keizai Shinbunsha, 1977), pp. 136–38.

54. Takeda, "Shihon chikuseki (3): zaibatsu," pp. 248–51.

55. *Mitsui Gōmei Kaisha rijikai kiroku* (Minutes of the Board of Directors of Mitsui Gōmei), held at Mitsui Bunko, Tokyo.

56. See ch. 6 of this book.

57. *Mitsui Gōmei Kaisha shokuin roku* (List of Mitsui Gōmei Officers), held by the Mitsui Bunko.

58. *Kabushiki Kaisha Mitsubishi Sha meibo, 1941* (List of the Officers of Mitsubishi Sha, 1941).

59. For more on the fact that most zaibatsu under exclusive family control were de facto managerial enterprises, see Morikawa Hidemasa, "Prerequisites for the Development of Managerial Capitalism—On the Basis of Cases in Prewar Japan," in *Development of Managerial Enterprise*, ed., Kesaji Kobayashi and Hidemasa Morikawa (Tokyo: University of Tokyo Press, 1986), pp. 11–16.

60. Mitsui Bunko, *Mitsui jigyō-shi,* vol. 3-1, pp. 289–90.

61. *Mitsui Hachirōemon Takamine den,* pp. 354–55.

62. Ikeda Seihin, *Zaikai kaiko* (Memoirs of the Business World) (Tokyo: Sekai no Nihonsha, 1949), pp. 130–31.

Chapter 8 Transformation, Collapse, and Postwar Dissolution

1. In September 1917 Japan followed the United States in instituting a gold embargo. The United States lifted its embargo in 1919, and the European countries, which had imposed embargoes after the outbreak of World War I, gradually removed theirs as well. The Japanese government, however, feared that a return to the gold standard would generate an economic downturn within Japan, and so Japan put off lifting its embargo until January 1930.

2. *Mitsui Ginkō 80-nen shi* (80 years of Mitsui Bank) (Tokyo: Mitsui Bank, 1957), pp. 252–53, 255.

3. *Kōhon Mitsui Bussan Kabushiki Kaisha 100-nen shi* (100 years of Mitsui Bussan) (Tokyo: Japan Business History Institute, 1978), vol. 1, pp. 536–40.

4. Ikeda Seihin, *Zaikai kaiko* (Memoirs of the Business World) (Tokyo: Sekai no Nihonsha, 1949), pp. 162–64.

5. Ibid., p. 186; *Mitsui Hachirōemon Takamine den* (Biography of Mitsui Hachirōemon Takamine) (Tokyo: Mitsui Bunko, University of Tokyo Press, 1988), p. 483.

6. *Mitsui Hachirōemon Takamine den,* pp. 477–78.

7. Morikawa Hidemasa, "1930-nendai ni okeru kigyōjin no ishiki" (The Mentality of Businessmen in the 1930s), *Shisō* (June 1976):860–61.

8. Udagawa Masaru, *Shinkō zaibatsu* (New Zaibatsu) (Tokyo: Nihon Keizai Shinbunsha, 1984), p. 62.

9. Ōshio Takeshi, "Shinkō Konzern" (New Konzern), in *Shakai Keizai Shigaku,* vol. 47, no. 6 (1981):71–90.

10. When Japanese scholars refer to "the war" that ended with Japan's defeat in 1945, they often mean "the fifteen-year war" that began with the Japanese military takeover of Manchuria in 1931–32.

11. Morikawa, "1930-nendai," p. 869.

12. Togai Yoshio, *Mitsui zaibatsu-shi: Taishō Shōwa hen* (History of the Mitsui Zaibatsu: The Taishō and Shōwa Eras) (Tokyo: Kyōikusha, 1978), pp. 179–81.

13. Hashimoto Jurō, *Dai kyōkō ki no Nihon shihonshugi* (Japanese Capitalism during the Great Depression) (Tokyo: University of Tokyo Press, 1984), p. 301.

14. *Mitsubishi Sekiyu 50-nen shi* (50 Years of Mitsubishi Oil Co., Ltd.) (Tokyo: Mitsubishi Sekiyu, 1981), pp. 7–12.

15. *Mitsubishi Kasei sha-shi* (History of Mitsubishi Chemical Industries Co., Ltd.) (Tokyo: Mitsubishi Kasei, 1981), pp. 37–44.

16. Ibid., p. 53.

17. Morikawa Hidemasa, *Makita Tamaki denki shiryō* (Biographical Materials on Makita Tamaki) (Tokyo: Japan Business History Institute, 1982), p. 305; *Iwasaki Koyata den* (Biography of Iwasaki Koyata) (Tokyo: University of Tokyo Press, 1957) pp. 224–25.

18. Holding Company Liquidation Commission, *Nihon zaibatsu to sono kaitai* (Japanese Zaibatsu and Their Liquidation) (Tokyo: Holding Company Liquidation Commission, 1951), p. 121.

19. Mishima Yasuo, *Mitsubishi zaibatsu-shi: Taishō Shōwa hen* (History of the Mitsubishi Zaibatsu: The Taishō and Shōwa Eras) (Tokyo: Kyōikusha, 1980), vol. 2, pp. 192, 202–3.

20. Togai, *Mitsui zaibatsu-shi: Taishō Shōwa hen*, p. 155.

21. Ibid., p. 156.

22. Ibid., pp. 168–70.

23. Ibid., pp. 177–78, 181–83.

24. *Sōgyō 100-nen shi* (100 years of Dōwa Mining) (Tokyo: Dōwa Kōgyō, 1985), pp. 301–7.

25. *Furukawa Jūjun-kun den* (Biography of Furukawa Jūjun) (Tokyo, 1971), pp. 183–84, 187–88.

26. Holding Company Liquidation Commission, *Nihon zaibatsu to sono kaitai*, p. 209.

27. *Yasuda Hozensha to sono kankei jigyō shi* (History of Yasuda Hozensha and Its Affiliated Enterprises) (Tokyo: Yasuda Fudōsan Kabushiki Kaisha, 1974), pp. 838–39.

28. Holding Company Liquidation Commission, *Nihon zaibatsu to sono kaitai*, pp. 156–58.

29. Togai, *Mitsui zaibatsu-shi: Taishō Shōwa hen*, pp. 212–15.

30. Ibid., p. 212.

INDEX

Aikawa Yoshisuke, 210, 226
aircraft production, 127, 152
aluminum industry, 158, 230
Ariga Nagafumi, 186, 187, 225
Asabuki Eiji, 31, 52, 108
Asahi Electric (Asahi Denka), 135
Asahi Glass, 149
Asahi Silk Manufacturing (Asahi
  Kenshoku), 150, 151
Asano Bussan, 133, 134
Asano Cement, 208
Asano Chūya Bank, 137, 138, 162,
  163
Asano Dōzoku, 207, 208
Asano Ltd., 207
Asano Shipbuilding (Asano
  Zōsensho), 130
Asano Shipping (Asano Kaisōten),
  19
Asano Sōichirō, 19, 82, 83, 84–86,
  130, 162–63, 175, 207, 208
Asano Steel Works (Asano
  Seitetsusho), 130
Asano zaibatsu: banking activities of,
  136–37, 138, 162, 163; coal
  mining activities of, 19, 82–83;
  diversification activities of, 54, 82–
  87, 92; establishment of, 19, 25; in
  iron and steel industry, 130–31,
  231; management of, 51, 104, 218;
  organizational structure of, 207–8;
  post-WWI performance of, 180–

81; in petroleum industry, 19, 84–
  85; in shipbuilding industry, 130,
  135
Ashio copper mine, 17, 18, 19, 74, 76
automobile industry, 151–52
Azuma Industries (Azuma Kōgyō),
  150
Azuma Leather, 127, 150

Bank of Japan, 20, 48, 98
Bank of Taiwan, 176–77
banking, 8–9, 30, 33, 68–69, 79,
  96–98, 136–38, 159–63. *See also
  under individual bank names*
bankruptcies, 10, 134, 141, 169
bantō, 21, 47, 48, 49, 54. *See also*
  managers
Besshi copper mine, 16–17, 40–41,
  81
Bōeki Shōkai, 31, 38

cartels, 143–44
cement industry, 19, 54, 82
Chandler, Alfred D., xxiii, 113
charity, contributions to, 225, 243
chemical industry, 67, 81, 129, 146–
  49, 153–56, 230
China, 61, 66–67, 89
Chōya Shirt Factory (Chōya Shatsu
  Seizōsho), 126
Chūō Wool Yarn Spinning (Chūō
  Keito Bōseki), 125

Claude-Process Nitrogen Industries
  (Claude-shiki Chisso Kōgyō), 150,
  155, 156, 177
coal mining, 28, 29, 30, 32, 38–39,
  41, 62, 68, 81, 143, 144
Commercial Code (1893), xx, 27, 43,
  44, 45, 46, 54, 57
Commercial Training School (Shōhō
  Kōshūsho), 101
compradors, 61
copper industry, 15–19, 28, 74, 75–
  76, 82, 90, 142, 143–44
copper wire production, 77, 81
cotton-spinning industry, 27, 57

Daigo Ginkō (Fifth Bank), 137
Daiichi Ginkō (First Bank), 74, 142,
  163
Daiichi Kokuritsu (First National)
  Bank, 9, 10
Daitō Bussan, 126, 133, 134, 169
Daiwa Bank, 126
Dan Takuma, 39, 65, 105, 108, 129,
  149, 186, 187, 219, 225

engineers, 50, 53, 104–5
exchange operations, 5–6, 36

family ownership, xxii, 114, 223–24,
  238, 245–46
financial services, 40, 41, 159–69
Fisher, Edward, 36
Fuji Communications Equipment
  Manufacturing (Fuji Tsūshinki
  Seizō), 158
Fuji Electric Company (Fuji Denki
  Seizō), 157–58, 180
Fujita Bank, 138, 141, 163, 209
Fujita Denzaburō, 12, 90–91, 208
Fujita-gumi, Gōmei Kaisha, 12, 42–
  43, 46, 236
Fujita Heitarō, 208
Fujita Hikosaburō, 210
Fujita Kotarō, 91
Fujita Mining, 208
Fujita Shikatarō, 12
Fujita Tokujirō, 208
Fujita zaibatsu, diversification
  activities of, 42–43, 92;
  establishment of, 3, 12, 25; land

reclamation activities of, 42, 90;
  management of, 51–52, 77, 90–
  91, 208–10, 217; in mining
  industry, 90; post-WWI
  performance of, 181
Fujitsu (FACOM), 158
Fujiwara Ginjirō, 100
Fujiyama Raita, 62, 100
Fukui Kikusaburō, 101, 186, 187,
  225
Fukuzawa Yukichi, 22, 30, 31, 52,
  99, 102
Furukawa Bank, 163, 204
Furukawa Electric Company
  (Furukawa Denki Kōgyō), 142,
  156, 157
Furukawa Gōmei Kaisha, 141–42,
  156–57, 204–5
Furukawa Ichibei, 17–19, 50–51,
  74, 75–76, 77
Furukawa Junkichi, 77–78, 136
Furukawa Mining, 78, 135, 142,
  143, 204
Furukawa Toranosuke, 78, 204
Furukawa Trading (Furukawa Shōji),
  133, 134–35, 141, 142, 156, 169,
  204
Furukawa zaibatsu: in banking, 137–
  38; in copper industry, 74, 81;
  decline of, 141–42; development
  of, 73, 74–78; establishment of,
  3, 17–19, 25; heavy industry
  activities of, 156–58; in life
  insurance, 166; management of,
  77–78, 135, 156–57, 204–6;
  organizational structure of, 137;
  post-WWI performance of, 180
Furuta Toshinosuke, 195
Fusō Marine and Fire Insurance
  (Fusō Kaijō Kasai), 138

gold standard, 224
Gotō Shōjirō, 29–30
government patronage, 3, 14–15,
  20, 25
Great Kantō Earthquake, 140, 143,
  157, 158

Hara Kei, 78, 135
Harima Shipyard (Harima
  Zōsensho), 129, 144–45, 177

Hasegawa Yoshinosuke, 52–53
Hashimoto Umetarō, 136–37
Hayakawa Senkichirō, 64, 186
heavy industry, 128–31, 150–59,
    229–33, 242
Hida Shōsaku, 29, 30, 33, 52
Hirose Saihei (Giemon), 16, 39, 40,
    49, 50
Hitachi mine, 91, 128
Hitachi Seisakusho, 210–11
Hōden Petroleum (Hōden Sekiyu),
    84, 85
Hokkaido Colliery and Railway
    (Hokkaido Tankō Tetsudō), 60
Hokkaido Colliery and Steamship
    (Hokkaido Tankō Kisen), 128,
    143, 187
Holding Company Liquidation
    Commission, 237, 238
Hōraisha, 29–30
Hozen Bank, 159–60
Hunter, Edward H., 130

Iba Sadatake, 49, 50, 78, 103
Ikeda Seihin, 100, 219
Imaizumi Kaichirō, 86, 104
Industrial Bank of Japan (Nippon
    Kōgyō Ginkō), 164
Inoue Kaoru, 9, 21, 36, 42, 43–44,
    64, 90, 99, 109, 115, 135
Inoue Kōji, 135, 205–6
Inoue Masaru, 35, 72
insurance business, 42, 87, 138–39,
    164, 166
iron and steel industry, 40–41, 79–
    80, 128–29, 130–31, 230–31
Irwin, Robert W., 36, 37, 102
Ishikari Coal (Ishikari Sekitan), 82–
    83, 130
Ishikawa Shichizai, 13, 54
Ishikawajima Zōsensho, 145
Isono Hakaru, 52, 53, 73
Itō Kumema, 51
Iwai zaibatsu, 125
Iwasa Iwao, 40–41
Iwasaki family, 34–35, 72–73, 117–
    18, 189
Iwasaki Hisaya, 46, 54, 71, 72, 95
Iwasaki Koyata, 95, 113, 188, 191,
    193, 216
Iwasaki Toshiya, 149

Iwasaki Yanosuke, 30, 31, 33, 46, 53,
    54, 71, 73, 95
Iwasaki Yatarō, 12–13, 22, 24, 28,
    29, 31, 52, 53, 99

Japan Brewery Company, 73
Japan Industrial Club (Nippon
    Kōgyō Club), 100, 157
joint-stock companies (*kabushiki
    kaisha*), xvi, 27, 43, 94, 212

Kadono Chōkurō, 104, 207, 216–17
Kaiseikan, 12, 13
Kajiura Kamajirō, 80, 81, 153
Kamaishi Kōzan Co., 129, 230
Kamioka mine, 39, 44
Kanegafuchi Cotton Spinning
    Company (Kanegafuchi Bōseki),
    27, 59, 62, 187
Kaneko Naokichi, 127, 134
Kansai Paint, 125
Kashiwazaki oil refinery, 84
Katō Takaaki, 52, 53
Katsuragawa Hydroelectric
    (Katsuragawa Suiryoku), 135
Kawada Jun, 169
Kawada Koichirō, 31, 53, 54
Kawakami Kin'ichi, 78, 79, 103
Kawasaki Kisen Kaisha, 126
Kawasaki Shipbuilding Co., 125–26,
    130, 144, 145, 146
Kawasaki Steel Corporation
    (Kawasaki Seitetsu), 130
Keiō Gijuku, 100, 105
Kimura Chōshichi, 51, 78, 135, 205
Kirin Brewery, 72, 73
Kita Matazō, 151
Kobe Copper Sales, 40
Kobe Paper Mill, 72–73
Kobe Steel Works (Kobe Seikōsho),
    127, 177
Kodama Ichizō, 61–62
Koiwai Farm (Koiwai Nōjō), 35, 72
Konda Bunjirō, 206
Kondō Renpei, 52, 53
Kondō Rikusaburō, 50, 78, 105,
    135, 205
Korea, 89, 92, 125, 129
Kuhara Fusanosuke, 90, 91–92, 133,
    211
Kuhara Honten, 210

Kuhara Mining Company (Kuhara
  Kōgyō), 91–92, 133, 210, 226
Kuhara Shōzaburō, 12, 42
Kuhara Trading (Kuhara Shōji),
  133–34, 169, 211
Kuhara zaibatsu, 125, 129–30, 141,
  143, 145, 181, 210–211, 226
Kyōdō Un'yu Kaisha (KUK), 22,
  23–24
Kyōsai Seimei Hoken (Kyōsai Life
  Insurance), 87, 164
Kyōsai Trust (Kyōsai Shintaku), 164
Kyushu Railway, 27, 126

land reclamation works, 86–87, 90
limited partnerships (*gōshi kaisha*),
  43, 45

Maebashi Silk Spinning Mill
  (Maebashi Kenshi Bōsekisho), 59
Makita Tamaki, 129, 149, 225
managers, role of, xxiv, 46–47, 54–
  55, 98–99, 218–19, 243, 247
Manchuria, 67, 89, 92, 226
Marunouchi business district, 33–34,
  69, 102
Masuda Takashi, 21, 36, 37–38, 48–
  49, 64, 100–102, 108, 110, 183,
  185, 186
Matsukata Kōjirō, 125
Matsukata zaibatsu, 125, 126, 130,
  144
Meidi-ya, 53, 73
Meiji Commercial Bank (Meiji
  Shōgyo Ginkō), 87
Meiji government, and
  industrialization, 4, 26, 57
Meiji Seimei, 164
Miike coal mine, 26, 34, 38–39, 44,
  60, 62, 67, 92, 129
Miike Coal Mining (Miike
  Tankōsha), 35, 39
Miike Dyestuff Works (Miike Senryō
  Kōgyōsho), xix, 147–48, 229
Miike Nitrogen (Miike Chisso), 156
mining industry, 3–4, 15–19, 32–
  33, 38–39, 68, 140, 229. *See also*
  coal mining, copper industry, iron
  and steel industry
Minomura Risuke, 44, 46, 48
Minomura Rizaemon (Rihachi), 7–
  8, 10, 20, 47–48

Mitsubishi Bank, 98, 161, 162, 166–
  69, 193, 194, 228
Mitsubishi Commercial School, 52
Mitsubishi Company (Mitsubishi
  Sha), 31–32, 53, 54, 68, 95, 111
Mitsubishi Estate (Mitsubishi Jisho),
  34, 188
Mitsubishi Exchange Office, 29, 30,
  69
Mitsubishi Heavy Industries
  (Mitsubishi Jūkōgyō), 231
Mitsubishi Internal Combustion
  Engine Works (Mitsubishi
  Nainenki Seizō), 152
Mitsubishi Iron and Steel (Mitsubishi
  Seitetsu), 129, 168
Mitsubishi Ltd. (Mitsubishi Gōshi
  Kaisha), 46, 68, 71, 72, 95, 111,
  117, 118, 133, 189–91, 193
Mitsubishi Mail Steamship Company
  (Yūbin Kisen Mitsubishi Kaisha),
  14–15, 30, 31
Mitsubishi Marine and Fire Insurance
  (Mitsubishi Kaijō Kasai), 139
Mitsubishi Mining, 143, 193
Mitsubishi Oil, 230
Mitsubishi Paper Mill (Mitsubishi
  Seishisho), 72–73
Mitsubishi Ship Repair Facility
  (Mitsubishi Seitetsusho), 28–29
Mitsubishi Shipbuilding and
  Engineering (Mitsubishi Zōsen),
  128, 145, 146–47, 152, 166
Mitsubishi Shōkai, 13
Mitsubishi Steamship Company
  (Mitsubishi Jōkisen Kaisha), 13–
  14
Mitsubishi Trading (Mitsubishi
  Shōji), 31, 72, 133, 134, 164, 169,
  173–74, 177, 238, 239
Mitsubishi zaibatsu: in agriculture,
  34, 35; in automobile industry,
  151–52; in banking, 30, 33, 52,
  96, 161, 162, 166–69; in chemical
  industry, 230; in coal mining, 28,
  29–30, 32, 68, 95, 143; diversification activities of, 28–35, 68–73,
  92; establishment of, 3, 22–24,
  25, 32; in iron and steel industry,
  33, 129; life insurance activities
  of, 164; management of, 52–54,
  71, 102–3, 117–18, 189–92,

199, 200–201, 215; in metals mining, 32–33, 68; in oil industry, 230; organizational structure of, xvii, 46, 105, 106, 111–14, 188–92, 212; in real estate, 33–34, 188; in shipbuilding industry, 33, 54, 69–71, 144, 145, 146–47, 233; in shipping, 5, 14–15, 22–24, 28–29, 30, 146; stockholdings of, 24, 27, 31–32, 35; in trading, 68, 72

Mitsui Bank: capitalization of, 10, 160, 161, 193; foreign exchange transactions of, 224, 225; history of, 10, 20–21, 35–36, 39, 43–44; as joint-stock company, 184; as limited partnership, 44–45; loans policy of, 96–98, 138, 166; management of, 47–48, 63, 100; stockholdings of, 59–60, 63, 64–65; as unlimited partnership, 43–44, 45, 100

Mitsui Board of Directors (Mitsui Shōten Rijikai, Mitsui Eigyōten Jūyakukai), 46, 108–10, 111

Mitsui Bussan (Mitsui & Co.): control of, 44, 45, 106, 184, 235–36; cotton division of, 62; criticism of, 225, 228; dissolution of, 238, 239; establishment of, 35–38; growth of, 66–67, 92, 169, 171–72, 177, 242; management of, 59, 101–2, 172, 186; mining activities of, 38–39; overseas offices of, 60–61, 66–67; relationship with Mitsui Bank, 63, 109; shipbuilding activities of, 129, 144, 147, 172; in shipping, 146, 147, 174–75; textile activities of, 59–60, 150, 151, 171; trading activities of, 60–61, 66–67, 131–32, 172–73, 224

Mitsui Chemical Industries (Mitsui Kagaku Kōgyō), 149, 229

Mitsui Exchange Bank, 8, 9, 10

Mitsui Family Constitution (Mitsui Kaken), 109, 115–16

Mitsui Family Council, 44, 46, 64, 106, 108, 109, 110, 111, 183, 184–85, 213, 235, 236

Mitsui Gōmei Kaisha, 111, 183, 184, 185, 186, 193, 213–15, 219, 225, 235

Mitsui-gumi Goyōsho, 7, 8, 9, 36

Mitsui Hachirōbei Takatoshi, 5, 114

Mitsui Hachirōemon Takamine, 45, 183, 185, 219

Mitsui Hachirōjirō, 45, 183, 185, 186

Mitsui Life Insurance (Mitsui Seimei), 164

Mitsui Marine and Fire Insurance, 138–39

Mitsui Mining (Mitsui Kōzan), xix, 44, 60, 62, 65, 67, 92, 106, 129, 130, 143, 148, 155–56, 184

Mitsui Morinosuke, 45, 186

Mitsui Saburosuke, 45, 183, 185

Mitsui Seimei, 164

Mitsui Shipbuilding (Mitsui Zōsen), 229, 233

Mitsui Shipping (Mitsui Senpaku), 175

Mitsui Takakimi, 225

Mitsui Takamine, 225

Mitsui Takayasu, 45, 183, 185

Mitsui Takenosuke, 36–37, 44, 45

Mitsui Trust, xix, 164

Mitsui Yōnosuke, 36–37, 44, 45

Mitsui zaibatsu: in banking and finance, 5, 7, 8–9, 10, 36, 96, see also Mitsui Bank; in chemical industry, 65, 67, 92, 129, 147–49, 155; in cotton spinning industry, 27; diversification activities of, 35–39, 92, 59–67; dye production activities, 147–49; establishment of, 3, 5–10, 20–21, 25; in insurance, 139, 164; in iron and steel industry, 128–29; management of, 45–46, 47–49, 100–102, 109–211, 114–16, 185, 186–87, 199–200, 213–15; in mining, 38–39; organizational structure of, xvii, xxi, 44–46, 105, 106–11, 113–14, 235–36; in shipbuilding industry, 144, 146, 147; in trading, 36–38; trust business of, 164

Mitsukawa Shōkai, 13

Mitsukoshi Gofukuten, xx, 8, 35, 44, 62, 65, 106

Mitsukoshi Tokuemon, 44, 45

Mizutani Rokurō, 71

Mori Kōzō, 203–4

Mori Tsutomu, 61
Mōri family, 36, 42–43, 90
Motoyama Hikoichi, 51–52, 99
Murai Bōeki, 125, 133, 134, 169
Murai zaibatsu, 125

Nagasaki Shipyard, 29, 30, 33, 70–71
Naigai Contractors (Naigai Yōtashi), 42, 43
Naigai Petroleum (Naigai Sekiyu), 180–81
Nakada Kinkichi, 103, 194, 195
Nakagawa Kamenosuke, 13, 54
Nakagawa Suekichi, 157, 205, 206
Nakajima Aircraft Company (Nakajima Hikōki Seisakusho), 127
Nakajima Kumakichi, 137, 157
Nakamigawa Hikojirō, 21, 44, 48, 48, 59, 63–64, 99–100, 101, 108
Nanboku Sekiyu, 84, 85–86
Nanbu Kyūgo, 52, 53
Nihon-koku Yūbin Jōkisen Kaisha (YJK; Japan National Mail Steamship Company), 14
Nippon Aluminum, 158
Nippon Celluloid and Rayon, 127
Nippon Chisso Hiryō (Nippon Nitrogenous Fertilizer), 73, 150
Nippon Denki (NEC; Nippon Electric), 196, 197, 229–30
Nippon Doboku (Nippon Construction), 42, 43
Nippon Hihaku (Nippon Tanning), 88
Nippon Keikinzoku (Nippon Light Metal Company), 158–59, 180
Nippon Kisen (Nippon Steamship), 129, 130, 133, 146
Nippon Kōkan (Nippon Steel Pipe, NKK), 86
Nippon Menka (Nippon Cotton Trading), 150, 151, 169
Nippon Railway, 27
Nippon Sangyō, 226–27
Nippon Sanso (Nippon Oxygen), 88
Nippon Seika (Nippon Shoemaking), 88
Nippon Seikōsho (Nippon Steel Works), 128, 187

Nippon Seitetsu (Nippon Iron and Steel), 230
Nippon Sekiyu (Nippon Petroleum), 84
Nippon Senryō (Nippon Dyestuff), 148
Nippon Sheet Glass, 196–97
Nippon Shōgyō Ginkō (Nippon Commercial Bank), 87
Nippon Soda Kōgyō (Tokuyama Soda), 125
Nippon Tar Kōgyō (Nippon Tar Industries), 230
Nippon Tetsudō Kaisha (Nippon Railway Company), 34–35
Nippon Yūsen Kaisha (NYK; Nippon Mail Steamship Company), 24, 29, 31, 35, 53, 69, 70, 71, 146, 175
Nishimura Katsuzō, 27
Nishimura Torashirō, 21, 48, 108
Nishinari Bōsekisho, 87
Nissan Motor, 151
Nissan Sangyō, 226–27
Nitchitsu, 227
Noguchi Jun, 150–51
Nomura zaibatsu, 125, 126, 133

Occupation, dissolution of zaibatsu by, 237–39
Odaira Namihei, 211
Odaka Kōgorō, 82
Ogura Masatsune, 103, 195, 198
Ōji Paper Company (Ōji Seishi), xix, 59, 62–63, 100, 187
Ōkawa Heizaburō, 63, 82, 84
Okazaki Kunisuke, 78, 135
Ōkubo Toshimichi, 22
Ōkuma Shigenobu, 22, 99
Ōkura & Co. (Ōkura Shōji), 132, 133, 134, 206
Ōkura Construction (Ōkura Doboku-gumi), 43, 51, 89, 206
Ōkura-gumi Co., 133
Ōkura-gumi, Gōmei Kaisha, 43, 46, 88, 89, 201, 206
Ōkura-gumi, Kabushiki Kaisha, 89
Ōkura-gumi Shōkai, 12, 43
Ōkura Kihachirō, 11–12, 42, 85, 207, 216
Ōkura Kishichirō, 207, 216–17

Ōkura Mining (Ōkura Kōgyō KK), 90, 206
Ōkura zaibatsu: diversification activities of, 43, 88–90, 92; establishment of, 3, 11–12, 25; management of, 104, 206–7, 216–17; organizational structure of, 46, 236–37; post-WWI performance of, 180; trading activities of, 12, 89
119th National Bank, 30, 33, 34, 52, 69
Ono, House of, 9, 10, 14, 17, 20
Ono Yoshizane, 35, 72
Onoda Cement, 187
organizational patterns, 44, 105, 106–14, 119
Oriental Steamship Company (Tōyō Kisen KK), 71, 83–84, 85, 130, 146, 175
Osaka Hokkō Kaisha (North Port Development), 136, 195
Osaka Shōsen Kaisha (OSK), 23, 40
Osaka Tekkōsho, 129–130, 134, 145, 210–11
Osaka Teppan (Osaka Sheet Iron), 125
ownership, patterns of, xv–xvi, 114–18, 243–46

petroleum industry, 19, 84–85, 230
political merchants, 3, 4–15, 20, 25
pollution problems, 50, 76, 80, 81

railways, 27, 31, 34–35, 73
Rakusan Trading Company (Rakusan Shōji), 30

Sakai Celluloid, 187
San'yō Railway, 27, 34, 99
Sansei Incident, 228
Sapporo Seifun, 127
Senkawa Suidō Kaisha, 31
Senshū Kaisha, 32, 36
Shibaura Engineering Works (Shibaura Seisakusho), xix, 59, 60, 62, 64, 187
Shibusawa Eiichi, 9, 17, 19, 42, 44, 45, 46, 63, 82, 208
Shidachi Tetsujirō, 103
Shijō Takahide, 204

Shinmachi Silk Spinning Mill (Shinmachi Kenshi Bōsekisho), 59–60, 62
shipbuilding industry, 33, 69–71, 129–30, 140, 143, 144–47
shipping industry, 5, 14–15, 22, 23–24, 28–29, 30, 40, 126, 146, 174–75
Shiraishi Motojirō, 51, 83, 86, 104, 137
Shōda Heigorō, 30, 31, 33–34, 52, 53, 70, 71, 73, 99, 102–3
Shōwa Depression, 180, 224
Soga Riemon, 15
Soma family, 17–18
state enterprises, sale of, 26, 27, 42, 82, 241
Suenobu Michinari, 52, 53
sulphuric acid production, 41, 80–81
Sumitomo Aluminum Refining (Sumitomo Aluminum Seiren), 230
Sumitomo Bank, 50, 79, 98, 103, 138, 161–62, 169, 195
Sumitomo Building, 198
Sumitomo Chemical Industries (Sumitomo Kagaku Kōgyō), 229
Sumitomo Coal Mining, 143
Sumitomo Copper Rolling (Sumitomo Shindōjo), 80, 81–82
Sumitomo Corporation (Sumitomo Shōji), 136
Sumitomo Electrical Wire (Sumitomo Densen Seizōsho), 82
Sumitomo family, 116, 194–95
Sumitomo Fertilizer Manufacturing (Sumitomo Hiryō Seizōsho), 155, 229
Sumitomo Honsha, 233–35
Sumitomo Life Insurance (Sumitomo Seimei), 164
Sumitomo Ltd. (Sumitomo Gōshi Kaisha), 194
Sumitomo Marine and Fire Insurance (Sumitomo Kaijō Kasai), 138
Sumitomo Masatomo, 15
Sumitomo Metal Industries (Sumitomo Kinzoku Kōgyō), 80, 229
Sumitomo Sōhonten, 135, 153, 169, 194

Sumitomo Steel Works (Sumitomo Chūkōsho), 79–80
Sumitomo Tomomochi, 15
Sumitomo Trust, 198
Sumitomo zaibatsu: in banking and finance, 40, 50, 79, 96, 98, 138, 161–62, 169, 195; in chemical industry, 80, 153–55; in coal mining, 41, 81, 143; in copper industry, 15–17, 80–81; diversification activities of, 39–41, 78–82, 92; establishment of, 3, 15–17, 25; family constitution of, 116; in forestry, 41; in iron and steel, 40–41, 50, 79–80, 179; in insurance, 138, 164; management of, 49–50, 103, 108, 118, 194–95, 197–98, 199, 200; organizational structure of, xviii, 195; post-WWI performance of, 179–80; in shipping, 40; trading activities of, 40, 135–36; in trust business, 164; in warehousing, 40
Suzuki Iwajirō, 127
Suzuki Masaya, 78, 79, 103, 135–36, 194, 195
Suzuki Shōten, 127, 129, 132, 134, 150, 155, 169, 175, 177, 181, 211
Suzuki Tsunesaburō, 206
Suzuki zaibatsu, 125, 129, 141, 144–45, 211

Taisei Corporation, 206
Taishō Kaijō Kasai Hoken, 138–39
Taiwan, 85, 125, 127, 176
Takada Shōkai, 169
Takahashi Yoshio, 21, 108
Takashima Coal Mine, 29–30
Tama Shipyard (Tama Zōsensho), 129, 229
Tamura Ichirō, 133
Tanaka Chōbei, 27
Tanaka Kōzan Co., 128–29
Teikoku Beer, 127
Teikoku Jinzō Kenshi (Imperial Artificial Silk; Teijin), 150, 177
Teikoku Kaijō Hoken KK (Imperial Marine Insurance Company, Ltd.), 42
Teikoku Kōhatsu, 236

Teikoku Seima (Imperial Linen), 87
Teikoku Seimei, 135, 166
Teikoku Steamship, 146
Tejima Eijirō, 51
Tenma Tekkōjo, 87
Terada Kōichi, 85
third-country trade, 61, 67, 72, 173
Third National Bank, 11
Tōa Paint, 135
Tōa Wool Spinning & Weaving, 125
Toba Zōsensho, 87–88
Tokio Marine and Fire Insurance (Tokyo Kaijō Kasai Hoken), 139
Tokudaiji Takamarō (Sumitomo Tomoito), 49, 50
Tokyo Bay reclamation project, 86–87
Tokyo Chochiku Bank, 163
Tokyo Furukawa Bank, 135, 137–38
Tokyo Imperial University, 103–4, 105
Tokyo Kasai Hoken KK (Tokyo Fire Insurance Company, Ltd.), 42
Tokyo Kōtō Shōgyō Gakkō, 101
Tokyo Rope Manufacturing (Tokyo Seikō), 130–31
Tokyo Shibaura Electrical Machinery, 233
Tokyo Shōgyō Gakkō, 101
Tokyo Sōko Kaisha (Tokyo Warehouse Company), 69
Tokyo Tatemono, 87
Tōshin Warehousing (Tōshin Sōko), 184
Tōyō Kōatsu (Oriental High Pressure), 156, 177, 229, 233
Tōyō Menka (Oriental Cotton Trading Company, Ltd.), xix, 62, 171
Tōyō Rayon, 150, 214
Toyoda Automatic Loom Works (Toyoda Jidō Shokki Seisakusho), 151
Toyokawa Ryōhei, 33, 52
Toyota Motor, 151
Tōzai Sekiyu, 85
trading companies, 12, 31, 131–34, 169–77. *See also under individual company names*
trust business, 163–64

Tsukumo Shōkai, 13, 28
Tsurumi Reclamation Company, 86–87, 130

Ueda Yasusaburō, 102, 108
unlimited partnerships (*gōmei kaisha*), 43, 45, 212

Walsh, John, 72, 73
Walsh, Thomas, 72, 73
Wanishi Iron Works, 128
warehousing, 40, 69
Watanabe Senjirō, 85, 101, 186
Watanabe Tōkichi, 85
World War I, effects of, 123, 128, 139

Yamaguchi Kisaburō, 157
Yamaguchi Takehiko, 88
Yamamoto Jōtarō, 102
Yamamoto Tatsuo, 52, 53, 103
Yamatake Shōkai (Yamatake Honeywell), 88
Yamawaki Masakatsu, 71
Yanagida Fujimatsu, 127
Yasuda Bank, 11, 42, 46, 87, 88, 116, 159–61, 177–79, 201, 203
Yasuda Hozensha, 42, 88, 116–17, 159–61, 163, 201, 202–3, 217–18, 237
Yasuda Motojime Yakuba, 87
Yasuda Seichōsho, 87, 88
Yasuda Shōten, 11, 41
Yasuda Trading (Yasuda Shōji), 87, 201

Yasuda Trust, 164, 203
Yasuda Unpan Jimusho, 87
Yasuda zaibatsu: in banking and finance, 10–11, 25, 41, 42, 46, 87, 88, 96, 116, 159–61, 164, 177–79, 201, 203; diversification activities of, 41–42, 87–88; establishment of, 3, 10–11, 25; in heavy industry, 242; in insurance, 41–42, 164; management of, 41, 51, 104, 116, 201–4; stock-holdings of, 42, 88
Yasuda Zenjirō, 10–11, 41–42, 116, 162–63, 201, 202
Yasuda Zenzaburō (Iomi Teiichi), 51, 104, 201–2
Yasukawa Yūnosuke, 225
Yawata Iron Works (Yawata Seitetsusho), 79, 89, 230
Yokohama Dock, 145
Yokohama Electric Wire Manufacturing (Yokohama Densen Seizō), 77, 156
Yokohama Rubber (Yokohama Gomu Seizō), 135, 142–43, 156
Yokohama Zōsensho, 130
Yoneyama Umekichi, 164, 187, 225
Yoshikawa Taijirō, 52, 53
Yoshimura Manjirō, 205
Yukawa Kankichi, 194, 195
Yūki Toyotarō, 164, 202–3, 217–18

zaibatsu: characteristics of, xviii–xix, 247; defined, xvii–xviii